Power Up Your Library

Power Up Your Library

Creating the New Elementary School Library Program

Sheila Salmon
Elizabeth K. Goldfarb
Melinda Greenblatt
Anita Phillips Strauss
Fund for New York City Public Education

1996
Libraries Unlimited, Inc.
Englewood, Colorado

LIBRARIES UNLIMITED, INC.
P.O. Box 6633
Englewood, CO 80155-6633
1-800-237-6124

Project Editors: Tama J. Serfoss, Kay Mariea
Copy Editor: Jason Cook
Proofreader: Ann Marie Damian
Layout and Design: Michael Florman

Library of Congress Cataloging-in-Publication Data

Power up your library : creating the new elementary school library
    program / Sheila Salmon . . . [et al.].
        xiv, 292 p. 22x28 cm.
        Includes bibliographical references and index.
        ISBN 1-56308-357-4
        1. Elementary school libraries--United States. I. Salmon,
    Sheila, 1931-   .
    Z675.S3P69 1996
    027.8'222--dc20   96-8836
                                                        CIP

Contents

Preface

This handbook is a response to the need for a practical document to help librarians implement the New York City Library Power Program. Library Power began in New York City in 1988 when the DeWitt Wallace-Reader's Digest Fund in partnership with the New York City Board of Education sought to reestablish elementary school libraries that had been devastated by a fiscal crisis in the 1970s.

A generous grant from the DeWitt Wallace-Reader's Digest Fund transformed 150 New York City public elementary school libraries over a six-year period. They were renovated, received additional resources, and were staffed by the New York City Public Schools with full-time library teachers in flexibly scheduled programs. The grant funded intensive on-site and off-site staff development to encourage collaborative teaching and learning and to convey a new vision of the library media center program as an essential component of school reform and restructuring efforts.

New York City Library Power, now in its seventh year, is a program of the Fund for New York City Public Education. The Fund is a private, nonprofit organization that mobilizes private sector support for public school reform to provide quality education for each child. In addition to Library Power, other Fund programs include New Visions schools, small new schools with personalized learning and high standards serving students of all abilities; participation in the Annenberg Foundation's New York Networks for School Renewal project; Real World Mathematics; and "School Close-Up," a school accountability project to help parents and the public learn more about individual schools and to build support for New York City's schools.

The condition of many of the 641 New York City elementary school libraries in 1988 was dismal. Some schools had no libraries. Many libraries were barren warehouses for dilapidated books or were used as classrooms. In schools that had libraries, librarians usually had rigid schedules, and their programs consisted of covering teachers' preparation periods. The Library Power Program addressed these conditions by establishing a support system for participating schools, updating facilities, and creating programs that modeled a new vision for library service.

Schools had to apply to participate in the New York City Program. Acceptance was based on a review process that included assessing the school and district administration's interest in restructuring its educational program by supporting an active library program administered by a full-time library teacher. The librarians, staff, and administrators of the selected schools faced issues of how to institute the changes that would make the library the center of the educational program. Concerns included establishing and increasing library access; initiating partnerships among librarians, teachers, and administrators; evaluating, weeding, and developing current, appropriate collections; creating educationally sound library programs; upgrading and designing library spaces; involving parents and the community; celebrating library accomplishments; implementing appropriate administrative routines; and supplementing inadequate budgets.

The original handbook, written specifically to deal with the issues facing the participants in the New York City Library Power Program, is now completely revised to reflect the changing needs of the Program and to broaden its relevance to a national audience.

Based on the success of the New York City Program, Library Power is now a national initiative of the DeWitt Wallace-Reader's Digest Fund and is established in 702 schools in 19 communities, serving 463,000 children. Library Power grants are awarded to local education funds that work with school districts to build community support for high-quality public education. The American Association of School Librarians, a division of the American Library Association and the Public Education Fund Network, provides expert technical assistance and program guidance to the sites. Each program is unique, but all share common goals that position the library as a catalyst for school reform.

Acknowledgments

Many people contributed to the creation of this book. Although we cannot thank each of them by name, we do want to acknowledge a few key supporters.

Many thanks to M. Christine DeVita, President of the DeWitt Wallace-Reader's Digest Fund, and the staff and trustees of the DeWitt Wallace-Reader's Digest Fund. They supported the vision that school library programs are a vital part of teaching and learning, established and generously supported the first Library Power Program in New York City, and initiated the National Library Power Program that has brought Library Power to 19 communities throughout the country.

Beth J. Lief, President and Chief Executive Officer of the Fund for New York City Public Education, has been a creative and innovative leader whose vision of school reform has influenced and strengthened our work in the schools.

It has been a tremendous pleasure to work with the New York City Library Power librarians, our first audience for this handbook, whose ideas permeate this book. Their professionalism, support, hard work, and willingness to institute change—and their concern for children—are gratefully and personally appreciated.

Carol Kroll, Director of the Nassau School Library System, and Kevin F. Daly, Supervisor of the Nassau County Board of Cooperative Educational Services Computer Center, have generously shared their knowledge and experience by authoring the chapter on OPACs and Circulation Systems.

Tracey Marie Allen, Library Power Program Assistant, has been tireless in helping to prepare this manuscript for publication. We thank her for her expertise, her skill, and her patience. Thanks to Marcel Assenza, Library Power Administrative Assistant, whose attention to detail keeps us all on the right track.

Julia Palmer, a tireless advocate for literacy, established the Library Connections Program and spearheaded the early Library Power efforts with Stanley Litow, Sara Schwabacher, and Robin Wilner.

Karen Breen, Judith May McGowan, and Eileen Newman generously shared their library expertise and their critical editorial skills.

We thank the many school superintendents, administrators, coordinators, teachers, parents, and children who have been part of the New York City Library Power Program and contributed so much to its success. We also thank everyone who assisted with various pieces of artwork in this book. Every effort was made to contact all copyright holders and to get model releases on the subjects of the photographs. We regret any oversights that may have occurred and would be happy to rectify them with a printed correction.

We also want to thank our husbands and families for their encouragement and sacrifice as we burned the midnight oil.

Introduction

This book is written for the school library media specialist, experienced or novice, who has or plans to have a library that conforms to today's vision of an effective school library media program. Library administration, collection development, technology, budgeting, teaching, scheduling, and other facets of the librarian's professional life are put into the context of a flexible, collaboratively planned teaching program that positions the library media center at the heart of the educational program of the school.

Each chapter addresses one aspect of school librarianship. Where cross-referencing is necessary, we have inserted a *See* reference. Chapters that deal with administrative routines may be adapted for training materials for volunteers or clerical support staff, or to support lobbying efforts. Each chapter is followed by a bibliography for more detailed information on a subject.

Chapter 1 outlines the roles of all the participants in the school library program, from the librarian to the library advisory committee. It may be useful to share this information when educating the school community of its rights and responsibilities regarding the program.

Chapter 2 details how to establish a collaborative, flexible program in a school with a fixed program, or how to extend the process in a school whose schedule is at least partially flexible. It also deals with the problems of time management, always an issue with overworked library media specialists.

Chapters 3 and 4 describe the instructional role of the librarian. Included are examples of interdisciplinary projects for small groups, whole classes, schoolwide celebrations, and workshops for the school community that may be adapted to local needs and curriculum. Projects are structured to appeal to children with differing learning styles. The issue of discipline is discussed, with many practical examples for eliciting positive behavior.

Chapters 5, 6, and 7 are important to share with administrators and the library advisory committee because the subjects of these chapters are particularly important to the entire school community. Chapter 5 explores the many types of evaluation, including student and adult perceptions of library services, student achievement, teacher involvement, documentation, record keeping, and planning for the future. Chapter 6 concerns collection policy, evaluation, and development. These are integral to positioning the library firmly into the school's educational framework and should be the subject of discussion among important participants in the school community. Upgrading the facility should involve the participation of others, particularly when renovations are needed. Chapter 7 gives many practical tips on making the most of the existing library space and points the way to more extensive renovations.

Chapter 8 deals with basic library procedures. It may be a helpful teaching tool to use with volunteers and library aides.

Although every library should be technologically advanced, many school libraries still are not. That situation is rapidly changing, and chapters 9 and 10 deal with planning for and using technology effectively. Chapter 9 describes the varied technologies available, describes how educational technology enhances the curriculum, and suggests ways to build a strong technology base in the media center. In chapter 10, Carol Kroll, Director of the Nassau School Library System and Executive Administrator of the Nassau Board of Cooperative Educational Services, and Kevin Daly, Supervisor, Nassau County Board of Cooperative Educational Services Computer Center, give step-by-step guidelines for planning and implementing an online public access catalog and circulation system.

Chapter 11 gives a general overview of the budget process. Specifics are determined by the policies of individual schools and districts, but all library media specialists should become experts in the budget process and make it work to their advantage.

Chapter 12 describes a number of ways library staff and volunteers can be effective in advancing the library program and gives many suggestions for recruiting and keeping a stable volunteer group.

Chapter 13 adds another dimension to the work of the library media specialist—making the library visible through a public relations program which enhances and supports the educational mission of the library.

The appendixes contain national policy statements to consult when materials or policies are challenged or when the library media specialist or advisory committee needs an important outside authority to help make policy changes.

School library media specialists have an increasingly important role to play in today's schools. They not only fulfill the traditional role of library administrator but also often serve as a school's technology expert, curriculum consultant, teacher, mentor, publicist, and lobbyist for enlightened change. We hope that this handbook will help librarians in their quest to make innovative changes and sustain educationally vital library programs that are essential to their students, their schools, and their communities.

Chapter 1

Working Partnerships

Introduction

Changing technologies, school reform initiatives, pressure to improve student performance, and all too often, budget reductions, all serve to focus attention on the school program. The media center, often a target of staff and budget reductions, must keep pace with current thinking and communicate its worth to the school and the larger community so that it can be central to educational reform and information literacy.

Administering the typical one-person library media center (with its complex mission of teaching classes, small groups, and individuals); organizing and developing the collection; circulating materials; and learning about and teaching new technologies in a school that may have 500 or more students is becoming increasingly difficult. Preparing an information-literate generation who can find, organize, evaluate, synthesize, and present information gleaned from a variety of print, electronic, and nonprint sources is especially challenging if you are juggling all the functions of a media center by yourself.

Now more than ever, it is imperative for you to develop a group of supporters who will help you establish library policy that addresses such issues as collection development, censorship, expansion of space, addition of materials, purchasing, new technologies, networking, automating, creating new and innovative library services, and integrating the library into teaching and learning. Administrators, parents, students, teachers, and community members can all have an important role in strengthening and expanding the school library media center's educational position in the school.

This chapter outlines many suggestions for partnership roles and responsibilities in the school library media program. Use the information to stimulate discussion, inform your constituency of its importance to the library, and solidify support for your work.

The Library Media Specialist

When the public thinks of the librarian, it is often solely as a book-finder who provides access and assistance. However, the American Association of School Librarians (AASL) and the Association for Educational Communications and Technology (AECT), in their publication, *Information Power: Guidelines for School Library Media Programs* (1988), breaks down the responsibilities of the school library media specialist into three categories: information specialist, teacher, and instructional consultant.

As Information Specialist

As an information specialist, the librarian:

△ Provides the school community with access to the world of information and information technology.

△ Determines user needs through formal and informal assessment.

△ Advises users of new acquisitions, relevant periodical articles, new technologies, new programs, and events of interest.

△ Provides access to and retrieval of resources beyond the school through networking with other institutions, agencies, and individuals.

△ Assists users in identifying needs and strengthening skills in the selection, evaluation, use, and communication of information.

△ Encourages users to take pleasure in learning: to develop lifelong reading, listening, and viewing habits, and to understand the need to be skilled in all modes of communication.

△ Develops flexible policies for the use of materials.

△ Protects the user's right to confidential and unrestricted access to information.

As Teacher

Although the school library media specialist has always taught library skills, that teaching responsibility is expanding as knowledge about how children learn changes teaching methodology in the library and in the classroom. Information literacy is much broader than library skills. It encompasses important strategies and life skills that apply to the whole process of understanding, collecting, synthesizing, and presenting data. In addition, the rapidly changing world of technology makes it imperative for librarians to provide opportunities for adults and children to become aware of and use new formats to promote communication and learning.

As a teacher, the librarian:

△ Instructs students in the skills, knowledge, and attitudes concerning information access, information analysis, and communication as an integral part of the school curriculum.

△ Instructs students in the use of various media and conveys the strength, limitations, and appropriate use of each.

△ Provides opportunities for students to evaluate their progress.

△ Creates opportunities for students to produce work in a variety of formats.

△ Works with teachers and administrators to plan the information curriculum and ensures its integration throughout the instructional program.

△ Provides opportunities for teachers and administrators to participate in resource selection, use, evaluation, and production.

△ Provides training in the use of new technologies.

△ Teams up with teachers and administrators in expanding and enhancing teaching methods to meet student learning needs.

△ Informs administrators, teachers, and parents about workshops and other learning opportunities.

△ Informs and advises parents about their children's learning needs and appropriate learning resources.

As Instructional Consultant

Your responsibility as an instructional consultant includes long- and short-term planning of curriculum and instructional teaching strategies. Knowledge of curriculum trends, local and state instructional requirements, and expertise in designing activities to promote learning is an essential part of your repertoire. The effective librarian plans instruction collaboratively, team teaches, and also:

△ Employs a wide range of resources, and teaching and evaluation methodologies to meet the intellectual and developmental needs of students.

△ Participates in school, district, departmental, and grade-level curriculum design and assessment projects.

△ Helps teachers develop instructional activities.

△ Provides expertise in the selection, evaluation, and use of materials and emerging technologies for the delivery of information and instruction.

△ Translates curriculum needs into library media program goals and objectives.

△ Integrates information skills into the curriculum in such a way to boost achievement in the content areas.

These guidelines were adapted from: American Association of School Librarians and Association for Educational Communications and Technology. *Information Power: Guidelines for School Library Media Programs* (Chicago and Washington: AL–AECT, 1988, pp. 26–42).

The Student

Students are active seekers of information and, when given sufficient opportunity for learning, need little encouragement to demonstrate their skills and proficiency in accessing information, using that information, and communicating their findings. Students also enjoy mentoring younger children and assisting adults. If students are not already dynamic learners in your library, give them the tools and the encouragement to be so. In the effective library media center, students:

△ Use the library frequently to pursue their own interests.

△ Learn about materials available in the library and how to access them.

△ Demonstrate a consideration for others by maintaining an atmosphere that is friendly and conducive to work and study.

△ Demonstrate a respect for information resources by using materials appropriately, checking them out properly, and returning them.

△ Demonstrate skills in using all forms of media and technology in their pursuit of learning and enjoyment.

△ Create and communicate information in many formats.

△ Assist in developing a library collection that meets their curricular and personal reading interests by requesting, reviewing, and evaluating material.

△ Use library resources to enhance their skills in critical thinking and inquiry.

△ Volunteer to help with ongoing library activities or special programs by:
  - Serving on the library squad.
  - Teaching adults and students to use library technology.
  - Tutoring or volunteering to be reading partners.
  - Mentoring younger children.
  - Preparing materials for displays, exhibits, and special programs.
  - Striving to achieve independence as lifelong learners.

The Teacher

The teacher is your partner in teaching and learning. The teacher knows the students' strengths and needs and can share that information with you so that together you can plan the best curriculum and activities for them. Finding time for planning in the busy school environment can be daunting, but persevere. Good relationships with teachers are essential for success. Teachers can be staunch advocates in promoting library use for information and pleasure. The teacher:

△ Identifies the learning needs of students and plans with the library media specialist the themes and units of study to address these needs. Planning includes:
  - Selecting a variety of teaching strategies.
  - Using appropriate resource materials.
  - Establishing student groupings: whole class, small groups, individual.
  - Evaluating student achievement.
  - Providing opportunities for students to participate in evaluation activities.

△ Participates in developing a library collection that meets curricular needs by requesting, reviewing, and evaluating material.

△ Works with the librarian and students to ensure that students use all appropriate formats of materials.

△ Knows the library policies and programs and assists in articulating them to the students.

△ Strives to integrate the curriculum with the library program to enhance student skills in critical thinking, inquiry learning, and research.

△ Provides opportunities for students to explore, share, and appreciate reading, writing, and literature of many types in every content area.

△ Encourages students to volunteer and share their expertise by serving as:
  - Library aides.
  - Peer readers or tutors.
  - Mentors for younger children.

△ Advises parents about their children's reading and information skills and encourages them to take an active role in the school library.

△ Encourages students to visit the library often and read for information and recreation.

△ Volunteers to serve on the advisory committee.

The Administrator

Your administrator may be your most powerful ally. He or she may control the library schedule, budget, and long-term goals. Regular meetings to share information will help him or her understand your goals, instructional objectives, and needs. His or her influence is important in making the library an integral part of the school instructional program. An effective and supportive administrator will involve the school community in the library program, encourage collaboration and teamwork, and create a climate conducive to learning. The administrator:

△ Knows the library media program and its significance to the school.

△ Articulates expectations for the library program including the:

- Role of the librarian in the instructional team.
- Importance of collaborative planning and teaching.
- Development of flexible access to materials, technology, and learning activities.

△ Facilitates full integration of the library program into the curriculum.

△ Schedules time for planning.

△ Works with librarians to:

- Set clear goals for the library.
- Evaluate progress.
- Encourage children to be independent library users.

△ Welcomes parent involvement in the library.

△ Includes the librarian in curriculum and governance committees.

△ Ensures the provision of adequate resources.

△ Provides necessary clerical assistance.

△ Creates a climate in which inquiry and independent learning are encouraged.

△ Establishes a library advisory committee composed of teachers, parents, students, and members of the community to work with the librarian to set broad policy and to support library programs.

△ Supports the American Library Association's "Library Bill of Rights."

△ Understands the role of technology in learning.

△ Promotes methods likely to increase student achievement and engagement in learning.

The Educational or Clerical Assistant

The library media specialist should spend his or her time working with teachers and children; nonprofessional tasks should be performed by the educational or clerical assistant. The clerical assistant is a crucial member of the library media center team and should be available throughout the day to ensure that the library remains open and accessible. The responsibilities of the clerical support staff include circulation and processing, maintenance of the collection, working directly with students, special projects, and technology support.

Chapter 12 provides a full description of how educational or clerical assistants work with the library media specialist to implement a dynamic library program.

The Parent

Parents are the backbone of the library. They serve as volunteers, fund-raisers, advocates for resources, and patrons. They are the most influential people in children's lives and are essential to promoting reading. Encourage parents to visit often. Use their special expertise in developing and evaluating the collection, technology planning, and grant writing. Provide services and incentives for them to continue coming. The parent:

  Δ Supports their children's reading and writing by reading to them and encouraging them to read to others.

  Δ Visits the school and public library to examine and borrow materials for use at home.

  Δ Serves as a role model for students by reading and by being lifelong learners.

  Δ Volunteers to help in the library to provide clerical, technical, and program assistance.

  Δ Assists in fund-raising activities.

  Δ Serves on advisory committees and helps with projects or special events.

  Δ Enriches library resources and delivery of services by sharing experiences including:
    - Career and work experiences.
    - Language and cultural heritage.
    - Travels, hobbies, and special interests.

  Δ Serves as an advocate for libraries, encouraging community support and funding for the library.

The Volunteer

Volunteers include people from outside the school community who, although they have no children in the school, wish to give service. Senior citizens may tutor or mentor children, help in the management of library routines, join the library advisory committee, or share their experience, knowledge, and talents with students and teachers. High school or college students may be offered work-study credits for their assistance. Business and professional people are often pleased to lend support by allowing student visits to their places of business, coming into the school to talk about their work, or providing awards and incentives for academic achievement. Volunteers can bring the excitement of the outside world into the school and become advocates for library services. Volunteers enrich library resources and delivery of services by sharing career and work experiences, language skills, ethnic and cultural heritage, travels, hobbies, and special interests. A volunteer:

△ Assists in the maintenance and circulation of materials.

△ Learns about resources, technologies, and teaching methods that can be applied to their own lives.

△ Contributes to the learning environment for all children who attend the school.

△ Serves as a role model for students.

△ Communicates information about library programs and services to the school community and beyond.

△ Assists in fund-raising activities.

△ Serves as a library advocate, encouraging community support and funding for library programs.

The Advisory Committee

A library advisory committee is a relatively new phenomenon in schools. The expansion of the library media specialist's role; the influx of expensive, complex technologies that radically alter the way students learn; and the shift to position the library at the center of instruction require that librarians develop a strong network for information, support, and advice. The advisory committee is such a vehicle; it can promote new ideas and communicate them to others more effectively than a single individual. The librarian should be a member of the committee (although not necessarily the leader); other members of the school community, including students, teachers, administrators, parents, and outside groups connected with the school, should also be involved on the committee. The committee's responsibilities include:

△ Helping establish short- and long-term goals for:
  - Programming and services.
  - Technology.
  - The remodeling or enhancement of library facilities.
  - The expansion of library resources.

△ Serving as a resource for library programs.

△ Promoting the use of the library.

△ Helping create schoolwide themes and celebrations.

△ Helping develop a collection policy and a collection development plan.

△ Modeling the use of the library in resource-based teaching and effective use of technology.

△ Communicating information about the library programs and services to the school community and beyond.

△ Grant writing and other fund-raising activities.

△ Advocating for libraries, encouraging community support and funding for library programs.

△ Developing a schoolwide plan for technology that connects classrooms, computer labs, the library media center, and the world.

Chapter 2

Flexible Access

Fig. 2.1. Students Work on Individual Projects in a Flexibly Scheduled Library.

Introduction

A visitor to a flexibly scheduled library might see students brainstorming ideas for an assigned social studies project on immigration, while others are looking for resources on recycling for a small multigrade committee project, and some are communicating with distant schools through electronic mail. One individual is browsing for a time travel fantasy; another is searching for an article in *Sports Illustrated for Kids* using a magazine index on CD-ROM. The school library media specialist is assisting where needed, with a full understanding of each child's assignment, because these activities have been planned in advance with teachers.

In *Information Power: Guidelines for School Library Media Programs* (pp. 27–28), the AASL and the AECT explain the importance of flexible access to school libraries:

The materials in the school library media collection and the expertise of the center's staff are central to meeting users' daily learning and information needs. Therefore, it is necessary that both be readily available to the school community throughout and beyond the entire school day. Class visits to the library media center are scheduled to facilitate use at the point of need. Any functions that restrict or interfere with open access to all resources, including scheduled classes on a fixed basis, must be avoided to the fullest extent possible.

This statement is a powerful tool for change for school library media specialists still working with a fixed schedule, particularly now when national interest in educational reform is high. Goals 2000, the Annenberg Network for School Renewal, the Coalition for Essential Schools, Charter Schools, the DeWitt Wallace-Reader's Digest Library Power Program and many other state, national, school, and district efforts strive to raise academic standards in American schools through school restructuring. Their presence and influence provide the philosophical and educational context to create flexibly scheduled or open access library media centers.

The flexible school library media program can help advance school reform efforts. Instructional design reformers advocate collaboration and team teaching. The librarian is an ideal partner in this endeavor. Resource-based learning encourages higher-level thinking skills and emphasizes the process of the information search. The library media center can provide resources. Heterogeneous and cross-age grouping, inclusion, and cooperative learning are easy to arrange within the flexibly scheduled media center. Multicultural and interdisciplinary curriculums can be implemented in a well-stocked media center. Projects using library materials and technology can be used for portfolio and performance assessment. Because library media specialists work with the whole school community, they are ideally placed to spearhead and participate in school reform.

Flexible scheduling provides the framework for students to learn about, explore, and use information from a variety of resources at point of need. Students may come when interest is high rather than having to wait for their class's scheduled time. Flexible access can enrich the partnerships between teachers and librarians who will share their knowledge of students' learning styles, curriculum, appropriate resources, and exciting learning activities. Flexible access can increase communication among students in different grades and among classroom teachers, specialized teaching staff, and the librarian. Student learning is strengthened, and the independent use of resources supports the development of lifelong learning skills.

This chapter will help you design a campaign to institute flexible access in your school library if it is currently on a fixed schedule, or strengthen a program already working on a flexible concept. It will also assist you in dealing with the time management problems that will arise from your success.

Initiating a Flexible Schedule

To interest your school community in converting to a flexibly scheduled program, you must be clear about how it works and why it would best serve students, teachers, and parents.

Getting Started

To begin, you should:

△ Collect professional material and read widely about the concept of flexible access and collaborative curriculum planning.

△ Discuss the concept with colleagues at the local, state, or national level.

△ Visit schools where librarians have implemented flexible schedules with positive results.

△ Develop strategies to convince other people in your school community.

△ Create an advisory committee if you do not already have one in place. This group should become the core of support for all library activities.

△ Share professional literature about the educational philosophy behind the concept of flexible access and the positive educational outcomes that are associated with it.

Lobbying for Change

Once you and your advisory committee believe that flexible access would be the most educationally sound alternative for your school, the campaign begins.

△ Introduce the concept of flexible access to your administrators or site-based management team, teachers, school board members, district office personnel, and parents.

△ Work with administrators, staff, and, where appropriate, union leaders on alternative scheduling of current class coverage responsibilities and other assigned duties. Share models of other schools' methods of providing flexible access.

△ Arrange for administrators and key teachers to visit nearby schools that are implementing flexible access.

Implementing Flexible Access

Some flexible access can begin even before the library has complete flexible scheduling. You and your committee should:

△ Discuss how the plan will be implemented with your administrator or management team. Then work out the details with school staff.

△ Attend Parent Association meetings with members of the library advisory committee. Explain flexible access, including the circulation of resources, to parents. Speak about the need for volunteers and encourage parents to borrow materials themselves and to ensure that their children are participating fully in the library program.

△ Plan how the access program will happen:
  - all at once
  - with a few teachers or grade levels
  - in a phased-in program

Setting Up a Schedule

Set up a schedule that reflects your school day. Provide opportunities for students in the breakfast program, after-school center, Saturday classes, school-day club programs, summer session, or any other activities that take place in the school building.

If there are more than 20 classes in the school, create a schedule so that teachers can sign up on a two- or three-week cycle. This will enable everyone to sign up for library time when it is appropriate for their curriculum plans. Some teachers will schedule class visits more than once and others not at all in a particular cycle. Small group access periods allow children from several classes to use the library during the same time slot.

The Flexible schedule should:

△ Accommodate individual students at certain times during the school day.

△ Block in time for circulation, browsing, and project work.

△ Include periods for classes and/or small group visits.

△ Vary your lunch and administrative time each day.

△ Establish lunchtime programs for children: story lunch programs, book discussion groups, crafts related to books, storytelling, library club, library newsletter, electronic mail projects, or browsing. (If your school has several lunch periods, schedule library time on alternate days or weeks for the grades or classes that eat during each lunch period.)

△ Indicate time for grade conferences and meetings (e.g., school governance committee, curriculum committee, library advisory committee, or others as needed).

If there are two librarians in your school, scheduling may be more complicated. If your library is limited in space, decide who will work in the library during each period. One librarian may visit classrooms while the other is in the library. One may be involved in a circulation program from a cart for primary-grade students when the library is being used for whole-class teaching. You may arrange a schedule so that one person comes in early and has a before-school program and then leaves early, while the other comes in later and has an after-school program. You may want to work with certain teachers and classes together.

Depending on the size and design of your media center, two different activities may be accommodated. One librarian might work with several small groups while the other library media specialist works with a whole class and its teacher. With two professionals or a library media specialist and a library assistant on staff, independent circulation and browsing can take place all day. The two library professionals should schedule time with each other for regular planning. Be prepared to make changes as you proceed.

A Case Study: The Excel School Library Media Center

The Excel School has approximately 500 students in grades K-5. There are three classes on each grade level, three mixed-grade classes (K/1, 2/3, 4/5) and three Spanish bilingual classes. The library is staffed with one professional librarian and one library clerk. Parent volunteers work in the library every morning.

The librarian and classroom teachers work closely together to plan curriculum-related activities. Formal planning takes place at weekly grade-level meetings and curriculum committee meetings. Informal meetings—short conversations, really—take place in the lunchroom or hallway during the teacher's or librarian's administrative periods or in the library when the teacher is visiting with his or her class.

Children visit the library individually for book exchange during the school day and after school each day. They may also visit the library with their class or as members of a small group or club. For example, during the two-week schedule shown in figures 2.2 and 2.3, a child in a fifth-grade class might come to the library three times to borrow books for recreational reading, twice with his class to work on a project about Canada and to meet an author, once to send an e-mail letter to a pen pal in Canada, and once to attend a meeting of a book discussion club.

WEEK ONE

	Monday	Tuesday	Wednesday	Thursday	Friday
8:40 – 9:10	Library Administration	Library Administration	Library Administration	Library Administration	Library Administration
9:10 – 9:40	Whole Class 3–Brown Japan-Introduction	Small Groups 2–Stone	Small Groups 5–Wells Environment	Small Groups 5th Gr. US Geography	Small Groups 3rd Gr.–Japan
9:40 –10:10	Small Groups 5th Gr. US Geography– Ongoing Map Project	Planets	Whole Class 3–Charles Rain Forest	2nd Gr.–Marine Life	Library Administration (Set up for afternoon workshop.)
10:10 –10:40		Small Groups 4–Jackson Native Americans	Small Groups 4–Jackson Native Americans	Whole class K–Ridge Nursery Bil. K/1-Perez Rhymes	
10:40 –11:10	Whole Class 1–Smith Folktales	Whole Class K–Levy Shapes Sp. Ed.–Brown	Small Groups 2–Reagan Stars	Whole Class 2–Tyler Marine Life Mural (with Art teacher)	Whole Class 1–Goodman Parents are invited to tell family stories.
11:10 –11:40	Whole Class 2–Johnson Marine Life	Small Groups 3–Brown Japanese 3–Cohen Games	Whole Class 1–Freedman Family Stories		
11:40 –12:10	Librarian's Lunch	Librarian's Lunch	Librarian's Lunch	Librarian's Lunch	Librarian's Lunch
12:10 –12:40					
12:40 – 1:10	Children's Story Lunch Gr. 3/4	Children's Story Lunch Gr. 3/4	Children's Story Lunch Gr. 3/4	Children's Story Lunch Gr. 3/4	Children's Story Lunch Gr. 3/4
1:10 – 1:40	Library Administration	District Meeting Librarian out of building until 3:10	Library Administration (Inventory- Ongoing Project)	Whole Class 4–Chester Poetry	Workshop for 4th & 5th gr. teachers How to use Hypercard
1:40 – 2:10	Newspaper Club (with Resource Room teacher.)	Teachers will bring in classes by themselves.			
2:10 – 2:40	Grade Level Meeting Gr. 3		Whole Class 5–Townes Canada (Print Research, Electronic Mail, Videos)	Meet with Goodman (Gr. 1) to discuss Family Unit.	Whole Class 5–Green Hypercard Autobiographies– Sharing Session
2:40 – 3:10	Small Group Peer Reading Gr. 1 & 5	5–Jones US Geography et al.		Peer Reading Gr. 1&5	
3:10 – 3:40	After-school Activities/ Individual Circulation	After-school Activities/ Individual Circulation	After-school Activities/ Individual Circulation	After-school Activities/ Individual Circulation	After-school Activities/ Individual Activities

Fig. 2.2. Week 1, Excel School Library Schedule.

Δ The aide and library volunteers handle circulation throughout the school day, including the librarian's lunch period.

Δ The librarian and aide are paid by the After-School Program to stay one-half hour each day for research, circulation, browsing, and computer activities. (Parents are encouraged to visit with their children.)

Δ When the librarian attends meetings, teachers use the library with their students.

Δ Small groups that require little assistance can work in the conference room, even while whole classes are present.

Δ When trained volunteers are available for story lunch, the librarian can work on other projects such as ordering.

Δ The librarian works with classroom teachers as well as specialists such as art and resource room teachers.

Δ The librarian usually attends one to two grade-level meetings per week.

Δ Special Education and bilingual classes are small. They often visit with children from other classes.

Δ Planning opportunities occur during library administration time and informally during lunch, grade-level meetings, and other school curriculum meetings.

Δ Parents are welcomed as volunteers, borrowers (especially before and after school), storytellers (See Friday, Class 1-Goodman), and Story Lunch readers.

WEEK TWO

	Monday	Tuesday	Wednesday	Thursday	Friday
8:40 – 9:10	Library Administration	Library Administration	Library Administration	Library Administration	Library Administration
9:10 – 9:40	Small Group Peer Reading Gr. 1 & 5	Whole Class/1–Beech Picture Books About Animals	Whole Class 5–Jones US. Geography	Peer Reading Gr. 1 with Gr. 5	Poetry Club meets with author. Librarian makes final preparations.
9:40 –10:10	Small Groups Kgn.-Gr.2 produce puppet play and Gr. 5 Students videotape the production.	Small Groups Gr. 5 Electronic Mail with Canadian Students	Whole Class 5–Green Canada	Small Groups Gr. 4 Local History	
10:10 –10:40			Poetry Club To brainstorm questions for author.		3–Brown Author 3–Cohen Visit
10:40 –11:10	Whole Class 2–Tyler Marine Life Mural (cont.)	Small Groups Kgn.-Gr.2 Continue puppet play	Whole Class 3–Brown Japan Research to prepare for video.	Science Curriculum Revision Meeting	Author Visit 3–Charles Sp. Ed. 4/5–Cook
11:10 –11:40	Whole Class 4–Jackson Native Amer. Presentation	Whole Class 5–Wells Environment			3–Jackson Author 3–Chester Visit
11:40 –12:10	Children's Story Lunch Gr. 1/2	Children's Story Lunch Gr.1/2	Children's Story Lunch Gr. 1/2	Children's Story Lunch Gr. 1/2	Luncheon for author.
12:10 –12:40					Teachers, parents and selected students are invited.
12:40 – 1:10	Librarian's Lunch	Librarian's Lunch	Librarian's Lunch	Librarian's Lunch	
1:10 – 1:40	Kgn., Sp. Ed K/1, Bil. K/2 Parent Workshop Reading Aloud	Library Administration (Training volunteers.)	Gr. 5 Planning Meeting	Library Administration (Prepares for author visit/Meet with Ms. Jackson (Gr. 4 to discuss local history)	Author Visit 4–Shea Bil. 4/5–Diaz
1:40 – 2:10					5–Green Author 5–Townes Visit
2:10 – 2:40	Parents bring their children to library to read to them.	Small Group Peer Reading Gr. 1 & 5	Book Discussion Club Gr. 4/5	3–Brown Japan Working on their "Reading Rainbow" Video.	5–Jones Author Visit
2:40 – 3:10		Whole Class Bil. 2/3–Garza Spanish Bil. 4/5–Diaz Poetry			Author Visit Committee- Evaluation
3:10 – 3:40	After-school Activities/ Individual Circulation	After-school Activities/ Individual Circulation	After-school Activities/ Individual Circulation	After-school Activities/ Individual Circulation	After-school Activities/ Individual Circulation

Fig. 2.3. Week 2, Excel School Library Schedule.

△ Most of Friday is devoted to a special event (e.g., an author visit). Grades 3-5 participate.

△ Parents are invited to the "Reading Aloud" Workshop (Kgn., Sp. Ed. K/1, Bil. K/1).

△ Parents are also invited for an author luncheon (supported by PTA).

△ The librarian attends a fifth-grade planning meeting and science curriculum committee meeting.

△ Poetry club meets with author on Friday morning in the conference room.

△ Parent/Teacher Committee meets to evaluate how the day has gone and begins planning for next year (Friday afternoon).

△ Parents who attend the Monday workshop will bring their children to the library (advance sign-up will enable the librarian to notify teachers).

△ Participants in the book discussion club (Wednesday) meet every two weeks.

△ On Monday, a skilled volunteer works with groups of children from different grades who are producing and videotaping a puppet play.

△ On Thursday, the same volunteer assists a third-grade class making a video.

Setting Up Administrative Procedures

Create a system for individual student access. This may include producing passes, arranging for adults or older students to accompany young children, or assigning particular hours for circulation. Develop a procedure for teachers to sign up. If the sign-up sheet is located in the office, the teachers will see it, but there will be little opportunity for direct communication with teachers. If the sign-up sheet is in the media center, you will have the opportunity to communicate directly with teachers, but not all teachers may see it. Create a user-friendly circulation system that encourages children to be independent borrowers.

Orientation

△ Teachers should sign up their classes to come to the library within the first few weeks of the school year for orientation. Use these briefing sessions to explain the new program to the children and encourage them to come to the library to borrow books and other materials. (You may want to create a flyer or letter especially for them; children are often the strongest advocates of open-access programs.) Teachers will also have another chance to hear about the procedures for the program.

△ Change some of the elements of the schedule, if modifications are needed.

△ Inform parents about flexible access. Flyers, articles in the PTA newspaper, and direct conversations with parents at orientations, workshops, and other meetings are good venues for publicizing the new schedule.

Creating Opportunities for Staff Development

Arrange workshops. If interest is high, ask your administrator to schedule curriculum planning meetings or workshops during the summer, after school, or on weekends. Groups may be formed according to grade level, subject interest, or other factors. Check on the opportunity to link with a local university that will provide expertise and graduate or in-service course credit. Meet with teachers before or after school, during grade-level meetings, and during faculty meetings. Informal lunch time meetings and workshops are other possibilities. Some districts have planning or staff development days preceding the start of school or during the school year. Work with your principal or school management team to schedule library workshops or planning sessions on those days.

Collaborative Planning

Flexible access enables librarians and teachers to provide the appropriate time, space, resources, and professional consultation to help students pursue their academic and personal goals. When the library media center is used in this intensive, creative way, planning is a necessity. A process in which teachers and librarians plan teaching strategies and learning activities together enhances student learning in ways that traditional library programs do not. Information literacy skills are most effectively learned within a subject context. Curriculum areas are enriched when the many resources of the library are woven into subject units or themes. Sometimes you will plan with one teacher. At other times all teachers in a grade or teachers from several grades will work together on a planning team. Whether you are working with one person or 10, the collaborative process includes many common elements.

The Collaborative Process

Fig. 2.4. Major Projects Require That the Participants Plan Together.

△ Arrange planning time. A quick idea might be generated during a hallway conversation, but major units require significant planning with the participants meeting several times throughout the unit.

△ Develop a collaborative unit planning sheet. You can use the form in figure 2.5 or modify it to fit your needs.

△ Discuss the instructional focus of the unit. Goals and objectives may come from national, state, district, or school curricula, but each teacher contributes suggestions to make the unit more meaningful. Take into consideration students' interests, learning styles, and academic level.

△ Brainstorm about how the unit will take shape.

△ Evaluate what skills students need to learn and what competencies they already have. If the unit requires research, determine students' competency in taking notes from written, oral, or pictorial sources; using print and electronic indexes and databases; and employing organizational tools such as webs and outlines.

△ Determine responsibilities for the teacher and the library media specialist, a timeline for completion of the project, and evaluation procedures.

△ Share information about available print, audiovisual, and electronic resources. Resources may include people, other libraries, and organizations. You may want to prepare a bibliography for current or future use.

△ Organize the learning activities that will be part of the unit. Some may be classroom based, others may be library based. The key to integration is to plan with the teacher and build on the experiences in both sites.

△ Determine the length of the unit and where teaching sessions will take place. Discuss who will be responsible for the teaching in each session.

△ Decide on grouping strategies. Will library visits be for the whole class? Small groups? Individuals? Or a combination?

△ Plan any related trips and decide who will accompany the students.

A Collaborative Planning Form (fig. 2.5) outlines the process of planning together and may be used formally, as a written document, or informally during planning discussions.

Collaborative Planning Form

Content Area:

Goals and Objectives:
    Content:
    Information Skills:
    Social Skills:
    Learning Strategies:

Learning Activities:
    Individual:
    Small Group:
    Whole Class:

Resources:
    Book:
    Nonbook:
    People:
    Community:

Responsibilities:
    Teachers: **Library Media Specialists:**

Product:

Evaluation:
    Teacher:
    Student:
    Librarian:

Fig. 2.5. Collaborative Planning Form.

Unit Implementation and Evaluation

While working on units with students, adapt your plans to fit the actual situations. You must be flexible and include additional sessions if the work takes longer than planned or find other ways to help your students successfully complete what you and the teachers have planned. Cut back or modify activities that are just too ambitious. Evaluate as you go along. Do you have the necessary resources? Are the students learning what you and the teachers expect them to learn? Are students able to complete the assignment in the time allotted?

Be aware of students' learning styles. Help students look at their method and strategies. Although classroom teachers may give the formal grades, you should be involved in assessing the students' progress. You may be able to give valuable insights into how students solve problems, interact with others, and organize their time and work. Students should evaluate their own processes and projects, too. Reflection stimulates metacognition.

Evaluate the unit in a final session with the teacher. Discuss perceptions about the unit with the participants, including students. You may want to ask some open-ended questions such as:

Did the work go as expected?
What was easy about the assignment?
What did you find difficult?

How would you modify the assignment if you were to do it again?

What did you learn?

Program Documentation and Dissemination ———

Collaboration with teachers on curricular units could be considered your "bottom line" just like a business declares its profits at the end of each year. Declaring your profit is not quite as easy as looking at the corner drugstore's ledger sheet, but it is no less important. Try the following technique and modify it over time as you share your successes and challenges with your administrators.

Create a three-ring binder for summary sheets of each resource-based collaborative teaching unit that was planned and carried out

Outreach Strategies

Some teachers are always eager to try new experiences. Cherish them. Teachers reluctant to become involved in the library must be courted. By learning about their interests and teaching styles, you may be able to find just the right approach. Sometimes teachers would rather collaborate in a subject area where they need help or lack interest rather than in an area in which they feel strong. The following are just some of the possibilities for drawing teachers into the process:

△ Reach out to teachers with specific suggestions for joint programs.

△ Newly appointed teachers need support and friends. They are usually very willing to collaborate and eager to use the methods they have learned in their education courses.

△ Link teachers who will benefit from sharing ideas and methods. Bring teachers together to discuss successful projects.

△ Connect teachers who are working on similar class projects.

△ Share a sample schedule with teachers and ask for their input. Suggest some lessons or units of study.

△ Entice teachers with the possibility of showcasing their students. Use highly motivated teachers and students as ambassadors.

△ Recognize all teachers who work on a collaborative project.

△ Before the schedule is posted, you may want to check with teachers who have not signed up recently.

△ Invite teachers, parents, and administrators into the library to see displays of children's work. Give students opportunities to perform and/or explain their projects.

△ Start a book discussion club for teachers. Focus on children's or adult literature.

in the library. You can also file the planning forms based on figure 2.5. These sheets contain accounts of the planning, the activities, and the evaluation of the unit. Over time, the notebook, organized by grade level or curricular theme will become a valuable log of learning activities for evaluation and analysis. Which teachers are served or underserved? What subject areas are covered or not yet reached by the library media program?

Time Management

When you speak to a library media specialist who has a highly successful program, you will find that there is usually one major problem: TIME! Time to plan with teachers, time to work with students, time to report to administrators, time to run the book fair, time to meet with the other librarians in the district, time to give parent workshops, time to supervise volunteers, time to fine-tune the new automated catalog. The schedule quickly gets filled beyond capacity.

If you are experiencing this very uncomfortable situation, then you know that you are doing a wonderful job. You must also recognize that it is now time to take a comprehensive look at your workload and begin to put your tasks in priority order, streamline routine tasks, look for additional help, delegate tasks where possible, and create timelines for long-term jobs.

These are components of time management. Because you are working largely on your own, without direct daily supervision, you must take the responsibility and the initiative to decide what can be accomplished immediately, what daily and weekly tasks must be done to continue the smooth functioning of the media center, and what long-term tasks must be finished by the end of the school year. You must decide with your supervisor how many periods are going to be allocated to whole-class and small-group visits, and how much time independent book circulation will require.

Depending on the staffing of your media center, you will have different options for creating time for administrative tasks. Many highly effective library media specialists put the program ahead of administrative tasks, at least in the short run. The more successful media centers have excellent librarians as well as other staff members who can keep up with the essential clerical tasks. Even if the library catalog and circulation system is fully automated, the books and other resources must still get back to the shelves in their correct order, and this takes person power, whether in the form of a paid library aide, parent or other adult volunteers who come in on a regular schedule, or a competent, well-trained student squad. In non-automated libraries, there are even more daily tasks associated with circulation and cataloging. Library media specialists cannot get the job done by themselves, yet in many localities they are struggling to do their jobs well without other support. Whether you are in a situation where you have assistance or work alone, it is helpful to analyze your management style in an effort to improve your efficiency in the future.

A first step in gaining control of your time is finding out how you spend your time in the library. Use a notebook and a 60-minute wind-up kitchen timer. Select one day to gather baseline data. Throughout the day, set the timer to buzz at 15-minute intervals. Whenever the buzzer sounds, stop what you are doing and record the time and your activities in the notebook. It is important to record exactly what you are doing at that time, not what you will be doing or what you think you should be doing. At the end of the day, you should have from 25 to 30 notations. Analyze and categorize your time notations into such groupings as unit planning, processing materials, direct instruction, equipment troubleshooting or repairs, student discipline, chatting with colleagues or students, answering office intercom messages, arranging furniture, and responding to teacher requests for materials.

Ask a colleague or your advisory committee to help you categorize time spent and suggest priorities. Talk with your administrator, too. Sometimes demonstrating on paper how your time is spent will clarify low-priority tasks and services that could be dropped, routines that could be streamlined or more effectively batched, tasks and services that could be delegated to staff in the library or other departments, and the need for additional library help.

The time management study grid (fig. 2.6) will assist you in examining how you spend your time. Using this grid, you will be able to track the time spent in reference and reading guidance, and that spent in instruction (direct teaching), collection development, teacher consultation and planning, library administration (managing and planning), staff development, library operations (circulation, cataloging, processing), personal time (lunch, breaks), and nonlibrary tasks. You may also spend time on tasks such as public relations, media production, and writing, which you may have to add to the form. Your time study should reflect what you are actually doing, not what you think you should be doing.

Time Management Grid Instructions

As a beginning step, do this study one day a week for five weeks. Although this may not be a true sampling of your work, it will provide you with enough information to make some of the decisions mentioned in the text on time management.

Use the sample provided or modify it by designating different time blocks (20 or 30 min.) or by changing the categories to reflect your specific duties (e.g., media production, other administrative duties, and clubs or special interest groups).

For each time break, check your activity. Try to do this at the exact time in order to ensure accuracy. If you forget, try to do it as soon after as possible. Remember that you are studying what you are actually doing, not what you think you should be doing. Do not reflect on patterns until the study is over.

Tally all sheets after the study is over. Daily tallies may influence the study.

For each day's sheet, add up the check marks for each category and check that the total of all columns equals the grand total of all time periods (28 in the sample).

Add up the total number of checks for each category, including data from all five days. These subtotals should add up to 140 if you are using the sample given.

To compute the percentage of your day spent in any of the various activities, divide the daily subtotal of each category by the total number of all daily time blocks (28 in the sample) and multiply by 100.

To compute the average percentage for each activity, divide the total sum of the five days for each category by the total number of time breaks in the study (140 in this sample) and multiply by 100. Round off your numbers. Present the results as an average percentage along with the range from lowest to highest percentages.

Look at the data that you have gathered. Are you spending too much time on clerical duties and too little time on direct instruction? Do you need to increase your teacher consultation time? Use the data to shape your schedule in the future.

This was adapted from appendix B of Curriculum Initiative: An Agenda and Strategy for Library Media Programs *by Michael B. Eisenberg and Robert E. Berkowitz (Norwood, NJ: Ablex, 1988), 163–66. The authors based their work on the lectures of Evelyn Daniel.*

When done in collaboration with other school librarians, data collection can be a useful tool for evaluation and training. It is concrete documentation that can be used to persuade administrators, teachers, parents, and funders that additional staff and resources are essential in meeting your school and library learning objectives. By analyzing the data, you should be able to identify four types of programs, determining which are:

1. High demand and high cost.

2. High demand and low cost.

3. Low demand and high cost.

4. Low demand and low cost.

In an environment where demand determines programs, the ideal would be to focus on programs in categories 1 and 2 and to reduce or eliminate those in categories 3 and 4. In the school, however, a program that is in low demand might be of high priority in meeting learning objectives. In that case, you would not seek to eliminate it but, perhaps, to publicize it more thoroughly and generate greater demand. A program that is low demand and high cost might be maintained because it reflects the extra effort required to modify the learning environment to meet the special needs or learning style of an individual student.

After you have filled in the grid and analysed your priorities, then order your activities. Add any others that you know come up during the year. Determine the approximate percentages of your time that should be spent on these tasks, given their relative importance in the priority listing that you created. Are you currently spending large amounts of time on tasks of relatively low professional impact? If you are, then this is the time *to make a break with the past.*

Reference & Reading Guidance	Collection Development	Teacher Consultation & Planning	Library Administration (Managing & Planning)	Instruction (Direct Teaching)	Library Operations (Circulation, Cataloging, & Processing)	Tasks not related to the library	Personal (Lunch Breaks)	Staff Development
8:00								
8:15								
8:30								
8:45								
9:00								
9:15								
9:30								
9:45								
10:00								
10:15								
10:30								
10:45								
11:00								
11:15								
11:30								
11:45								
12:00								
12:15								
12:30								
12:45								
1:00								
1:15								
1:30								
1:45								
2:00								
2:15								
2:30								
2:45								
3:00								
Total =								
28 blks.								
Percent = 100%								

Fig. 2.6 Time Management Chart. Adapted from *Curriculum Initiative: An Agenda and Strategy for Library Media Programs,* by Michael B. Eisenburg and Robert E. Berkowitz.

△ Delegate the tasks that can be done by someone else:
  - Technical assistant
  - Paid library aide
  - Parent or other adult volunteer
  - Library school intern or student teacher
  - High school volunteer
  - Member of library squad

△ Lobby for additional staff or more staff time by showing your administrator what could be accomplished with additional personnel.

△ Recruit and train volunteers, including more students on your squad.

△ Automate all possible library clerical operations including purchasing, processing, circulation, cataloging, management routines, and so on.

△ Simplify by looking at your technical processes. Break down tasks so that others can help.

△ Eliminate tasks that are continued because they have always been done (e.g., acquisition of books).

△ Postpone tasks that cannot be finished within your regular workweek. Some of these may have to be done before or after the school day. Others may be scheduled at times of the year when business is slow because of testing or end-of-year activities.

△ Set short-term goals. Try a three-month period at first and see if that works for you. Make a list of "to-do" items every week. Check them off as they are accomplished.

△ Create blocks of time when you can work on big projects. You can put together your own lunch and administrative time on particular days if you give them up or shorten them on other days.

△ Communicate with other librarians. They may be able to offer suggestions or shortcuts. Speak candidly with your administrator about what needs to be done. Administrators are not always aware of the librarian's workloads, especially if the librarian is working on a flexible schedule.

△ Be professional. You must devote time outside the school day to planning, preparation, and collection development just as every teacher must spend time in preparation, thinking, and correcting homework.

There will probably never be a time when the busy library media specialist feels that there are enough hours in the school day to accomplish everything necessary for successfully administering the library program. However, a careful analysis of how you spend your time and an aggressive campaign to streamline operations and delegate responsibilities will go a long way to make the impossible more possible.

Bibliography

American Association of School Librarians and Association for Educational Communications and Technology. 1988. *Information Power: Guidelines for School Library Media Programs*. Chicago and Washington, D.C.: ALA-AECT, pp. 27-28.

Buchanan, Jan. *Flexible Access Library Media Programs*. Englewood, CO: Libraries Unlimited, 1990.

Dobrot, Nancy L., and Rosemary Cawley. *Beyond Flexible Scheduling: A Workshop Guide*. Castle Rock, CO: Hi Willow Research and Publishing, 1992.

Eisenberg, Michael B., and Robert E. Berkowitz. *Curriculum Initiative: An Agenda and Strategy for Library Media Programs*. Norwood, NJ: Ablex, 1988.

Lance, Keith Curry, Lynda Welborn, and Christine Hamilton-Pennell. *The Impact of School Library Media Centers on Academic Achievement*. Castle Rock, CO: Hi Willow Research and Publishing, 1993.

Turner, Philip M. *Helping Teachers Teach: A School Library Media Specialist's Role*. 2d ed. Englewood, CO: Libraries Unlimited, 1993.

Chapter 3

The Librarian as Teacher

Fig. 3.1. The Library Media Specialist Is a Full Partner in Teaching and Learning.

Introduction

To understand the role of the librarian as teacher, it is important to reflect on the historical development of the library media center, the library program, and the educational issues that influence teaching and learning in schools today.

Until midcentury, school libraries, where they existed, tended to be collections of academic reading and basic reference tools. There was little organized effort to define or teach a library curriculum. The librarian was the keeper of the collection, a literature expert, and a materials manager.

In 1950s and 1960s, the school libraries took on their first curricular role. The space race and the perception that the United States was "falling behind" other countries in educating youth caused public pressure to increase resources for schools. Research on learning styles influenced the kinds of instructional materials purchased. Early childhood programs focused on "disadvantaged learners" and the need for providing enriched environments and hands-on experience.

School library collections benefited from additional funding and librarians were given new responsibilities. They continued to be literature experts, but were also expected to develop a set of skills designed to help students access the library collection and use reference materials. Librarians had responsibility for acquiring audiovisual materials and training staff and students in their use. The librarian instructed teachers and students in local media production and the library began to be known as the library media center.

The curriculum was formalized into a sequential list of skills for children in grades pre-K through 12 with units of instruction, measurable objectives, and tests. Children came to the library, usually for one period a week, to receive library instruction. The librarian often shared a story, gave a library skills lesson, and circulated books. "Library" became a separate subject or content area.

Planning with teachers was accidental or incidental. Librarians engaged in parallel teaching, often presenting units or lessons covering the same content as the lessons used by the classroom teacher. Because the library curriculum was not viewed as central to the educational curriculum, the library position was often viewed as nonessential, and staffing was reduced or eliminated to effect savings.

In the late 1970s and early 1980s, society again placed emphasis on excellence in education and educational innovation. Attention was paid to the "different learner" and the child who was "not achieving." Curriculum became less teacher-centered and more learner-centered, with attention to process as well as content, and resource-based teaching replaced or supplemented textbooks.

Adding computers to schools symbolized for parents and administrators that the schools were "preparing students for tomorrow." In many schools, students were "taught computer," just as they were "taught library." The informational function of computers was separate from the library program and few schools had a computer in the library. At the same time, schools were separating "computer" and "library" into discrete subjects, and graduate schools of library education were changing their titles from "School of Library Science" to "School of Library and Information Sciences."

The whole-language movement empowered classroom teachers to nurture literacy and create learning environments that met the needs of individual students. Basals were replaced by literature as texts for teaching reading. Many schools developed extensive classroom libraries to support the new reading program. Some schools diverted funding from the school library to create these collections or dismantled the central school library and distributed books to the classroom. The professional literature in language arts discussed the changing role of the library media center, and there was a disquieting theme that perhaps school libraries were no longer needed.

In 1988, the American Library Association published *Information Power: Guidelines for School Library Media Programs*. The guidelines stated: "The mission of the school library media program is to ensure that all students and staff are effective users of ideas and information." The document asserts that information technology is not only appropriate in the library, it is essential, and insists that students and teachers have the opportunity not only to use but to create information in various formats. The document stressed the need for physical and intellectual access to information in all formats and identified the role of the librarian as information specialist, teacher, and instructional consultant. For many administrators and librarians, the basic tenets of the document were, and still are, revolutionary.

Today, the professional literature stresses collaboration between the librarian and the classroom teacher to develop thematic, resource-based units. The library media specialist is a full partner in teaching and learning. Library media specialists and teachers are encouraged to plan together from the initial objectives through the final assessment of student outcomes. This chapter addresses some of the key issues of the librarian's responsibility as teacher including how children learn, how you create an environment for learning, and how learning experiences can be enhanced through structured and informal activities in the library media center.

How Children Learn

Basic tenets that have emerged from research on learning and observation of children's behavior are that children are:

△ Questioners. After the age of three, most conversations are well seasoned with "Why?"

△ Compulsive seekers and processors of sensory information.

△ Relentless imitators, modeling their language and behavior after those around them.

△ Masterful processors. In the first five years of life, children process thousands of bits of information and use language to shape and pattern the world around them in meaningful ways.

△ Confident learners. Most four-year-olds are convinced they can talk, dance, sing, write, build, repair, and become almost anything, real or imaginary.

△ Social learners who enjoy interaction with peers, siblings, parents, and others.

△ Concrete, tactile learners in their early years, who use their bodies and real objects to verify and extend what they know about the world around them.

△ Manipulators of ideas. In middle years children are able to evaluate sources and explore different points of view.

△ Diverse in learning styles.

△ Egocentric and only able to see other points of view as they mature.

△ Different in temperament.

△ Varied in their rate and ease of learning.

△ Joyful learners.

Seven major factors influence how children learn and need to be considered when selecting resources and creating programs:

1. past experience

2. maturation

3. learning rate

4. temperament

5. learning modality

6. information processing ability

7. intelligence

Past Experience

Children come to school from varied backgrounds and with different experiences. Because learning requires building or scaffolding new information on prior knowledge, materials and experiences must provide opportunities for children to build on their own background knowledge. You should use not only the resources in the school but also the experiences and knowledge of teachers, parents, and the community. Encourage discussions that help children connect what they know with what is new.

Maturation

Children of the same chronological age may differ greatly in maturation. Compare two six-year-olds with the same date of birth. One is reading and socializing with peers; the other is not. One has developed fine motor skills and holds a pencil easily; the other cannot.

There are differences in maturation between children of the same age and there are also great differences within each child. A bright six-year-old, who uses an extensive vocabulary and has superior social skills, may not have developed the eye-hand coordination to tie his shoe. Another six-year-old may already be reading and have fine motor coordination but lack the social skills to interact appropriately with peers.

Learning Rate

Children learn at different rates. Some children will require that content or skills be taught and re-taught. Others learn after one presentation and require extension or alternative activities or they could become restless, bored, or disruptive.

Temperament

Temperament is important in learning, too. Children may be outgoing or shy, persistent or easily discouraged, fearful or fearless, aggressive or passive, social or solitary. Many children exhibit combinations of these traits depending on their mood, time of day, and the task. Temperament influences how children relate to each other and the staff, facility, resources, and program of the library media center. You need to modify materials, environments, activities, and groupings to meet student needs and also help children understand their own temperament and that of others.

Learning Modality

Children have different learning modality preferences. Some are auditory learners; they learn best by listening. Others are primarily visual; they have to see information or ideas graphically presented. Still others are kinesthetic; they need to build models, perform, or demonstrate. Learning modality research is still in its infancy. It is not yet clear what impact modality has on learning, but there is evidence to suggest it influences how children select, process, synthesize, and communicate information. Children who "can't seem to sit still" may be kinesthetic learners who literally can't sit still. The children who "never listen" may be unable to use the aural modality effectively. Mixed-modality learners adjust to specific information and assignments and learn effectively whether the information is presented orally, visually, or kinesthetically.

As children mature, mixed-modality learning becomes more common and children can perform or cope in two or more modalities. They also learn to identify situations that best fit their learning style. The self-aware learner in the upper-elementary grades can tell you whether he or she would rather communicate information by writing, demonstrating, or drawing.

Information Processing Ability

In addition to having different learning modality preferences, children process information in different ways. Global learners prefer a holistic view; they are deductive, thematic, and multidisciplinary. Give them an overview of the whole concept, then gradually fill in the details. Analytic learners need to be taught sequentially. They are specific, inductive, and linear. Children can learn more about their processing styles through questionnaires and dialogues. Knowing how they learn can help children take control of their learning. The self-directed learner is more able and more likely to generalize and apply learning strategies to new learning situations.

Intelligence

To reach and teach the whole child in the library, you need to be aware of multiple intelligences and their implications for learning in the library. Thomas Armstrong in *Multiple Intelligences in the Classroom* describes seven different categories or intelligences:

  △ Linguistic—a capacity to use words whether orally or in writing.

  △ Logical-Mathematical—the capacity to use numbers effectively and reason well.

  △ Spatial—the ability to perceive the visual-spatial world accurately and perform transformations upon those perceptions.

  △ Bodily-Kinesthetic—expertise in using one's whole body to express ideas and feeling and facility in using one's hands to produce or transform things.

  △ Musical—the capacity to perceive, discriminate, transform, and express musical forms.

  △ Interpersonal—the ability to perceive and make distinctions in the moods, motivations, and feelings of other people.

  △ Intrapersonal—self-knowledge and the ability to act adaptively on the basis of that knowledge.

Armstrong suggests that each individual has all these intelligences and others in some degree. With training, these intelligences can be developed to a level of competency, then mastery. Providing an environment with activities, materials, and processes to stimulate and develop the multiple intelligences is a continuing challenge for educators in general and, in particular, for you in the library.

All of these factors affect how children learn and influence how you organize and use your space, select materials, and structure your program. The task may seem daunting, but the goal is familiar: to present each child with a variety of appropriate learning experiences and opportunities that will promote and enhance intellectual and social growth. One of the primary tasks is to provide an environment that is welcoming to active, curious young minds.

Creating the Learning Environment

Creating the learning environment is also known as classroom management or discipline. Experienced teachers and professors of education will tell you that teachers who have good classroom management skills do not have problems maintaining an environment for learning. They say that if a child is engaged in learning, you will not have discipline problems. That is true for some children, some of the time. For the rest of the time, it is useful to have a large repertoire of strategies and skills at your disposal. You can discover these skills if you:

△ Ask teachers and administrators about their classroom management techniques.

△ Observe teachers and others as they work with children.

△ Attend workshops and conferences.

△ Read a variety of professional literature.

△ Adopt techniques consistent with your personal philosophy, teaching style, and sound educational practices.

Not all techniques successful in the classroom will apply to the library space and program. When developing a library media center that is child-centered and where child-directed learning is expected, it is necessary to establish some common rules for appropriate behavior that are understood by administrators, teachers, and children. It is much easier to manage the environment if everyone is clear on expectations.

Rules and Expectations

The library serves the whole school. Children of different ages and classes use the space at the same time and in many different ways. Students may come into conflict with their peers and test how firmly you enforce rules and practices. Children may also have misperceptions about your role based on their teacher's classroom management techniques.

State the library rules positively during orientation, making it clear that different rules may apply in their classroom or elsewhere in the school. Set a few rules that you really believe in and can enforce, rather than creating rules for every situation. Be clear in your own mind how you will enforce the rules you make and be sure enforcement is consistent with the rules and policies of the school. Positive reinforcement works better than punishment to control behavior and it is more pleasant for the children and for you.

Be sure children understand the rules and, whenever possible, discuss why the rules are in place. Emphasize that the library is a place for serious work. Everyone is a scholar, entitled to respect for his or her work, and everyone is expected to care for the space and the resources. Students must not disturb others. The librarian, teachers, and peers can guide, coach, and facilitate but should not do the work for students. This brief framework covers almost every situation in the library without ever having to spell out what will happen if John uses a CD-ROM disc as a Frisbee.

Teachers and administrators may have concerns about the informal atmosphere of the library media center. You need to communicate the reasons behind your rules. Invite teachers, administrators, and parents to visit the library media center when multiple activities are in progress. Let children know in advance that guests will be coming to see how well they work independently. Ask children to be prepared to answer questions about what they are doing and how they are doing it. Invite children to explain how they direct their own learning. You will be reinforcing self-discipline, self-directed learning, and metacognition skills.

Strategies for Effective Discipline

Watch children interact in the library space. You will learn a lot about the teaching styles and classroom management techniques used by teachers in your school. This information will help you when you plan units with teachers. It will also help you plan and structure learning experiences for children so that all children have the opportunity to move toward greater independence and self-directed learning. For example:

Do children ignore quiet requests? If teachers raise their voices when they want attention, children may feel the teacher is not serious if the request is softly spoken. Continue to speak at a decibel level you feel is appropriate, and children will learn that you are serious.

Does permission for quiet talk result in a roar? Children may need practice in modulating their voices when talking is permitted.

Do children leave resources littered around the room? If the teacher stresses the importance of keeping the classroom neat, encourage children to view the library as an extension of their classroom. Ask for their help and leave sufficient time to clean up.

Do children wait for you to supply them with resources or repeatedly approach you asking, "Is this right?" "What do I do now?" These children need to become more independent. They may be used to a high degree of structure and may need practice setting their own goals and monitoring their own behavior. Reward them when they do so. Gradually extend their areas of responsibility.

Do children squabble over a book or a chair and come to you to settle the disagreement? Do they fight, cry, interfere with others, or display other immature behavior? Are there clashes between children of different classes, genders, or age groups? Encourage discussions that help children learn positive ways of settling conflict. Helping children settle conflicts in positive ways gives them independence and furthers educational goals. Provide rules and guidelines so children feel secure and gradually extend the areas for which they are personally responsible. Help them internalize control. Praise mature behavior and give positive reinforcement.

Do children squabble when working in a group or complain that group members don't help, are supercritical, or too bossy? Use the cooperative learning model. Assign roles and teach social skills.

You cannot insist that teachers use particular classroom management techniques or adopt a common teaching style, but you can use the library as a demonstration laboratory for different models. You may supply some of the models, and by encouraging teachers to work together on multiclass and cross-grade projects, you will give them an opportunity to experience other models. The goal is to establish an environment in which children become inner-directed, responsible for their behavior, and in charge of their own learning.

Discipline problems are reduced when students are encouraged to take charge of their own learning. Support their efforts, validate their discoveries, and reward the achievement of autonomy. Here are some strategies for creating an environment that is appropriate for learning:

△ If discipline problems occur more frequently in one area or near one resource, you may be able to reduce conflict by rearranging the resources or modifying the traffic patterns.

△ Provide signs and location keys for common materials (paper, scissors, tape, stapler, pencils, etc.). Advise children to locate these items early in the year and then expect them to find the items on their own. This will reduce many disruptive and nonessential questions.

△ Simplify general directions and rules, such as "Please return all reference books to the shelving truck." "Sign up to use the computer." "Rewind videotapes." "Take the bathroom pass if you need to leave the room."

△ Establish cues for focused listening. "When I flick the lights, listen for important announcements."

△ Develop routines. "When I give this signal, you know there are 10 minutes left in the period. Put materials away and come to the discussion area so that we can talk about what you have learned."

△ Model and reinforce appropriate behavior. "Table one got right down to work." "Notice how everyone in the room is engaged in purposeful work."

△ Support peer cooperation. "Help each other. If you discover a better way to do it, share it." "Become an expert in the topics you enjoy."

△ Encourage reflection. Question students to determine what they found out and what strategies they used. "What worked? Why? Why not? What would you do differently next time?"

△ Analyze what didn't work. In real life and in research, it is as important to know what doesn't work as what does work. By reflecting on what worked and what didn't, children can learn strategies for the future.

There are times when additional techniques are needed to maintain an atmosphere of productive learning. Start by analyzing the discipline problem. Is there too much movement, noise, or insufficient time on task? Are many children exhibiting these behaviors, or only a few? Can you discern a pattern?

Identify those individuals who are causing the disruptions. Are the disruptions deliberate or inadvertent? (That child using his desk top as a drum may not even be aware of the sound. A child snapping his fingers may be unconsciously imitating an action of an adult.) Are these behaviors interfering with student learning or your ability to help students? If not, you may wish to ignore the behavior.

Is the problem the task? Is it too hard? Do the students have the necessary skills to accomplish it? Do they know what they are supposed to do? Are there sufficient suitable materials? Are there other materials or other formats that would help? Is it too easy or not stimulating enough?

Discuss problems with teachers and students. Break the assignment down, simplify it, and provide additional materials. Teach the material in a different way if it has not been learned. Develop extension activities if it is too easy.

When you are working with another teacher, it is important to discuss discipline. Explain the atmosphere you would like to maintain in the library, your techniques or rules, and the behavior that is acceptable in the library environment concerning talking with peers about the assignment or materials, moving around the room to obtain materials or work with peers or staff, using and sharing resources, and requesting help from teachers and peers.

Ask how your standards and rules are similar to or different from the classroom rules and how this information can be conveyed to students. Ask the teacher to give you background information on children in the class: their ability to work in groups, preferred learning styles, and special problems or needs.

Techniques for Working with a Class or Large Group

Body language. Use eye contact, facial expression, body posture. Stand to enhance control, sit to establish eye contact when you share or conference. Move closer to individuals who are engaging in disruptive behavior.

Positive reinforcement. Place the emphasis on behavior, not personality. "You are really listening." "That was an excellent question."

Reduce stimuli. Speak in a quiet voice, slow the pace, or lower your tone.

Use silence and eye contact. "We'll wait until it is quiet."

Change the atmosphere. "Lights out until it gets quiet." "Rest until it gets quiet." These methods become less effective if used too frequently.

Offer new activities to students who have finished options. Suggest quiet reading time, computer time, audiotapes, helping others, and so on.

Exclude temporarily. "Please leave the circle, table, or group and go to that area (specify) until you are ready to work."

Appeal to a sense of fair play. "When *you* are sharing, you want others to listen."

Working with a Small Group

Use the same techniques as above but direct them to the group. A careful structuring of small groups at the outset may prevent problems from developing. The person who knows the students best should make the group designations. Groups may be formed to: include both higher and lower functioning children; enhance social interaction (shy and aggressive); blend children with various learning style preferences; include children with different frustration levels, background knowledge, interests, motivational levels. When working with a group:

△ Be sure that you, the teacher, and the children are clear on the assignment.

△ Move between tables. When two or more teachers are present, all should circulate and monitor group activity. Discipline can deteriorate if you do paperwork or engage teachers in private conversation. Direct a quiet question to someone who seems to have trouble focusing on the task. Ask how the work is going. Offer an additional source. Compliment a child working on the task.

△ Discuss group progress with the groups at the end of each or several sessions. Peers will encourage unproductive group members so that their group doesn't fall behind.

△ Pair a child who has successfully mastered a point with a child still struggling. Be sure to give every child a chance to be tutor and tutee.

△ Tell a nonfunctioning member of a group to work alone until he or she is ready to cooperate.

△ Reassign the nonworking student to another group or give a different task.

△ Invite groups that are making progress to share strategies with other groups.

△ Offer additional work slots to groups that need more time and optional or extension activities to groups that are finished. Offer them options: quiet reading time, time on the computer, or listening to an audiotape.

△ Compliment the group in their teacher's hearing, in an administrator's hearing, or in a parent's hearing.

△ Display the work of the groups. Highlight children's efforts and achievements.

△ Ask for suggestions from students on improving group productivity.

△ Learn more about individual interests and preferred learning styles.

△ Talk about problems with a child or group in private.

△ Offer an alternative assignment or task to a disruptive or unengaged student, if feasible.

Strategies for Working with Teachers

Some teachers avoid team teaching and collaboration for fear of being judged. You are a colleague and peer, and it will require tact and careful planning to develop a working relationship that is comfortable for both of you. Teachers use the techniques that have proved successful in the past and that they find most comfortable. Broadening their repertoire requires a willingness to change and to take risks. They are more likely to attempt to change if they feel that you respect their expertise, value their insights, and are nonjudgmental. If you are trying to incorporate new classroom management techniques into a joint project with a classroom teacher, here are some opening lines you might try:

"I am having a little trouble with . . . do you think we could try . . ." (Help me, you're the expert.)

"Would you suggest . . ." (It is really your idea not mine.)

"I noticed that you are very successful at . . . could we . . ." (Describe good techniques, don't judge, suggest an alternative.)

"I'd like to try an experiment using . . ." (Just evaluate, don't participate.)

"I'm trying to get children to . . ." (That's why we shouldn't intervene.)

"Will you watch when I try . . . and see if you think it works?" (Evaluate me.)

"I read this technique in a journal article." (Power of the outside expert.)

"*Information Power* suggests I do . . ." (Power of the written word.)

"Do you think it would be better to try x or y?" (Forced choice.)

It is better to decide in advance the rules and techniques to use when managing the group in the library space. Discuss your classroom management techniques that use positive reinforcement and encourage children to be self-directed and responsible for their behavior and learning. Agree on signals to cue each other during lessons. Identify children who may need additional structure or guidance. Develop groups that enhance learning. Present the rules and guidelines to children jointly, stressing that Mr. X and you have agreed on how to proceed.

What if you have jointly decided on classroom management techniques, carefully planned the unit, assigned responsibilities, are in the middle of an activity and find that the teacher is reverting to management techniques that you feel interfere with student learning? Try the following strategies:

Describe a positive situation. "It really worked well when you . . ."

Divide the unit between you to be sure at least some sections use your model. At the end of the project, compare results.

Empathize with the teacher and brainstorm alternative solutions for problem kids or situations.

Volunteer to work with one or two disruptive students while the teacher works with the others, or visa versa.

Intervene. It may be necessary to step in calmly to defuse a situation. It is not easy, but it is a professional obligation.

Talk about differences privately.

Developing the Inquiry Process

You have created an environment for learning and have stocked it with beautiful and useful resources. Now it's time to develop the instructional component. Effective teaching begins with planning. When you collaborate with teachers, you pool expertise about curriculum, resources (people, materials, places), how students learn, and assessments of individual students (what they know and what they need to know). Deliberate over the objectives: content, skill, strategy, and social. Consider real-life constraints of the schedule, time frame, physical spaces, and limited resources. Design a vehicle and process for meeting your objectives including the teach-reteach component; practice sessions and practice environment; student demonstration of learning, sharing, and extending learning; evaluation and assessment; and reflections by students and teachers on the process and products of learning.

The teaching role of the librarian and teacher will vary with the objectives determined. In the early elementary grades, units frequently emphasize strategy and social objectives. Strategies are directly taught and modeled, for example, "These are some things you can do if the words are too difficult." Social interactions are also taught directly through use of cooperative learning. Content is usually familiar, unambiguous, and frequently provided by the teacher or the librarian. The teacher and librarian model the processes and structure the learning.

As the student matures and consolidates skills, the emphasis shifts to activities that provide opportunities to practice and reflect on social interactions and strategy use. Unfamiliar and more ambiguous content will be introduced. Students take a greater responsibility for directing their own learning. They spend more time analyzing, synthesizing, repurposing, creating, and sharing information.

Fig. 3.2. Children Learn as They Work with Partners.

Teaching the Inquiry Process

In school, inquiry is guided by the teacher, who replaces parents as the source of information. The teacher also introduces a more formal way of conducting inquiry and labels the process. Gathering children for a "meeting" or sharing session, the teacher may present the topic or pose a question: "We are going to get a class pet. What kind of pet should we get?" Children's responses are written onto an experience chart, attributing comments carefully to the individual child. "Andrew says, 'I think we should get a dog.' Seline says, 'I think we should get a rabbit.' " Suggestions might also be webbed by the teacher.

Children might be asked to draw a picture of the pet they would like for the class. These pictures, with the child's comments dictated to the teacher, could be put around the room for other children to see and think about. In the days that follow, the pet investigation continues throughout the curriculum. For mathematics, the children might make a list of animals or pets using background knowledge and library resources, vote for their preferred pet, and tally the results, which can be displayed on a picture graph. For language arts, children could interview a parent, teacher, or friend about a pet. They might bring in photos of family pets, find and cut out pictures of pets from magazines, or display books and magazine articles about pets.

Stories read aloud by the teacher and librarian may focus on pets, too. A variety of pet books, videos, and stories could be borrowed from the school library and be available for individual use.

When children have gained background knowledge, the teacher initiates the next step in investigation. "What will the pet need?" "Would the pet you recommend be a good classroom pet?" "Why or why not?" Children brainstorm and the teacher puts comments on an experience chart or the chalkboard. Comments may be grouped by category: "What kinds of food does the pet need?" "What kind of home or cage will it need?" The teacher solicits questions from the children or further structures the investigation by supplying children with questions to answer about the pet they recommend. Children may work individually or in small groups. They may use background knowledge and interview peers, family members, or members of the school community. They may choose books and materials from home, the classroom, or the school library, dictating their findings to an adult or older child. Classmates are invited to discuss the presentation and reach conclusions about the pet described. They may compare and contrast pets, give judgments about the best pet based on the information presented, and finally use the information to vote on and select a class pet. Once a pet has been decided upon, further investigation may be needed to identify necessary equipment, means of obtaining the pet, and developing routines for animal care.

You may be puzzled that this scenario is labeled "inquiry." It is, after all, the kind of teaching that happens in most early childhood classes that are experientially based. In the inquiry model, there would be additional steps: The teacher would formally plan aspects of the unit with the librarian and others. He or she would review and label the steps of the process, making children aware that there is a procedure for obtaining and evaluating information. The teacher encourages the children to generalize from the process and apply it to other information-gathering situations. The teacher also provides opportunities to practice the model with support. The school library media center is one site for supported practice. Finally, the teacher encourages the children to evaluate and reflect on the process. This thinking about the process is the first step in metacognition.

Teaching Inquiry in the Early Grades

In the early grades, emphasis on inquiry is placed on practicing and developing skills and strategies that help the student develop a process for dealing with information. The emphasis is on the process rather than the content. The children are taught the steps of the process and are given many opportunities to practice the process using content from every curriculum area. As they become familiar and comfortable with the process, they are encouraged to generalize the process and apply it to new learning situations.

The teacher and librarian:

△ Obtain baseline information on students (what they know, what they need to learn next).

△ Provide much of the background information on the topic or theme.

△ Model and develop the questions for the research.

△ Teach subskills needed for the activities and unit.

△ Identify appropriate sources: people, places, books, and nonprint materials.

△ Discuss the outcomes and products.

△ Structure how information will be shared.

△ Label the steps of the process and specialized "research terms."

△ Provide many practice sessions.

△ Provide ongoing assessment that is used to develop additional minilessons.

△ Provide feedback to students on their progress.

△ Provide an audience and forum for students to share their learning.

Because reading is a difficult process in the beginning years, it is important to structure activities to include visual, auditory, tactile, and oral components with a limited reliance on reading and writing. Include skills instruction in mathematics, oral communication, reading visual images, sequencing, listening, and working with a partner or group. The classroom, library, and larger community can provide new experiential opportunities.

The teacher and librarian help focus the listening and the understanding of the process through guided discussion and questions. They also teach and model cooperative learning and social skills. They establish rules, roles, and responsibilities for group work. Some assignments might include designating one student in each group as director or facilitator, recorder, presenter, timekeeper, and resource gatherer. Children should be encouraged to evaluate their individual and group participation. This self-evaluation and group evaluation are valuable steps in metacognition. Children learn from interacting with materials, personal observation, and through asking and answering questions.

Once the teacher and librarian have modeled the process, much of the discussion can take place in small cooperative learning groups with children helping peers. When young children work together, the discussions may be oral or visual. Children can share with their partner or small group, and then share with the whole class, if desired. Practice at selecting, organizing, rehearsing, and presenting information orally is important for future literacy development.

Cross-age collaborations can also be developed with older and younger children paired as research buddies, reading buddies, and the like. Older children working with younger children can guide discussions, encourage strategy use, read aloud, and act as scribes or recorders. Children are excellent teachers of their peers and younger children, but they need training prior to working with other children and time for guided reflection after working sessions. Helping older children understand the role of tutor or teacher and encouraging them to reflect on how children learn stimulates metacognitive awareness. Such sessions give the older child additional chances to practice and generalize strategies they have learned. Cross-age mentoring is a powerful tool for enhancing cognitive development and social skills; it helps both the tutee and the tutor.

The teacher and librarian monitor the progress of the student interactions, moving from group to group to question, coach, facilitate, and provide additional help as needed. They take advantage of the "teachable moment," providing focused attention and skillful direct questioning at the point of need to help the young child move forward in his or her intellectual development.

Piaget noted that children are motivated to restructure their knowledge when they encounter experiences that conflict with their predictions. He called this condition "dis-equilibrium" and suggested that educators help children to acquire knowledge developing methods that encourage dis-equilibrium and permit children to work their own way to reestablish equilibrium. Piaget suggested that children be encouraged to explore their personal interests to maximize opportunities for dis-equilibrium to occur.

Children also need to be provided with a structure, a process for exploration and guidance. Without guidelines and focus, children easily become frustrated and discouraged. The world is complex and the child feels powerless. The child ceases to think of himself or herself as an observer, researcher, and powerful part of the information process: "Adults know everything; when I am an adult, I will know everything too. Tell me what to do-think-believe." Or "The world is magic; things happen without plan or pattern." Neither belief will help the child become an effective user and creator of information. Small group projects using a structured inquiry process and offering the child some choice provide an ideal opportunity to investigate and study the world in a controlled way and to develop the skills and strategies to tackle other real-life information needs in the years ahead.

The worksheet on page 38 suggests a simple structure for a first inquiry project. Prereading children would get oral instructions—questions and answers can be dictated to an adult or older child.

Studying Animals Worksheet

1. With a partner, choose an animal about which you want to learn more. Find two pictures that show the animal.

2. What did you find out about the animal?

   _____

   _____

   _____

   _____

   _____

   _____

   _____

3. Share your pictures with another pair. Think about questions you might like to explore on the subject.

Questions:

1. _____

   _____

2. _____

   _____

3. _____

   _____

Fig. 3.3. Studying Animals Worksheet.

Subsequent activities to a first inquiry project might include:

△ Finding additional information from observation, pictures, and text.

△ Creating models, dioramas, and drawings based on information found.

△ Presenting the information in oral, written, visual, or electronic format.

△ Using the information to create poetry, riddles, or stories.

Teaching Inquiry in the Upper Grades

During the middle and upper grades, inquiry projects can be structured to give the students more control over the process, content, and products. The teacher and librarian may provide the broad theme, but students will be encouraged to develop their own hypotheses and questions. Standard "study skills strategies" are used as part of the process to help students gather, analyze, and synthesize information.

It is important to discuss with teachers how "study skills" or "strategies" are taught throughout the curriculum and which strategies are emphasized. It makes sense to use inquiry activities to practice strategies that have already been taught. A simple reminder to students can help them generalize a strategy to a new situation. For example, if a student comes to the library to begin a research or inquiry project on Egypt but has trouble getting started, a suggestion by the librarian to "Use KWL," or the simple worksheet shown on page 40, may be all that is needed to help the student get on track.

Too often study skills and strategies are something students learn to use in a workbook and never transfer to other information-gathering situations. As you converse with students during projects and determine where they are getting stuck, share this information with the classroom teacher. You may want to suggest direct teaching of a particular strategy. The instruction can be given by you or the teacher. It may be given to the whole class, a small group, or even an individual child as needed. Some standard titles that introduce study skills are suggested in the bibliography. Strategies include:

△ KWL (what you *Know,* what you *Want* to learn, and what you have *Learned*).

△ QAR (Question, Answer, Relationship).

△ Venn diagrams/Boolean search strategy.

△ Two-column note taking, note taking from lectures, interviews, or visual materials.

△ Story mapping, story grammar.

△ Using visual clues, maps, graphs, photos, drawings.

△ Using special features: index, glossaries, keys, format cues.

△ Webbing/brainstorming.

△ Keyword.

△ Main idea/summarization.

△ Skimming.

The following worksheet will help children focus on the initial stages of inquiry, selecting a topic.

"Your Research Topic"

1. What is your topic?

_____

_____

_____

_____

2. Why are you considering this topic?

_____

_____

_____

_____

_____

3. What do you already know about this topic?

_____

_____

_____

_____

_____

4. What have you learned about it so far?

_____

_____

_____

_____

_____

Projects in which students take control of their learning are useful because, in general, students are more motivated to learn about a subject in which they are already interested. Frequently they have some background knowledge, personal experiences, or sources of information about the topic. Because students develop their own questions, they are less likely to open the encyclopedia and copy a few paragraphs to find the answers. Children will frequently ask questions to which there are no clear answers. Helping children understand that all questions do not have answers is sometimes difficult.

Progress toward information literacy is often uneven. While it is impossible to establish a strict sequence of skills, strategies, and content that must be mastered as the child becomes a skilled user and producer of information, some schools and school systems are developing a framework or guide that can be used by teachers, parents, and students. Giving teachers a clearer understanding of when particular skills and strategies are introduced, reinforced, and mastered can help them integrate these activities into the classroom. The list can also serve as a check when evaluating units and student products. Sharing these documents with parents and students encourages students to take greater charge of their own learning and to think about what they know and what they need to learn.

Even with a schoolwide scope and sequence, it is impossible to assume that two children in the same class at the same time are equally prepared for the task you are presenting. Children frequently move from school to school, from one end of the country to another. Teachers and librarians must make frequent baseline assessments. Whenever possible, children should be pulled into the evaluative process. It helps the teacher and librarian function as coaches and facilitators rather than judges and juries.

As with inquiry projects for younger children, the activities for older students begin with the librarian and teacher planning a unit or project and setting objectives. Units will vary in their duration, organization, and intensity. Different aspects will be directed by the classroom teacher or the librarian. Increasingly, students will take responsibility for the process of their learning. The students will monitor and document progress with a flowchart, learning log, or journal entries. These documents will be used by the teachers to encourage and support metacognition. There will be times set aside for conferences with peers, teachers, and the librarian. New strategies will be introduced through direct teaching, modeling, and reteaching at the point of need.

In the middle and upper-elementary grades, teachers and librarians will also stimulate higher-level thinking skills as they use the materials under discussion to focus on:

△ Bias and point of view of the information producer.

△ Reliability and validity of information.

△ Differences between fact and opinion.

△ Authority of the sources.

△ Evaluating media.

△ Strengths and weaknesses of different formats.

△ Effective ways to share the information gathered.

△ Ways to analyze the information and apply it to new situations.

For a discussion of various ways to introduce and teach these topics, read Kay Vandergrift's *Power Teaching: A Primary Role of the School Media Specialist* and other titles in the bibliography. Sometimes the teacher or librarian will provide direct instruction in one of these areas. You may show a film or video clip and stimulate discussion or read aloud from several sources discussing the same event or issue. You may make data available and ask students to discuss or analyze it.

Frequently, an activity will be structured so that students gather information in the library and present information to the class. The librarian serves as mentor or facilitator, assisting students in the library informally, helping them locate information sources, develop questions, and evaluate and synthesize essential elements, and modeling or suggesting formats for presentation or sharing. Information will be shared in class in debates, discussions, and oral or written reports. As with other inquiry projects, it is essential that you understand the teacher's objectives for the unit or project so that you can give appropriate help and guidance to the student. Thoughtful dialogue and questioning can stimulate and encourage critical thinking. You may also be asked to join the classroom teacher to facilitate the discussion and questioning, or to evaluate students.

The school library may serve as the on-site learning laboratory, but other facilities in the school will also be incorporated. The librarian is frequently the conduit to other facilities. Perhaps the exhibit case or bulletin boards will be used to document the project. Information may be repurposed in the photography lab, computer lab, music room, or school radio or television station. There may be a culminating activity in the classroom, auditorium, gym, or a community site—the mall, city hall, or a nursing home.

Outcomes of Inquiry Learning

There are many products and outcomes of inquiry-based learning. Some of them are planned as part of the projects; others are unexpected and come as a result of the work. Outcomes and products may include:

△ Published books.

△ Data collected by students are used by adult researchers.

△ A page on the World Wide Web.

△ Reports.

△ Literary magazines.

△ Computer multimedia presentations.

△ Students use a variety of resources outside the school building.

△ Mentors from the professional community may support students with special interests.

△ Audiences view products of student learning within the school, the community, and beyond.

Integrating Inquiry with Language Arts

The writing process encourages children to write about what interests them. Often that is their family, a pet, or their last birthday. They may also select a topic that sparks an interest about which they want more information. A first-grader may write about how he helped his mother make a peanut butter sandwich and then want to explore where peanuts come from, how they grow, and how "Skippy" makes peanut butter. Having seen a television special about whales, a child may start a story about a whale mother and then need to find out more about baby whales.

When questions arise and children need information, they should be able to go to the school library. For young children and beginning readers, there must be someone to help them find the information they need. In some schools, a child who goes to the library for help with an immediate informational need wears a button that states, "Researcher." That button alerts adults and older children that the child needs help. Library and classroom orientations for both younger and older children have established that the button wearer may approach any older child or adult. The person approached helps locate the needed information and explains the process.

The questioner and the person supplying help benefit from this activity. Both younger and older students become aware that research is a serious and important business. The questioner gets information and practice in inquiry and the helper gets added practice at interpreting questions and locating information. The library media specialist is able to monitor a great many inquiry searches, intervening when children get stuck and suggesting additional resources and formats. The librarian can compliment the helper, extend the search, and encourage reflection on the strategies used.

The writing process also encourages children to look at the writings of others for models and inspiration. The librarian can provide resources for independent reading, author studies, and genre studies; share stories; invite special guest storytellers and authors; and provide a forum to celebrate and share the written work of professional writers and student authors.

Integrated Language Programs and Inquiry

Integrated language programs, or whole language, also provide many opportunities to involve the inquiry process and the library. The integrated language approach encompasses much more than a literature-based reading program. It links the communication arts: reading, writing, and oral language. Frequently, the content is derived from classroom and community happenings and the background and interests of the children. A morning meeting or sharing may begin with a discussion of Shane's loose tooth and lead to reading, writing, drawing, and talking about dentists, baby teeth and big teeth, tooth fairies, dinosaur teeth, shark teeth, who else has lost a tooth, and more. Many of these explorations would be enriched with resources from the library.

The Librarian as Literature Teacher

In addition to teaching information skills and critical thinking, the librarian has responsibilities as a literature specialist. For some activities, you will be the organizer and lead teacher. You may schedule the activity or event, select the materials, structure the event, and invite the audience. For other activities, you will be drawn in to assist classroom teachers, subject specialists, or children. In other cases, you will be asked to advise administrators, parents, teachers, and children. Literary activities encompass all curriculum areas, all reading levels, all learning styles. There are many excellent professional titles to help you develop a repertoire of curriculum-based activities listed in the bibliography. Other literature-based programs can be found in chapter 4, "Programming." Some events, like a play, will take months of planning and rehearsing. Others, like a spontaneous booktalk for the child who wants a good scary book, may take 30 seconds.

Keeping up with literature—titles, authors, and genres—is a continuing challenge for all school librarians. It is important to read professional journals and books, attend conferences, and participate in staff development. It is essential that you read the books as well as the reviews. There is no substitute. You must also practice your craft. You become a good storyteller by listening to stories, reading widely, selecting carefully, rehearsing, and telling them again and again. Practice telling your story before a mirror or into an audiocassette or video camera. Evaluate your performance. Tell your story to a friend, colleague, or member of your family.

Amateurs may assume reading aloud to children is easy. Just pick up a book. Anyone who can read should be able to read aloud to a group of kids! But effective reading aloud is a complex skill akin to professional acting. It is a delicate harmony of material, reader, voice, pacing, language, mood, and audience. You need to select with care, evaluating different versions with attention to language and literary quality. Analyze the mood, characters, and plot, and practice diction, pacing, voice, and presentation. You must be aware of your audience, their previous experiences with stories and listening, and their attention span. You must respond to audience cues to decide when to speed up, slow down, pause, and stop.

Storytelling and reading aloud are just two of the activities that come to mind when thinking about the librarian's role as literature specialist. But there are many other activities including:

- Δ Selecting books and other media.

- Δ Gathering resources for thematic study.

- Δ Developing reading lists and bibliographies.

- Δ Suggesting titles for teachers and parents to read aloud.

- Δ Suggesting titles for recreational reading.

- Δ Serving on the curriculum, assembly, textbook, book club, or trip committee.

- Δ Supervising or coaching student storytelling, reading aloud, or peer tutoring.

- Δ Developing and presenting booktalks.

- Δ Evaluating student booktalks.

- Δ Judging oratory contests, debates, poetry, and prose reading or writing.

- Δ Organizing book and media discussions for children, parents, and teachers.

- Δ Sharing poetry.

- Δ Supervising writing contests or clubs.

- Δ Assisting with plays, performances, and dramatizations.

- Δ Advising the literary magazine staff.

- Δ Coordinating author celebrations and author studies.

- Δ Developing genre or theme studies.

- Δ Assisting with displays and exhibits.

- Δ Supervising television, radio, multimedia, or video productions.

Developing Teaching Opportunities

For some programs, the librarian might be the organizer, gatherer of materials, primary teacher, and evaluator; for other programs, the librarian might find the presenter, assist with materials, arrange for space and materials, or document the program with video or still photos. At times, the librarian may only make the space available. Often the library will be used by several small groups at the same time. The librarian needs to supervise and oversee the activities without interfering with independent learning. Achieving the delicate balance of oversight is a continuing challenge.

Children will also come to use the library for recreational reading and other independent interests. Sometimes they come for a friendly word or a warm and inviting place of respite from the rest of the school. Make children feel welcome and comfortable. Take the time to talk with children and to really listen to them. A quiet greeting, a question, or an offer of help can humanize a large and alien environment for young children. It can also be some of the most valuable teaching time of the day. It is an opportunity for individualized instruction at the point of need.

As the library media specialist, you are the role model for all sorts of learning. Children are recording everything you say and do. Your gestures, expressions, and body language become a part of their repertoire. Observe children who have observed you as you go about your routines. You will find they mimic your words, movements, and even attitudes. It is an awesome responsibility and one that imbues each minute with meaning and purpose. There is no downtime for the school media specialist. Help children become self-sufficient in locating and circulating materials and in using equipment. Demonstrate ways of accessing, modifying, and using information. Put learning in the context of where it will be used. Encourage children to help peers, older and younger children, teachers, and parents. Invite and value questions, stimulate their interests, open the world to their exploration.

Students need to demonstrate what they have learned by teaching others. They also need to reflect on the processes and products. By developing opportunities for students to increase their expertise and share it in productive, practical ways, you further their intellectual growth. You may be called upon to develop, organize, and supervise a variety of groups, projects, and events. You need to examine each opportunity and maximize the learning value of each assignment. Some of these are discussed in chapter 4, "Programming." These may include service clubs, special interest clubs, discussion groups, contests, special events, and happenings.

As the librarian, you need to help administrators, teachers, parents, and students understand the importance of giving students a more active role in teaching and learning in the school. Administrators may question the participation of students. "Are they really learning anything as research buddies, or are they just free labor?" Teachers may complain that having students released from class to work on the computer squad or to serve as peer tutors is a "waste of teaching time." They may want to send only the brightest students who "can spare the time." Conversely, parents may complain that their bright students should be doing "advanced work," not "baby-sitting" or "doing the teacher's job." You have an important role educating administrators, teachers, and parents about the value of student activities. It is also important to help students understand the importance of the work they do. You must structure the experience for students so that their participation is a useful learning opportunity for tutors and tutees.

Create teaching environments in which you may not be an active participant and for which the audience is less defined. You may set up:

△ Displays of books and media that explore a theme, juxtapose points of view, stimulate discussion, or challenge ideas.

△ Exhibits of student writing, art, models, or science fair projects that extend peer learning.

△ Biomes like terrarium, aquarium, cactus garden, or hamster and cage with response journals to encourage observation and reflection.

△ Realia: shell collections, seeds, feathers, rocks, dried leaves, or flowers with related books that invite children to examine, classify, and compare.

△ Science and math tools like prisms, magnifying glasses, mirrors, magnets, calculators, tangrams, geoblocks, balance beam, and the like to facilitate inquiry.

△ A listening center and viewing center for self-directed learning.

△ Photos, postcards, maps, and other items to facilitate self-directed visual learning.

△ Puppets, masks, costumes, and animal noses to encourage creative self-expression.

△ A museum corner in which students, teachers, and parents can display special collections or artifacts of interest.

△ Computer and CD-ROM programs for student and teacher use.

△ Puzzlers: Post literary riddles, crossword puzzles, geography questions, or odd facts selected by students or teachers.

△ A wonder wall: Put up a large sheet of blank paper and encourage children to post questions or answer questions you post.

The Librarian as Instructional Consultant

The librarian must become familiar with the whole school curriculum. You work with teachers and students at every grade level and serve as an instructional consultant. Sample projects for the librarian as instructional consultant are presented in chapter 4. Others are discussed in titles mentioned in the bibliography. The librarian:

Δ Selects and circulates professional books and magazines.

Δ Locates and purchases materials to meet the teaching and learning needs of the whole school.

Δ Maintains a file of community resources.

Δ Meets regularly with teachers to plan programs and activities.

Δ Serves on curriculum and other schoolwide planning committees.

Δ Helps organize schoolwide special programs and events.

Δ Provides access to resources beyond the school.

Δ Documents student learning and school events.

Δ Communicates frequently with the school administration about resource and equipment needs.

You are in a unique position to know who is teaching what, how teachers teach, what resources are needed, and common problems and concerns. Informal staff development might include a brief conversation with a teacher in the hallway about new materials just received. You might:

Δ Let a first-grade teacher know that the fourth grade is also studying endangered animals and might like to share the products of their research.

Δ Photocopy the table of contents of professional magazines and post them over the time clock in the office to encourage teachers to continue staff development. Maintain a bulletin board with professional development opportunities in the school, district, or county.

Δ Assist with grant writing: It's a great way to learn more about other teachers and encourage collaboration.

Δ Post information on conferences, workshops, college courses, trips, museum exhibits, and the like.

Δ Send away for resource packets, free materials, and curriculum guides advertised in professional magazines.

Δ Display recent professional titles or book jackets in the teachers' lunchroom. Suggest a great new title for reading aloud.

Δ Invite teachers to come to the library during their preparation periods, lunch periods, or before or after school.

Δ Plan formal staff development sessions, which might include participation in grade-level conferences and teacher planning meetings. You may provide in-service training for new teachers or sessions in using the new information technologies.

△ Speak at an orientation for new teachers to discuss the library program and resources, and encourage collaboration.

△ Gather resources, help develop objectives, and plan units or themes. Use your expertise on the curriculum committee or technology planning committee.

△ Circulate a questionnaire to teachers asking for their suggestions for workshops, materials, and assistance.

△ Offer to team-teach, providing teachers with models of different learning styles, materials, and methods.

△ Provide an annotated book list; display or give a two-minute booktalk at staff meetings.

△ Present or help organize an after-school or lunchtime workshop on a issue of concern to teachers.

△ Develop a workshop for parents, or for parents and their children.

△ Attend conferences and report on what you learned.

Bibliography

Armstrong, Thomas. *Multiple Intelligences in the Classroom*. Alexandria, VA: Association for Supervision and Curriculum Development, 1944.

Bodart, Joni Richards. *Booktalk! 4*. New York: H. W. Wilson, 1992.

Burkle, Candace, and David Marshak. *HM Study Skills Program. Level 1*. Alexandria, VA: National Association of Elementary School Principals, 1989.

California Media and Library Educators Association. *From Library Skills to Information Literacy: A Handbook for the 21st Century*. Castle Rock, CO: Hi Willow Research and Publishing, 1994.

Carletti, Silvana, Suzanne Girard, and Kathlene Willing. *The Library/Classroom Connection*. Markham, Ontario: Pembroke/Heinemann, 1991.

Chapman, Anne. *Making Sense: Teaching Critical Reading Across the Curriculum*. New York: College Entrance Examination Board, 1993.

Cullinan, Bernice E. *Children's Literature in the Reading Program*. Newark, DE: International Reading, 1987.

Dublin, Peter, Harvey Pressman, Eileen Barnett, Ann D. Corcoran, and Evelyn J. Woldman. *Elementary Education: Integrating Computers in Your Classroom*. New York: HarperCollins College, 1994.

Dunn, Rita. "Now That You Know Your Learning Style—How Can You Make the Most of It?" *Early Years* (February 1983): 49–52.

Eisenberg, Michael B., and Robert E. Berkowitz. *Information Problem Solving: The Big Six Skills Approach to Library and Information Skills Instruction*. Norwood, NJ: Ablex, 1990.

Freeley, Mary Ellen, and Janet Perrin. "Teaching to Both Hemispheres." *Teaching K-8* 18 (August-September 1987): 67–69.

Frender, Gloria. *Learning to Learn: Stregthening Study Skills and Brain Power*. Nashville, TN: Incentive, 1990.

Hancock, Joelie, and Susan Hill. *Literature-Based Reading Programs at Work.* Portsmouth, NH: Heinemann, 1987.

Haycock, Ken. *School Library Program in the Curriculum.* Englewood, CO: Libraries Unlimited, 1990.

Hill, Susan, and Tim Hill. *The Collaborative Classroom: A Guide to Co-operative Learning.* Portsmouth, NH: Heinemann, 1990.

Johnson, Lauri, and Sally Smith. *Dealing with Diversity Through Multicultural Fictions: Library Classroom Partnerships.* Chicago: American Library Association, 1993.

Kuhlthau, Carol C. "Information Search Process: A Summary of Research and Implications for School Library Media Programs." *School Library Media Quarterly* 18 (Fall 1989): 19–25.

Laughlin, Mildred Knight, and Letty S. Watt. *Developing Learning Skills Through Children's Literature: An Idea Book for K-5 Classrooms and Libraries.* Vol. 1. Phoenix, AZ: Oryx Press, 1986.

Loughlin, Catherine E., and Joseph H. Suina. *The Learning Environment: An Instructional Strategy.* New York: Teachers College, 1982.

Lovitt, Charles, and Ian Lowe. *Investigations: Chance and Data.* Vol. 1. Carlton, Australia: Curriculum, 1993.

McCarney, Stephen B., and Janet K. Tucci. *Study Skills for Students in Our Schools: Study Skills and Instructional Intervention Strategies for Elementary and Secondary Students.* Columbia, MO: Hawthorne, 1991.

McCarney, Stephen B., Kathy Cummins Wunderlich, and Angela Bauer. *The Teacher's Resource Guide: The Staff Development Guide to the Most Common Learning and Behavior Problems Encountered in the Educational Environment.* Columbia, MO: Hawthorne, 1994.

Stripling, Barbara K., and Judy M. Pitts. *Brainstorms and Blueprints: Teaching Library Research as a Thinking Process.* Englewood, CO: Libraries Unlimited, 1988.

Swan, Susan, and Richard White. *The Thinking Books.* London: Falmer Press, 1994.

Turner, Philip M. *Helping Teachers Teach.* 2d ed. Englewood, CO: Libraries Unlimited, 1993.

Vandergrift, Kay E. *Power Teaching: A Primary Role of the School Library Media Specialist.* Chicago: American Library Association, 1994.

Wadsworth, Barry J. *Piaget's Theory of Cognitive Development: An Introduction for Students of Psychology and Education.* 2d. ed. New York: Longman, 1979.

Watt, Letty S. *Developing Learning Skills Through Children's Literature: An Idea Book for K-5 Classrooms and Libraries.* Vol. 2. Phoenix, AZ: Oryx Press, 1994.

Weiner, Esther. *Dirt Cheap Science: Activity-Based Units, Games, Experiments and Reproducibles.* New York: Scholastic Professional Books, 1992.

Chapter 4) Programming

Fig. 4.1. Library Media Specialists Are Collaborative Partners in Planning and Implementing Programs.

Introduction

Programming is an important vehicle for meeting the learning objectives and the educational goals of your school. As the librarian you will be called upon to plan, facilitate, produce, publicize, evaluate, and document a wide variety of programs for many different audiences. You will need to become an expert at managing time, space, and scarce resources. Programming in the school library for the twenty-first century will challenge you to use your expertise as an information specialist, master teacher, and superior communicator.

Your primary goals are to ensure that students and staff are effective users of ideas and information, foster the love of reading, and encourage lifelong learning. As the school library media specialist, you also need to be aware of the larger school goals and the goals enumerated in state and local curriculum guides. Many schools have a formalized mission statement that articulates the school's goals. They also have a collection of the curriculum guides used in the school. These documents are valuable tools when planning programs and allocating time and resources. Consider how each program fits into the overall goals of your school and its curriculum and how it helps students meet their learning objectives.

If your school does not have a formal mission statement, you may wish to develop one in cooperation with administrators, teachers, and parents. If you do not have the curriculum guides used by your school for all grades and content areas, make an effort to acquire them. The library media center should have those resources that help teachers make thoughtful planning decisions.

The programs included in this section were adapted from some of the many programs developed by school librarians. There are programs that:

△ Address many teaching styles and learning preferences.

△ Enhance skills, strategies, and content objectives.

△ Use high tech and no tech.

△ Accommodate large and small groups and spaces.

△ Involve the whole school, a single grade or class, small groups, and individuals.

△ Involve same and mixed age groups.

△ Involve students, teachers, administrators, and parents.

Figure 4.2. on page 51 summarizes graphically the various programs discussed on pages 52 to 75.

Small Group Programs

The library is a great place for small groups and special interest activities. These can occur during lunchtime, before or after school, and during the school day. You may organize a club or group in response to a personal interest or an interest expressed by students, teachers, administrators, or parents. Possible clubs include kites, creative writing, early-bird reading, book buddies, puppets, quilting, weather, drama, or book discussion. The teacher or the librarian may select children to participate or children may volunteer. Sometimes, older and younger children from several classes participate in the same activity. Other groups may include only children of a single age or class. A group may meet weekly, monthly or, if there is a project under way, every day until the project is completed.

You may direct the activities, or teachers, volunteers, or students may be in charge. For example, in the Puppet Club, the librarian instructs the children, but in the Reading Buddies program, older students monitor younger students.

If a whole class is studying or researching a topic, special interest groups may be established to pursue different aspects or to create different products. Because many groups from many classes may be competing to use the very limited library space, time, and resources, it is essential that you meet with teachers early in the planning process. For example, a class studying Haiti may be divided into four to five groups: one focusing on music, another developing a puppet show, a third using maps or needing information on folk costumes, and so on. Planning and careful scheduling are important.

A program objective may be to introduce children to a literary genre or provide opportunities for oral language, collaborative learning, or socialization. Some projects provide in-depth study in a content area or provide opportunities to develop a particular information skill. Some enable children to explore a new technology.

For some programs, the process is paramount; in others, there will be a final product, display, or performance. In still others, desired outcomes may be introducing a new idea, opening a window for students, teachers, or parents. The variety of activities is limited only by your imagination!

Program	Participants						Subject Content							Outcome			
	Special Interest Groups	Individual Class	Multi-grade	Parents	Teachers	Community	Using Technolgy	Art	Math	Social Studies	Science	Language Arts	Social Skills	Written	Oral	Visual	Kinesthetic
Puppet Club	✓			✓	✓	✓		✓	✓			✓			✓	✓	✓
Kite Club	✓		✓	✓	✓	✓	✓		✓	✓	✓	✓	✓	✓	✓	✓	✓
Book Buddies Online	✓		✓		✓	✓	✓			✓	✓	✓	✓	✓	✓	✓	✓
Lunch Bunch	✓			✓	✓	✓		✓		✓		✓	✓	✓	✓		
Radio Show: The Immigrant Experience		✓		✓	✓	✓			✓	✓	✓	✓	✓		✓		✓
Pigs on Parade				✓	✓	✓		✓	✓		✓				✓	✓	✓
Hands-On Science			✓		✓	✓			✓		✓	✓			✓	✓	✓
Book Pals			✓		✓	✓						✓			✓		
Video: Columbus		✓		✓	✓		✓	✓		✓		✓	✓	✓	✓	✓	✓
Journeys		✓	✓	✓	✓	✓		✓		✓			✓		✓	✓	✓
Investigating Animals		✓	✓	✓	✓	✓	✓	✓			✓	✓				✓	✓
Celebrate Reading Month					✓	✓		✓				✓		✓	✓	✓	✓
Math Fair			✓	✓	✓			✓	✓		✓	✓	✓	✓	✓	✓	✓
Bug It!			✓		✓			✓			✓				✓	✓	✓
"We Hate English"			✓	✓	✓	✓	✓	✓		✓		✓	✓	✓	✓	✓	✓
Oral History	✓		✓	✓	✓	✓		✓		✓			✓	✓	✓	✓	✓
Project SPROUT			✓	✓	✓	✓		✓		✓	✓	✓	✓	✓	✓	✓	✓
Parent and Child Workshop				✓			✓									✓	
"We Hate English": Teacher Workshop			✓		✓			✓	✓	✓	✓	✓		✓	✓	✓	✓
Showcase P.S. 72					✓	✓	✓	✓	✓	✓	✓	✓	✓	✓	✓	✓	✓
Thematic Planning					✓			✓		✓		✓	✓	✓	✓	✓	✓
Showcase J.H.S. 47					✓		✓										
Journeys: Teachers Workshop					✓	✓	✓	✓		✓		✓		✓	✓	✓	✓

Fig. 4.2. Shows Graphically Each of the Many Facets of Programs Discussed in This Chapter.

Lunchtime Puppet Club

Students Involved: 20 fourth- and fifth-graders, five first-grade classes

Major Content Area: Language arts

Objectives: To stimulate oral language, cooperative learning, and performance skills; encourage reading; and provide opportunities for creating art.

Needs Addressed: Many of the students in this school speak English as a second language. Students need practice in using English to facilitate fluency. In the workshops, students read silently and aloud, discussed the story with peers, turned the text into dialogue, rehearsed, and performed. Finally, they answered questions from the audience about their performance.

Skills: Reading, adapting, and synthesizing a story for performance. Cooperative learning, oral language, writing, performance, art construction.

Description: Children signed up for the Puppet Club and came to the library during two lunch periods each week for eight weeks. Children read a variety of fairy tales and, working in small groups, selected one to perform. They assigned parts, wrote a script, created puppets, rehearsed, and performed for other members of the Puppet Club. Performances were also held for other students and parents. At the end of each performance, puppeteers answered questions from the audience. Puppets and fairy tale books were kept on display in the library.

Planning: Publicity flyers and sign-up sheets were sent to classrooms. The librarian displayed a variety of fairy tales and books on puppet making. Materials such as markers, yarn, paper bags, sticks, and cardboard cartons were gathered.

Instructional Roles—Students: Signed up. Selected and read fairy tales, adapted one to perform, developed scripts, constructed puppets, props, and backdrops. **Librarian:** Advertised and scheduled the program, gathered books and materials; demonstrated several simple methods of constructing puppets, facilitated group activities, and invited classes to attend performances. **Teachers:** Attended performances with classes, facilitated questioning after each performance. **Parents:** Provided puppet and stage materials and videotaped some performances.

Learning Styles Addressed—Materials: Visual. **Process:** Visual, auditory, tactile. **Products:** Visual, auditory, tactile.

Evaluation: The librarian reported that more spontaneous language was used by students as the Puppet Club progressed. Teachers indicated that children involved were more willing to participate in other oral projects in class.

Resources: Books of fairy tales, books on puppets, and puppet stages.

The Kite Club

Students Involved: 25 fourth- and fifth-graders

Major Content Areas: Language arts, social studies, math, science, and art

Objectives: To stimulate oral and written language, enhance research skills, foster multicultural awareness, and use mathematics in the creation of art.

Needs Addressed: Children from many countries attend the school. Teachers are interested in fostering cooperative learning, multicultural awareness, and an interdisciplinary approach to learning.

Skills: Note taking from encyclopedias, magazine articles, and interviews. Expository and creative writing using computer word processing and publishing programs. Using math (measuring) to enlarge original kite designs and construct kites. Working cooperatively to build a large box kite.

Description: Children requested a Kite Club. For eight weeks, they came to the library for two-hour sessions twice a week to read about and research kites in many cultures. Children wrote poems, stories, a play, and nonfiction pieces on kites, and made books in both English and Spanish using the library computers. Parent volunteers assisted students in building an enormous box kite and each child designed and built a personal kite. On field day, children flew their kites in a local park.

Planning: The librarian met with classroom teachers to discuss the integration of the Kite Club with other classroom objectives. The librarian located information on kites and found a parent volunteer willing to help with kite construction. Classroom teachers agreed to help with written projects, and the art teacher offered assistance with the art construction aspects. The librarian began collecting materials useful for kite making from parents and children.

Instructional Roles—Librarian: Planned the activities of the Kite Club in cooperation with classroom teachers and a community volunteer, gathered book and nonprint resources on kites and materials for kite making, scheduled sessions and culminating activities, facilitated small group activities in the library, documented activities with still photos and videotape, and created a display for the library. **Community Volunteers:** Assisted with the design and construction of kites. Served as content resources, describing how kites were made and flown in their country of origin. **Teachers:** Helped with planning, content, skills, and follow-up activities. Specialists assisted with art and computer components. **Students:** Initiated the club; assisted each other's reading, writing, researching, and construction; interviewed parents and relatives on kites from their culture; used the library computers to write and edit stories and poems and make books; wrote a script for a play about kites from around the world with the librarian and classroom teacher; rehearsed and presented an assembly program about kites; made kites with the help of the parent volunteer and designed a personal kite with the help of the parent volunteer and art teacher. Measured, cut, constructed, and decorated a personal kite.

Learning Styles Addressed—Materials: Visual, auditory, tactile. **Process:** Visual, auditory, tactile. **Products:** Visual, auditory, tactile.

Evaluation: Each child in the club produced one book or writing sample. Many reflected an awareness of kites in other cultures. Every child participated in building both the group kite and a personal kite. Every kite flew!

Resources: Books, magazines, family photos, and a video on kites; oral interviews with parents and students and sample kites from several countries.

Book Buddies Online

Students Involved: 23 fifth-graders from six classes

Major Content Area: Language arts

Objectives: To stimulate an interest in reading and writing, and increase skills in using the computer for telecommunications.

Needs Addressed: Some students were fascinated by computers but were less interested in reading books. This project was designed to encourage reading and to provide access to the computer for online telecommunications.

Skills: Reading, writing, computer telecommunications, and peer tutoring.

Description: Students selected books to read and wrote reviews to share with students in other schools via computer telecommunications. The librarian taught students how to use e-mail. As the program progressed, experienced students taught other students how to send and receive messages. Students worked with peers who helped them edit their book reviews. Children recommended titles to buddies in different schools and received recommendations from their buddies.

Planning: The librarian obtained and installed computer software for telecommunications and opened an account for online time, identified a buddy school willing to communicate, informed teachers of the new program and invited students to select books for sharing and to come for training sessions on the computer.

Instructional Roles—Librarian: Trained students to use the word processing and telecommunications program, organized and scheduled student reading and editing buddies. **Students:** Trained other students on computer telecommunications and assisted each other as reading and editing buddies.

Learning Styles Addressed—Materials: Visual, tactile. **Process:** Visual, auditory, tactile. **Product:** Visual.

Evaluation: The librarian reported that children borrowed and read more books during the project as evidenced by their reading logs. Teachers examined reviews and indicated that the book reviews got longer and more coherent as the project progressed. After three training sessions, half of the students could use telecommunications without assistance.

Resources: Books, computer hardware and software, and online connections.

The Lunch Bunch

Students Involved: 24 students from four classes, each cycle, grades 1-5

Major Content Areas: Language arts, social studies, science

Objectives: To stimulate interest in reading and listening, provide opportunities to evaluate factual information, identify the main idea and create art based on ideas and information from books.

Needs Addressed: Teachers wanted students to practice listening skills and critical thinking activities in a fun-filled informal setting. They wanted to give students in the same grade but in different classes a chance to socialize, and they wanted to incorporate an art activity based on a curriculum theme.

Skills: Listening and reacting to books, paraphrasing, locating the main idea, evaluating factual material, and transforming ideas and information into a visual presentation.

Description: The librarian met with teachers and decided on a project related to the classroom curriculum. Six children from each of four classes volunteered to come to the library for a half hour each day after their lunch for a special project. A project took 6 to 12 sessions to complete. When the project was complete, the librarian invited another group of children from the same grade until every child in the grade who wanted to participate had done so. Then a new grade and a different project were selected.

Sample Projects—Fourth-Grade Project: The librarian read aloud two biographies of Benjamin Franklin. Students discussed Franklin, compared the information in the two sources, and selected a part of Franklin's life to illustrate. Each then made one square of a paper "Biography Quilt." The quilt was laminated and is on display in the library.

Third-Grade Project: Focusing on Earth Day, the librarian read *The Lorax* by Dr. Seuss aloud. Students brainstormed the causes of waste and pollution, suggested ways to reduce pollution, and suggested the ways children, parents, the school, and city could help solve the problem. Children made a hallway mural about their own ideas to reduce pollution.

First-Grade Project: The librarian read aloud some of her favorite picture books. Children listened to the stories and suggested their own favorites. They compared and contrasted stories; analyzed characters, events, art, setting, plot, and more; predicted endings; and discussed sequels. Then they selected a favorite story to illustrate for the "Parade of Picture Book Characters." Children made posters, puppets, and murals and came costumed as a favorite character. They were prepared to tell other students and guests who they represented, something about the story in which they appeared, and why they liked the story or character.

Planning: The librarian met with teachers to decide on the curriculum area, gathered books and related materials, arranged with the kitchen for students with passes to be given "priority lunch," and gave each teacher six passes for students.

Instructional Role—Librarian: Introduced topic, books, and activities; worked directly with children; read aloud; discussed the books; and focused student responses to enhance critical thinking skills.

Learning Styles Addressed—Materials: Visual, auditory. **Process:** Visual, auditory, tactile. **Products:** Visual, auditory, tactile.

Evaluation: Teachers reported that children eagerly participated in the program and passes were quickly given out for each cycle. Children groaned when a session was canceled due to holidays or weather. Teachers reported that children discussed the project with peers in the classroom and that there seemed to be some transfer of the critical thinking skills to other activities.

Resources: Books, magazines, videos, markers, paper, fabric, and other craft supplies.

Radio Show: The Immigrant Experience

Students Involved: 15 fifth-grade students from three classes

Major Content Areas: Social studies, language arts, music, drama

Objectives: To encourage research, reading, and writing about immigrant populations and family history, to provide opportunities for oral language, translating facts into a docudrama for sharing via a radio show.

Needs Addressed: As part of their fifth-grade social studies curriculum, students study U.S. history and patterns of immigration in their Brooklyn community. Teachers wanted students to research, study, and reflect on their roots and forge links with other immigrant groups, past and present.

Skills: Note taking from written, visual, and oral sources; writing a script based on research; and developing a radio docudrama.

Description: Students met with the librarian during lunchtime to create a half-hour program for the local educational radio station based on their research about immigrants in their community. Working cooperatively, students developed a script, rehearsed under the direction of the librarian, and traveled to the radio station to tape their production. The production was aired on educational radio and shared in the school.

Planning: The librarian suggested using ongoing research about immigrants to develop a radio program for a local educational radio station. She approached teachers and invited interested students to a lunchtime workshop.

Instructional Roles—Librarian: Scheduled workshops, facilitated script writing and rehearsals, supervised children during the trip to the radio station, and taped copies of the production for sharing. **Music Teacher:** Located and taught songs for the program to the chorus. **Parents:** Were interviewed by students at home and at school and participated in a panel discussion for an assembly.

Learning Styles Addressed—Materials: Visual, auditory. **Process:** Visual, auditory, tactile. **Product:** Auditory.

Evaluation: The completed cassette tape served as the assessment of oral language, research, and synthesis of facts on immigration.

Resources: Fifth-grade social studies curriculum, books, magazines, filmstrips, oral interviews, and audiotapes.

Whole Class Programs

Many programs involve whole classes or grades and more than one curriculum area and skill. The librarian and teachers should plan the unit together, identify resources, note the skill and content objectives, and decide who will do what. Joint projects lighten the load and are excellent ways to continue professional development as teachers learn from each other and share their expertise. Either the classroom teacher or the librarian might introduce the unit. It depends on space, time, special interests, and the skills of the individuals involved. For some projects, the whole class comes to the library for an initial browsing or brainstorming session, then is divided into small groups for additional sessions in the library and the classroom. In other projects, the librarian will work more directly with one group and the teacher with another.

A small group may work with the librarian on a dramatic retelling of a folktale, while another group locates pictures of African masks needed to design papier-mâché masks with the help of the art teacher. Other students may prepare a written report, a mural, a rap song, or a diorama with the classroom teacher.

Parents and community people may come to the library and be interviewed by children on a topic of special interest or the librarian, teacher, and students may videotape a student performance for sharing with other classes. Student-produced videos, audiotapes, books, and art can be added to the library collection for other students to use. The library becomes a place of performance, celebration, sharing, and display. It is a center for ongoing independent learning.

Pigs on Parade

Students Involved: 35 first-graders

Major Content Areas: Language arts, science, art, music

Objectives: To encourage reading for pleasure, introduce the basic classifications of fiction and nonfiction, study the life cycle of pigs and other animals, promote oral language and improve oral speaking, introduce basic library research skills, and provide opportunities for self-expression through art and writing.

Needs Addressed: An enthusiastic group of first-graders went "hog-wild" after hearing a story about an imaginary pig. The teacher and librarian used the enthusiasm to introduce children to beginning research skills, library location skills, and to explore the pleasures of reading. They also used the pig motif to stimulate creative writing, expository writing, and art projects.

Skills: Reading, listening, oral language, writing, research strategies, and art.

Description: During the course of the school year each child read and listened to dozens of stories and accounts from nonfiction books on pigs, then selected a favorite pig character to build and decorate. They found facts about pigs in a variety of library sources. They worked with older children to write "piggericks" (poems and stories) and built a 6' papier-mâché pig. They visited a pork store and interviewed a pig farmer who came to school with pigs. The culminating activity was a "Pig Parade" song and dance festival with pig stories, book reviews, "piggericks," and pig refreshments.

Fig. 4.3. "Pigs on Parade" Culminating Activity—Pig Refreshments.

Planning: The librarian and teacher met to discuss a vehicle to introduce beginning research and location skills. The pig story was shared for fun. The pig was used to introduce concepts and skills throughout the year.

Instructional Roles—Librarian: Introduced the first pig story and found fiction and nonfiction materials on pigs, taught pig poems and songs, found directions for making bleach-bottle pigs, encouraged older students to mentor young pig enthusiasts in research and writing, arranged rehearsals and the final celebration in the library, assisted students in locating information on pigs, documented the programs with photos and videos. **Teacher:** Introduced writing, drawing, and scientific information about pigs; monitored book reviews and assisted in the library. **Parents:** Provided costumes, materials for art projects, and refreshments. **Students:** Served as scribes and mentors.

Learning Styles Addressed—Materials: Visual, auditory, tactile. **Process:** Visual, auditory, tactile. **Products:** Visual, auditory, tactile.

Evaluation: Teacher evaluated written and oral work products.

Resources: Books, magazines, videos, filmstrips, pictures, audiotapes, experts, live pigs, puzzles, models, trips, and tours.

Hands-On Science

Students Involved: 10 classes, grades 1-5

Major Content Area: Science

Objectives: To provide students with hands-on science experience using the scientific method and to stimulate oral language, writing, reading, and thinking.

Needs Addressed: The school has no science specialist. Classroom teachers felt they lacked the time and resources to conduct hands-on science with their students.

Skills: Applying the scientific method to problem solving—orally, experimentally, and in writing; developing a hypothesis, testing, observing, recording, modifying the hypothesis, and further testing.

Description: The librarian invited classroom teachers to sign up for hands-on science activities in the library. The librarian identified simple experiments in books and magazines from the library, and contacted the local high school for volunteers. High school volunteers assembled materials, practiced the experiments, and set up three or four science tables in the library. Classes were scheduled to come to the library with their teachers. The high school student introduced the topic, demonstrated the experiment, and provided materials for students to explore further. Students kept a record of their hypothesis, experiments, results, and conclusions. The high school students, the librarian, and classroom teachers facilitated experimentation and dialogue. If time permitted, students rotated to another science station. At the end of the period, students reported to the whole class on their findings. Teachers borrowed materials and books for further exploration in the classroom. Student notes were formalized as a science journal in the classroom.

Planning—Librarian: Contacted the local high school for student volunteers to help with hands-on science and met with the student coordinator to discuss the needs and schedule of the science program. Contacted teachers regarding science curriculum areas and scheduled group visits, located appropriate experiments and related books, and trained volunteers.

Instructional Roles—Librarian: Helped facilitate oral communication, writing, and thinking activities; provided follow-up resources for the classroom teacher. **High School Volunteers:** Introduced and demonstrated science experiments and facilitated dialogue. **Teachers:** Facilitated experiments and oral communication, conducted follow-up activities in the classroom, and helped students revise and edit their science journals.

Learning Styles Addressed—Materials: Visual, auditory, tactile. **Process:** Visual, auditory, tactile. **Products:** Visual, auditory.

Evaluation: Teachers used student science journals and worksheets to evaluate student understanding of science concepts introduced through the experiments. The high school teacher coordinating the teen volunteer placement came to the school to observe students working with younger children. The librarian completed an evaluation questionnaire for the teen volunteers.

Resources: State Elementary Science Curriculum, magazines, books and science videos, batteries, balloons, prisms, copper wire, magnets, and so on.

The librarian says:

This is a win-win program. Children had opportunities for hands-on science, a reason to read, write, and think scientifically. They met some wonderful role models as they worked with successful high school seniors from their community. Classroom teachers had help in teaching an important curriculum area. I was able to share with teachers and children some of the great books, magazines, and video resources for science learning. One of our high school volunteers reported to me [that] his volunteer work here was very important in helping him get a full college scholarship aid package.

Book Pals

Students Involved: 90 multiple handicapped children ages 5 to 21

Major Content Areas: Language arts, social skills

Objectives: To encourage enjoyment of books and stories, improve listening skills, and enhance oral language and social skills.

Needs Addressed: The students in the school have multiple severe and profound handicaps. They need exposure to books and stories and opportunities to interact with peers and adults.

Skills: Listening and attending to the speaker, responding orally or though special apparatus when appropriate, and interacting with books, peers, and teachers.

Description: An actor from the Screen Actors Guild volunteered weekly, coming to the school to read, act out stories, and talk with the students. Students, their teachers, and aides came to the library where the actor worked with a small group for 15 to 20 minutes sharing books, stories, songs, and conversation.

Planning: The librarian met with the actor to discuss appropriate materials and stories and to provide information on the special needs of the students he worked with. The librarian also passed on comments and ideas from classroom teachers who attended previous sessions. The librarian prepared a schedule for classes to visit the library and gathered related books, stories, toys, objects, and visual materials.

Instructional Roles—Librarian: Provided appropriate books and guidance for the professional actor; gave him information about the needs of the students, appropriate materials, and presentation techniques; and passed on suggestions and critiques from teachers attending past sessions. **Actor:** Rehearsed and adapted his performance to meet the needs of his special audience. **Teachers:** Observed and assisted their students throughout the program to maximize the learning experience and provided feedback to the librarian and actor about the program and classroom follow-up.

Learning Styles Addressed—Materials: Visual, auditory, tactile. **Process:** Visual, auditory, tactile.

Evaluation: Teachers met with the librarian to discuss the success of the program for each of their students. They suggested follow-up activities. Teachers reported that children were enthusiastic about the program.

Resources: An actor, books, visuals, toys, sound makers, and other objects related to the stories and concepts under presentation.

Student-Produced Video: Columbus on Trial

Students Concerned: 20 sixth-grade ESL students

Major Content Areas: Social studies, oral and written language, drama

Objectives: To enhance oral and written language for English as Second Language students, develop research skills and critical thinking skills using social studies, transform facts into drama, and videotape the results.

Needs Addressed: The teacher wanted an interdisciplinary project that would involve library research, note taking, oral and written language, and drama. She also wanted her students to work cooperatively in planning, producing, filming, and editing a video production.

Skills: Researching to find information to support ideas; note taking from various sources; selecting, verifying, and synthesizing facts and presenting them as drama; establishing a point of view; and scripting, rehearsing, filming, and editing a docudrama.

Description: The teacher wanted a fresh approach to the study of Columbus. After reading about Columbus, students brainstormed about his life, times, and the personalities of his world. Working in interest groups, students researched the issue of exploration from the point of view of the participants: Native Americans, Queen Isabella, Spanish sailors, and so on. Committees took notes, summarized, and shared their findings. Students wrote a script, rehearsed, gathered costumes and props, and videotaped their docudrama. The video was shared with other classes and submitted to a citywide social studies fair, where it won top honors.

Planning: The teacher met with the librarian to discuss the curriculum objectives, time frame, and resources. They decided who would teach what. They scheduled sessions for whole and small groups.

Instructional Roles—Teacher: Determined the content area and the student skills; reviewed student logs; monitored progress; taught students filming techniques and how to use the video camera; supervised staging, costumes, props, rehearsals, and filming; supervised student editing; prepared the finished video for showing. **Librarian:** Located resources; assisted students with their use and interpretation; taught note taking skills, critical thinking skills, and bibliographic forms; scheduled small group research sessions and performances in the library. **Students:** Worked with their groups sharing expertise and information, coached student actors, videotaped, and edited.

Learning Styles Addressed—Materials: Visual, auditory. **Process:** Visual, auditory, tactile. **Product:** Visual.

Evaluation: Teacher evaluated notes, log entries, script, editing, and the final video. The video was used to evaluate the research and oral language and to demonstrate the students' understanding of points of view.

Resources: Books, films, videos, and audiotapes.

Journeys

Students Involved: 30 third-graders

Major Content Areas: Language arts, social studies, art

Objectives: To encourage writing based on family experiences and oral history, stimulate visual literacy and cooperative learning, and produce a three-dimensional art construction.

Fig. 4.4. Children Describing Their "Journeys" Project and Accordian Book.

Needs Addressed: The teacher wanted an interdisciplinary activity that would combine social studies, writing, oral language, and art.

Skills: Interviewing, note taking, writing, layout and design, and cooperative learning.

Description: Students met for five two-period sessions with their teacher, the librarian, and a book artist from the Franklin Furnace, Inc., an arts organization. Each student interviewed a family member who had taken a journey, took notes, and wrote a prose piece or poem on a significant event in that person's life. Working in small groups, students determined the elements needed to share the event visually. The classroom teacher assisted with the content and mechanics of writing and the artist focused on the layout and design of the 36" x 36" accordion book. Several books were assembled and shared with classmates, parents, and guests at a celebration in the library.

Planning: The librarian, classroom teacher, and artist met to plan the project and discuss who would do what.

Fig. 4.5. Completed "Journeys" Book Art.

Instructional Roles—Artist: Designed and assisted children in constructing the sculpture books, used questioning skills to help children develop ideas and concepts as they wrote and illustrated family history experiences, and worked with the librarian and teacher planning activities and follow-up. **Teacher:** Worked on the writing component with children and assisted throughout. **Librarian:** Assisted throughout, coordinated the culminating activity in the library, and assisted with evaluation.

Learning Styles Addressed—Materials: Auditory, visual, tactile. **Process:** Auditory, visual, tactile. **Products:** Visual, tactile.

Evaluation: The teacher, artist, and librarian discussed the project at the conclusion. Students wrote evaluations and demonstrated an understanding of the design considerations of creating a book and transforming written text into visual ideas. They could list the sequence of the process and could critique art made by peers.

Resources: State Social Studies Curriculum Guide, books, tapes, interviews, photos, and objects from family members.

Investigating Animals

Students Involved: 65 second-grade students

Major Content Areas: Science, language arts

Objective: To introduce beginning research.

> **Needs Addressed:** Classroom teachers and the librarian developed this project as a library research project for second-graders. Because many of the students were not yet fluent, independent readers, most components were auditory, visual, or verbal rather than written. Support was offered throughout the process so that every child experienced success. The process was the most important part of the project.

> **Skills:** Distinguishing between fact and fiction; brainstorming; writing questions; developing search strategies; using pictures, filmstrips, experts, and audiotapes for information; identifying the information that answers questions; indicating the source of information; and organizing, presenting, and sharing the information.

> **Description:** The teachers and librarian introduced and modeled the research process. Children selected an animal and brainstormed to determine what they already knew. Teachers, the librarian, or older students acted as scribes. Children formulated four or five questions about their animal, and then small groups came to the library to begin work. The librarian helped students locate two sources of information. She modeled reading pictures for information and taking single word and picture notes. After finding answers to their questions, children created pictures, murals, models, and dioramas. Children shared projects and answered questions. Questions often stimulated further research so it was back to the library.

> **Planning:** The classroom teacher and librarian met in advance to discuss available resources, who would teach what, and to plan the schedule.

> **Instructional Roles—Teacher and Librarian:** Determined the content and skills needed, and shared the responsibility for teaching and modeling specific skills, conferred with students throughout the process, and monitored student progress.

> **Learning Styles Addressed—Materials:** Visual, auditory. **Process:** Visual, auditory, tactile. **Products:** Visual, auditory, tactile.

> **Evaluation:** The classroom teacher and librarian evaluated the process through continuing dialogue. The teacher evaluated the final product.

> **Resources:** Audiotapes, pictures, filmstrips, books, magazines, videos, and experts.

Multiclass and Schoolwide Celebrations

Schoolwide celebrations are powerful instruments for stimulating cross-grade, peer, and whole school learning. However, schoolwide events require extensive planning, cooperation, teamwork, stamina, and enthusiasm. Because they require so much time and effort, only those projects that are educationally sound and that support the goals and missions of the school should be considered.

Meet with teachers, administrators, and parents to decide which programs will be undertaken. Make sure that resources are available, that the time frame is realistic, and that many people are willing to do the work. You do not have to be in charge of the whole event to make an important contribution. Use your expertise as a resource specialist, master teacher, and communicator to help make the schoolwide celebration an effective instrument of learning. Properly planned and implemented, schoolwide events provide excitement, a sense of community, and joy in learning that extend beyond the particular event and enrich participants in many different ways.

Celebrate Reading Month

Students Involved: 700 students in 30 classes

Major Content Areas: Language arts, social studies, art

Objectives: To promote reading, writing, and oral language; provide opportunities for creating works of art based on reading; and heighten the awareness of books and stories from many different cultures.

Needs Addressed: The activities were developed to stimulate children's enthusiasm for reading a variety of books for pleasure.

Skills: Reading, writing, cooperative learning, and oral and visual expression.

Description: A monthlong celebration of reading was planned by the assistant principal, librarian, reading specialist, and staff developers. All classroom teachers and children were invited to participate. The steering committee developed the guidelines and information on each activity. Whole classes and individual children participated in events. All children attended opening and closing assemblies.

Planning: The steering committee determined objectives, time frames, rules of participation, and culminating activities. Teachers and parents were asked to help in providing assistance, materials, and prizes.

Instructional Roles—Assistant Principal: Chaired the steering committee; coordinated communications, activities, and scheduling; and participated as a "pop-in" poet, guest reader, and judge. **Reading Teacher:** Suggested books and discussion questions. **Librarian:** Worked with the steering committee to develop activities and objectives; gathered resources; assisted with scheduling; documented all events; and displayed banners, art, and writing projects. **Teachers:** Scheduled reading aloud, silent reading, and participation in activities by whole classes and small groups; assisted with gathering materials, construction of projects, rehearsals, and assembly performances; served as "pop-in" poets and guest readers. **Parents:** Encouraged nightly silent reading and reading aloud and served as guest readers and "pop-in" poets. Provided materials for costumes and banners and supplied prizes. **Students:** Assisted with read-aloud groups and activities.

Evaluation: Varied. Some activities had formal judges; for others, classroom teachers evaluated the work product and process.

Resources: Books, filmstrips, videos, audiotapes, and guest readers.

The Annual Math Fair

Students Involved: 40 classes, grades 1-8

Major Content Area: Math

Objectives: To celebrate the use of math and math concepts in all areas of the curriculum and in real-life situations; challenge children to use math concepts in new and different ways; demonstrate how math is used in music, science, social studies, language arts, economics, physical education, and art; and encourage discussion about math and sharing of ideas.

Needs Assessed: Teachers expressed concern that children did not see the use of math in real-life activities. They did not generalize math skills and concepts to other areas of the curriculum, for example, making or reading graphs in social studies, using measurement in art, using ratios in reducing or enlarging recipes in cooking or making art materials, and using information on angles to help sink a basket in basketball. Children said math was boring and useless. Teachers wanted children to see math as exciting, useful, and fun.

Skills: Any area of math skills could be explored.

Description: The math coordinator, assistant principal, teachers, and the librarian met and set the guidelines for the Math Fair. All children in grades 1-3 were invited to participate through individual or group projects, and children in upper grades were required to enter a project that would be evaluated as part of their math grade. Projects could focus on any use of math and involve any math concepts. Children could create models, dioramas, visual representations, audio or videotapes, performances, games, puzzles, computer samples, or written reports. During the four weeks preceding the Fair, children were encouraged to examine the books and related materials in the school and public libraries. Small groups came to the library to browse and gather ideas and resources for projects. Children were also encouraged to interview family members and community people about math in their lives. Special guests who used math were invited to school to speak with interested students. The librarian read aloud stories with math concepts and displayed books of famous mathematicians, math games, and puzzles. During the Fair, held in the gym, students presented their projects and answered questions.

Planning: The math coordinator met with an advisory group that included administrators, teachers, and the librarian to set the time frame, objectives, and criteria. Parents were notified by letter of the guidelines. The librarian prepared resource lists for classroom teachers.

Instructional Roles—Math Coordinator: Provided guidance for the classroom teachers and coordinated the event from setting criteria for projects through judging. **Teachers:** Assisted children with locating appropriate math-related projects and monitored follow-through, used discussions and brainstorming to emphasize the use of math in all subject areas, and helped evaluate Fair entries. **Librarian:** Located resources, assisted with scheduling, worked with small groups on related projects as needed, provided book displays and related stories, and helped judge the Fair.

Learning Styles Addressed—Materials: Visual, auditory, tactile. **Process:** Visual, auditory, tactile. **Products:** Visual, auditory, tactile.

Evaluation: Classroom teachers and the math coordinator provided formal assessment.

Resources: Books, magazines, audio and videotapes, computer programs, manipulative math materials, interviews, art and construction materials.

Bug It! A Schoolwide Celebration of Insects

Students Involved: 30 classes, grades pre-K-6

Major Areas Concerned: Science, language arts, art

Objectives: To introduce the scientific method and techniques of observation and journal writing, stimulate an interest in reading about and studying insects, provide students with an opportunity to share what they learn with peers and adults, and create art and writing products based on scientific observation and study.

Needs Addressed: The school recently strengthened its science focus with a new emphasis on hands-on activities. The administration and science teacher wanted to publicize the new program and also give students a chance to share what they learned in an eight-week study of insects.

Skills: Observation; the scientific method; reading, writing, and oral language; locating facts; evaluating; paraphrasing; note taking; synthesizing; presenting information in new formats; sharing information; and constructing models and dioramas.

Description: Students on all grade levels worked with the science teacher, classroom teacher, and librarian exploring insects. They read about, researched, kept journals and logs, and wrote poems and stories about insects. They selected one insect for in-depth study, gathered information, and presented it in a new way. Some students worked with the librarian, building huge models of favorite insects. Students studied common home and school insects, helpful and harmful insects, and those with complete and incomplete metamorphosis. For the *Bug It!* celebration, each child or group of children researched, designed, displayed, and presented a project related to insects. Children and parents toured the displays and asked questions of student presenters.

Planning: The science teacher, administrator, classroom teachers, and librarian met to plan activities, time frame, evaluation criteria, and the culminating event. The librarian served on several committees: resources, scheduling, publicity, and refreshments.

Instructional Roles—Science Teacher: Prepared lessons and experiments on insects for all grade levels, led small group discussions, modeled the scientific method, and facilitated and evaluated projects. **Teachers:** Continued science activities related to insects in the classroom and supervised related reading and writing projects. **Librarian:** Gathered materials to support the teachers and students; made exhibits of related books and videos; worked with small groups on research, information skills, and art-related projects; encouraged the use of scientific classification keys and journal writing with a table magnifying lens and mystery insect; displayed giant insects and arachnids made by students; hosted gatherings for "buggy" stories, "buggy" poems, and "buggy" riddles; and included several student projects in the library collection for use in future years.

Learning Styles Addressed—Materials: Visual, auditory, tactile. **Process:** Visual, auditory, tactile. **Products:** Visual, auditory, tactile.

Evaluation: The science teacher evaluated research products and bug exhibits according to criteria set by the advisory committee. The classroom teacher evaluated writing and art projects. Students gave written evaluations of the *Bug It!* celebration with suggestions for next year. More than 90 percent of all students participated in some aspect of the project, and nearly 200 parents toured exhibits during the day.

Resources: Books, magazines, videos, filmstrips, pictures, audio and videotapes, insects (living and dead), special guests, models, games, art, and construction materials.

We Hate English Memoirs Study

Students Involved: 10 classes, grades 1-5

Major Content Areas: Language arts, technology

Objectives: To develop language skills through memoirs study and to enhance technology skills of English as Second Language students.

Needs Addressed: In order to promote language development, ESL students were immersed in reading and writing, spending at least one period a day reading, writing, and gathering oral history. The librarian worked with children studying the conventions of picture books, and each child took home a book a night to read aloud.

Skills: Listening, reading, and writing skills; analyzing the language, grammar, and images of literature books and their own writing; using the new technologies of computer software (HyperCard and HyperStudio) to create their own memoirs or oral history works.

Description: Students worked with their classroom teachers and with the librarian, reading, listening to, and analyzing literary works. During the course of the 16-week program, every child wrote two picture books based on personal or family history, one using traditional bookmaking techniques, and one using the computer programs of HyperCard and HyperStudio to add animation, sound, and drawings to the text. Older children read aloud to younger children; parents were encouraged to read aloud at home and at school. Monthly special events included storytellers, parents, and students sharing their books.

Planning: The principal, teachers, and librarian met to discuss the implementation of the program. Teachers requested help in gathering materials for memoir studies and using the new technologies. The librarian volunteered to gather books for reading aloud, classroom and home borrowing, and to conduct workshops after school for teachers on various literary genres. The principal set up a series of 16 workshops in cooperation with the district computer specialist to help the teachers and librarian become proficient with the new technology. Parents were sent a letter asking for their help in reading aloud, sharing oral history, and supporting their children's reading and writing.

Instructional Roles—Librarian: Prepared background material on genre study for teachers, gathered appropriate books for study, organized nightly read-aloud books for all classes, assisted teachers with technology and other reading and writing activities. **Teachers:** Facilitated student reading, writing, bookmaking, and use of computers; hosted author celebrations and read-in programs. **Parents:** Read to their children nightly, attended author events, wrote books. **Students:** Served as coaches and editors.

Learning Styles Addressed—Materials: Visual, auditory. **Process:** Visual, auditory, tactile. **Products:** Visual, auditory, tactile.

Evaluation: Classroom teachers evaluated progress in writing and using the computer technology.

Resources: Books, magazines, visuals, audio and videotapes, experts, computer software, art materials.

Programs for Parents

Programs for parents may serve many purposes. Some programs are organized for parents and caregivers without children in attendance. At these programs, the librarian, teachers, or administrators might present information about the school and discuss teaching methods, testing, parenting strategies, and new technologies. Guest speakers from the public library, health department, and local agencies or museums can help parents become acquainted with community resources. Informal social gatherings encourage parents to reach out and meet others with similar interests and concerns.

Reading-aloud workshops, toddler programs, and hands-on science (or other subject matter) sessions introduce parents to the school and demonstrate good teaching techniques that will help parents become more effective teachers of their own children. Programs for parents and children help improve communication and skills for both parent and child. They enhance the loving-learning bond.

The parent may be the content or skills expert in some programs, such as career days, oral history projects, or immigrant studies. In others, the student or child is the learning expert. Both parents and children benefit when there is consistent communication and sharing between the school and home.

Oral History, Literature, and Quilt-Making Project

Students Involved: Third fourth and fifth-grade students in five classes

Major Content Areas: Language arts, social studies, art

Objectives: To promote reading, writing, and oral language; stimulate an interest in oral history, using family members as sources for historical information; provide opportunities for children to create art and writing projects based on literature and oral history.

Needs Addressed: The teachers were interested in stimulating recreational reading by students. They wanted to involve parents as curriculum resources in school projects, sharing family histories. Because many parents and children are recent immigrants with diverse backgrounds, teachers felt all students would have an opportunity to hear different points of view on current issues and past events. They also hoped that by exploring other cultures and discovering similarities they could foster cooperation rather than conflict.

Skills: Reading, questioning, interviewing, note taking, and writing; differentiating fact from fiction; peer tutoring and editing; evaluating information sources; transforming literary images and ideas to visual formats via quilting and other art projects; and developing oral presentation skills.

Description: Parents were invited to participate in a variety of oral language and quilt-making projects. Some parents were interviewed by their children at home and some came to school to be videotaped or interviewed. Parents discussed events from their family history or their recollections of events from their lifetime. Parents shared their skills in quilt making, cooking, and crafts. Children asked questions, gathered notes, and created prose, poetry, quilt squares, and drama based on the interviews. Culminating projects included quilts, a rap song, video and audiotapes, poems, prose, short dramas, a museum, and books based on oral history interviews.

Planning: The librarian met with the staff developer, teachers, and parent representatives to discuss strategies for involving parents in an oral history and literature project. Based on their suggestions, a letter was sent asking parents to participate. The librarian gathered resources to enhance the project and circulated titles to teachers.

Instructional Roles—Parents: Shared their personal and family history with individual students and classes; assisted with quilt making, cooking, and craft making. **Librarian:** Assembled the advisory committee, scheduled classes and small groups, gathered and shared resources, trained student tutors and editors, scheduled parent visits and gave them orientations to the oral history project and quilting activities, displayed finished projects, scheduled performances, and documented activities with still photos and video. **Teachers:** Shared literature with classes, encouraged discussion, facilitated prose and poetry writing, scheduled peer tutors and editors, and organized follow-up activities.

Evaluation: Teachers evaluated writing and drama projects. Teachers reported that student writing became more fluid and descriptive as the project progressed and that the writing evidenced a greater sensitivity and awareness of cultural differences. Children showed a high level of interest in peer writing projects. Videotapes made by students were the assessment tool for parts of the project. Children and parents also filled out questionnaires.

Resources: Books, magazines, slides, audio and videotapes produced by parents and students, interviews, guest visits, art and construction materials.

Project Sprout

Students Involved: 15, with parents

Major Content Areas: Language arts, parenting, technology

Objectives: To introduce parents to the school, its teachers, teaching practices, and the technology used by their children; involve parents in sharing experiences; foster self-help groups, introduce community resources, and help parents become literacy models for their children.

Needs Addressed: Many of the parents were recent immigrants who felt isolated because they did not speak English and were unfamiliar with programs and services that could help them. They wanted a good education for their children but were not sure how to help.

Skills: Oral and written communications, computer skills, and parenting.

Description: Parents came for lunch in the library each Thursday. The parent coordinator arranged programs and special activities with the help of the librarian, teachers, and community specialists. Programs included hands-on activities and crafts, lectures and demonstrations, trips, and parent and child activities. Parents made quilts, masks, and books and learned about storytelling, reading aloud, and helping with homework. Parents received instruction in using computers. They heard about community health programs and summer camps; shared books, puppets, and nursery rhymes with their children; and took trips with them to museums and parks. Parents in the program provided a support system for new parents in the school.

Planning: Parent coordinator met with the librarian, teachers, and parents to determine needs and to gather program ideas and suggestions to advertise the programs for parents.

Instructional Role—Parent Coordinator: Planned and scheduled activities with the assistance of teachers and the librarian, arranged lunches, gathered materials, and facilitated the programs. **Librarian:** Modeled reading aloud, storytelling, and homework assistance for parents; encouraged parents to borrow books with their children; and to share books in English and Spanish. **Teachers:** Presented special programs as needed. **Parents:** Served as mentors to each other, supported and trained new parents.

Evaluation: The parent coordinator kept questionnaires and evaluations filled out by parents. Teachers reported that since the parent program had been in operation, there was greater participation by parents at all school functions. There was more communication of all types between parents and the school.

Resources: Books, magazines, newspapers, computers, bookmaking and art materials, guest speakers.

Parent and Child Workshops

Students Involved: 15 children of one grade level for each program, grades 1-5 participating

Major Content Areas: Science, language arts, social studies

Objectives: To promote communication between the school and parents, engage parents in positive learning experiences with their children, and demonstrate instructional techniques used in the school.

Needs Addressed: The parent committee wanted to get more parents actively involved in the school and in their children's education. They suggested that workshops given by teachers at school and held during the day would be helpful in getting more parents to participate in their children's education. The librarian circulated a questionnaire and offered to organize the workshops around themes suggested by parents and teachers.

Skills: Cooperative learning, hands-on science, oral language.

Description: The librarian scheduled a series of daytime workshops for parents and their children. Parents could sign up to attend with their child. The librarian gathered materials, arranged for facilitators and speakers, and provided refreshments with the help of the parents' organization. Children were given passes to attend workshops with their parents. Sample workshops included: "Hands-On Science" (working with magnets, batteries, acids, and bases), "Hands-On Puppets" (making a puppet and performing a play), "Tell-Me-a-Story" (joint oral history and writing projects by parents and children), and "How-to-Take-a-Test" (strategies for parents and children).

Planning: The librarian sent an interest questionnaire to parents based on the suggestion of the parent groups. He scheduled workshops for parents and children and arranged for speakers and presenters.

Instructional Roles—Librarian: Conducted programs or facilitated programs directed by other teachers.

Evaluation: Parents filled out a questionnaire after attending each session.

Resources: Books, magazines, filmstrips, videos, arts and craft materials, guest speakers.

Programs for Teachers and Administrators

Fig. 4.6. Librarians Share Expertise with School and District Colleagues.

The effective librarian participates in and provides ongoing staff development for teachers and administrators. Programs might include an introduction to new materials or technologies, a summary of findings on new teaching strategies from professional magazines or conferences, or information on upcoming professional workshops or courses.

As the librarian you are aware of the programs and projects throughout the school, and you are in an excellent position to encourage collaboration and to facilitate sharing between classes, grades, and specialties.

Your involvement in staff development may be as minor as mentioning to the first-grade teacher that a fourth-grade class is also studying Native Americans or asking a second-grade teacher who has prepared a puppet show if her children will give an additional performance for a kindergarten class. You could model a booktalk, or book discussion, in the class of a new teacher and open up whole new teaching vistas. You might see an article in a professional journal that discusses a concern or answers a question a teacher asked in the teachers' lunchroom. Copying the article and placing it in the teacher's mailbox with a note indicates your interest in his or her professional growth and development.

Participate in workshops organized and presented by others to keep abreast of new resources, teaching techniques, and technology. When you become a student again, you may be more aware of the barriers of anxiety, ignorance, and frustration that your students face. It reminds you that it is only easy when you already know how.

You may be asked to share your expertise with colleagues in the school or the district. There is no better way to learn what you know or don't know than to prepare for a presentation before your peers. Plan ahead, no matter how well you know your material. Rehearse, alone and then with a friend. Ask for feedback. Encourage your colleagues to evaluate your presentation, letting you know what helped them learn, what required more or less time, and what would have made the whole presentation more useful to them. If you enjoy giving workshops for your colleagues, consider submitting a proposal to present at a city, state, or national conference. Sharing your ideas and strategies will help others. Communicate! Celebrate! Help others connect!

We Hate English: Memoir and Computer Study: Teacher's Workshop

Audience: Teachers

Major Content Areas: Technology, language arts

    Objectives: To train teachers in HyperStudio and other interactive video and computer technologies and to give teachers an opportunity to practice the computer skills being taught to children in their classes.

    Needs Addressed: The teachers expressed the concern that they were not keeping up with the new technologies the children were being taught in their computer classes. Teachers said they could not get access to practice on the computers during the school day and did not have the new technology at home. The principal and the district computer coordinator organized a series of 16 workshops that were offered to five teachers and the librarian during the school day. A computer station was set up in the library so that teachers could use it at different times during the day. The librarian received training so that she could assist other teachers as needed.

    Skills: An introduction to the computer—basic operations, using word processing programs, HyperCard, video imaging, transferring drawings and slides to the screen, adding voiceover, text and animation, printing text, and making a video book.

    Description: Teachers and the librarian met with the computer coordinator for a double period each Monday for 16 weeks. The first part of each program was a lecture demonstration by the computer specialist, while the second part of the session was devoted to hands-on work with the computers and programs. Teachers and the librarian were given an assignment to complete before the next session.

Planning: Workshops were planned by the principal, computer teacher, and district computer coordinator. Classes were scheduled so that teachers could be free for a block of time to attend workshops. A computer station was set up in the library so that the librarian and teachers could use it to practice new skills.

Instructional Roles—District Computer Specialist: Directed lecture and hands-on workshops for teachers and the librarian. Gave additional assistance to the librarian so that she could assist other teachers during their free time using the computer station in the library. **Librarian:** Participated in workshop and provided follow-up for teachers.

Learning Styles Addressed—Materials: Visual, auditory, tactile. **Process:** Visual, auditory, tactile. **Products:** Visual, auditory, tactile.

Evaluation: Teachers participating in the workshops reported in their evaluations that they felt more confident about using the technology and more proficient in their ability to help students.

Resources: Computer stations, HyperCard and HyperStudio software.

Showcase

Audience: 32 librarians in the Library Power Program

Major Content Areas: Language arts, math, social studies, technology, art

Objectives: To share with other librarians information about ongoing programs involving the library; demonstrate new ways to organize the library space, routines, and activities; provide ongoing staff development and opportunities for networking.

Needs Addressed: School librarians complain about isolation, lack of opportunities to meet with colleagues, and lack of continuing professional development. Librarians in the Library Power Program have monthly, daylong staff development workshops to address training needs and foster communicating and networking. Periodically, individual librarians volunteer to organize and present a showcase of their activities at these training meetings.

Skills: Collection management, collaborative planning, scheduling, promoting and publicizing, documenting, and displaying.

Description: The librarian gave a tour of the library and several classrooms and described programs in progress: Open Access, Reading Buddies, Storytelling Contest, Library Squad, and the schoolwide Read-In Day. She demonstrated the new library computer with CD-ROM and online communications program. She invited different teachers to tell about projects they were working on with the library. The math coordinator discussed the Math Through Literature Project and School Math Fair. A sixth-grade special education teacher described a research project on herbs that resulted in a big book and a project of growing and selling potpourri samples. A first-grade teacher described a writing unit in which the librarian read a related story to one group while others worked with the teacher writing their own books. A social studies ESL teacher described how students came to the library to research Columbus and then produced a video. Students in the Reading Buddies Program described how they selected books to read aloud, practiced with peers, and then read aloud to small groups of younger children. Library squad members described their jobs. First-graders presented a brief puppet show they had written using picture book fairy tales. The principal spoke about the dramatic effect the library programs have had on the entire school.

Planning: The librarian planned the program, scheduled teachers' presentations, arranged teachers' visits with help from the assistant principal, arranged for refreshments, and alerted the teachers to possible drop-in visitors.

Instructional Role—Librarian: Introduced topics and guests, answered questions, gave additional information on programs, and directed tours. **Teachers:** Presented information on their programs. **Students:** Described projects and programs in which they were involved and answered questions.

Learning Styles Addressed—Materials: Visual, verbal, tactile. **Process:** Visual, verbal.

Evaluation: Librarians filled out written evaluations. They were very positive about the visit.

Resources: Books, displays, CD-ROM, computers, student-produced materials, guests.

Thematic Planning

Audience: Teachers and elementary school librarians attending the National Council of Teachers of English Conference, March 1993

Major Content Areas: Language arts, science, social studies, art

Objectives: To discuss schoolwide and districtwide planning of cross-disciplinary multicultural programs and stimulate educational change.

Needs Addressed: Teachers are interested in discovering ways to integrate the curriculum to maximize meaningful learning for students.

Skills: To identify student objectives and curriculum themes that can be united in a cross-disciplinary multicultural model, encourage collaboration between teachers, and apply and adapt models from a districtwide project to other schools.

Description: The librarian participated in a series of districtwide workshops that focused on developing models for cross-disciplinary multicultural programs involving students in all the elementary grades. When the project was completed she was asked to present the process through which the models were developed and share the finished models with elementary school librarians in New York City. She also presented the process and product as part of a workshop given for teachers and librarians at the National Council of Teachers of English Conference, Spring 1993, in a workshop entitled: "Every Which Way to Learn."

Planning: The librarian used materials already developed and shared them with these new audiences.

Instructional Roles—Librarian: Introduced concepts and models of thematic planning, lectured on the process, facilitated small group discussion, answered questions, and encouraged participants to experiment in their own schools. She also displayed student products from her school developed using the cross-disciplinary approach.

Learning Styles Addressed—Materials: Visual, auditory, tactile. **Process:** Visual, auditory. **Product:** Auditory.

Evaluation: Teachers attending the workshops were enthusiastic in their written evaluations.

Resources: Books; professional journals; sample projects made by students; District 22, Brooklyn, New York, Thematic Planning Guide.

Showcase: J.H.S. 47, A School for the Deaf and Hard-of-Hearing

Audience: 25 librarians

Major Content Areas: Language arts, social studies, careers, technology

Objectives: To share information with librarians about working with deaf and hard-of-hearing populations to suggest ways of adapting materials and programs for hard-of-hearing students in the general education setting, and to provide ongoing staff development.

Needs Addressed: The school serves deaf and hard-of-hearing students from infancy to 21 years. With more special populations being mainstreamed into the general education program, it is essential that all teachers become familiar with materials, techniques, and services that can maximize learning for these children and sensitize librarians, teachers, and children.

Skills: Adapting programs, services, materials, and space to meet special populations.

Description: Many students and staff sign with great fluency and speed; others use some oral speech or cued speech. The librarian described reading and signing a story for younger children and helping teens with very low reading levels, using captioned films and videos, and the difficulty of locating materials in American Sign Language (ASL). The librarian, in cooperation with teachers, is producing a collection of video kits that children may borrow. Each kit contains a book and a videotape of the story told in ASL. Teachers sign the stories and the media specialist adds sound and captions. The committee is working on identifying short curriculum segments that can be produced and presented by students. She also discussed work with a ninth-grade teacher whose students are dramatizing selections of *Romeo and Juliet* in sign as part of their Shakespeare study. She discussed online services that will make it possible to communicate with students in other schools and to teach via visual materials. Librarians were taken on a tour of the computer media print shop where students are designing an interactive dictionary of ASL with text, sound, and video clips of students demonstrating the signs.

Planning: The librarian organized the program, scheduling teachers and arranging tours.

Instructional Role—Librarian: Presented with help from other teachers.

Learning Styles Addressed—Materials: Visual, verbal, tactile. **Process:** Visual, verbal.

Evaluation: Written evaluations by participants were extremely positive.

Resources: Books, magazines, pictures, videos, computers, CD-ROM, guest speakers.

Journeys: Teacher Workshop

Audience: Elementary school teachers

Major Content Areas: Language arts, social studies, teaching methods

Objectives: Professional development.

Needs Addressed: To foster educational change and promote effective innovative teaching methods, it is essential that teachers have an opportunity to hear from other teachers about successful projects.

Skills: Collaborative teaching, communication.

Description: The classroom teacher and the librarian met with teachers interested in learning about the cross-disciplinary unit described in Journeys. During the informal lunch meeting, the program was described. Teachers were encouraged to ask questions, to plan together for possible future collaborations, and to suggest adaptations that would make the program more useful to their students.

Planning: The librarian scheduled the meeting for lunchtime in the library and invited all interested staff. The teachers and librarian met to discuss who would teach particular skills.

Instructional Roles—Librarian and Teacher: Presented together.

Learning Styles Addressed—Materials: Visual, verbal, tactile. **Process:** Visual, verbal, tactile.

Evaluation: Informal comments by participants were positive. According to the librarian, many teachers expressed an eagerness to develop and implement similar projects involving language arts, social studies, and art, using the library as a key component.

Resources: Books, writing and art samples produced by students, the finished student-made books, video of the Parent Celebration in which the books were unveiled and shared.

Permission to publish these programs was granted by the following elementary school teachers, librarians, and specialists: Edward Clinton, Mary Coppinger, Rhoda Fishbein, Iona Flamm, Catherine Gustaitis, Sybil Habib, Merril Lugoff, Julia Matlaw, Judith Mercado, Lorraine Mollahan, Sally Savedoff, Judith Schaeffner, Connie Simari, Herbert Strauss, and Nancy Vega.

Bibliography

General Guides to Programming: Philosophy

American Association of School Librarians. *Kaleidoscope: New Visions for School Library Media Programs*. Video (Follett Software). Chicago: AISLE, 1993.

Barron, Ann E., and Gary W. Orwig. *New Technologies for Education: A Beginner's Guide*. Englewood, CO: Libraries Unlimited, 1993.

Bennet, Barrie, Carol Rolheiser-Bennett, and Laurie Stevann. *Where the Heart Meets the Mind*. Toronto: Educational Connections, 1991.

Connor, Jane Gardner. *Children's Library Services Handbook*. Phoenix, AZ: Oryx Press, 1990.

Hill, Susan, and Tim Hill. *The Collaborative Classroom: A Guide to Co-Operative Learning*. Portsmouth, NH: Heinemann, 1990.

Lazzaro, Joseph J. *Adaptive Technologies for Learning and Work Environments*. Chicago: American Library Association, 1993.

Loertscher, David V. *Taxonomies of the School Library Media Program*. Englewood, CO: Libraries Unlimited, 1988.

Miller, Elizabeth B. *The Internet Resource Directory for K-12 Teachers and Librarians, 1994/95 Edition*. Englewood, CO: Libraries Unlimited, 1994.

Wilson, Patricia J., and Ann C. Kimzey. *Happenings: Developing Successful Programs for School Libraries*. Littleton, CO: Libraries Unlimited, 1987.

Periodicals

Arithmetic Teacher. National Council of Teachers of Mathematics. 1954- . Monthly, September-May.

Art and Activities: Creative Activities for the Classroom. Art and Activities. 1932- . 10 issues annually.

Book Links: Connecting Books, Libraries and Classrooms. American Library Association. 1991- . Bimonthly.

Classroom Cable. Connell Communications, a division of IDG Communications. Monthly, except July and August.

Classroom Connect: Internet Activities and Resources. Wentworth Worldwide Media. 9 issues annually.

Computing Teacher: Journal of the International Society for Technology in Education. 8 issues annually.

Gifted Children Today. G-C-T Publishing. 1978- . Bimonthly.

Learning: Creative Ideas and Insights for Teachers. Springhouse. 1972- . 9 issues annually.

Multimedia Schools. Online publication. 1994 - . 5 issues annually.

Science and Children. National Science Teachers Association. 1963- . 8 issues annually.

Social Studies and the Young Learner. A Quarterly for Creative Teaching. K-6. National Council for the Social Studies. 1988- . Quarterly.

Teaching Exceptional Children. Council for Exceptional Children. 1968- . Quarterly.

Wonderscience: Fun Physical Science Activities for Children and Adults to Do Together. American Chemical Society/American Institute of Physics. 1987- . 8 issues annually.

Recipes for Programming

Bailey, Sally Dorothy. *Wings to Fly: Bringing Theatre Arts to Students with Special Needs*. Rockville, MD: Woodbine House, 1993.

Bauer, Caroline Feller. *The Poetry Break: An Annotated Anthology with Ideas for Introducing Children to Poetry*. New York: H. W. Wilson, 1995.

Beaty, Seddon Kelly, and Irene Fountas. *Butterflies Abound! A Whole Language Resource Guide for K-4*. Menlo Park, CA: Addison-Wesley, 1993.

Bower, Bert, Jim Lobdell, and Lee Swenson. *History Alive! Engaging All Learners in the Diverse Classroom*. Menlo Park, CA: Addison-Wesley, 1994.

Braddon, Kathryn L., Nancy J. Hall, and Dale Taylor. *Math Through Children's Literature: Making the NCTM Standards Come Alive*. Englewood, CO: Libraries Unlimited, 1993.

Brewer, Chris, and Don G. Campbell. *Rhythms of Learning: Creative Tools for Developing Lifelong Skills*. Tucson, AZ: Zephyr Press, 1991.

Butzow, Carol M., and John W. Butzow. *Science Through Children's Literature: An Integrated Approach*. Englewood, CO: Libraries Unlimited, 1989.

Cook, Sybilla Avery, and Cheryl A. Page. *Books Battles and Bees: A Readers' Competition Resource for Intermediate Grades*. Chicago: American Library Association, 1994.

Cravotta, Mary Ellen, and Savan Wilson. *The Media Cookbook for Kids.* Englewood, CO: Libraries Unlimited, 1989.

Diehn, Gwen, and Terry Krautwurst. *Scientific Crafts for Kids: 50 Fantastic Things to Invent and Create.* New York: Sterling, 1994.

Dublin, Peter, Harvey Pressman, Eileen Barnett et al. *Integrating Computers in Your Classroom: Elementary Education.* New York: HarperCollins College, 1994.

Eric Carle: Picture Writer. 27 min. New York: Searchlight Films/Putnam Publishing Group, 1994. Video (VHS).

Farmer, Lesley S. J. *Cooperative Learning Activities in the Library Media Center.* Englewood, CO: Libraries Unlimited, 1991.

Farmer, Lesley S. J., and Jean Hewlett. *I Speak HyperCard.* Englewood, CO: Libraries Unlimited, 1992.

Gallery Association of New York State. *Children's Film Programming: A Handbook.* Fort Atkinson, WI: Highsmith Press, 1992.

Goldfarb, Elizabeth K. "Library & Hands-On Science: A Winning Combination," *Appraisal: Science Books for Young People* 26, no. 4 (Fall 1993): 1-7.

Goldfarb, Elizabeth, and Merril Lugoff. "Linking Students and Social Action: Quilts for AIDS Babies," *The Whole Idea: Newsletter for Innovative Teachers* V, no. 3 (Spring/Summer 1995): 22-24.

Goldfarb, Liz, and Terry Cambridge. "Signing Shakespeare: Romeo Loves Juliet," *Perspectives in Education and Deafness* 13, no. 3 (1995): 12-16.

Goldfarb, Liz, and Sheila Salmon. "Enhancing Language Arts for Special Populations: Librarians & Classroom Teachers Collaborate," *Language Arts* 70 (November 1993): 567-572.

Hall, Susan. *Using Picture Storybooks to Teach Literary Devices: Recommended Books for Children and Young Adults.* Phoenix, AZ: Oryx Press, 1994.

Hamilton, Martha, and Mitch Weiss. *Children Tell Stories: A Teaching Guide.* Katonah, NY: Richard C. Owen, 1990.

Heller, Norma. *Projects for New Technologies in Education: Grades 6-9.* Englewood, CO: Libraries Unlimited, 1994.

Irvine, Joan. *How to Make Super Pop-Ups.* New York: Morrow, 1992.

Kovacs, Debroah, and Peter Preller. *Meet the Authors and Illustrators: 60 Creators of Favorite Children's Books Talk About Their Work.* New York: Scholastic, 1991.

Laughlin, Mildred Knight, and Kathy Howard Latrobe. *Readers Theatre for Children: Scripts and Script Development.* Englewood, CO: Libraries Unlimited, 1990.

Laughlin, Mildred Knight, and Terri Parker Street. *Literature-Based Art and Music: Children's Books and Activities to Enrich the K-5 Curriculum.* Phoenix, AZ: Oryx Press, 1992.

Lazear, David. *Seven Ways of Teaching: The Artistry of Teaching with Multiple Intelligences.* Tucson, AZ: Zephyr Press, 1991.

Lewis, Barbara A. *The Kid's Guide to Social Action: How to Solve the Social Problems You Choose— And Turn Creative Thinking into Positive Action.* Minneapolis, MN: Free Spirit Press, 1991.

Livo, Norma J., and Sandra A. Rietz. *Storytelling Activities.* Littleton, CO: Libraries Unlimited, 1987.

Love, Ann, and James Drake. *Take Action: An Environmental Book for Kids.* New York: Tambourine/Morrow, 1993.

MacDonald, Margaret Read. *Tom Thumb.* Phoenix, AZ: Oryx Press, 1993.

McGlathery, Glenn, and Norma J. Livo. *Who's Endangered on Noah's Ark? Literary and Scientific Activities for Teachers and Parents.* Englewood, CO: Libraries Unlimited, 1992.

Marantz, Sylvia S. *Picture Books for Looking and Learning: Awakening Visual Perceptions Through the Art of Children's Books.* Phoenix, AZ: Oryx Press, 1992.

Montgomery, Paula Kay. *Approaches to Literature Through Theme.* Phoenix, AZ: Oryx Press, 1992.

Raines, Shirley C. *450 More Story Stretchers for the Primary Grades: Activities to Expand Children's Favorite Books.* Mt. Rainier, MD: Gryhon House, 1994.

Robertson, Deborah, and Patricia Barry. *Super Kids Publishing Company.* Englewood, CO: Libraries Unlimited, 1990.

Shepard, Aaron. *Stories on Stage: Scripts for Reader's Theater.* New York: H. W. Wilson, 1993.

Sierra, Judy. *Flannel Board Storytelling Book.* New York: H. W. Wilson, 1987.

Sierra, Judy, and Robert Kaminski. *Twice upon a Time: Stories to Tell, Retell, Act Out, and Write About.* New York: H. W. Wilson, 1989.

Sklar, Daniel Judah. *Playmaking: Children Writing and Performing Their Own Plays.* New York: Teachers and Writers Collaborative, 1991.

Stowell, Charlotte. *Making Books.* New York: Kingfisher, 1994.

Terzian, Alexandra M. *The Kids' Multicultural Art Book: Art and Craft Experiences from Around the World.* Charlotte, VT: Williamson, 1993.

Weiner, Esther. *Dirt Cheap Science: Activity-Based Units, Games, Experiments and Reproducibles: Life. Earth. Physical Science. Grades 1-4.* New York: Instructor, 1992.

Weitzman, David. *My Backyard History Book.* Boston: Little, Brown, 1975.

Westridge Young Writers Workshop. *Kids Explore America's Hispanic Heritage.* Sante Fe, NM: John Muir, 1992.

Winnett, David A., Robert A. Williams, Elizabeth A. Sherwood, and Robert E. Rockwell. *Discovery Science: Explorations for the Early Years. Grade K.* Menlo Park, CA: Addison-Wesley, 1994.

Winters, Nathan B. *Architecture Is Elementary: Visual Thinking Through Architectural Concepts.* Tucson, AZ: Zephyr Press, 1985.

Zarnowski, Myra. *Learning About Biographies: A Reading-and-Writing Approach for Children.* Urbana, IL: National Council of Teachers of English, 1990.

Chapter 5 〉 Assessment

Introduction ─────────────────────────────────

Educators, parents, government and business leaders, and the general public are deeply concerned about the state of education. They are debating the schools' ability to educate students to function in today's increasingly information- and technology-rich society. Everyone seems to have ideas, many of which are contradictory, about what constitutes quality education, how to measure student achievement, what outcomes to evaluate, and how best to measure the results.

Experts in the school library media field are also reviewing the function of the media center in view of current educational needs and practices. Carol Kuhlthau, Judy Pitts, Barbara Stripling, and others have studied how students approach assignments requiring the search for information. Their work is leading to a deeper understanding not only of what skills and approaches teachers and librarians must focus on to help children become informed users of information, but also how to assess the products and the process of the information search.

In an article in *Reading Today* (1995) describing a professional development program prepared by the International Reading Association "to help teachers stay on top of the latest developments in this fast-changing field," we learn that, "Assessment continues to be one of the hottest topics in reading education." Reflective educators are seeking alternative means to assess their own work, and researchers are studying portfolio assessment and simulation exercises as alternatives to traditional evaluation measures.

Library evaluation traditionally has centered on administrative policies, technical services, budget allocations, collection development, patron satisfaction, and in school libraries, curriculum integration. The current emphasis on student assessment may also affect the school library media center. Librarians in some school districts are required to grade students using traditional reporting methods such as report cards. Whether or not you participate formally in assessing student progress, you should become familiar with current trends, distribute that information to staff, and evaluate aspects of your library program regularly.

Reporting devices used to convey assessment information are important communication tools. The data shared on student learning can give library media specialists and library services the visibility to highlight the integration of the library program with the instructional mission of the school and justify additional expenditures for the program. Information gathered with assessment tools can:

△ Aid teachers and librarians in evaluating student learning.

△ Help students evaluate their own progress.

△ Determine program and scheduling needs.

△ Determine collection needs.

△ Help the planning committee formulate a technology plan.

△ Allow parents to assess their school's library facility, staffing, schedule, and collection.

△ Assist in long-term planning.

△ Determine the allocation of resources.

△ Help planning committees advocate for additional funds for staff, materials, and technology.

Assessment procedures should be administered on a regular basis. In addition to your individual evaluation program, many school districts and state departments of education require a yearly collection of data pertaining to staffing, the collection, funding, and populations served. The focus on the librarian as an essential partner in the teaching and planning of instruction, and the important link of the library to student learning, makes the examination of the library's teaching function an essential element of schoolwide evaluations.

This chapter describes a few recently devised assessment strategies, developed by practitioners in the field, that will help you measure the products, processes, and progress of the library media program.

Assessing Student Learning

Traditionally, the method to determine what children have learned is testing. Although objective testing continues to have a function in the total assessment plan, today's educators, who are as interested in the process of learning as they are in the mastery of content, often require learners to demonstrate competency through performance. Performance assessment gives teachers the means to understand students' thinking skills, attitudes, and group behavior. It also helps teachers involve children in shaping and understanding their own learning.

A major component of performance assessment is that the students perform in a "real-life context." They may select a topic related to an investigation of a community concern, join a group of students on the Internet investigating acid rain in their area, or select a design project for which they must measure, calculate, draw to scale, and build the finished project. To be successful, students must have flexible use of time and resources, opportunities for collaboration with peers and adults, and input into the evaluation criteria. Assessment occurs throughout the learning process. There are a number of terms you may see in the literature relating to assessment. They include:

Performance assessment. The act of producing a product that can demonstrate learning through music, dance, theater, film, or the visual arts. It may be an individual or group project performed for an audience, an athletic performance, science fair presentation, or other demonstration of student work.

Direct assessment. Personal interactive contact between the teacher and student. Assessment tools may include questionnaires, observations, and interviews with students contributing ideas and feedback.

Authentic tests. Measurement of problem solving, thinking, and writing stressing depth rather than breadth. Scoring is based on elements of understanding and has a self-assessment component.

Portfolio assessment. A collection of student work that demonstrates work in progress, completed projects, logs, journals, writing samples, and other selected pieces that give a whole picture of students' progress and demonstrated learning over a semester, a school year, or many years.

These alternatives share the philosophy that it is better to evaluate actual student processes and products than to rely on data from test scores alone. Proponents of these forms of evaluation believe that they are superior to standardized testing because they are more comprehensive, ongoing, and directly related to classroom work. They allow students to be involved in their own learning. They can be opportunities to build better final outcomes or projects because reflection, revision, and evaluation are part of the process. Portfolio assessment is particularly relevant to work done in the school library media center.

The School Library Media Specialist and Portfolio Assessment

Library media center research activities fit naturally into the framework of portfolio assessment. Collaborating with teachers in the assessment process will lend another dimension to the integration of the library media center into the mainstream of instruction. Students can be active learners who shape their learning and present their findings to others. Library media specialists assist students and evaluate their work. Usually, this assistance is informal and takes place as students search for information, or when they encounter stumbling blocks in their work. Responses to verbal and nonverbal requests for assistance often focus on problem-solving strategies and lead to the reflection that is so important to learning.

The librarian's ability to focus on the process by which students find and use information is an essential component in an evaluative process that goes beyond looking only at the product. Skills include:

△ Defining informational needs.

△ Developing a hypothesis.

△ Defining criteria to examine and evaluate information sources.

△ Locating needed information.

△ Extracting data that support the hypothesis.

△ Documenting information.

△ Organizing and presenting information.

△ Using a variety of formats, sources, technologies, and resources from inside and outside the media center.

Adding or emphasizing additional skills and refining and formalizing them in the context of a holistic assessment is a logical next step. These skills include:

△ Articulating search strategies.

△ Comparing new work with past searches.

△ Applying past experiences to new learning situations.

△ Reflecting and sharing.

Portfolio Contents

In addition to demonstrating end-products, portfolios give teachers and students insight into the learning process. Portfolios are collections of work and generally:

Δ Are selected by the students, in consultation with adults or peers.

Δ Include works in progress, observations, self-evaluations, and peer evaluation.

Δ Are comprehensive evaluations of students' work.

Δ Show student development over several months, semesters, or years.

Δ May be arranged in a variety of ways (e.g., chronologically, by topic, in folders or boxes, in print, electronic, graphic, or nonprint formats).

Δ Should be based on students' and teachers' goals.

Δ Should be evaluated on objective standards or rubrics that can be described and supported by the evidence.

The inquiry process can be documented from the first brainstorming efforts to the finished work. Kuhlthau suggests that self-assessment, process assessment, and product assessment are all necessary to determine what worked and what could be improved. Documentation might include:

Δ A list of topics initially considered for the inquiry with a journal entry describing how each topic was evaluated and why the final topic was selected.

Δ The defining questions used.

Δ Journal entries of sources consulted with explanations of why sources were chosen and how pertinent they were for obtaining the desired information.

Δ Learning logs that reflect the note-taking process.

Δ Computer discs, audiotapes, video clips, preliminary drawings, models, or other nonprint formats that document work.

Δ Drafts of written products or evidence of process for other products (e.g., storyboards).

Δ The final product.

The classroom teacher may ask you and other teachers to evaluate their students' work, but even if you are not an evaluator, you should know the criteria for successful completion of assignments so that you can coach students effectively.

Assessing Individual Projects

Students and teachers decide in advance how a project will be assessed. Students should be active in this process, and discussions will relate to their own expectations and joint agreement on the organization, content, inclusions, sources of information, evidence of creativity, reflection, clarity of purpose, and so on. These discussions help shape the project and give students direction and clarity of purpose. A set of descriptive statements, or a rubric, is devised so that evaluators can assess each project consistently and students know the basis on which they will be evaluated.

In the following example, the library media specialist and teacher work together to plan the unit activities and the evaluation criteria. After a visit to the local museum to view the dinosaur exhibit, the teacher and librarian introduce a project that requires students to make observations based on the exhibits they saw. Two choices of projects are proposed:

1. How did the environment affect the life of a specific dinosaur? What biome today would suit the dinosaur you select? How would the dinosaur have to adapt to survive in this environment? Could people and dinosaurs coexist in the natural world?

2. If people could create a dinosaur park, what would be the special conditions needed? Interview another student, share information on your dinosaurs, and decide how the dinosaur park would have to be modified to accommodate both species.

Students are asked to select a problem; develop a hypothesis; research the data through observation, interviews, and written sources; and present their findings in a model, oral argument, or written presentation. The purpose of this activity is to use known data to create new information and hypotheses.

Evaluation of the project can be achieved through a rubric that is known in advance and examines the components of the process. Evaluation by peers or teachers or both would occur at the end of each step. If a student has not met the conditions for successful completion of the task, give individual assistance and provide mentoring so that every student will succeed. This process makes students feel good about their learning, motivates them to reach for a higher level of competency, and avoids the ineffective method of giving students a poor grade at the end of a substantial project, which feeds into a cycle of failure. Components of this project include:

△ Defining informational needs.

△ Developing a hypothesis.

△ Defining criteria to examine and evaluate information sources.

△ Articulating search strategies.

△ Locating needed information.

△ Extracting data that support the hypothesis.

△ Defending the hypothesis.

△ Documenting information.

△ Organizing and presenting information.

△ Using a variety of sources, technologies, and resources from inside and outside the media center.

Each of the components could have a separate set of criteria for evaluation, or one set of criteria can incorporate all the elements. To evaluate the component of "extracting the data that support the hypothesis," you could require that students make a chart that lists the necessary conditions for life in the dinosaur's original environment and in the environment the students have created. If no data exist, students are to make a plausible argument based on known data. Students should include data on:

△ Climactic requirements.

△ Dietary needs.

△ Ability to reproduce.

△ Ability to protect itself.

The criteria that form the rubric for successful completion of this portion of the assignment are:

△ All four components are included.

△ All information is factually correct and documented.

△ Conclusions are logically drawn from the scientific data presented.

△ The chart is clear and understandable.

Levels of competence can be measured by either a numerical scale from 1 to 5 or descriptive evaluations, such as additional work required, satisfied requirements, or exceeded requirements.

In the example cited above, a child who had included all four components, documented his or her facts accurately, completed a chart, but drew few conclusions from the scientific data would be assessed as having satisfied the requirements. Any omitted or inaccurate elements would lead to an evaluation of additional work required, and the child would be given additional assistance to complete the work successfully. A child who accomplishes all the requirements and exhibits a high level of competency in all four of the elements would be assessed as having exceeded requirements.

Assessment Tools

Checklists, flowcharts, and timelines are useful graphic illustrations of work in progress. Students may keep logs in which they reflect on what they have learned about doing research, or what paths they used successfully, or unsuccessfully, to get to the information they wanted. They may also look at their participation in the group, if they are working in a cooperative learning situation. Students participate in the evaluation process, depending on their age and level of sophistication.

A learning log (see fig. 5.1) is one device to help students reflect on their learning process. Its purpose is to encourage students to think critically about what information they are noting and how that information supports their research. Logs can also serve to document students' feelings about what they are learning. Other types of useful records include progress logs in which students record and reflect on their success or lack of success in finding information, and process logs in which students reflect on what they are learning about the research process. You may use one or more of these types of logs, depending on the developmental level of the student and the extent of the research project. If the formal log is not appropriate for students with limited facility in language, you may help students reflect on their research during individual interviews or in small group discussions that may be audio- or video-taped. These media logs can be examined by teachers or students at a later time. Even the youngest children can think about the strategies they used to find information.

A checklist (see fig. 5.2) helps students visualize what activities they need to do and when tasks need to be completed. It may help them organize their work and it also serves as a way for adults to discuss the work in progress with the students. Coaching students at each step will facilitate learning and help you and the teacher evaluate students' understanding.

Learning Log

Students write information gathered
in this column

Comments, questions, other reactions
in this column

Notes	Reactions

Fig. 5.1. Learning Log.

Investigation Checklist

Name: _____ **Topic:** _____ **Date Due:** _____

Task	Students Initials	Teacher's Signature and Date	Evaluation
KWL sheet			
List of questions			
Log (up-to-date, specific)			
Evidence of public library visit			
Resources			
Completion of any intended phone calls— letters/ interviews/trip arrangements			
Log (up-to-date, specific)			
Note cards begun			
Partner interview (shared information, listened, and responded helpfully to partner)			
Log (up-to-date, specific)			
Draft due (with entire folder)			
Conference with partner			
Evidence of revision			
Log completed			
FINAL COPY SUBMITTED (including bibliography and entire folder)			

Fig. 5.2. Investigation Checklist.

Cooperative learning groups can reflect on the group process by using assessment tools that examine the principles of cooperative learning. A simple questionnaire filled out by individuals in the group by answering "yes" or "no" or by drawing a smiling, frowning, or neutral face can help even the youngest student examine his or her own social skills. Ask if the student:

△ Participated in the group activity.

△ Took turns.

△ Asked questions.

△ Maintained a quiet voice.

△ Summarized out loud.

△ Listened actively.

△ Gave encouragement.

Supporting Alternative Assessment

You can learn more about assessment techniques and encourage colleagues to adopt some of these methods if you:

△ Subscribe to professional journals and share information with colleagues.

△ Facilitate or plan workshops to help staff gain expertise.

△ Plan assessment activities with classroom teachers in the context of student assignments.

△ Assume responsibility for teaching some of the skills and strategies students need to complete their assignments. These may include: extracting and evaluating data from an online database, demonstrating production or presentation skills, comparing data from differing formats, interviewing, and working in cooperative groups.

△ Assume responsibility for some of the small group discussions during which students discuss processes and reflect on learning.

△ Encourage the use of the library as an inquiry laboratory in which children can practice skills, strategies, and the acquisition and use of content.

△ Evaluate student products with teachers.

Assessing the School Community's View of the Media Center ─────────

Surveying the school community will help library media specialists, teachers, and administrators determine if the library is used to support resource-based learning and teaching. This assessment is extremely important in schools that profess to support active learning, research and inquiry, resource-based learning, and collaborative teaching. Where the library is considered a separate enrichment program, the documentation gathered may bring attention to the need to change teaching practices and the library's role in the school.

David Loertscher (1988) has designed a taxonomy of the LMS's involvement in instruction. The responses of teachers, students, administrators, and the school library media specialist will give a clear picture of how the school community perceives library media services. They will serve as a focal point for discussion and provide guidelines for future action. Analysis of the responses may spur change on the part of a school community that has become comfortable with the status quo or may be an affirmation of the collaboration that exists.

The library media specialist's taxonomy is a school self-assessment tool. You may find that you cannot pinpoint your library's place on the taxonomy. It is likely that the library functions on a number of different levels depending on the personalities and needs of individual teachers and students, but most responses will fall within a range on the taxonomy. Once you have determined the range, decide your short- and long-term goals for moving up. Think about strategies to attain your goals.

Library Media Specialist's Taxonomy

1. NO INVOLVEMENT
   The library media center is bypassed entirely.

2. SELF-HELP WAREHOUSE
   Facilities and materials are available for the self-starter.

3. INDIVIDUAL REFERENCE ASSISTANCE
   Students or teachers retrieve requested information or materials for specific needs.

4. SPONTANEOUS INTERACTION AND GATHERING
   Spur-of-the-moment activities and gathering of materials occur with no advance notice.

5. CURSORY PLANNING
   Informal and brief planning with teachers and students for library media center involvement.

6. PLANNED GATHERING
   Gathering of materials is done in advance of class project at teacher request.

7. EVANGELISTIC OUTREACH
   A concerted effort is made to promote the philosophy of the library media center.

8. SCHEDULED PLANNING IN THE SUPPORT ROLE
   Formal planning is done with a teacher or group of students to supply materials or activities for a previously planned resource-based teaching unit or project.

9. INSTRUCTIONAL DESIGN, LEVEL 1
   The library media specialist participates in every step of the development, execution, and evaluation of a resource-based teaching unit. LMC involvement is considered as enrichment or as supplementary.

10. INSTRUCTIONAL DESIGN, LEVEL II
    The library media center staff participates in resource-based teaching units where the entire unit content depends on the resources and activities of the LMC program.

11. CURRICULUM DEVELOPMENT
    Along with other educators, the library media specialist contributes to the planning and structure of what will actually be taught in the school or district.

Fig. 5.3. Library Media Specialist's Taxonomy. Adapted from *Taxonomies of the School Library Program,* by David V. Loertscher.

After completing the taxonomy, you may want to match your findings with what other people perceive as the library's place in their professional lives. The Teacher's Survey below is a similar tool that will gauge how teachers see themselves in relation to the library program. If there is a wide divergence between how you see the program and how the teachers rate their usage, it's time to do some serious thinking about why your perception and your colleagues' perceptions are far apart. If there is congruence, involve your colleagues and plan strategies to move up on the taxonomy. The following survey is adapted from Loertscher's Teacher's Taxonomy of Resource-Based Teaching. The teacher's survey focuses on resources rather than skills, strategies, or processes. You may want to adapt these statements to place greater emphasis on these aspects of student learning.

Teacher Survey

Level 1. I use texts, workbooks, or instructional packages. I have no real need for library media center facilities or materials.

Level 2. I have a classroom library. There is little need to interact with the school library media center.

Level 3. I borrow material from the library media center, the public library, or other sources for use in my classroom.

Level 4. I rely on the library media staff for ideas and suggestions for new materials to use and training on the use of media, professional materials, and information.

Level 5. I use the library media center facilities, materials, activities, and staff to supplement unit content—to provide the "icing on the cake" for a unit.

Level 6. LMC materials/activities are integral to unit content, rather than supplementary in nature. Students are required to meet certain objectives while using library media materials.

Level 7. I work with the library media staff to construct a unit of instruction that will use the resources of the library media center fully.

Level 8. My colleagues and I consult with the library media specialists as curriculum changes are being considered. We plan curriculum changes together and discuss their impact on LMC materials, facilities, and activities.

Fig. 5.4. Teacher Survey

Students are the raison d'être of the media center program, and you should always look for ways to get student reaction. Loertscher's "Student Taxonomy" from the Student's Taxonomy of Resource-Based Learning has been adapted to produce the Student Survey on page 90. This survey can be adjusted to suit your own situation and can give you insight into how students see your library. Students are asked to check all statements that apply. Many negative comments are signals that you need to make programmatic or public relations changes. Other kinds of student surveys focus on student proficiencies in locating, using, evaluating, and presenting information. You may also want to ask students for their ideas about what materials and services the library should offer.

Student Survey

Level 1. I never come to the library media center.

Level 2. I browse and find materials I like.

Level 3. I ask the librarian to help me find what I'm looking for or to teach me how to use the equipment.

Level 4. I come to the library for special programs.

Level 5. I learn how to find information in different formats in my school or public library or from people in the community.

Level 6. My teachers give me assignments that I do in the library.

Level 7. I go to the library alone or with a few people that I am working with on a project. I enjoy using the library for reading, working on a computer, creating my own projects, and finding information.

Fig. 5.5. Student Survey.

Discuss with your administrator how and when to administer these taxonomies in your school and what follow-up activities should result. Loertscher suggests a number of methods to collect and disseminate the information. Select the ones that are most appropriate for your situation. (See the bibliography, page 95.)

Collaborative Planning

Evaluation of the collaborative planning process will strengthen future planning efforts and provide direction for needed change. After each collaboratively planned instructional unit, think about the process that created it. Some elements to look at include:

△ *Time:* Was there sufficient planning time? How much of the planning was formal, informal? Was one type of meeting more useful than another? Was the time spent productively? If not, why not?

△ *Participants:* Who participated in the planning sessions? Should other school staff or volunteers have been involved? Were students involved in planning? What was my role: initiator, facilitator, or resource person?

△ *Teaching strategies:* What strategies were used to teach skills? How were students grouped: small groups, whole class, or individual at point of need? Peer tutoring? What worked well? What should be changed or strengthened?

△ *Teaching responsibilities:* Who taught particular skills? How were teaching responsibilities divided? Was the teaching effective? Did teachers work together as a team?

△ *Student reaction:* Did students react to the project as expected in the planning stages? Were student learning needs determined accurately? Were students able to complete the assignment as planned?

△ *Evaluation:* Were the evaluation tools selected adequate for the purpose? Was evaluation ongoing? What recommendations do the participants have to improve the planning, teaching, and learning process?

School Close-Up: School Library Resources

Many methods of assessing the school library media center's programs, services, and facilities are found in the professional literature. The bibliography listed at the end of this chapter will point you to many different kinds of evaluation forms. A new reporting device to inform parents about the facilities of the media center is now being field-tested. The Fund for New York City Public Education developed *School Close-Up: School Library Resources,* a tool for school communities to use to examine their own library facilities. The Fund anticipates that portions of the survey will be reported to parents as part of the *Annual School Report* that each New York City public school distributes to the community.

The *Annual School Report* documents the school population, number of teachers, their years of teaching experience, degree of space utilization, reading and math scores, and demographic information. The *School Close-Up* surveys are self-assessment forms that examine instructional philosophy, parent involvement, and school library strengths and needs.

The *School Close-Up: School Library Resources* evaluation surveys (see figs. 5.6 and 5.7) are designed so that teachers and library media specialists can describe the media center in terms of their own needs and perceptions. A library media specialist may perceive that the program and services of the LMC have a more positive or negative impact on the school community than the teaching staff. Where there are perceived differences, it is important to close the communication gap. Administrators, teachers, and the library media specialist must find ways to address the school community's concerns and make the appropriate changes.

No matter what assessment tools you use, be sure to use them regularly and in a way that will promote increased understanding of the program's importance to student learning. You and your administrators, teachers, parents, and students need to have that information to build a more vital and effective connection to the school community.

SCHOOL CLOSE-UP: School Library Resources
Pilot Survey for School Library Staff Members
Page 1 of 2

School _____   District/Borough _____

Position _____   Date _____

LIBRARY HOURS
What hours are your school library open and available to students?

NUMBER OF STUDENTS
On the lines below, please indicate the number of students enrolled at the following grade level in your school and also provide an overall total.

_____ Pre-K to 2
_____ 3 - 5
_____ 6 - 8
_____ 9-12
_____ Total number of students

NUMBER OF PERSONNEL ASSIGNED TO LIBRARY
Please indicate how many personnel in the different categories listed below (including yourself) are assigned to your library.

_____ Full-time certified librarians	_____ Full-time aides or paraprofessionals
_____ Full-time teacher-in the library	_____ Part-time aides or paraprofessionals
_____ Part-time certified librarian	_____ Part-time aides or paraprofessionals
_____ Part-time teacher-in the library	_____ Volunteers
_____ Other (please specify)	

SCHOOL LIBRARY PHYSICAL ENVIRONMENT	**Yes**	**No**			
Is your library wheelchair-accessible?	O	O			

Check only one box for each of the following questions.

	Excellent	Good	Fair	Poor
Attractiveness of physical facility (freshly painted, good lighting, etc.)	O	O	O	O
Sufficient furniture in good repair	O	O	O	O
Ability to accommodate both large and small group activities at the same time	O	O	O	O
Availability of independent study areas	O	O	O	O
Availability of reading areas with comfortable seating	O	O	O	O
Creative arrangement of print and non-print materials to encourage use	O	O	O	O
"Face-out" displays of books to break up conventional shelving	O	O	O	O

ACCESS TO YOUR SCHOOL LIBRARY	**Yes**	**No**
Do all students have access to the library?	O	O
Do family members have access to the library?	O	O

*Please check the box that most accurately describes how your library is scheduled. Please check only **one** box.*

O The librarian has complete flexibility in scheduling the library for classes, small groups, and individuals.

O The administrator schedules classes in the library part of the day, but it is flexibly scheduled for the rest of the time.

O The administrator schedules classes in the library all day and individual students have limited access to it.

O Other (please describe).

School Close-UP: School Library Resources, *Pilot Survey for School Library Staff Members, Page 2 of 2*

INTEGRATION OF THE LIBRARY INTO THE SCHOOL PROGRAM AS A WHOLE
Please check the box that best describes the degree to which the school library is integrated into your school's program as a whole.

	Always	Often	Some time	Rarely or never
The librarian is an instructional leader in this school.	O	O	O	O
The library is a center for school-wide activities.	O	O	O	O
The librarian and teachers collaborate on projects and activities.	O	O	O	O
Teachers give classroom assignments that require the use of the library.	O	O	O	O
Students use the library voluntarily for their own purposes and interests.	O	O	O	O
Pupils' work is displayed in the library.	O	O	O	O
Teachers accompany classes to the library for whole class activities.	O	O	O	O

SCHOOL LIBRARY RESOURCES

_____ How many books do you have in your collection? (If you do not have an exact count, please estimate.)
_____ How many computers do you have in your library?

Please mark the box that best describes the quality of various characteristics of your school library collection.

	Excellent	Good	Fair	Poor
Diversity of collection (e.g., is it responsive to different ages, interests, languages, and curriculum content?)	O	O	O	O
Up-to-dateness of the books in your collection	O	O	O	O
Condition of collection	O	O	O	O
Availability of magazines	O	O	O	O
Availability of non-print resources (audio, video, etc.)	O	O	O	O
Availability of electronic resources (CD-ROM, software, online databases, etc.)	O	O	O	O
Support for curriculum needs of school	O	O	O	O

TECHNOLOGY AVAILABLE IN THE LIBRARY
Please mark the correct box to indicate whether or not each of the items below is available in your school library.

Yes	No		Yes	No	
O	O	telephone line	O	O	automated catalog
O	O	computers with CD-ROM	O	O	automated circulation system
O	O	computers without CD-ROM	O	O	audio-visual equipment
O	O	equipment providing access to online services	O	O	other (please describe)
O	O	equipment enabling students to create their multimedia			

Fig. 5.6. *School Close-Up: School Library Resources.* **School Library Staff Members Survey.**

SCHOOL CLOSE-UP: School Library Resources
Pilot Survey for Teachers

School _____ District/Borough _____ Date _____

Are you a special education teacher? ____ yes ____ no
Is your classroom self-contained? ____ yes ____ no.

If not, please describe (e.g., cluster teacher, instructional specialist, etc.)

SCHOOL LIBRARY RESOURCES
___ How many books do you have in your collection? (If you do not have an exact count, please estimate.)
___ How many computers do you have in your library?

Please mark the box that best describes the quality of various characteristics of your school library collection.

	Excellent	Good	Fair	Poor
Diversity of collection (e.g., is it responsive to different ages, interests, languages, and curriculum content?)	O	O	O	O
Up-to-dateness of the books in your collection	O	O	O	O
Condition of collection	O	O	O	O
Availability of magazines	O	O	O	O
Availability of non-print resources (audio, video, etc.)	O	O	O	O
Availability of electronic resources (CD-ROM, software, online databases, etc.)	O	O	O	O
Support for curriculum needs of school	O	O	O	O

ACCESS TO YOUR SCHOOL LIBRARY

	Yes	No
Do all students have access to the library?	O	O

*Please check the box that most accurately describes how your library is scheduled. Please check only **one** box.*
O I am able to schedule whole class or small group instruction when I need to.
O My students have access to the library on an individual basis.

INTEGRATION OF THE LIBRARY INTO THE SCHOOL PROGRAM AS A WHOLE
Please check the box that best describes the degree to which the school library is integrated into your school's program as a whole.

	Always	Often	Some time	Rarely or never
The librarian is an instructional leader in this school.	O	O	O	O
The library is a center for school-wide activities.	O	O	O	O
I collaborate with the librarian on projects and activities.	O	O	O	O
I give my students classroom assignments that require the use of the library.	O	O	O	O
Students use the library voluntarily for their own purposes and interests.	O	O	O	O
Pupils' work is displayed in the library.	O	O	O	O
I accompany classes to the library for whole class activities.	O	O	O	O

SCHOOL LIBRARY PHYSICAL ENVIRONMENT

	Yes	No
Is your library wheelchair-accessible?	O	O

Check only one box for each of the following questions.

	Excellent	Good	Fair	Poor
Attractiveness of physical facility (freshly painted, good lighting, etc.)	O	O	O	O
Sufficient furniture in good repair	O	O	O	O
Ability to accommodate both large and small group activities at the same time	O	O	O	O
Availability of independent study areas	O	O	O	O
Availability of reading areas with comfortable seating	O	O	O	O
Creative arrangement of print and non-print materials to encourage use	O	O	O	O

Fig. 5.7. *School Close-Up: School Library Resources.* **Teacher Survey.**

Bibliography

ALA, AECT. *Information Power: Guidelines for School Library Media Programs.* Chicago: American Association of School Librarians; Washington, DC: Association for Educational Communications and Technology, 1988.

Au, K. H., J. A. Scheu, A. J. Arakaki, and P. A. Herman. "Assessment and Accountability in a Whole Literacy Curriculum." *The Reading Teacher* (April 1990): 574–78.

Federer, Adele. *Practical Assessments for Literature-Based Reading Classrooms.* New York: Scholastic Professional Books, 1995.

Hopkins, Dianne McAfee. *School Library Media Programs: A Resource and Planning Guide.* Madison: Wisconsin Department of Public Instruction, 1991.

"IRA Launches Professional Development Program on Assessment." *Reading Today* 12, no. 4 (1995): 1.

Kuhlthau, Carol Collier, ed. *Assessment and the School Library Media Center.* Englewood, CO: Libraries Unlimited, 1994.

Loertscher, David V. *Taxonomies of the School Library Media Program.* Englewood, CO: Libraries Unlimited, 1988.

"Portfolios." *Language Arts* 71, no. 6 (October 1994): 404–44.

"Reporting What Students Are Learning." *Educational Leadership* 52, no. 2 (October 1994): 4–58.

Stripling, Barbara. "Learning-Centered Libraries: Implications from Research." *School Library Media Quarterly* 23, no. 3 (Spring 1993): 163–70.

Turner, Philip M. *Helping Teachers Teach: A School Library Specialist's Role.* Englewood, CO: Libraries Unlimited, 1985.

Udall, Anne J., and Joan E. Daniels. *Creating the Thoughtful Classroom: Strategies to Promote Student Thinking.* Tucson, AZ: Zephyr Press, 1991.

Wolf, Kenneth. "The Schoolteacher's Portfolio: Issues in Design, Implementation and Evaluation." *Phi Delta Kappan* 73, no. 2 (October 1991): 129–36.

Chapter 6 〉 The Collection

Introduction

The library media collection includes all those resources available in the media center as well as those accessible through interlibrary loan, satellite, telecommunications, and cable. The collection includes print and nonprint materials in a variety of formats, the equipment needed to utilize them, and the technical assistance to make the resources accessible.

The collection development process includes:

△ Systematically analyzing and evaluating the existing collection.

△ Examining materials and removing outdated, worn, or inappropriate items.

△ Selecting the best materials in the most appropriate format based on curricular needs.

△ Investigating alternative services, sources, and products to meet information and recreational needs.

△ Continuing evaluation.

Each collection grows and changes to reflect the school's curriculum and to meet the informational and recreational needs of the students. Because demand for new and different resources frequently exceed budgetary allotments, it is essential that the librarian work in cooperation with teachers, administrators, parents, and students to set priorities, evaluate existing materials, and determine what materials and services are needed. Developing a collection may involve cooperative planning between school librarians and public librarians and may extend to a school district, region, or state.

A balanced collection includes materials in which a variety of viewpoints and values are represented. Diverse ethnic, cultural, religious, and political materials must be available. Materials that are free of stereotypes concerning gender, sexual orientation, race, ethnic and religious backgrounds, age, and disabilities should be included.

Every school library should have a written collection policy developed in cooperation with the librarian, the administration, and teachers. The policy should, of course, be reviewed periodically. The policy should reflect the school's philosophy, curriculum, and the needs and interests of all learners. It should establish criteria and priorities for acquisition of materials in various formats, set guidelines for gifts and for discarding materials, and set procedures for challenging materials. A clearly written collection policy is the best defense against censorship.

Considerations for Writing a Collection Policy

△ What are the aims and objectives of the library media center?

△ Who will participate in the selection of materials (e.g., special education teacher, bilingual coordinator, reading teacher, and so on)?

△ Will there be a selection committee that meets regularly? This may be especially important in the selection of materials that may be considered controversial in your community.

△ What is the librarian's responsibility for materials selection?

△ What types of resources are in the library media center and what criteria will be applied to their selection? Include computerized databases and online services, the Internet, as well as software, CD-ROM, and other nonprint material.

△ How will your school's personnel and student body comply with the fair use guidelines of the copyright regulations?

△ How will your school share its resources with other libraries? What networks will it join?

△ What are the areas of the collection that will receive special attention (e.g., materials to support the subject of a magnet school, parent collection, professional periodicals)?

△ What specific topics in the curriculum will warrant major allocations of resources?

△ How will you address issues of great importance to educators (e.g., critical thinking and lifelong learning)?

△ What selection aids will be used?

△ What are the policies concerning gifts, weeding, duplication of materials, and replacement for lost or damaged materials?

△ What are the procedures for handling complaints?

Evaluation of the Collection

After the collection policy has been established, examine the existing collection to assess immediate and long-term needs. Your collection may not meet the numerical standards for excellence set by state or national guidelines. However, excellence is not determined by quantity alone. Weed those materials that are worn, outdated, inaccurate, and irrelevant to your school community. Judge your collection on how well it meets student needs for academic and recreational purposes and teacher needs for professional purposes. Currency; variety of formats; visual, aural, and literary appeal; and the quantity of materials in requested areas are important factors in evaluating the collection. Ask the students and staff if the collection reflects their needs.

Find out what your students and teachers need and like. Build up those areas of the collection until there are consistently high ratings on evaluations filled out after the completion of collaborative units. Concentrate on only a few areas each year, choosing themes or topics based on the school's curriculum and your knowledge of special projects. Remember that themes or special emphasis collections may include materials located in many areas of the collection. For example, a focus on a country might include books, videos, slides, CD-ROMs, student-produced books, Internet sites, and realia. It would also include books cataloged in the 300s (costume, holidays, folklore), 600s (cookery, industries), 800s (poetry, literature), and 92 (biographies) in addition to the 900s (travel, description, geography). There might also be picture books, concept books, or novels to complement study.

Collection Mapping

David Loertscher and May Lein Ho (1995) have written a detailed book that outlines the steps needed to create a graphic representation of your collection's strengths and needs. This can be used in your collection development work and should be used as an advocacy tool to generate more support for your collection. Use your data and charts with your administrators, parents, district personnel, school board members, or legislators to lobby for more funding. The collection map should also help you focus on areas for grant writing proposals. The basic steps in this process are:

1. Collect data on the various segments of your collection by estimating the number of items in your library in all the different categories such as reference, folklore, fiction, science, technology, biography, etc. Count nonbook resources, too: CD-ROMs, periodicals, computer programs, cassette recordings, etc. You may want to include resources found elsewhere in the school, including classrooms and computer labs. Distance resources might be included, too: telecommunications services and cooperative purchasing or lending groups. List your totals for each category on a chart. Calculate the number of items per student in each category. Add information concerning age of the collection category and quality of each segment.

2. For some parts of the collection, age is a very significant factor. This is especially true in the 300s, 500s, 600s, 900s, biography, and reference sections. Start with these sections and average the copyright dates found on your shelflist or automated catalog database for each segment. Start with 25 randomly selected items. Compute the average age and then add 10 additional dates and compute again. Continue adding 10 dates at a time until there is no significant difference in the average date.

3. Quality is probably the most important factor, and Loertscher and Ho suggest that you can only evaluate the quality of a collection segment when a collaborative unit has been completed and you, the teacher(s), and the students determine how useful the collection has been in a particular situation. This can involve evaluation of online resources and interlibrary loan materials. You can use a rubric with a 1 to 5 rating scale for different factors, and an overall average rating.

4. Rather than build the kind of general collection that librarians used to assemble, Loertscher suggests creating a collection that is responsive to your school's individual needs. Determine your existing general emphasis and specific emphasis collections. General emphasis collections are those broad areas such as animals or folklore. Dinosaurs or pioneer life might be specific areas of emphasis in your library. Decide which themes or subject areas will be built up, which will stay the same size, and which will be smaller as a result of de-emphasis. (Sometimes you will weed large numbers of items in a particular subject area and not replace them, because the topic is no longer covered in the curriculum.) Decide if there are new areas that you need to emphasize.

5. Create a collection map, in the form of a bar graph or a series of pie charts that will show your colleagues and other interested parties what the collection looks like now and how it will change when specific purchases are made. Include stars or other symbols to show the quality of certain segments.

6. Compare your collection size with regional, state, or national standards. Use a bar chart or divide the quantitative standard that you are using by 5; label each part of the bar using ratings ranging from "in progress" to "exemplary." Chart your progress from year to year.

Figure 6.1 is based on the Loertscher and Ho model and was adapted to meet the specific needs of an elementary school library in New York City. The specific emphasis on multicultural resources was important because the collection was deficient in those areas.

PS:___ D:___ Name:___________ # of Students:___ total # of Items in the collection:___ # of total collection items per student:___

COLLECTION MAP

	Total	Grade Level					Specific Emphasis								Pub. Date
		Pre K-K	1-2	3-4	5-6	7-8	African-Amer.	Latino	Asian	Holiday					post-1985
Reference (General)															
Reference (Encyclopedias)															
000															
100															
200															
300															
398.2															
400															
Language															
500															
590															
600															
700															
800															
900															
920															
Biography															
Easy															
Fiction															
Picture															
Periodicals															
Professional Col.															
Parent Col.															
Total															

Fig. 6.1. Collection Map.

Collection Building

△ Keep a record of areas that need an infusion of materials or that need a major weeding.

△ Use a notebook or loose-leaf binder at your desk to record requests that could not be filled or particular subjects that need attention.

△ Keep a record of units and themes planned with teachers in the past and plans for future programs. When evaluating units or special projects with students and teachers, check how well your collection filled needs.

△ Discuss curricular trends with faculty and administration representatives to decide how to focus the collection in terms of the curriculum.

△ Create a desiderata file on a computer database or on 3" x 5" cards that includes titles found to fulfill your specific needs. Include student and teacher requests.

△ Add copies of reviews of materials in all media from such journals as *Booklinks, Technology and Learning,* and *School Library Journal* to your file so that you can compare several titles on the same topic.

△ Create a file of bibliographies from various sources, including textbooks used in your school.

Book Formats

Selecting the content of the collection is only one aspect of collection building. The variety of bindings, proliferation of toy and paper construction books, and nonstandard sizes and shapes challenge the selector. Electronic formats are discussed in chapter 10. Some special consideration for print materials are discussed here.

Trade Books

The term refers to standard hardcover books published for the bookstore market but often used in libraries. Generally they have a paper dust jacket and come in all sizes and shapes. These bindings can be bought at the highest school and library discount rate. Some books are also available in "Reinforced Trade" editions. When these are available for the same high discount (often 40 percent), they should be purchased, as the reinforced bindings are more durable.

Pre-Binds

Two general types are available from companies that specialize in this format. Hardcover books recovered with special reinforced bindings are one type. This process does not always capture the colors or clarity of the original cover and therefore produces a less attractive book. These books are tightly bound and do not always lie flat. The other type of pre-bind is a paperback that has been attached to a laminated binding, incorporating the original paperback cover. The paper quality and size of the individual volumes need to be examined before purchase, as they usually differ from the original hardcover edition. The binding may also outlast the paper stock and the value of the content.

Publishers' Library Bindings

These specially bound editions are usually sold to public and school libraries. They sometimes have paper dust jackets, but usually have an illustration printed directly on the cover. They often have special guarantees on wearability. Because discounts are limited, these bindings often are more costly than trade editions. Some books, especially nonfiction titles, are only published in library bindings. Discounts usually range from 10-20 percent.

Paperbacks

Quality of paper and covers varies from publisher to publisher. Low costs and high discounts will help stretch book budgets. Multiple copies of popular books and books that may become dated quickly also may be purchased in this format. Some books, especially those from small presses, may only be available as paperbacks. This is a very appealing format to children. Try to observe your users' patterns. Do they prefer the paperback version of a novel that is also available in your hardcover fiction section? If so, you may want to invest more in your paperback collection. There is always the option of putting laminated covers on the paperbacks to increase attractiveness and number of circulations.

Big Books

Oversized (as large as 17" x 23") paperbacks are often used in literature-based reading programs. These can be used for read-aloud sessions in the library or loaned to classes. Companies that trade in these materials usually sell sets of small versions of the same book. Big books can be very effective when used with beginning readers. Predictable language patterns and lilting rhythms are the hallmarks of good quality in this format. Visual appeal and the size and clarity of the type are important factors. Discount policies vary. Nonfiction titles and titles in Spanish are also available in the "Big Book" format. Consider storage options when purchasing.

Board Books

Printed on heavy cardboard pages, these are usually intended for very young children. Schools with day care programs, classes for three-year-olds, special populations, or parent collections may wish to purchase these. Because they often have only one or two lines of text on a page, they can be used by beginning readers who want to read to younger brothers or sisters.

Pop-Up Books and Toy Books

Books with many moving parts, extra pieces, or cutouts sometimes designed in unusual shapes are fascinating to children, even though text quality is not always on a par with visual and tactile appeal. Because they are expensive and fragile, a limited number should be purchased and placed on display or used with small groups in the library, as they are easily torn in circulation. Encourage students to create their own pop-up books.

Guidelines for Weeding

While your selection policy and collection plan are the best guides for decision making about what materials should be included in your collection, the following basic guides should help in deciding what to discard.

0-100: Keep almanacs three years, space permitting. Keep computer books five years. Keep bibliographies of children's books a maximum of 10 years.

200: Keep mythology and Bible stories. Keep introductions to world religions. Examine works on religious services, festivals and holy days, sacraments, and so on and replace as necessitated by changes in practice. Ask teachers and parents of various religions to advise.

300: Keep five years: books on urban problems, pollution, energy, communications, technology. Keep transportation 10 years except for historical treatments. Keep 10 years: city workers and community helpers. Examine to see that races and genders are adequately represented.

372: Discard professional titles, how-to-do-it manuals, and curriculum guides after 10 years. Discard educational textbooks and readings on educational theories and practices after 10 years. Supplement this area with professional journals and vertical file materials from conferences and seminars.

394: Discard materials on holidays and customs as interest wanes. Examine customs of other cultures for currency and accuracy with the assistance of teachers and parents from the culture.

398: Keep standard works of fairy tales, especially those that are indexed and those that provide sources and notes. Discard titles that are untrue to the original in language or plot. Examine and discard those with stereotypes. Early collections of Native American stories "for young audiences" were often altered by editors. Discard those in which dialect or illustrations are demeaning.

400: Keep a selection of dictionaries at various levels of difficulty and in several languages. Make sure that contemporary words in common use are included. Keep books of word origins, idioms, homonyms and antonyms, and the like. Discard grammar textbooks and style manuals after 10 years.

500: Keep botany, natural sciences, math history, and books on the physical sciences such as simple machines. Discard those with outdated theories and facts and chronologies of "recent discoveries" that are older than 10 years. Examine other titles closely; most should be discarded after five years. Examine titles lacking sources, notes, or indexes and replace with titles that give documentation. A few exceptions: Keep the excellent, very easy series like Let's-Read-and-Find-Out and the photo essays of Seymour Simon.

600: Keep historical treatments on transportation. Discard space travel after five years. Discard after 10 years: planes, trains, ships, and automobiles. Keep 10 years: farming, manufacturing, construction. Keep longer: pets, farm animals, cookery, gardening.

700: Keep fine arts and works on artists. Keep how-to arts and crafts, games, and sports unless interest does not support it. Keep historical works on music: jazz, rock, pop, folk, heavy metal. Supplement with recent works. Discard books on sports, TV, movie, and music personalities after 10 years, sooner if subjects retire. Discard price guides to coins, stamps, and sports cards after five years.

800: Keep standard poetry works that are indexed. Keep literature, poetry, and prose from other cultures and in other languages that support the curriculum. Keep some classical works in original and adapted versions: *Robin Hood, The Odyssey, Canterbury Tales,* Shakespeare. Examine poetry collections; many do not age well. Discard poems that are overly sentimental or didactic. Examine titles with biographical notes on the authors to see that they are current. Purchase visually appealing editions to replace those with unattractive or dated illustrations.

900: Discard as interpretations of facts, people, or events change. Update historical works on the decade, century, and so on. Discard multiple volumes on events or issues and replace with a single summary volume when the topic is no longer of high interest.

910-12: Examine maps and atlases carefully for accuracy and date of issue. Purchase paperback atlases for circulation. Discard frequently.

913-19: Discard books on countries, unless they are primarily historical, after 10 years, sooner if major changes occur in name, boundaries, government, and so on. (Recent examples: the government of South Africa or the dissolution of the USSR.)

920: Discard collective biographies after 10 years unless they are primarily of historical figures (explorers, great painters, football greats).

Biography: Discard multiple copies of former leaders and popular figures (past presidents, TV personalities, rock stars). When an important figure dies, replace existing titles with one that provides a summary or evaluation of the individual's contributions. Discard titles with extensive invented dialogue.

Picture Books: Discard marginal titles by major authors or illustrators. Discard television and movie tie-ins after the fad has waned. Discard titles that have stereotypic views. Discard where illustrations, theme, or text are dated.

Easy Books: Discard early efforts that mirror basals, formula titles with questions to answer, bold highlighted vocabulary, and so on. Discard "hot" topics and media tie-ins that are no longer hot.

Fiction: Discard abridgments, adaptations, and works that are too long or difficult for students. Discard those with dated themes, illustrations, or incorrect information about careers, countries, world issues, or other topics.

Reference Materials

Note: The titles cited here are examples of types of available reference material that must be examined for weeding.

Encyclopedias: Keep general encyclopedias five years. Encyclopedias more than five years old but not older than 10 years can be circulated or used in classrooms. Discard those older than 10 years.

Annuals: Keep one year; circulate two to three years if interest warrants (*Guinness Book of World Records, Sports Records*).

Index to Poetry: Keep volumes covering those years represented in the collection.

Primary Search: Magazine index on CD-ROM, three updates annually.

Almanacs: Keep most current year in reference; keep two past years in circulating collection.

Elementary School Library Collection: Replace after five years.

Children's Catalog: Replace every five years when the annual supplements cease.

World Religions: Examine and consider for replacement when new edition is available, if use warrants.

World Mythology: Keep.

Holidays and Anniversaries Around the World: Keep edition 10 years.

Index to Fairy Tales: Keep those volumes covering years reflected in the collection.

Background Notes of Countries: Keep most current. Discard older sheets as new editions become available.

Costumes: Keep.

Unabridged Dictionary: Replace after 10 years. New words become part of common usage; biographical and geographical entries become outdated.

Science Encyclopedias: Keep five years. Examine articles of current importance from the edition in your collection; compare to the same topic in the newest edition. A new copyright date does not mean the articles have been updated.

Field Guides to Trees, Shells, Animals, Birds: Keep 15 years or until titles with superior photographs or illustrations are available.

Stories of Operas, Ballets, and so on: Keep.

Rules for Sports and Games: Examine; after five years consider for replacement.

Companions to Music: Keep.

Familiar Quotations: Keep.

Lands and Peoples: Examine; after five years consider for replacement.

Geographical Dictionaries: Examine; after five years replace.

Atlases: Examine; after five years replace.

Junior Author Series: Examine carefully. Determine if the series is used. If you are keeping up the series, keep older volumes as well.

Flags: Keep five years.

Books of Presidents: Replace when new edition becomes available.

African-American History: Replace as new editions become available.

Native Americans: Keep.

Books of Hispanic Americans, Chinese-Americans, Famous Women: Examine for currency. Keep 10 years.

State Seals, Flags and Symbols: Keep unless a new state is added.

Periodicals

Establish policies based on space, use, and availability in other formats. For example, you might determine that:

Popular Juvenile Magazines (*Seventeen, Hispanica, Karate Illustrated*) would be kept on display one month and circulated for one year or until they disintegrate.

Juvenile Research Titles (*Odyssey, Ranger Rick, Zoobooks, Cobblestones*) would circulate to teachers and would be kept on file five years.

Reference Titles (*Newsweek, World in Focus*) would be kept on display, would not circulate, and would be kept one year.

Teacher Titles (*Reading Teacher, Instructor, Technology & Learning*) would be displayed one month, circulated to teachers, and kept five years.

Newspapers: Keep one month, space permitting.

Other Formats

Note: Ask borrowers to assist in evaluating the condition and continued usefulness of materials in non-print and electronic media. Ask users to fill out a media evaluation sheet for returning materials.

Filmstrips, Filmloops: Are the visuals still crisp, accurate, and timely? Is the audiotape audible and appropriate? Are suggested readings and related activities current and useful? Do you have the equipment necessary to play the filmstrips and loops? Is this the best and most cost-effective format for the content?

Videos: Many videos purchased for school use were not produced for the school market. Replace tapes purchased from commercial markets and those intended for older audiences as superior material becomes available. Programs taped from commercial or educational television must adhere to copyright regulations. Do not accept for school use pirated or illegally made copies of commercial videos. When videos are produced within the school, request that the supplier fill out a media form indicating who, what, when, how long, suggested subject headings, and recommendations for shelf life.

Games and Realia: Discard if parts or pieces are missing or damaged and cannot be replaced.

Study Prints, Transparencies: Evaluate for the continued usefulness and currency of the content. Discard warped, damaged, brittle, faded items.

Maps and Globes: Place names should be current, accurate, and readable. Maps should indicate the date of drawings and sources.

Puppets: Shabby, dirty, torn, or damaged puppets should be discarded, as should puppets related to movies or television shows that are no longer shown or remembered.

Audiotapes and Sound Recordings: Discard those that are scratched, cracked, warped, or otherwise damaged. Transfer albums to cassette tape if record players are no longer available. You may make one copy of an album on tape without violating copyright laws, if only the tape is circulated and the album recording is placed in storage.

Electronic Media: Many materials in electronic format come from publishers with restrictions on use, copying, discarding, and so on. Copy and save all warranties and agreements. Attach one copy of the agreement to the physical material and keep one copy on file. As with other non-print media, it is helpful to have your borrowers assist with evaluating for continued usefulness. For additional suggestions on selecting, evaluating, and weeding titles in electronic formats, you may wish to consult *The Challenge of Technology: Action Strategies for the School Library Media Specialist* (Wright 1993), *Selection and Evaluation of Electronic Resources* (Dickinson 1994), and other titles in the bibliography of this chapter.

Computer Programs: Careful note must be taken of the original purchase or leasing agreements. Determine whether replacement is needed and cost effective: Is there a reduced price for upgrading? Can you continue to keep or use the superseded version? Is the upgrade compatible with your existing systems and hardware? What has been changed? Has the producer mostly eliminated bugs or speeded up access, but not substantially changed the content? Ask users to help you evaluate existing software and recommend weeding or keeping.

CD-ROM Encyclopedias: Just because the copyright is altered each year doesn't mean the content has been upgraded. Examine the new edition and compare it to your current edition. You can often see the new products at computer stores and educational conferences or examine them online using telecommunications services. Ask colleagues to put a message on e-mail when new CDs are received so that you can pool your expertise. Ask them to conduct a sample search for you and print out the results. Select a topic with which you are familiar: your hometown, a current science topic, a high-profile government official, then print out and compare the articles from both editions. Are the facts current? Is the information readable? Many reviewers of CD-ROM encyclopedias focus on the bells and whistles rather than the content. They report on enhanced graphics and the number of sound and video clips with little attention to the text. Photos may be abundant but of little use in understanding the articles.

The CD-ROM encyclopedia is a useful tool for teaching research strategies and Boolean logic. It is highly motivating for students who enjoy cruising the new technology, even when the text is too difficult. They also enjoy printing out maps, photos, and sections of texts. Where available, the note-taking function can enhance careful reading and paraphrasing. Is the upgrade compatible with your existing systems and hardware? As with computer programs, many upgrades may require additional memory.

CD-ROMs: As with all materials, ask if this is the most useful, cost-effective and best format for the content. Does it offer distinctive features for strategy or skills development? Does it fill a need for students or faculty with different learning styles? Do you have the equipment to support its use? Some CD-ROMs may be received free with equipment purchases or as part of a bundle. Keep only those titles that meet your materials' selection standards. Find a written review or personally examine titles added to your collection.

Materials Selection

Materials selection is one of the major ongoing tasks of a library media specialist's professional career. With the proliferation of electronic formats, you will have to make some complex choices, considering not only the quality and suitability of an individual item, but whether a particular medium is the best format for the content.

All materials should be written or produced by people with an in-depth knowledge of their subject. Based on school need, some materials should also be available in various languages, both for children to use by themselves and for parents who read different languages to use with their children. You should also select materials that will facilitate your students' ability to create new information, and materials that assist children in developing new learning strategies. Factors that should be considered are the usefulness, relevance, and importance of a particular item to the collection, especially if a high price tag is attached. Figure 6.2 provides a list of many criteria to use in the selection process.

Try to examine materials before you purchase them. Books may be seen at libraries, bookstores, conference exhibits, and at local previewing sites. Multimedia and other audiovisual materials may usually be previewed for a short period. Contact individual companies about preview policies. Video producers are often reluctant to send their products out on preview. Recordings, too, usually cannot be previewed. Check with the company about return policies if you are not satisfied with materials that are purchased sight unseen.

CRITERIA FOR THE PURCHASE OF ALL LIBRARY MATERIALS		
Intended Audience and Usage	**Content**	**Format and Technical Qualities**
Students' interests.	Accuracy.	Print and Non-Print
Teachers' curriculum.	Currency and timeliness.	Type of visuals.
Professional reference.	Tone and style.	Quality of visuals.
Parents' interests.	Appeal.	Clarity of design.
Grade levels.	Organization.	Clarity of graphics.
Reading levels.	Logical sequencing.	Durability.
Ethnic groups.	Reflect cultural diversity.	Quality of narration.
Languages spoken.	Reference features.	Effective music.
School programs.	Authors' and illustrators' credentials	Realistic sound effects.
Cost vs. usage.	Unique to the collection.	User-friendly.
Past usage.	Complements or supplements other material.	Flexible usage.
Future needs.		

Fig. 6.2 Criteria for All Library Materials

Selection of Nonprint Materials

Audio Formats

Audios come in three formats: record, cassette, and compact disc (CD). Records are being replaced by CDs and cassettes. Cassettes are probably the format of choice for most elementary schools because they are easy to use and moderately priced. If you have records in your collection, you may want to copy them on cassettes for greater ease of handling. This is not a violation of copyright. As more children's materials come out on CD and as prices have come down for both the discs and the players, this format has become more popular because of its better sound quality and durability. You can also play audio CDs on the CD-ROM drive connected to your computer.

School systems may place different emphasis on music in the curriculum. Some schools stress singing and choral performance. Others give children experience in learning and playing instruments. Students may also hear live performances by a variety of musicians. Recent studies have shown a correlation between early music education and intellectual development. Music can stir students' imaginations and may have some positive effects on problem-solving abilities.

Library collections that include a full range of musical recordings, both instrumental and vocal, give teachers and students access to the rich body of music created through the ages and around the world. The musical selections should be excellent examples of different musical periods and styles: classical, folk (representing cultures from around the world), jazz, contemporary, and so on. Recordings with songs that include repetitive lines or verses, cumulative songs, call-and-response songs, action songs, and silly songs should be in the collection. Curriculum-related songs can also please children, provided that the lyrics rise above didacticism and the music is appealing.

Many books, folktales, and poems are available on cassette tape. Children enjoy listening to stories read by a professional narrator, an actor, or the author. Whether the child only follows the pictures or actually reads along in an accompanying book, this activity can be very positive for beginning readers, reluctant readers, and even eager, experienced readers.

Picture books and easy-to-read books are often recorded in their entirety. Stories and folklore are most commonly offered, but some easy nonfiction is also available. Novels for older children are sometimes fully recorded or may be abridged or adapted. Publishers or distributors may package cassettes with a hardcover or paperback book. Some companies supply several paperbacks to use with a small group. Occasionally, the tape may be purchased separately, if you already have the book.

Storytellers have also recorded their work in various formats. Sometimes these stories are available in books and sometimes they are not. Encourage children to listen to these recordings and read related books to further their enjoyment.

CRITERIA FOR SELECTING MUSICAL RECORDINGS

△ Liner notes should include information on the style, performers, sources of selections, and any relevant historical background information.

△ Musical selections should inspire children to participate by listening, singing along, or dancing.

△ Playing time for each selection should be indicated on written material accompanying the recording. Selections should be of appropriate length for the intended audience.

Fig. 6.3. Criteria for Musical Recordings.

Visual Formats

Videos and films must stand on their own merits as creative works. Beautiful or arresting images, excellent acting, and appropriate and interesting techniques can all be used to produce videos and films of high quality. You should introduce students to videos and films in which technical quality, style, and content are artfully woven together to create new experiences for viewers. Select those films that instruct most effectively.

Videos and films correlate with every area of the curriculum. Your students can travel around the globe, experience life in another century, go with astronauts to the moon, view a music or dance performance, or find out about AIDS from a person who has the disease or a doctor trying to cure it. Few media bring today's world into the classroom or library as well, if the films and videos you choose are current, accurate, and well-crafted. Films and videos that are based on books and traditional stories can open up another dimension of discussion for your students and can also inspire students to create their own productions.

Videos have enjoyed increased usage in recent years because of their convenience and availability. Some videos cost $10-$30, making them even more attractive. These are generally videos that have been produced for the home market and include films that have been shown in theaters or on television. Beware, however, of the Hollywood feature film, which rarely has a place in a curricular setting. Videos produced primarily for the school and library market tend to be more expensive, in the $50-$300 range, and are usually not available in commercial video outlets. These may be borrowed from public libraries, rented from universities, or be available through cooperative purchases by district or regional agencies. Consider how you will use the video, the size of the audience, and the value of the contents.

Taping television programs may be another source of video material, although this practice must follow copyright laws. Be aware that there are restrictions on the use of duplicated video materials. For more information, contact the original producers of the materials. Some of the programs aired on PBS and other stations are produced for instructional television stations across the country and may be taped, providing that you obey the guidelines for fair use.

Many audiovisual companies are making filmstrips newly available as "videos." Although this is indicated in their catalogs, remember that many of these "videos" may be static in quality as they are still photographs recorded on tape. Some videos have "enhanced visuals," which means that a special technique has been used to add a sense of movement to the original filmstrip frames. Carefully consider that the price of these "new" videos are generally higher than the original filmstrips that are often still being sold.

Videos in different languages and captioned videos for students who have hearing disabilities are available. Nonnarrative videos may also be included in your collection and these can be viewed with enjoyment by many types of students. Always preview videos and encourage teachers to do so, even if they are using a video on your recommendation. You can also stop and start videos to accommodate class discussion or use only an appropriate section.

Electronic Formats

Reference materials in electronic formats are being produced in all subject areas for children at every age level at an astounding rate. Children are excited by these formats and quickly learn the searching techniques needed to locate information. Many standard encyclopedias and other reference materials and books are produced both in electronic format and print, and librarians are faced with the choice of evaluating and deciding whether to buy the print or electronic version of a particular reference tool, or perhaps to buy both. Cost factors (including the cost of equipment) must be considered when evaluating reference materials as well as usage (20 children using different encyclopedia volumes versus one or two children at a single computer terminal).

Consider purchasing one or more of the following programs:

△ Publishing and word processing programs give librarians, students, and teachers the ability to produce reports, newsletters, newspapers, magazines, and books in a variety of type sizes and fonts. When using these programs, students become more proficient at editing and are likely to produce multiple drafts of materials.

△ Database programs enable users to assemble and categorize information in a variety of ways, giving students opportunities to analyze and synthesize information. Librarians can also use database programs to create desiderata files, orders, bibliographies, overdues, library statistics, and reports of all types.

△ Games motivate student learning in different subject areas. Many educational computer games require reading, the use of reference skills, and critical thinking.

△ Graphics programs are used to create posters, charts, timelines, and illustrations for academic and recreational purposes.

△ Multimedia programs enable students, teachers, and librarians to bring together video clips, audio pieces, text, and graphics to create their own brand new pieces of information.

CRITERIA FOR SELECTING NONPRINT MATERIALS

Format	Considerations	
All formats	Age appropriate. Format appropriate for content. Technically excellent, including sound, graphics and visuals. Appealing to users. Challenging and creative in its approach to content.	Offer positive experiences. Invite repeated use. Materials that are comprehensive and clear. Authentic. An abridgment or adaption should be faithful to the original work.
Audio	Pleasing and well-timed narration. Sound signals audible, but not jarring.	Clear sound reproduction. Sound should complement the narration, not overpower it.
Visual	Effective visuals or photographs. Excellent animation.	Visuals work well with text.
Electronic	Creative use of the medium. On-screen directions are clear. Text is legible. Documentation. Student work can be saved, displayed, or printed.	Vivid graphics. Support services that are free or inexpensive. Adaptable to individual and group use.
Globes	Scale indicator included. Legends and indexes clearly indicated. Effective use of color contrasts to portray dimension and topography.	Surface finish that can be marked and easily erased. Readable print. Accurate place names. Portable. Durable.
Study Prints/Art Prints	High quality of reproduction. Excellent choice of photographs or illustrations used in study prints.	Appropriate text and typeface used in captions. Durable mounting and surface finish.
Realia (authentic natural specimens or authentic cultural artifacts)	Accurate accompanying information. Educational value. Encourage the use of critical thinking and logic.	Durable and safe. Well-written instructions. Adaptable to different levels. Packaged for display, examination, storage, and circulation.
Puppets	Durable and safe. Easy to use. Easy to clean. Appeal to students.	Adaptability to different characters. Authenticity, if meant to represent a particular ethnic or cultural group.
Manipulatives	Related to the curriculum. Durable and safe.	Accompanying materials with clear instructions and ideas for multiple uses.
Slides	Quality of photography. Documentation, sources. Relevance to the curriculum.	Clear accompanying text in print or on audio.

Fig. 6.4. Criteria for Nonprint Materials.

Selection of Print Materials: Fiction

The elementary school library media center must satisfy a great many requirements when providing readers of various abilities and ages with literature and stories. The youngest students need access to beautifully illustrated picture books. Whether the books are read aloud to them, explored alone, or shared with a friend, vivid illustration and brief evocative texts will kindle an appreciation of language and a love of story in children too young to read on their own. As students acquire some reading skills of their own, they continue to explore picture books, but easy-to-read books give them the confidence they need as they "practice" their new abilities by engaging in the real task of reading whole books.

The wider variety of first chapter books that are now being published satisfy the next transitional stage. Some children will move quickly to reading novels of varying length and complexity, while others may spend more time reading the shorter, easier chapter books. Still other students, commonly called reluctant readers, have mastered the mechanics of reading but are not motivated to read. Entice them and support their efforts by selecting high-interest/low-reading books. Select action-filled, brief fiction, and visually appealing nonfiction materials of interest to their age. This is an important group to cultivate. Give them exciting selections on appealing topics so they will want to read for pleasure. As you select fiction titles for your library, it is vital that you address all audiences: your brand new listeners and readers, your eager "bookworms" who can't wait to curl up in a corner and immerse themselves in the words of their current favorite author, and those students who haven't yet discovered the wonderful attraction of a good story. With the right selections at hand and a warm, personal approach, you will have the tools to bring those children into the community of readers.

Picture Books

Picture books are among the most widely used materials in schools today. As more pre-K children enter public school, easy concept books and very simple stories are needed in large quantities for read-alouds by teachers, librarians, parents, and for children's own forays into reading.

The visual quality and appeal of a picture book are paramount. Illustrators are currently using many styles and mediums including somber, Renaissance oils; vivid, Matisse-like paper cutouts; sensitive, traditional watercolors; unusual materials in collages; and bold interpretations of modern art. With the development of better production techniques, photography has become an important element in picture books. The visual images convey the sense of action, character development, and theme, but the text of a picture book should not take a secondary role.

Picture books produced with the adult gift market in mind should be evaluated carefully. The book must appeal to children, not to adults' sometimes inaccurate conceptions of children's interests. The very best picture books have a timeless quality that elevates them to the "classics" category—those books that have been enjoyed by several generations.

Wordless picture books are useful for a variety of age levels. Young children can "read" these books themselves, while wordless books for older children can serve as a starting point for writing projects. Parents with limited reading skills can use these books with their children.

Include specialized picture books in your collection: alphabet, counting, and math concept books; color, shape, and other visual discrimination concept books; picture search; and puzzle books. Some picture books appeal to a wide age range, going beyond the traditional picture book audience. Many teachers are using picture books in conjunction with their introduction to the "writing process." Some contemporary picture books explore mature themes, such as war, the environment, and historical concerns. Purchase them to satisfy older students' needs. Students with high reading levels and those who are experiencing difficulty in moving on to other types of books for the upper elementary grades will find picture books with mature themes inspiring. See figure 6.5 for selection criteria.

CRITERIA FOR SELECTING PICTURE BOOKS

Of interest to children.
Use of color (or black and white).
Use of line.
Style (realistic, abstract, modern, naive, adaptation of a specific ethnic style).
Medium (oils, pastels, crayons, ink, photographs, etc.).
Use of unusual materials (collage, natural materials, etc.).
Book design, including type size, style, and placement.
Paper quality and durability.
Quality of text and pictures.
Amount of text.
Use of rich, rhythmic language, appropriate for intended audience(s).
A stimulating plot.
Themes and settings that enlarge a child's sense of the world.

Fig. 6.5. Criteria for Picture Books.

Easy-to-Read Books

Children who are learning to read need a wide variety of easy-to-read books for reading at school and at home. Books with limited text and vocabulary (although not bound by the kind of word list once imposed by some publishers) are usually more appealing than textbooks that control not only the vocabulary but the phonetic sounds that are introduced.

Although poor examples of this genre are stilted and boring, the best easy readers are often quietly humorous such as, the Frog and Toad books by Arnold Lobel, or lively and engaging books such as Alvin Schwartz's *Ghosts!* Select many of books from this genre so that children can read several or even many of them each day. Familiarity is an important factor in a child's selections. Look for quality series. This stage in a child's reading career is crucial for developing reading for pleasure.

CRITERIA FOR SELECTING EASY-TO-READ BOOKS

Visual appeal.
Engaging plot.
Short sentences.
Generous use of white space.
Repetition is used to encourage the reader, but not to bore.
Variety of subjects including sports, history, animals, and crafts.

Fig. 6.6. Criteria for Easy-to-Read Books.

First Chapter Books

First chapter books are a relatively new phenomenon in the publishing world. Meant to serve as a bridge between easy readers and full-fledged chapter books, they provide attractive, interesting-looking books for those who are either reluctant readers or who are eager to read about the same characters again and again. In some cases, the predictability only means that the style and reading level will be the same from title to title. But by far the most successful are those that feature the same characters in a series.

Once looked down upon by those who wished to provide only the best reading for children, the newer series and individual titles provide good reading as well as popular appeal. While many of these series are available in hardcover, the most attractive format for many children is the paperback.

Novels

Traditional and modern classics, mysteries, science and historical fiction, romances, fantasy, adventure stories, contemporary fiction, and stories set in a variety of cultures and countries should all be part of your collection. If your collection lacks a strong fiction section, use the sources listed at the end of the chapter to strengthen it, but remember to use your students' reading and interest levels to guide you.

Use review journals to select the best new novels and stories. Read as many of these as you can. There is no substitute for really knowing your fiction collection. You may need to promote certain titles through formal booktalks, informal "shelf" talks with individuals, reviews in a library newsletter, or recommendations to teachers seeking read-alouds.

Speak to public librarians about books. Compare notes about what's popular in your respective libraries and also discuss books that have more literary merit. Attend conferences that offer opportunities to discuss children's literature and allow you to meet authors and illustrators.

Selecting fiction in other languages is challenging. Reviews will help, but assistance in selecting appropriate foreign-language novels should be sought from people who know the language and the reading audience. Seek out bilingual teaching specialists and public librarians who have foreign-language collections.

As students move from first chapter books, help them find enjoyable books that will also expand their horizons. Librarians often feel a tug-of-war between the need for popular materials (e.g., the Goosebumps series, the Babysitters Club books, Encyclopedia Brown) and more literary materials that may have to be "sold" to make them inviting to students. You'll probably want to buy several paperback copies of fiction series titles that your students request. You can use school book fairs to help fill in on the ephemeral popular titles.

CRITERIA FOR SELECTING NOVELS

Of interest to children.
Believability, coherence, and creativity of plot.
Authenticity of setting.
Character development.
Originality.
Intellectually and emotionally challenging.
Use of rich and beautiful language.
Intrinsic interest of the theme.
Life affirming.
Interesting point of view.

Fig. 6.7. Criteria for Novels.

High Interest/Low Reading-Level Books

Some children in the upper-elementary grades need materials written at a lower reading level, although their interests have expanded beyond that of primary school students. "Reluctant readers" are defined as upper-elementary students (fourth- to sixth-graders) whose independent reading levels are significantly below their chronological age. The label also applies to students who can read at the appropriate level but are not motivated to read.

Many reluctant readers have short attention spans and may have a history of academic failure with resulting low self-esteem. These students are afraid to fail. Reluctant readers need titles that are suitable for their level; are exciting to them in appearance, format, and subject matter; and promote reading success.

Format must also be considered, because students of this age do not want to be seen reading a "baby" book. Size and illustration style must be similar to materials intended for students reading on grade level. With success, students who have been limited to these materials will move into the other areas of your collection. A high-interest book of particular relevance will be read by a child no matter how difficult the vocabulary, often surprising teachers, librarians, or parents.

Reading levels may be determined by skimming through the book, using reviews and publishers' estimated levels, or using a readability formula such as the Fry Readability Formula. Librarians need not provide books that are at the student's exact level, but it is helpful to estimate the reading level of books when recommending them to reluctant readers.

CRITERIA FOR SELECTING HIGH/LOW BOOKS	
Short paragraphs.	Access to content.
Easy vocabulary.	Detailed index.
Simple plots of information.	Accessible captions and subject headings.
Logical grammatical constructions.	Appropriate design.
More action, less descriptions.	Visual appeal of the title.
Language flows.	Precisely defined glossaries.
Format must match audience.	Vivid writing.
Themes must be age-appropriate.	Interesting subject matter.

Fig. 6.8. Criteria for High/Low Books.

Selection of Print Materials—Nonfiction

When adults think of pleasure reading, many think of fiction. But ask children what they like to read and they will often tell you they like "true" books about dinosaurs, sports stars, drawing, or outer space. Today's children can find nonfiction titles with superb, full-color illustrations or photographs and accurate texts written by experts on almost any topic. Quality nonfiction titles rival fiction works in their literary quality. Indeed, several recent nonfiction titles have received Newbery Honors.

In the following pages, nonfiction books are discussed and special selection considerations are given for different categories, including poetry and folklore. Biographies now offer ever-younger readers carefully documented introductions to important people, living and dead, from many cultures. Many new titles combine primary source material, appealing photographs, and very brief texts.

Science and social studies books have undergone a revolutionary change. Publishers like Dorling Kindersley pioneered the technique of cutting out separate, distinct images from color photographs and placing the images in sharp contrast to the white space on the page. Other titles use computer simulations, stop-action photography, and photos taken through electron microscopes and space satellites to make the unknown visible.

Improved book production techniques and author-illustrators such as Gail Gibbons, Aliki, and Douglas Florian make nonfiction accessible and appealing to young students as they combine brief text and colorful illustrations. David Macaulay's detailed studies of architecture and technology open up new worlds for visual learners. And the many museum publications, often combining poetry and literature with excellent color reproductions of well-known masterpieces, have all contributed to an exciting new world of nonfiction for children.

Folktales

Although folktales in picture book format are now in great demand, many excellent story collections, old and new, can be used by older children, teachers, and librarians searching for stories to tell and read aloud. Several versions of the same tale may be used effectively to examine the nature of folklore and the universality and diversity of the human experience. Comparing many tales from one culture may illuminate values of the people from that culture.

When selecting folktales, check their authenticity. Does an author's note include information about the origin of the tale? The illustrations and use of language should appropriately convey the cultural and historical setting of the tale. In cases where the author and/or illustrator change the traditional setting, a statement about their particular version of the story should be included. Contemporary settings sometimes provide an amusing counterpoint to traditional stories, but traditional versions of the same tale should also be available.

Poetry

Poetry is an important part of the written and oral tradition for children around the world. It should be purchased in multitheme anthologies and specialized single-subject collections (e.g., holiday poems, nature poems, etc.). Purchase collections by a single poet or group of poets, books that contain examples of various poetic forms (e.g., haiku, cinquain, etc.), and beautifully illustrated picture book versions of individual poems. Buy poetry in languages spoken by your students. Mother Goose rhymes and other traditional rhymes from a variety of cultures (some in bilingual versions) should also be in your collection. Collections of poetry by children can be purchased.

CRITERIA FOR SELECTING POETRY ANTHOLOGIES	
Scope	**Arrangement**
Number of poems included. Types of poems (theme, mood) and poetic forms.	How the poems are organized (by poet, theme, mood, poetic form).
Poets represented.	Logical, cohesive, appealing arrangement.
Diverse cultures represented.	Arrangement enhances the appreciation of the poems.
Literary quality.	Usefulness of indexes.
Illustrations extend the text.	Special content (e.g., biographical information, critical analysis).

Fig. 6.9. Criteria for Poetry Anthologies.

Reference Materials

Reference materials in both print and electronic form are costly and should be chosen with particular care, using recognized review sources and personal review of the material to check reading level and scope of material in relationship to your school's needs. Discussions with other librarians may be enlightening. Some expensive reference materials can be shelf sitters, while others may be in constant demand. See figure 6.10 for selection considerations for reference materials.

It is advisable to purchase new print encyclopedias every 5 years, and to discard them every 10 years. Electronic encyclopedias may be updated annually. You will need dictionaries at levels ranging from picture dictionaries to at least one unabridged dictionary, foreign-language dictionaries, thesauri, atlases (including one or more children's atlases), current almanacs, and specialized references on a variety of topics. Look for some of these tools as components of word processing and desktop publishing programs.

Traditionally, reference materials did not circulate. Today, overnight checkout is a must. Also, purchase site licenses for electronic reference materials so they are available over networks for access in the library, the classroom, and at home.

CRITERIA FOR SELECTING REFERENCE MATERIALS
The information is well organized and easy to use.
The information is primarily for student or teacher use.
The anticipated usage justifies the cost.
The information is accurate and current.
The material is available via networks in electronic versions.

Fig. 6.10. Criteria for Selecting Reference Materials.

Biography

Accuracy and a lively, interesting style are necessary for the successful presentation of a famous person's life, in any format. The best authors of biographies for children and young adults not only realistically describe their particular subject but also evoke an entire era through the introduction of fascinating historical details.

Collective biographies are important, too. In recent years, the growing interest in historical and contemporary figures from many ethnic groups and the emphasis upon women's history, collective biographies have often been the best source of information for curriculum-related projects. Students who have a particular interest in an area such as sports or music may also find useful biographical material in CD-ROMs, filmstrips, videos, and recordings. For popular figures, you will need several biographical treatments at different reading levels.

CRITERIA FOR SELECTING BIOGRAPHIES
Biographee's whole life or just a period, such as childhood.
Easy access to information.
Illustrations are accurate and appealing.
Index.
Meaningful chapter headings.
Chronology of important dates.
Literary and interesting writing.
Realistic portrayal of people as human beings.
Notes and sources, including citation of primary source materials.

Fig. 6.11. Criteria for Selecting Biographies.

Science

Science titles are of great interest to elementary school children. Natural disasters, unusual phenomenon, science personalities, and scientific discoveries described in the media are frequently the subject of children's books a scant year later. An explosion of exciting, vividly written, visually beautiful titles for beginning and experienced readers have expanded opportunities for science literacy as never before.

Curriculum goals stress the need for hands-on learning, higher-level thinking skills, and science literacy for all students. At the same time, adults must make decisions about their daily lives, which require an understanding of scientific principles. What are the consequences of logging in the rain forest? Saving the spotted owl? Sending satellites to Venus?

Children can develop an understanding of the scientific method and scientific principles by reading about present and past discoveries, learning about scientists and their work, collecting and analyzing data, and exploring through experimentation and observation.

CRITERIA FOR SELECTING SCIENCE MATERIALS

Vivid and beautiful, clear without oversimplification.

Adheres to the scientific method.

Distinguishes between fact, theory, and opinion.

Stimulates further exploration by the reader.

Includes primary source material where available.

Avoids anthropomorphism (attributing to animals the emotions and values of humans)
and teleological explanations (suggesting that organic life or physical changes result from design rather than mechanical or natural causes).

Illustrations are carefully labeled.

Indexes provide access to the information by scientific and common name, by theory and scientific principle, by the discoverer.

Title inspires, excites, and involves the reader.

Fig. 6.12. Criteria for Selecting Science Materials.

CRITERIA FOR SELECTING SCIENCE PROJECT BOOKS

Materials test and demonstrate what they purport to test.

Materials and equipment needed are readily available.

Adequate safety warnings provided.

Procedures are clearly labeled and easy to follow.

Procedures specify necessary equipment, materials, safety considerations, space and time required to complete, setup and cleanup.

Following the procedures result in the outcomes suggested by the author.

Explanations are given for the scientific principles demonstrated.

Extension and follow-up activities are provided.

If living organisms are used in experiments they are treated humanely.

Fig. 6.13. Criteria for Selecting Science Project Books.

World Cultures

Most books and multimedia materials on the countries and cultures of the world are produced in series format. Although the ethnocentrism sometimes evident in the history and geography books of earlier decades has largely been eliminated, many current books are superficial, especially those written for the primary and middle grades. Whenever possible, purchase individual titles written by authors who have spent significant time living in and/or studying the country or region described in the material. In addition to books in the 300 and 900 sections, consider picture books, fiction, poetry, folklore, biographies, cookbooks, arts books, films and videos, and multimedia materials for a fully rounded view of many cultures. See figure 6.14 for selection criteria.

CRITERIA FOR SELECTING BOOKS ON WORLD CULTURES
Currency (political and social changes are rapidly making some books obsolete).
Sensitivity to the customs and traditions of different cultures.
Quality of illustrations and/or photographs.
Inclusion of material of special interest to children—information about school life, games and sports, holidays, how children spend their time, and so on.
Reference features—maps, indexes, bibliographies.
Organizational features—chapters, subheadings.
Readability (students on different levels can "read" the pictures in heavily illustrated volumes).
Correlation of text and illustrations.

Fig. 6.14. Criteria for Selecting Books on World Cultures.

The Visual Arts

In schools that have neither a trained art teacher nor nearby museums, the only contact that children have with art may be in your library. Therefore, this becomes an important section to develop and promote. If your school has an arts program, work with the art teacher to select appropriate materials.

As the quality of both color printing and art direction in the children's publishing field has improved, the books available have changed dramatically. There is an increasing number of books that share the excitement and beauty of the arts with children. The major art museums are active in publishing books about artists and artistic concepts. Artists of many cultures are the subjects of recent biographies. Textile arts, photography, and other media are represented in addition to painting, drawing, and sculpture. The CD-ROM materials from museums are astounding, providing tours and collections of artworks on disc never before available. See figures 6.15 and 6.16 for selection criteria for books on the visual arts.

CRITERIA FOR SELECTING VISUAL ARTS MATERIALS
Excellent reproductions, true to the original in color.
Reproductions should be as large as possible.
Size of the original work should be indicated.
Sources are noted.
Art should evoke strong aesthetic, emotional, and intellectual responses from the viewer.
The art is successful in conveying a story or creating a mood.
Visually engaging page or screen layouts.
Text or audio guides extend the viewing experience, highlighting historical, geographical, and social background information.
Text or bibliography provides access to materials such as museum catalogs or other scholarly materials.

Fig. 6.15. Criteria for Selecting Visual Arts Materials.

OTHER CRITERIA FOR SELECTING VISUAL ARTS MATERIALS	
Scope	Arrangement
History: Art of the world, of a country, of a century. Artists: Individual, schools of art, periods, countries. Themes: Children, work, play, animals. Concepts: Line, shape, color, composition. Medium: Collage, watercolor, fresco, oil, photography, clay, stone.	Chronological. Thematic. Country or region.

Fig. 6.16. Other Criteria for Selecting Visual Arts Materials.

In developing your art section, provide a balance between materials that will give your patrons viewing and reading experiences about the artistic heritage of the world and materials that show them how to produce their own works of art. "How To" books on the arts and crafts should have step-by-step instructions, clear photos or illustrations, and safety guidelines.

CRITERIA FOR SELECTING "HOW-TO" ART BOOKS
Projects are of interest to the intended audience. Projects stimulate further exploration. All materials and tools are safe to use by the intended audience as directed. Includes a list of all materials and tools needed as well as sources for those not readily available. Indicates the level of difficulty of the project, approximate time needed to complete it, and any special preparation or clean-up directions needed. Provides excellent photos and drawings of materials, tools, procedures, and finished products. Includes background information that links project to historical periods and geographic regions. Materials are as much as possible authentic to the craft, period, and culture that generated them. Projects can be accomplished by the intended age group. Projects are aesthetically pleasing.

Fig. 6.17. Criteria for Selecting "How-To" Art Books.

Summing Up

As we approach the twenty-first century, information is changing at an astronomical rate. It is impossible to predict what infrastructure will be essential, what tools will be available, and what format resources will take in the next decade, or even the next few years. Planning is essential and challenging. No one person can be solely responsible for steering the course. Develop a network of colleagues, local and long distance, and a committee of experts to help in the work ahead. Experts can be found on your administration and teaching staff. Experts are also found in the parent body, the local community, and the world outside. You can be the catalyst who finds other experts to help, who focuses and shapes the dialogue in light of the school's mission and philosophy, and who helps transform teaching and learning in the school to meet the changing information needs of these challenging times.

No school library can meet all the needs of the school community alone. Collection sharing and cooperative collection development have existed in different areas of the country for some years. If you are not involved in any of these initiatives yet, now is the time to investigate any possibilities that are available to your school or actively campaign for your district, region, or state to create such projects. Some cooperative collection development programs offer grants for schools to build up special theme collections that will be shared through interlibrary loan; to set up district media evaluation centers; to create networks of libraries that share periodical articles via fax (within copyright regulations); to institute networks that connect schools, public libraries, and university libraries; to produce district or state-wide union catalogs that facilitate interlibrary loan possibilities; and to create district computer networks that enable users to share resources and curriculum projects. Projects have usually been funded with state or national funds, but private grants should be considered. These days, you cannot run an exemplary library, or even a good library, without looking beyond the walls of your individual building.

Bibliography

Note: Starred items are basic tools and should be priority purchases for your collection.

Professional Journals

AAAS Science Books and Films. American Association for the Advancement of Science. Published nine times a year by the American Association for the Advancement of Science. Reviews print, audiovisual, and electronic resources intended for use in science, technology, and mathematics education. Reviewers are science specialists and librarians. Includes science television shows and reviews by children.

Appraisal: Science Books for Young People. Published quarterly by the Children's Science Book Review Committee. Sponsored by Boston University, School of Education, 605 Commonwealth Ave., Boston, MA 02215. Provides reviews of nonfiction science books for preschool through high school by librarians and subject specialists.

*Booklist. American Library Association. Published twice a month, September through June, and once a month in July and August. Listing constitutes recommendation. Often has bibliographies on special topics that may include older titles. Includes media reviews. "Editors' Choice," a listing of their top books of the year, is published each January. Includes reviews of computer software, CD-ROMs, and audiovisual materials.

Bulletin of the Center for Children's Books. University of Illinois Press. Eleven issues per year. Reviews about 70 books per issue, assigning codes ranging from highly recommended to not recommended to books meant for specialized collections or only suitable for "unusual readers."

Horn Book. Published six times per year. Includes positive reviews of high-quality picture books and fiction. A limited number of nonfiction titles are included. It also contains interesting articles about children's literature, authors, illustrators, and publishing. Occasional audiovisual reviews.

*Horn Book Guide to Children's and Young Adults Books. Created in 1990, the Guide attempts to list all new hardcover trade books published each season. The two issues a year include brief reviews, a numerical rating system, and excellent subject indexes. Very useful.

Kirkus Reviews of Children's and Young Adult Books. Published once a month. Cumulates twice a year. Fiction and nonfiction. Reviews prior to publication. Monthly, six-month, and annual indexes. Includes pre-K to young adult.

MultiMedia Schools. Online Inc., 462 Danbury Rd., Wilton, CT 06897-2126. Published five times per year. A new journal specializing in articles about technology in the educational community, the Internet, and multimedia production. Includes reviews of technological resources for K-12.

*School Library Journal. Published monthly. One of the best sources for current reviews. Positive and negative reviews are written by practicing school and public librarians who often cite other useful books on a subject. Also reviews computer software, CD-ROMs, and audiovisual materials.

*Technology and Learning. Peter Li, Inc., P.O. Box 49727, Dayton, OH 45449-0727. Published eight times per year. Includes individual reviews of software and CD-ROM products and very useful articles and charts comparing resources on different curriculum topics. Their annual award list is an excellent source for beginning collections.

Technology Connection. Linworth Publishing, Inc., 480 East Wilson Bridge Rd., Suite L, Worthington, OH 43085-2372. Published 10 times per year. A new journal directed to school library media specialists to assist them in planning for the new technologies. Includes reviews for K-12.

Other Selection Guides

Barstow, Barbara, and Judith Riggle. *Beyond Picture Books: A Guide to First Readers.* 2d ed. New Providence, NJ: Bowker, 1995.

> More than 2,500 books are included with a selective list of 200 outstanding books for children at a first- or second-grade reading level. Brief annotation and reading level are given. Indexed by subject, readability, illustrator, and series.

Berger, Pam, and Susan Kinnell. *CD-ROM for Schools: A Directory and Practical Handbook for Media Specialists.* Wilton, CT: Eight Bit Books, 1994.

> More than 300 CD-ROM titles have been selected for inclusion in this basic guide to the use of CD-ROM for educational purposes. The authors have chosen 100 titles for their "core collection" and further highlighted their 10 favorites.

*Book Links. Chicago: American Library Association.

> Published bimonthly. A wonderful way to encourage theme-based projects and a useful tool for locating titles on all sorts of subjects. Each issue includes annotated bibliographies on themes often used in elementary and middle schools. Teaching ideas are included.

Carroll, Frances Laverne, and Mary Meacham. *More Exciting, Funny, Scary, Short, Different, and Sad Books Kids Like About Animals, Science, Sports, Families, Songs, and Other Things.* Chicago: American Library Association, 1992.

> A subject arrangement of books with brief annotations for children grades 2-5, including 100 popular children's topics. Indexed by author and title. Companion volume to *Exciting, Funny, Scary, Short, Different, and Sad Books Kids Like About Animals, Science, Sports, Families, Songs, and Other Things* (Chicago: American Library Association, 1984).

*CCBC Choices. Madison, WI: Cooperative Children's Book Center.

> Annual. A selective list of new books arranged in many different categories, chosen by the staff of the Cooperative Children's Book Center, University of Wisconsin-Madison. Send $4 plus a self-addressed 6" x 9" envelope with $.65 postage to Friends of the CCBC, Inc., P.O. Box 5288, Madison, WI 53705-0288.

Children's Books of the Year. New York: Child Study Children's Book Committee.

> Chosen by the Child Study Children's Book Committee at Bank Street College with some advice from a group of "young reviewers." Annual. Organized by age group and subject category. Send $4 plus $1 per order for postage and handling to Child Study Children's Book Committee, Bank Street College, 610 West 112th St., New York, NY 10025.

*Children's Books: 100 Titles for Reading and Sharing. New York: New York Public Library.

> Annual. Annotated list of outstanding books of the year. Order from: Office of Branch Services, New York Public Library, 455 Fifth Ave., New York, NY 10016. Send $3 plus $1 shipping and handling. The Library also publishes other specialized bibliographies for children and young adults. Write for information.

The Children's Catalog. 16th ed. New York: Wilson, 1991.

Published every five years and supplemented in each intermediate year with a paperback volume. Usually available in the reference section of your local public library. Most useful feature may be its references to individual sections of books, especially as an index to collective bibliographies. Each elementary school library should own updated copies of this or *The Elementary School Library Collection.*

Children's Reference Plus. New Providence, NJ: Bowker.

A CD-ROM resource that includes the full text of many Bowker bibliographic products, including *Children's Books in Print, Subject Guide to Children's Books in Print, Children's Video* from *Bowker's Complete Video Directory,* reviews from *School Library Journal, Booklist* and complete contents of books like *Best Books for Children* (4th ed.), and *Books Kids Will Sit Still For* (2d ed.). A useful resource if your budget will permit. For IBM only. Bowker updates this resource annually.

Dickinson, Gail K. *Selection and Evaluation of Electronic Resources.* Englewood, CO: Libraries Unlimited, 1994.

Includes selection considerations for electronic resources such as CD-ROM encyclopedias and other reference materials, online databases, and magazine indexes. The author also discusses the relationship of electronic resources to the library collection and program.

The Elementary School Library Collection. 20th ed. Williamsport, PA: Brodart, 1996.

Annotated guide to selecting books, professional materials, magazines, and computer and audiovisual materials. An excellent resource for every school library. Updated every two years. Dewey arrangement with author, subject, and title indexes.

Friedburg, Joan Brest, et al. *Portraying Persons with Disabilities: An Annotated Bibliography of Non-fiction for Children and Teenagers.* New Providence, NJ: Bowker, 1992.

Titles are arranged in broad categories. The book covers more than 350 titles from 1984 to 1991.

*Gallant, Jennifer Jung. *Best Videos for Children and Young Adults: A Core Collection for Libraries.* Santa Barbara, CA: ABC-CLIO, 1990.

Includes 350 curriculum and recreation videos. Videos have either won awards or had excellent reviews in general sources.

*Gillespie, John T., and Corinne J. Naden. *Best Books for Children.* 5th ed. New Providence, NJ: Bowker, 1994.

Annotates some 17,000 titles for preschool through middle school, with multiple recommendations from major reviewing sources. Not as selective as *The Children's Catalog* or *The Elementary School Library Collection.* Most useful for gathering information on titles that you later review yourself. General subject arrangement. Annotations include interest levels. Indexed by subject, author, and title. *Best Books for Junior High Readers* is also available.

Katz, Bill, and Linda Sternberg Katz. *Magazines for Young People: A Children's Magazine Guide Companion Volume.* 2d ed. New Providence, NJ: Bowker, 1991.

Formerly entitled *Magazines for School Libraries,* this volume reviews more than 1,100 magazines in 75 subject areas. Includes a core list of recommended magazines. See *Magazines for Libraries,* 8th ed., by Bill Katz and Linda Sternberg Katz (New Providence, NJ: Bowker, 1995).

Kobrin, Beverly. *Eyeopeners II! Children's Books to Answer Children's Questions About the World Around Them.* New York: Scholastic, 1995.

Annotations for more than 500 nonfiction books for children. Includes age range, tips for parents and teachers, and quick-links to other books. Indexed by author, title, and illustrator.

*Kruse, Ginny Moore, and Kathleen T. Horning. *Multicultural Literature for Children and Young Adults.* Madison, WI: Cooperative Children's Book Center, University of Wisconsin-Madison, 1991.

Send $16 and postage ($3.50) to Friends of the CCBC, Inc., P.O. Box 5288, Madison, WI 53705-0288, or call (800) 243-8782 to inquire about Bulletin 1923, or write to Publication Sales, Wisconsin Department of Public Instruction, P. O. Box 7841, Madison, WI 53707-7841.

*Lima, Carolyn W., and John A. Lima. *A to Zoo: Subject Access to Children's Picture Books.* 4th. ed. New Providence, NJ: Bowker, 1993.

More than 14,500 titles are categorized under more than 800 subject headings, arranged alphabetically. The authors state: "The picture book, as broadly defined within the scope of this book, is a fiction or nonfiction title with illustrations occupying as much or more space than the text and the text vocabulary or concepts suitable for pre-school to grade two." Please note that this is not specifically a selection guide, but the authors have read the great majority of books included and deem them suitable for the indicated audience. Indexed by title, author, subject, and illustrator.

*Miller-Lachman, Lyn. *Our Family, Our Friends, Our World: An Annotated Guide to Significant Multicultural Books for Children and Teenagers.* New Providence, NJ: Bowker, 1992.

Arranged by world region, this is an excellent selective bibliographic guide to fiction and nonfiction published since 1970 on every part of the world. The U.S. section focuses on major ethnic groups including Native American, African American, Asian American, and Hispanic American.

Nicholas, Margaret Irby. *Guide to Reference Books for School Library Media Centers.* 4th ed. Englewood, CO: Libraries Unlimited, 1992.

Includes almost 2,300 recommended reference titles and uses a code system to indicate grade level. Covers books published from 1985 to early 1991. Some older titles have been included if they have not been superseded.

Notable Children's Trade Books in the Field of Social Studies. New York: National Council for the Social Studies-CBC Joint Committee. New York: Children's Book Council.

Annual. An excellent selection of fiction and nonfiction books related to social studies, chosen by the National Council for the Social Studies-CBC Joint Committee. Send a self-addressed envelope with $.52 postage and $2 to Children's Book Council, Attn: Social Studies Books, 568 Broadway, Suite 404, New York, NY 10012.

Outstanding Science Trade Books. New York: Children's Book Council. Annual. Selected by the National Science Teachers Association-CBC Joint Committee. Send a self-addressed envelope with $.52 postage and $2 to Children's Book Council, Attn: Science Books, 568 Broadway, Suite 404, New York, NY 10012.

Richey, Virginia H., and Katharyn E. Puckett. *Wordless/Almost Wordless Picture Books: A Guide.* Englewood, CO: Libraries Unlimited, 1992.

Annotated bibliography that includes alphabet books, number books, and concept books as well as those books in which the pictures tell the story. Comprehensive subject index.

Robertson, Debra. *Portraying Persons with Disabilities: An Annotated Bibliography of Fiction for Children and Teenagers.* New Providence, NJ: Bowker, 1992.

More than 650 titles are included with annotations that both describe plots and critically review the way in which the disabilities are presented. Picture books are included. Covers 1983–1991.

Rudman, Masha K., Kathleen Dunne Gagne, and Joanne E. Bernstein. *Books to Help Children Cope with Separation and Loss: An Annotated Bibliography.* 4th ed. New Jersey: Bowker, 1993.

Includes 750 fiction and nonfiction books, including folklore and poetry on these important themes.

Sherman, Gale W., and Bette D. Ammon. *Rip-Roaring Reads for Reluctant Teen Readers.* Englewood, CO: Libraries Unlimited, 1993.

Books that will attract reluctant readers in grades 5-8 and 9-12. The 40 titles are augmented by activity suggestions and reproducible bookmarks with additional suggestions.

Sinclair, Patti K. *E for Environment: An Annotated Bibliography of Children's Books with Environmental Themes.* New Providence, NJ: Bowker, 1992.

More than 500 books are included on topics related to this timely subject. Books published since 1982 are emphasized.

*Teachers' Choices. Newark, DE: International Reading Association.

Annual. Outstanding books useful for curriculum-oriented projects are selected and annotated by seven regional teacher teams. Reviewing project is coordinated by the International Reading Association (IRA). Send $1 and $.98 postage to International Reading Association, Attn: Teachers' Choices, P.O. Box 8139, Newark, DE 19714.

Trelease, Jim. *The Read-Aloud Handbook.* 4th ed. New York: Penguin, 1995.

An annotated list of books for reading aloud includes annotations, reading level, and interest level. Indexed by author and title.

**Van Orden, Phyllis J. *The Collection Program in Schools: Concepts, Practices and Information Sources.* 2d ed. Englewood, CO: Libraries Unlimited, 1995.

A comprehensive source of information on collection development, collection policies, and issues such as censorship. Includes a very complete bibliography of selection guides and a useful list of agencies and associations that provide information and bibliographies.

Wright, Keith. *The Challenge of Technology: Action Strategies for the School Library Media Specialists.* Chicago: American Library Association, 1993.

Wynar, Bohdan S., ed. *Recommended Reference Books for Small and Medium-Sized Libraries and Media Centers.* Englewood, CO: Libraries Unlimited.

Published annually. Books that meet the needs of smaller libraries have been selected from *American Reference Books Annual* (Libraries Unlimited), coded with an indication that they are suitable for school library media centers and public and small college libraries. Libraries Unlimited also publishes *A Guide to Reference Books for Small and Medium-Sized Libraries, 1983-1993,* edited by G. Kim Dority.

Periodicals That Include Reviews of Resources

Arithmetic Teacher (National Council of Teachers of Mathematics)

Childhood Education (Association for Childhood Education International)

Children's Software Review

Educational Leadership (Association for Supervision and Curriculum Development)

Instructor

Language Arts (National Council of Teachers of English)

Media and Methods

Parents' Choice

Phi Delta Kappa

Primary Voices (National Council of Teachers of English)

Reading Teacher (International Reading Association)

Science and Children (National Science Teachers Association)

Social Studies and the Young Learner (National Council for the Social Studies)

Teaching Exceptional Children (Council for Exceptional Children)

Teaching K-8

Video Rating Guide for Libraries

Young Children (National Association for the Education of the Young Child)

Children's Literature

The books listed below, often used as textbooks in children's literature courses, will give you a good working background in the history of children's literature and an introduction to different aspects of contemporary books for children. Many recommended titles are cited. These books are generally updated every few years.

Huck, Charlotte, et al. *Children's Literature in the Elementary School.* 5th ed. Fort Worth, TX: Harcourt Brace Jovanovich, 1993.

Sutherland, Zena, et al. *Children and Books.* 8th ed. New York: HarperCollins, 1991.

Collection Mapping

Loertscher, David V., and May Lein Ho. *Collection Mapping for School Library Media Centers.* Castle Rock, CO: Hi Willow Research and Publishing, 1995.

Chapter 7

The Facility

Introduction

The library media center is the center of learning in your school, the physical access to information, and the gateway to the outside world. It should provide space for large and small group instruction, quiet reading, conferences, research and study, media production and viewing, and performance and display. The library is a learning laboratory where teachers facilitate students' mastery of information literacy and critical-thinking skills. Students locate materials for recreational reading, process information in a variety of formats, work together, read, write, perform, share, create, and display projects. They practice and use information-gathering skills and strategies, operate computers, participate in telecommunications activities, produce videos, socialize while learning, have fun, and teach others.

Teachers, librarians, other professionals, and parents gather to plan, develop, and implement curriculum; extend professional development; and share expertise. The library provides access to resources and colleagues beyond the school through electronic mail, telecommunications, and interlibrary loan services. The library media specialist and library staff must order, process, arrange, use, and circulate books, media, equipment, and other materials to serve the needs of the school community.

Administrators use the space for professional development, as a meeting area, as a focal point for visitors to showcase what is happening in the school, and as a source for their own information needs. Parents view the process and products of their children's learning, and borrow books and materials to read themselves and use with their children. They also participate in workshops and share their knowledge, skills, and time with students.

When you assess your current library, ask yourself this important question: Does this space enhance access for students, teachers, administrators, parents, and others? Size, furnishings, equipment, arrangement, merchandising, signage, storage, color, shelving, noise barriers, and security are necessary components of a comfortable space and an atmosphere conducive to active learning.

This chapter discusses basic facility and equipment needs. It will help you evaluate your present space and develop a plan to make improvements. It will offer recommendations for changes requiring little or no cost, additional ideas if some funding is available, and finally, suggestions for a major revitalization or renovation.

The Basics

The Space

National and state guidelines suggest how much space is required for the library media center. Formulas based on population suggest adequate seating for 10 percent of the school population or three square feet for each student. Guidelines may indicate minimum size requirements regardless of school population. Jane P. Klasing (1991) suggests a minimum space allotment for an elementary school library of 1,850 square feet. In reality, however, the physical space available for your library is probably fixed. The space may have been designed before state standards were in place, before your student population expanded, and before the proliferation of nonprint media made the 110 wiring and single electrical outlet woefully inadequate. Regardless of the adequacy of your existing facility, it is essential that you examine, evaluate, and plan for optimal utilization.

The Library Facilities Checklist (fig. 7.2 beginning on page 129) that follows will help you look at your library and become more knowledgeable about your space. Additional checklists are provided for standard library equipment (fig. 7.1) and furniture needs (fig. 7.3). The checklists will help you evaluate your facility and compare it to exemplary libraries. It will suggest some renovations or purchases required to meet the standards of the twenty-first century.

The Equipment

The following checklist outlines the basic requirements of a well-stocked media center.

Equipment Checklist

_____ Amplifier

_____ Art print, big book, and poster storage

_____ Camcorder with tripod and portable battery pack

_____ Camera, 35 mm, with flash

_____ Cassette recorder, portable, dual with AM/FM radio

_____ Computer printers (laser, color)

_____ Computers for LMS, staff, parents, and students

_____ Computer workstations (CD-ROM, scanners, fax-modem)

_____ Digital, still filmless camera for computer

_____ Easels (portable dry mark or chalkboard, folding display)

_____ Electronic signs

_____ Filmstrip/cassette automatic player

_____ Globes on sturdy bases

_____ Headsets and jack strips

_____ Laminating machine

_____ LCD computer projection panel

_____ Microphones

_____ Modem (28.8 baud minimum)

_____ Photocopier

_____ Projectors and screens (overhead, opaque, slide, filmstrip)

_____ Puppet stage

_____ Record player, CD player

_____ Surge protectors

_____ Telephones (touch-tone, speakerphones, data lines)

_____ Television, VCR, and cable box

_____ Video display projector, large screen

_____ Video tape recorder (VCR), four head

Fig. 7.1. Equipment Checklist.

The Furniture

The quantity of furniture is determined by the population of the school, square footage of the library media center space, and the intended usage, but a basic furniture inventory would include the items on the Basic Furniture Inventory (see figure 7.3 on page 131).

Library Facilities Checklist

Use the following five-point scale to rate your library; 5 means your library is outstanding in this respect; 1 means the library is substandard.

Physical Space

5 4 3 2 1   The space supports individual, large, and small group uses.

5 4 3 2 1   The library can support circulation for many individuals concurrently.

5 4 3 2 1   The space has ample seating.

5 4 3 2 1   There are computer work areas for students and staff.

5 4 3 2 1   There are rooms for conferences and small groups.

5 4 3 2 1   There is sufficient work space for technical and professional services.

5 4 3 2 1   The room supports multiple uses, including media production, performances, and special events.

5 4 3 2 1   The space has a sink and a bathroom.

5 4 3 2 1   There is an unrestricted view of the main library space.

5 4 3 2 1   There is sufficient open and closed storage for media, equipment, personal belongings, and materials.

5 4 3 2 1   Children's work can be easily and attractively presented in formal and informal displays.

5 4 3 2 1   The library is barrier-free and accessible to the whole school.

5 4 3 2 1   It is available to the community off hours, with direct or easy access to the street.

5 4 3 2 1   There is adequate security.

Lighting

5 4 3 2 1   All areas of the library receive sufficient light.

5 4 3 2 1   It meets lumen standards for reading areas.

5 4 3 2 1   It contains multizone dimmers.

5 4 3 2 1   It has incandescent lighting.

5 4 3 2 1   It has nonglare fixtures.

Climate

5 4 3 2 1   Windows open and close properly.

5 4 3 2 1   Windows provide adequate ventilation and light.

5 4 3 2 1   The temperature is easily regulated and controlled.

Sound

5 4 3 2 1   Acoustical ceiling tiles are in good repair.

5 4 3 2 1   There is carpeting or a carpeted area.

5 4 3 2 1   The library has good acoustics and is insulated from classroom and corridor noise.

Library Facilities Checklist *(cont)*

Electrical Wiring

5 4 3 2 1   Electrical wiring has adequate current for present and future use of equipment.

5 4 3 2 1   Outlets work, are appropriately placed, and are flat to the floor.

5 4 3 2 1   Phone and cable lines are installed and properly placed.

Ambiance

5 4 3 2 1   The library looks cheerful and inviting.

5 4 3 2 1   The library is uncluttered.

5 4 3 2 1   The library is clean and organized.

5 4 3 2 1   Walls and ceilings are in good repair, without holes or leaks.

5 4 3 2 1   Paint is bright and fresh, without flaking or peeling.

Merchandising

5 4 3 2 1   The arrangement of the collection is logical.

5 4 3 2 1   The collection is well merchandised.

5 4 3 2 1   The top shelf of tall bookcases is used for display.

5 4 3 2 1   New books are integrated into the collection.

5 4 3 2 1   Attractive, relevant books are displayed face out on every shelf.

5 4 3 2 1   Books occupy no more than two-thirds of a shelf.

5 4 3 2 1   Signs are clean, clear, correct, and attractive.

Furnishings

5 4 3 2 1   Window coverings are in good repair and can be used to darken the room effectively.

5 4 3 2 1   There is adequate shelving for current needs and future growth.

5 4 3 2 1   Bookshelves have adequate shelf supports.

5 4 3 2 1   Furnishings are in good condition.

5 4 3 2 1   Tables and chairs are the appropriate size for the population.

5 4 3 2 1   There is appropriate furniture for computers, media, and other equipment.

If your space rated mostly 4s and 5s, congratulations! Few changes may be necessary. Read on to learn what you can do to improve your space.

If your space scored lots of 1s and 2s, there's work ahead. Start with changes you can make yourself. Then explore the changes that will require collaboration and outside funding. These changes are dealt with in the rest of this chapter.

Fig. 7.2. Library Facilities Checklist.

Basic Furniture Inventory

_____ Seating for at least one-and-a-half classes of children (preferably oak, walnut, or other durable wood chairs)

_____ A combination of rectangular and round wooden tables

_____ A multipart circulation desk with a librarian's chair or a smaller, one-piece circulation desk

_____ Magazine, display, and paperback racks (that can contain paperbacks of varying sizes)

_____ Two or more book trucks

_____ Shelving for the current and future collections

_____ Chairs, sofas, beanbags, or other informal furniture

_____ Carpet

_____ Computer work stations

_____ Storage for materials, equipment, and media

_____ File cabinets

_____ Carts for media equipment

Optional furniture can include such items as:

_____ A "reading roost," created by three 42"-high bookcases surrounding a 36" x 72" carpeted seat, with a lower shelf for display or books

_____ Big book rack

_____ Electronic signs

_____ Hanging bag display racks for media

_____ Opaque projector

_____ Picture book table (for early childhood center with abundant space)

_____ Electrified carrels

_____ Display cases

_____ Newspaper racks

_____ Rocking chair

Fig. 7.3. Basic Furniture Inventory.

Improving the Facility: Low-Cost Options

The library's appearance can be improved without a substantial outlay of funds by eliminating clutter, changing the signage, renewing or replacing displays, merchandising the collection, and creating a thoughtful arrangement of furniture. This face-lift will improve the visual appeal and functional quality of the library media center, even before additional funding further enhances the space.

Stand at the door of your library and look at the room with the eyes of a newcomer. Can you see from one side to the other, or is the room blocked with tall shelves, file cabinets, or other obstructions? Are posters neatly attached or have they begun to peel around the edges? Are signs faded and torn; are letters missing? Are your plants straggly and neglected? Are the books on your shelves falling down or shelved haphazardly?

Listen to your borrowers. If you are hearing the same questions again and again, you may need to rearrange some sections or improve signage so that borrowers can locate materials independently. Think about the impression your facility makes on those who walk through the door.

Remember: If it's no longer useful—discard it! If you can't bear to throw it out, offer the item to a colleague in trade. Here are some common examples of items that should be discarded:

△ Tables and chairs that are splintered, cracked, or have splayed or wobbly legs.

△ Dictionary, television, or typewriter stands that are tucked away in corners and are no longer necessary.

△ Unused chalkboards, torn screens, bookcases, and dated maps or globes.

△ Those tall bookcases, protruding from the middle of the 900s section, that were needed for an unweeded collection.

△ Empty aquariums, old scenery, book displays, and projects.

Eliminate Clutter

As you get busier, it becomes difficult to find time to regroup, organize, and straighten up. Without noticing, suddenly you can be confronted with: a desk spilling over with catalogs, mail, and books awaiting action; shelves whose contents are dated or inappropriate; tables being used as work desks; aisles blocked with cartons of work; forgotten projects; all those treasures you might need some day; construction paper; stencils; old books for clipping; and outdated promotional pieces from suppliers. What is your message to borrowers who view your space? Be assured, it will not occur to them that you are too "busy" to pick up. It is often surprising how little you really see when you work in a space, day after day.

Merchandise

A library can be thought of as a marketplace. The goods we offer are as marketable as clothing, groceries, or furniture. Your goal should be to make these materials readily available. One of the more effective ways of moving merchandise (in this case circulating books) is by presenting it in a bold, aggressive way. The Dewey number on a book need not dictate its placement in the collection. We will discuss later the methods of bookstore-like shelving, but consider the simple remedy of changing a Dewey number on a book to rescue it from oblivion. You can pull the obvious picture book from the nonfiction shelves, move the mistakenly labeled fiction book out of the picture books, and change the placement of a beautiful photo essay that will never be seen if it's shelved with photography (don't forget to change all records of these materials in your catalog).

The next step is to show off the books and media you want your students to discover by creating displays on your countertops, bookshelves, and tables. Supermarkets and other stores use the checkout counters to tempt you to buy one more thing you didn't know you needed. The same principle can be applied to a library. If your bookshelves are jammed from end to end, all the children will be able to see is the spine of each book. Empty some space and turn books around to face the room. A good rule of thumb is to leave one-third of the space on each shelf open for display. Use the top shelf of tall bookcases to display a few books, videos, CDs, student projects, or appropriate realia.

Publishers spend a lot of money on book covers; take advantage of the art. If you have more than one copy of a quality book, put several face out on the end of the row. "Viola!"—instant display and interest. But be prepared! These are the books that will circulate the quickest, so it means that you will have to replace them often. Don't fall victim to the trap of grabbing any book to show off. This is an art show and part of your room decoration, but you should display books that you really want children to read. If you can't find a book on the shelf worth showing off, consider what this says about your collection. Tired, hackneyed, and unappealing? Who would want to use it? Then it's time to weed. Spend a few minutes each day evaluating and weeding the collection, print and nonprint, eliminating the dead wood. This allows the fresh, beautiful, and appealing to shine, and leaves room to display!

Improve Signage

Your merchandising will not be effective if the signs that identify the sections are shabby, faded, missing, or inaccurate. Too many styles of signs (colors, lettering, homemade mixed with professionally made) can detract from the overall look of a room. Decide what you want to say and then say it in simple, clear, contrasting colors that can be repeated throughout the room. Digital signs, once only seen on highways, are now available for libraries. Use your computer to program a short message for users or celebrate a poem written by a student. Printed or engraved signs are available from most suppliers of library equipment. Signs can also be designed in the school and made with stencils, commercially available letters, or computer lettering on quality poster board. Art teachers, skilled parents, or students may have calligraphic talents to offer.

Be sure the message sent is the one you want to deliver. When you look at your room, are there signs pointing to nonexisting sections that are leftovers from some previous arrangement? Is the "Catalog" sign where the catalog used to be? Is the "Return Books Here" sign over the new listening center? Keep perfectly positioned signs crisp and fresh; peeling letters, faded paper, and curling or torn edges announce neglect.

Create Displays

Librarians have been creating displays of associated titles for decades. Merchandising suggests establishing some new revolving and permanent sections of the collection. Try keeping all the science projects books and media together in one area, or placing the easy readers in their own section. Move the collective biographies and the individual biographies into a unit of their own. Create a changing display of multicultural books and videos, but rotate some of them back into their assigned space so that the borrowers can find them. Should you put videos and cassettes face-out in floor and tabletop browsers or place them with their related subjects? Much will depend on the extent of the collection and the space in your room.

You may combine media, realia, and picture books by theme. Display the *American Sign Language Dictionary* CD-ROM (HarperCollins) with related books, games, and posters. Identify mysteries, science fiction, sports fiction, humor, historical fiction, or adventures by labeling them. Keep most of the media and books in each genre shelved with the fiction to encourage student browsing. Make temporary displays highlighting genres, seasonal displays, and current interests. Your users' interests and special requests are candidates for new arrangements. Break free of traditional shelving and start moving the materials around.

Formal displays of children's work and products demonstrate that children's work efforts are valued and make it possible for them to learn from their peers. Bulletin boards showcase children's projects and library materials of interest. Shelving and tops of bookcases and windowsills allow for attractive displays of projects. Glass display cases protect fragile objects. Commercially produced strips of metal, Velcro, and cork are available from school supply stores. A strip attached from one corner to another and clothespins or clips can be used to suspend projects. Be aware of local fire and safety regulations. Avoid an overabundance of displays, as too many can become overpowering.

Collection Arrangement

Books are shelved from left to right and from top to bottom within each bookcase. Usually nonfiction books, those with "Dewey" numbers, are shelved in a continuous pattern so that the numbers get larger as you move from left to right in the room. Fiction books may be separated into novels, easy books, and picture books. Each section is arranged by the author's last name, from left to right and top to bottom in each bookcase, from A to Z. This may seem obvious to you, but many staff members over a long period of time may have made modifications to the arrangement of the collection. Librarians may have shifted areas of the collection to accommodate changing needs, but these may not work with your current program or population. Or, on the other hand, no change in the collection arrangement may have been made in years, and rethinking the arrangement may be necessary.

When planning to shift the collection, consider how libraries are generally arranged. You want to make your space inviting and functional for the user, but you also want the user to learn library skills and strategies that can be transferred and applied to other libraries. Use the section below to determine if shifts need to be made and if these shifts create a need to move shelving to create a logical arrangement of materials.

Library Sections

Picture Books

Arrangement: Alphabetical by author's last name. Many libraries interfile all As together, Bs together, and so on to save time, rather than by each letter of the last name. Try to keep all of an author's books together. If you have a large squad that has the time for this task, alphabetize in exact order of the author's last name. This saves time when you want to find a particular book or author.

Special Considerations: Picture books should be placed on low bookcases (preferably 42" high), keeping in mind the height of the readers, but should not be placed below fiction books. Place the first letter of the author's last name in bold print on spine labels to facilitate shelving.

Other Options: Special sections may be created for alphabet books, counting books, and other concept books for young children. Make appropriate signs and color-code these books if you want to make this a permanent change in your picture book area.

Some libraries have developed a subject arrangement scheme for all picture books, using a color-coding system. Examples of subject sections are: animal stories, family and school stories, and scary stories. This can be a difficult system to set up because many books fall into more than one category, and strategies will have to be devised to find specific books when they are requested. A letter code can be used for automated catalogs or color coding can be added to the catalog card.

Easy Readers

Arrangement: Alphabetical by author's last name.

Special Considerations: Place easy readers on low shelving, near the picture books.

Other Options: Even though many picture books are labeled "E," you should limit this section to books in the "easy reader" format, found in such series as HarperCollins I Can Read books and Greenwillow Read-Alone books. These books are intended for students reading independently on a first- or second-grade level. Color-code this section to distinguish these books from picture books.

Fiction

Arrangement: Exact alphabetical order by author's last name. For ease of shelving, spine labels should contain at least the first three letters of the author's last name. Most distributors will accommodate this request. If yours doesn't, find one who will.

Special Considerations: Begin or end this section near picture books and easy readers. These books can be placed on bookcases that are taller than those of the picture book area.

Other Options: Use color-coding (or other special spine labels) to highlight specific types of books: science fiction, mysteries, historical fiction, adventure stories, multicultural novels, beginning chapter books, or any other genres or themes appropriate to your school's needs. Some librarians create separate shelving units of "beginning chapter books" and use color codes for easy identification as with the easy readers. These codes should be highlighted on a poster or chart so that your readers will be able to find the materials they want easily.

Folklore

Arrangement: Numerically by Dewey number; within each number, alphabetically by author's last name. Numbers will range from 398–398.8. Folklore is often housed within the nonfiction section in its correct Dewey location in the 390s but there are also other considerations and options.

Special Considerations: Place folklore in the same part of the room as picture books. It is also an excellent section to put in an arrangement of freestanding bookcases. (For example, four bookcases can be placed in a square or H-formation.)

Other Options: Some librarians like to shelve the anthologies by Dewey numbers at the beginning or end of the folklore section. The individual picture book versions can then be alphabetized by title, thus grouping together versions of the same story (provided that they start with the same word). You may also want to create changing displays of variants of the same tale that may have different titles (e.g., Cinderella variants from around the world).

Nonfiction

Arrangement: In exact Dewey order. When several books have the same number, alphabetize by author's last name.

Special Considerations: Include sufficient space in the nonfiction area to allow the entire run of numbers to flow naturally from beginning to end. Student worktables should be near the nonfiction books.

Other Options: Create a "discovery shelf"—a changing display of easy, high-interest books on various nonfiction topics. This will attract browsers to your nonfiction. Place this near your picture books and easy readers or near your nonfiction. Better yet, make two such displays. Some libraries are shelving the 900s together by continent and then in alphabetical order by country. This may be an effective way to deal with many social studies project needs.

Biography

Arrangement: Alphabetical by the subject's last name.

Special Considerations: Place biographies in their own section at the end of the nonfiction area. They can be placed after a doorway or other break in the wall. Biographies also can be placed in a freestanding grouping of shelves.

Other Options: Biographies may be placed within the nonfiction area, following 920. This is particularly true if the spine label reads 92 rather than "B."

Collective Biography

Arrangement: Alphabetical by author's last name, unless Dewey number is fully expanded. Then shelve by number and then by author.

Special Considerations: Place these books at the beginning or end of the biography section. Use signs to ensure that users and shelvers are aware of their location.

Other Options: Collective biographies also can be placed in the general nonfiction area, following 919, but they may be utilized more if they are located near the biographies.

Reference

Arrangement: Place all encyclopedia sets first. Locate encyclopedias for young children on lower shelves. Arrange all other reference materials in Dewey order.

Special Considerations: The reference section should be located near the computers. Place a table nearby that can be used for research.

Professional Materials

Arrangement: Shelve materials in Dewey order.

Special Considerations: Place the professional collection near a teachers' meeting space, if there is one in the library. If space is a problem, these materials can be placed on shelves behind the librarian's desk.

Other Options: Curriculum guides and other materials can be arranged in the major subject areas and assigned codes. For example, use SS for Social Studies and LA for Language Arts. Color-code professional materials to separate them from the children's or parent's collection.

Parents/Parenting

Arrangement: Arrange books as you would in other sections of the library: picture books in alphabetical order, fiction in alphabetical order, nonfiction in Dewey order, and so on.

Special Considerations: Use appropriate spine labels for each type of book. Use a color code to denote parents' books. If you have room, place this section near the professional section. Teachers may also want to use some of these materials.

Magazines

Arrangement: Place current copies alphabetically by title on magazine racks, and back issues of magazines that you wish to save in magazine boxes.

Special Considerations: Racks for students' magazines can be placed near the recreational reading area. Professional magazines can be displayed on racks, if you have the room, or placed near the professional collection. If you are purchasing CD-ROMs with retrospective collections of magazine issues, storage boxes will become obsolete.

Paperbacks

Arrangement: Place paperbacks, with covers displayed, on revolving stands and other paperback racks. Many librarians do not put paperbacks in any particular order.

Special Considerations: Spine labels are not necessary for paperbacks used on browsing racks unless you have multiple racks and plan to separate fiction from nonfiction, or alphabetize them by title or author. Place stands or racks in your recreational reading section, near a carpeted area if you have one. Keep them neat, attractive, and well stocked. If you have multiple copies of a title for book discussions or holidays, you need not keep them all on the open shelves.

Other Options: If you plan to integrate paperbacks into the general collection, use the appropriate spine labels. When you purchase these fiction and nonfiction paperbacks, process, catalog, and interfile them in your collection. (Craft books, song books, and other books may be published in paperback editions only.) You can make displays for paperback mysteries, science fiction, and so on. Use the same color coding as used in your hardcover fiction section.

If your current collection includes "Permabound" or other similar paperbacks rebound in hard laminated covers, house them either in the paperback section or the other appropriate areas in the library. Base your decision on whether these books have been purchased as extra copies of materials already purchased for the library in hardcover editions, or whether they form the bulk of your collection. Purchase regular paperbacks and hardcover trade editions in the future. (See chapter 6, "The Collection.")

Media

Arrangement: Several factors affect the arrangement of media in your collection: access, control, space, and the size and shape of the materials. Use Dewey order for informational materials and alphabetical order by title for fictional materials. You may shelve series materials together under the name of the series (e.g., "Reading Rainbow"). Because of the differing physical shapes and sizes of the cases involved, and the control that you need over certain items (videotapes, for example), you may choose to house media in several areas, in both open and locked cabinets. (Remember to weed your media collection. Many materials are out of date, incomplete, or physically damaged.) Place recordings, CDs, and cassettes in cabinets, on shelves, or in browsing units or bins. Arrange them according to type of music (e.g., folk, classical, opera, children's songs). Place story recordings in a section of their own, alphabetically by title. Place videos on shelving behind your desk or in a locked cabinet or storage area. Borrowers can access the collection by using a computer listing that you prepare giving title, length of time, grade level(s), and a short annotation, if possible.

It would be most helpful to have a subject arrangement for this listing, either using the Dewey system or general curriculum areas such as math, social studies, and science. Arrange videos alphabetically by title or match the subject arrangement of the list. Handle computer software, including CD-ROMs, in the same way that you handle videos. House filmstrips and media kits in a media section near the professional section. Filmstrip sets often come with Dewey cataloging and this section can be arranged in Dewey order by curriculum area. Media display racks can feature cassette and book sets or individual filmstrip and book sets. If you have several, you may want to use different racks for materials to be borrowed by children, materials to be borrowed by teachers, or for different subject areas. Appropriate signage should indicate what is on the rack.

Special Considerations: Media can also be interfiled in every part of the library. This is difficult to achieve primarily because of the need for security and the difficulty in housing materials of varying sizes. However, you can try to make this concept work for you. You will have to assign all nonfiction items Dewey numbers and arrange all other materials just as you would if they were print materials. Add a media code to the first line of each label (e.g., CAS=cassette, VID=video, and so on). Try to interfile all materials in correct alphabetical or Dewey order. Shelve oversized materials flat on the bottom shelf of the correct section. Make users aware that this system is being used. This system works best if all materials are cataloged.

Developing a Room Plan

If you are pleased with your initial efforts to spruce up your facility and collection, it is time to consider more extensive change. With careful planning, you can create new interest in the room by designing a more logical and intelligent arrangement of furniture, equipment, materials, and resources.

If you would like separate areas for research, listening, reading, computers, or small group discussions, see how you can stretch existing space. Consider:

△ Discarding one table, a storage cabinet, the magazine rack that is too tall, or obsolete card catalogs.

△ Using only one side of two-sided bookcases and placing the other side against a wall. This reduces the amount of usable shelving but increases floor space.

△ Removing a unit of the charging desk, now that you don't need the circulation drawers, to make it fit near the door.

△ Switching 42" or 60" bookcases currently lodged against the walls with taller bookcases, moving the smaller ones into clusters.

Plan on paper before shifting furniture or the collection. If possible, locate the original architectural blueprints or plans of the library. They may give more details than you need, but the outline and details of fixed features like closets, radiators, windows, doors, and electrical notations will be helpful. If plans are not available, draw your own diagram for the library. An architect's ruler and graph paper can be used to draw to scale, or use one of the many room design computer programs or home design kits available. The computer specialist, teachers, custodian, district office, or parents may have a program that is suitable for design. Tap into their expertise. Older children can help obtain the measurements. Give them an 80' carpenter's measuring tape or use a ball of string and a yardstick.

Measure all furniture you intend to keep. Measure the height of bookcases and indicate how many shelves each case holds. You will also need to map and count your book collection. An average 36"-long shelf generally holds 30 to 35 books of average size when filled to the recommended two-thirds capacity. Approximately 18 reference books and 60 picture books can be accommodated per shelf. Leave shelf space for rotating displays of new books, special themes, and other special interests. Shelves do not have to be of consistent height throughout the room. In each area, indicate the number of shelves needed (e.g., fiction, 25 shelves; picture books, 15 shelves). It is not necessary to know exactly how many picture books you own; rather, count the number of shelves used to house them currently. Remember to weed before counting and to anticipate areas of collection growth. If you decide to shift the whole collection or create new centers, you will need to be sure that the appropriate number of bookshelves will be located where needed. If you'd like to move the biographies to a freestanding cluster of four 42" bookcases, will you have enough shelves? If you expand your picture books, is there room for growth near the new relaxed-reading area?

Transfer fixed features to your plan. Computer programs make it easy to drag and drop icons representing different items of furniture. When working on a paper drawing, use tracing paper, a clear plastic overlay, and an erasable pen or graph paper on heavy plastic that can be purchased as a kit, with colorform-like furniture that you can move until you are satisfied. Photo marking pens can be erased. If graphite pencils are used, you can reverse the paper, place it on top of the plain paper, and rub the graphite markings onto the fresh sheet. Move furniture about on the drawing. Be sure to consider aisles, and sufficient space for wheelchair users, as well as doors and the placement of electrical outlets. Are there electrical outlets and phone jacks near the proposed computer area? If you plan to move the charging desk, will you create a bottleneck for borrowers? Are the tables so close together that students can't get in and out of their chairs? Are dinosaur books or other popular items up high or squeezed in narrow, dead-end aisles? Is new shelving necessary?

Have your library advisory committee help you plan the rearrangement of the space. Counting floor or ceiling tiles will give approximate measurements. When you have a plan that makes sense, make several copies. Ask staff and students to help you anticipate problems. Use "Post-it" notes to indicate where new material will be located (for example, the encyclopedias will be here; dinosaur books will be here). Use masking tape to mark off possible placement of furniture.

Does the new arrangement work better than the current setup? Is it visually appealing? Functional? Logical? Does it meet current and future needs?

Shifting the Furniture and the Collection

Discuss the plan with your administrator and advisory board before taking action. A committee's decisions about change can provide a stronger impetus than an individual's. Shifting furniture and the collection will require time and help. If items need moving, your custodian, a valuable collaborative partner (and possibly an advisory committee member), or a member of his staff may be able to move them. Local rules about custodial duties differ, but it often helps to bring these staff members in on the planning process. Schedule the rearranging for off-peak times, especially if you will be reducing borrowing or access for a period of time. Alert the staff and students. Gather a team of volunteers, students, and others.

You may be able to move smaller cases with the books on them. In other cases, it may be easier to move the cases without the books. As far as possible, plan the shift so each book is moved only once.

Demonstrate how to move books within a small range (section), for instance, from 550-551.5, so that you do not end up with your books out of order. Instruct your staff and volunteers to rearrange the books one section at a time, removing the books in the order that they appear on the shelves and placing them directly onto their new shelves. An alternative method is to move books and media on library carts in Dewey or alphabetical order.

Once the collection has been moved, create new signs to help borrowers locate materials and find new services. It will take some time to determine if the new arrangement improves service and access. Continue to monitor and evaluate the changes.

Improving Appearance with Moderate Funding

Some funding may be necessary to create an improved facility. Conduct a needs assessment and use the Renovation Notation Form (fig. 7.4 on pp. 141-42) to help evaluate your existing facility. Once you have implemented the previous suggestions and your advisory committee has decided what else needs to be accomplished, determine how much funding you have and what you can anticipate in the foreseeable future.

Consult an architect or interior designer who is familiar with school library design. If paid consultation is not possible, there may be community or parental help you can solicit. If not, create your own design. Plan carefully before you make major physical changes in the library. Research the literature on library renovations, visit schools and public libraries, and request that library furniture vendors submit recommendations for room layout plans and costs. Become familiar with the various styles of furniture that are available within your price range.

Set priorities. Do you need furniture, equipment, painting, carpeting, storage, additional electrical wiring, a wall removed? Some projects can be completed in stages. Document each step of the renovation process with photographs, notes, and staff and student comments. Photographs can be powerful tools.

Painting

Perhaps the most important single improvement you can undertake is to paint the library. Libraries should look vibrant. You want the children to appreciate the facility that houses a treasure trove of literature, information, media, and technology. The space should be inviting. Peeling, flaking, drab paint does not inspire confidence nor does it make users feel welcome. A freshly painted room with vivid colors beckons. If painting is on your agenda consider the following:

△ Premium paint is long-lasting and wears well.

△ Leaks must be repaired before painting or the paint will chip or peel.

△ Plastering must be done properly to prevent bumpy, cracking walls.

△ Prime the walls to prevent peeling.

△ Use two coats of paint (Additional coats may be required if painting over dark colors).

△ Painting can camouflage old magazine racks, utility cabinets, or bookcases.

Paint after other maintenance, such as pointing of bricks, installation of a new intercom system, phone or cable lines, or electrical wiring upgrading has been completed.

If funding is not available for professional painters, parents, teachers, and/or community members might collaborate and paint the library. The color or design scheme need not be intricate, but the results should indicate that change has occurred. Pure white paint contrasted with primary color accents draws attention to the space. Initially, the changes may lure the children, staff, and parents, but the wonderful program and materials will ensure that people return.

Renovation Notation Form

Indicate problems, needed repairs, and possible purchases.

Paint
(Plaster, prime walls, ceiling, bookcases, window frames, doors, trim, peeling, cracks, leaks. Paint scheme and colors.)

_____

_____

_____

Carpentry and Maintenance
(Secure bookcase backs, table legs, build shelves and storage, repair stripping, remove discarded furniture.)

_____

_____

_____

Electric
(Additional in-wall wiring; surface cabling; repair, replace, add outlets; replace lighting fixtures. Purchase surge protectors, upgrade current service, additional circuits, 220 wiring.)

_____

_____

_____

Refinishing
(Desks, tables, chairs, bookcases, new laminate for tables or counters.)

_____

_____

_____

Carpet
(Note location and size. Wash and repair, replace, area or full room.)

_____

_____

_____

Floors
(Repair or replace tiles or wood floor, remove wax barriers.)

_____

_____

Renovation Notation Form *(cont.)*

Window Treatments
(New shades. Wash, repair, replace blinds or curtains, replace mountings.)

_____

_____

Storage
(Repair doors or locks on closets and cupboards, buy or build additional storage, note location.)

_____

_____

Plumbing
(Repair faucets, drains, toilets, drinking fountain.)

_____

_____

Displays
(Secure, repair, replace bulletin boards, mounting rails; add cork strips and display cabinets.)

_____

_____

Furniture
Discard

Item _____ move to room _____ or remove from building _____
Item _____ move to room _____ or remove from building _____
Item _____ move to room _____ or remove from building _____
Item _____ move to room _____ or remove from building _____

Keep

Item _____ height x length x width _____
Item _____ height x length x width _____
Item _____ height x length x width _____

Purchase

Item _____ Description _____ Price _____
Item _____ Description _____ Price _____
Item _____ Description _____ Price _____

Fig. 7.4. Renovation Notation Form Adapted from Renovation Notes developed by Deborah Berke Architect.

Repairing and Refinishing Furniture

Tables or other wooden items such as chairs, bookcases, or magazine racks can be given new life if you repair, refinish, or laminate them. A school vocational program might be able to refinish dilapidated pieces and the only cost to the school might be materials and trucking. If help is not forthcoming in that area, parents and/or the custodial staff might be recruited to refinish tired but still serviceable furniture. Plants, book displays, student artwork, colored cloths, and tiles add texture and color. They also hide the scratches, stains, and gouges that make furnishings look decrepit.

It usually costs less to repair furniture than it does to replace it, especially if the school system already employs skilled carpenters. Carpenters can separate attached bookcases (that divide rooms and make reasonable furniture placement difficult) by removing the screws that attach them to each other and building (or you might be able to purchase) end panels to create individual bookcases.

If sections of your circulation (charging) desk are in disrepair, unscrew and remove the objectionable sections from the unit. Unless there is one continuous countertop, you could repair or discard the pieces. If your desk is in good repair, but takes up too much room, ask the carpenters or custodial staff to remove unnecessary units, then reconfigure it. The end panels also may have to be moved. Some charging desks have a small cabinet in the front of the corner piece that is too small for good storage. Remove the door and the shelves become an open-faced unit to display books, realia, or students' work.

If your library has inadequate shelving, look above or below the sink or below bookcases for underutilized built-in or freestanding cabinets. If they are currently used for storage, they might be converted to bookcases by removing the cabinet doors. Cabinets that are too high for students can be used for professional, parent, or personal collections.

Storage

Storage should be included in the library design and be located within the library. If available storage is limited, locked cabinets can be purchased to accommodate software and materials. The New York City Library Power Program and the New York City Board of Education's skilled mechanics, in collaboration with Deborah Berke Architect, created attractive "Little Houses" (figs. 7.5 and 7.6) to keep and secure materials and hardware.

Figs. 7.5. and 7.6. Photographs of a "Little House."

Two framed 60"-high x 72"-wide x 10"-deep bookcases are the sides of the house. A peaked roof (with wood strips for book displays) and a locked, corked door complete the structures. The house is brightly painted in coordination with the color scheme of the room. The house is lodged against a wall so as not to impede access, light, and vision. The inside of the house is used to store materials, equipment, scenery, and so on. In a few instances, the house door has been removed and children sit inside and read. Some houses have chimneys, others have skylights, but all are charming and utilitarian. They often are located near the carpeted reading area, and the bookcases adjoining the carpet house the picture book, easy, or fairy tale collections. The schematic drawing is shown in figure 7.7.

Furnishings

Furniture should be sturdy, durable, attractive, appropriately sized, and safe for those who will use it. Shelving, in particular, should be purchased with care to ensure that it will maintain the weight of a full load of books without warping, buckling, or splintering. This is an important

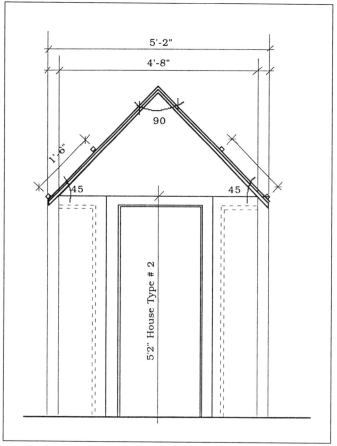

Fig. 7.7. Schematic Drawing of the Little House.

safety consideration; falling shelves, loaded with books, can be dangerous.

In her excellent 1989 guide on selecting furniture for the library, Carol R. Brown discusses furniture construction. Chairs should be constructed of wood to withstand heavy use over a long period of time. Sled-based chairs are generally the strongest, but four-legged chairs can compare favorably. Consider the strength of the joints when selecting chairs. The strength of the chair is also affected by the size of the rails. The wider the front rail, the greater is its potential for strength. Generally, the cost of a chair is determined by its design rather than its strength, and the cheapest chair is not necessarily the weakest. If only one size of furniture is being planned, 16" chairs can be used by people of most heights.

If your school is an early childhood center, you might prefer to buy 14" chairs and 25" tables. Consider informal seating such as beanbag chairs, child-sized couches, and armchairs, as well as traditional chairs and tables. You might purchase 18" chairs and 29" tables for schools whose students are predominantly in middle, junior high, or high schools.

Informal seating is important, but be aware that it does not last indefinitely. Purchase beanbag chairs that can be refilled and ensure that they conform to health and safety guidelines. Test foam or other leisure chairs before you purchase them, as many are not comfortable.

People in wheelchairs need tables that are at least 29" high. Some computer desks and tables are adjustable (including expensive, automatic tables that adjust heights with a switch). When you are arranging your library furnishings, allow at least 8' of turning room for wheelchairs.

Tables should be constructed from wood and be strong and resistant to wear from normal use. Joints should be well constructed with metal-to-metal joints used to attach the leg to the mounting plate. Tables should be braced or reinforced along their length for additional support and strength. Tabletops should be easy to maintain. Tables that are 27" high serve a wide range of students and adults and are used with 16" chairs.

Bookcases, tables, and chairs should be constructed of five-ply hardwood lumber core. Five-ply hardwood lumber has the advantages of structural strength to withstand long-term loading and a solid edge that can be shaped and finished and provides good holding power for fasteners. Particleboard is less expensive, but may sag or warp under the weight of books. Another major disadvantage is that particleboard does not hold screws securely. Steel shelving is durable and less expensive than wood, but it has a slippery surface that does not hold books as well as wood.

Bookcases are usually purchased in three standard heights. Those that are 82" high and 10" deep should be secured to the walls. One individual bookcase (starter) plus add-ons can be connected and is less expensive than using only starters. If you expect that you will need to reconfigure the bookcases or wish to use some individually, you should purchase starters. A starter has two end panels and the add-on has one end panel. Bookcases should have backs. Consult manufacturers' catalogs to determine if sway braces are needed for stability with tall shelving units.

Bookshelves that are deeper than 10" take up extra space. Books are not easily displayed because they slip to the rear of the bookcase. If you plan to use 60" bookcases be careful that they do not obstruct the view of the whole space. The 60" and 42" bookcases should all be starters, single-faced, and with backs to promote flexible use.

The 42" bookcases are particularly helpful if you need to add books to a particular area of the collection. Use 42"-high bookcases to house a specific collection of books, such as biographies or easy readers. They extend visibility and promote a spacious, open look. Place them under windows, at the edge of a carpeted area to define a listening space, or arrange them into groups of two or four bookcases. They can be moved as collection needs change or space is needed for various activities.

Charging or circulation desks also should be constructed of wood and appropriately sized. Elementary school circulation desks should be 32" high. The essential units are a charging unit for a manual circulation system, or a flat surface and open shelf for an online system. Additional units include book drop, open or closed storage, and knee space units. Charging desks for middle school or older students are 39" high. The charging desk should have individual counter tops rather than a continuous one, in case a unit is damaged or you choose to rearrange them. Small school libraries might consider purchasing stand-alone charging desks that are 6' long. These units are economical and useful, especially when space is limited.

You will need racks to display books, magazines, paperbacks, media, and software. Student magazines often are housed separately from parent or professional magazines. If space is an issue, magazine holders that are affixed to walls or sides of bookcases can be purchased. Computers with cables and peripherals (printers, scanners, external modems, backup drives, etc.) require furniture, too. Rolling computer and media carts should be considered so that equipment may be used where needed, or stored and secured when not in use.

Carpeting and Decorating

A carpeted area is an asset for reading and listening and for students who prefer nontraditional seating. It encourages recreational reading and informal small group learning.

A carpeted area can be purchased for a nominal expense. The carpet should seat at least a full class and should be located apart from dense shelving. To extend the life of the carpet, children should not have to step on it to access the collection.

Carpeting the whole library media center provides excellent sound insulation and a warm, pleasant ambiance, but it is expensive. The carpet can be difficult to maintain; it should be vacuumed often and cleaned regularly.

Purchase a patterned, commercial carpet that meets fire and health regulations and is durable, hides dirt, can be glued or tacked to the floor, and has rubber stripping to prevent tripping.

Special attention should be paid if carpet is to be used in areas where computers, security devices, and other sensitive electrical equipment are used. Static electricity can interfere with data transmissions and other operations. Check with manufacturers before purchasing.

Decorating

Personal decorating touches make the library a warm, inviting place. Plants, small pets, a puppet basket, a gallery area for display of student art, glass cases for fragile three-dimensional projects, a minimuseum and realia, mobiles, stuffed toys, art materials, science tools, puzzles, and games create a user-friendly environment that encourages and celebrates learning. These final touches need not be expensive, yet they can set the tone for the space.

A plan for a library renovation that required moderate expense included the removal of two non-load-bearing (retaining) interior walls, new furniture arrangement, furniture purchases, repairs, and repainting. Details of the renovations and the list of furnishings to be kept, discarded, or purchased are noted on the "punch list" shown in figure 7.8 on pages 147-48.

Extensive Renovations

If extensive renovations are needed, funding has been secured, and space is available, it is often possible to expand or improve an existing site. Sometimes a more suitable space in the building can be found for the media center. Consider kindergarten rooms. They are often large, located on low floors, and have sinks and toilet facilities. Sometimes two or more rooms can be joined, or a new library space can be created as part of an addition.

Major upgrades of old buildings can be a challenge, though. When major renovations are being considered, an architect or engineer must survey the space, draw the blueprints, and verify that:

△ Floors and walls can support the additional furniture, tall bookcases attached to the walls, and heavy books, and equipment.

△ State and local building and fire codes are observed.

△ Walls that must be removed or have archways or doors cut into them are not weight-bearing or laden with asbestos.

△ Windows and radiators are in good repair.

△ Wires, beams, and pipes in walls to be removed can be relocated.

△ Electrical wiring is adequate for present and anticipated use or can be upgraded. The library can be wired to classrooms, the computer lab, and other learning centers.

△ Outlets are placed strategically throughout the library media center.

△ Floor outlets are flat to the floor.

(List continues on page 149.)

Punch List

The Excel School: Library Renovation Project, Rooms 109, 109A, 113.

Furniture

Keep

— 5 42" round tables
— 1 36" round table
— 2 book trucks
— 1 rocking chair
— 1 AV cart
— 22 84"h x 36"w bookcases
— (relocate as shown on plan)

— 6 42"h x 36"w bookcases
— 1 34"h x 40"w painted wood
    bookcase (repaint blue)
— 1 54"w x 24"d x 28"h computer table
— 1 metal vertical file 18"w x 28"d x 30"h

Discard

— 1 3' x 5' table
— 1 librarian's chair (missing slats)
— 1 metal vertical file (broken)
— 36" bookcases
— existing carpet

— 1 magazine rack 12"d x 36"w x 29"h
— 1 typewriter stand
— 1 outdated globe
— 1 84" x 20" x 72" bookcase

Purchase

— 40 chairs, 16"h	style number
— 1 librarian's swivel chair	style number
— 1 revolving paperback rack	style number
— 1 magazine rack	style number
— 2 beanbag chairs	style number
— 1 4-unit circulation desk	style number
— 1 sq. comp. station	style number
— 2 3' x 5' tables	style number
— revolving video rack	
— floor globe (brass stand)	
— 86" conference table	

Carpentry and Maintenance

— remove entire wall in Room 309/309A as indicated on plan
— remove 20' of wall between rooms 309 and 313 as indicated on plan
— relocate 84" high bookcases as indicated on plan
— remove hooks from the north wall of room 309A

Carpentry and Maintenance (*cont.*)

— build steps at window wall of carpeted area

— repair plaster on east wall as indicated on plan

— remove existing carpet in Room 309

— repair all window sashes, ensuring proper operation (2nd and 3rd windows don't open)

— remove discarded furniture

Electrical

— remove surface mount (old)

— relocate existing electrical outlets where wall is removed

— relocate 309A outlet

— repair surface mount in 309A

— install quad outlet on circulation desk

Windowshades

— replace all shades with white shades cut to fit windows

Floors

— wax floor

Carpet

— cut and install free-form carpet (18'8" x 11'8" overall) as per plan

— steps for carpeted area

Paint

— 8" base molding at walls blue

— 3" picture moldings at 7'1" above floor and 11'6" above floor blue

— wall between picture moldings yellow

— all other walls white

— ceiling white

— ceiling beams yellow

— all radiators blue

— all window sashes and frames red

— all window mullions yellow

— revarnish wood bookcases, cabinetry, doors, and door trim

— vertical piers blue

— paint library doors red

Fig. 7.8. Punch List Developed by Deborah Berke Architect for the Library Power Program.

△ Phone and cable lines are installed in appropriate areas to facilitate use in a variety of ways.

△ Materials are used to enhance acoustics.

△ Services such as lavatories, elevator access, and ramps are adequate.

△ Ample security devices including reinforced doors are installed.

△ Unimpeded views of the public areas of the library including partitions of clear glass or Plexiglas are possible.

△ Leaks and outside pointing are repaired.

△ The media center is located on a low floor convenient to the whole school and to the community during off hours.

The architect or engineer should plan a library space, taking into consideration elements of good design, fire and safety codes, and good building practices. You will need to supply information on the school population, the school mission and philosophy, and the library program so that the architect will know if you require:

△ A large performance area with excellent acoustics because teachers and students frequently gather in the library for storytelling.

△ A T-1 line with router because most students use telecommunications for assignments.

△ Additional secure storage for an archive housing student work.

△ Sufficient electrical outlets placed throughout the room so that students can work on multimedia projects in many locations simultaneously.

△ Formal, secure display areas for student projects.

△ A defined space to house a proposed center for aviation study.

△ A media center that can accommodate a 10 percent enrollment increase in the next four years, as indicated in a recent demographic study.

Your library advisory committee should participate in every stage of research, planning, decision making, and leveraging funds. A strong advisory committee convinces the various constituencies that an improved library is for the good of the school. The proposal should include specific costs for architectural services, construction, equipment, and furniture. It can also identify potential funding sources.

If an architect is chosen to design the plans, make sure that your advisory committee clearly articulates the facility and program needs. You should be included in every phase of the design and implementation process and understand exactly what the architect is planning. Architectural drawings are technical and may be difficult to grasp. To prevent future problems, ask for explanations of every item that confuses you. Ongoing involvement reduces design flaws, which are expensive and hard to change in the final stages of construction. Some examples of problems to watch out for include:

△ The placement of the bathroom in the center of the library.

△ The installation of minimum standard electrical wiring, which limits future equipment purchase and use.

△ Storage rooms and offices that are poorly located and limit visibility and access.

△ Furniture (circulation desk, bookcases, computer stations, carrels) that are bolted to the floor, limiting flexibility in room design.

△ The installation of a single telephone line instead of multiple lines and jacks.

△ Furniture purchases that do not meet school and program needs.

△ Decorative steps that limit wheelchair access and movement of equipment.

△ The location of the office restricts visibility of the main room.

△ Windows that leave too little space for bookcases underneath them.

The library committee's renovation proposal to the board of education should describe how the improvement of the physical space will further the school's educational objectives. The proposal should demonstrate how:

△ Furniture purchases will facilitate resource-based learning.

△ Removing a wall will allow you to service more students.

△ Computer workstations will provide greater access for technology-related activities.

△ A carpeted area for relaxed reading will encourage reading for pleasure.

If the school or district cannot accomplish a full renovation in one fiscal year, develop a three- to five-year plan. Start with what you most urgently require, or decide what can be purchased with available funds. The early renovations may excite the desire for more extensive renovations.

Creating a new design for a school library media center requires an enormous amount of energy, resources, and collaboration, but the benefits to students, staff, and the community are immeasurable. Figure 7.9 is adapted from an elementary school library plan created for the New York City Board of Education by the School Construction Authority. The library is spacious, contains small and large group areas, and can be used for a variety of programs, activities, and celebrations. Groups and individuals can use the space simultaneously. Bookcases that are not secured to walls are low, individual, and can be relocated for collection and organizational purposes. Meeting rooms provided access for the community.

Whether you develop a new library, renovate or enhance an existing one, or merely weed and rearrange furniture, the physical space is only a room until a dynamic, energetic library media specialist, a supportive administration, collaborative teachers, curious students, and involved parents make it the hub of the school and the center of learning.

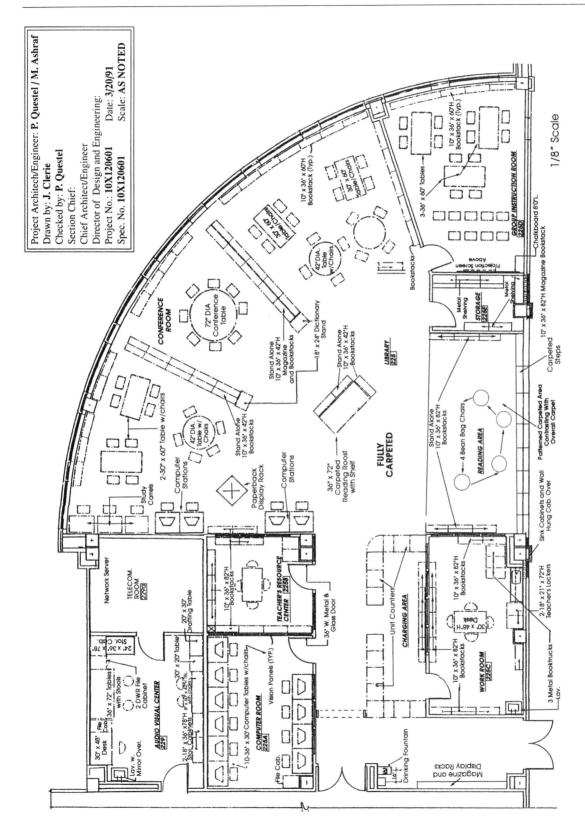

Fig. 7.9. Possible Plan for a New Media Center

Bibliography

American Association of School Librarians and Association for Educational Communications and Technology. *Information Power: Guidlines for School Library Media Programs.* Chicago and Washington D.C.: ALA-AECT, 1988.

Brown, Carol R. *Selecting Library Furniture: A Guide for Librarians, Designers, and Architects.* Phoenix, AZ: Oryx Press, 1989.

Klasing, Jane P. *Designing and Renovating School Library Media Centers.* Chicago: American Library Association, 1991.

Klasing, Jane P., and Daniel Callison, eds. "Planning Learning Environments for Library Media Programs: An Introduction." *School Library Media Quarterly* 20, no. 4 (Summer 1992): 204–10.

Knirk, Frederick G. "New Technology Considerations for Media Facilities, Video Technologies and Space Requirements." *School Library Media Quarterly* 20, no. 4 (Summer 1992): 205.

Robertson, Michelle M. "Ergonomic Considerations for the Human Environment: Color Treatment, Lighting and Furniture Selection." *School Library Media Quarterly* 20, no. 4 (Summer 1992): 211–15.

Walling, Linda Lucas. "Granting Each Equal Access." *School Library Media Quarterly* 20, no. 4 (Summer 1992): 216–21.

Woolls, Blanche. *Managing School Library Media Programs*: Littleton, CO: Libraries Unlimited, 1988.

Chapter 8

Library Operations

Introduction

Every successful business or organization must examine its operating procedures to maximize service and efficiency and minimize cost, time, and labor. You are the CEO of a very important enterprise. As you examine the current systems in place, you need to look at the present and future needs of your teachers and students and determine the best ways to organize the procedures and routines that make the media center run smoothly and efficiently. These systems generally include acquiring and processing all resources and equipment (including software, hardware, and online services), cataloging, inventory, circulation, materials acquisition, and deselection (weeding). Integrating the use of technology into library routines and educational services is essential as you organize your time so that you can perform the roles of information specialist, teacher, and instructional consultant. You must streamline operations, find the personnel to do the work (paid assistants, student library squads, and volunteers), and evaluate the changing needs of your library media center. A change in one system or service often necessitates changes in other routines.

Are you are switching to a flexible schedule? Consider a different method for handling circulation.

Are you planning for automation? Decide how operations will change. What will remain the same? How will you handle retrospective conversion?

Has your school suddenly increased in size? Added another grade level? This may affect purchasing, ordering, budgeting, circulation, and overdue procedures.

Has your school cut back or added aides or paraprofessionals? You may need to attract more volunteers. Rethink how you deploy your "staff."

Library media specialists have the multiple roles and responsibilities outlined above. You must ensure that library operations serve the needs of your school community, especially the students, and not merely stay in place to serve the institution of the library media center.

Systems Analysis

What should you do first when walking into a new position or when taking a fresh look at how your media center meets today's challenges? The system of library operations or "routines" includes a number of discrete tasks that must be accomplished within a regular structure in order to keep the library media center working properly. Systems analysis, a useful tool common to commercial enterprises, not-for-profit organizations, and educational institutions, is a process of breaking down an already existing structure into its component parts, examining the necessity for each of these parts, and then reconstructing these components or tasks in a different and improved way.

Remember, this is not change for the sake of change. Ask yourself these questions about a new procedure:

Δ Is it cost effective?

Δ Does it save time?

Δ Does it save labor?

△ Is it user friendly?

△ Is it easier?

△ Is it self-regulating?

△ Does this new way of doing things make it easier to serve the needs of students, faculty, and parents?

△ Does it release you from nonprofessional tasks?

If new procedures raise the cost of running the library media center (for example, installing a new automated catalog), will the expenditure benefit student learning? Will it enable your students to use Boolean logic and various search strategies that will help them become more effective users of information?

If you follow the basic steps of systems analysis, you will find the evidence to convince the constituencies in your school that the changes you want will improve services. Use the steps below to begin your analysis.

Analyze the current system:

△ Break the system into pieces and diagram or map the component tasks or steps.

△ Ask yourself if the tasks are necessary and performed as efficiently as possible.

△ Document the time and cost involved in the current system.

△ Think carefully before you alter a system that is necessary and efficient. If it's not broken, don't fix it!

Investigate alternatives:

△ Examine other models.

△ Request assistance from experts.

△ Ask users to reflect on improvements to the current system.

Develop a new model:

△ Explain it.

△ Test it.

△ Evaluate it.

△ Make adjustments.

Institute the new system:

△ Introduce it.

△ Teach others to use it.

△ Evaluate it.

Monitor the system with periodic redesign in mind:

△ Measure the positive or negative effects and eliminate any problems.

△ Redesign until the procedure works better than the old system.

The following is an example of a magazine circulation system, and how changing the system can benefit the library and its patrons:

Current System

1. Check in magazines upon arrival and produce and paste in card and pocket.

2. Insert current issue in magazine cover.

3. Student selects magazine, writes name and class on book card, and takes it to the circulation desk.

4. The library media specialist or assistant stands at the desk and stamps the cards and pockets.

5. Card is filed.

6. When the magazine is returned, it is carded. If the magazine is not returned on time, an overdue notice must be written.

New System

1. The magazine is checked in.

2. The bar code is attached.

3. Student takes the magazine to the desk.

4. The bar code is scanned.

5. The date due is stamped on the card and on the magazine cover.

6. When the magazine is returned, the barcode is scanned. Overdues can be generated by computer. Circulation figures are kept automatically.

Comments: Time spent on magazine processing is significantly reduced. In addition, circulation records may be helpful in determining future reorders.

Modifications: Reader demand may necessitate purchasing magazines on CD-ROM.

Common Systems in the Library Media Center —————

Many books on library media center administration supply detailed procedures for acquisitions, cataloging, processing, circulation, inventory, and weeding. Some of these are listed in the bibliography at the end of this chapter. In this chapter, you will not always be provided with the standard solutions to common library media center needs, but with the means to analyze the systems in place in your center and the points you need to consider when redesigning any of your systems.

Library operations or routines should maximize:

△ The timely delivery of the best resources to students, teachers, and other members of the school community.

△ The availability of the appropriate equipment necessary for the library media center and the efficient delivery of equipment to the entire building (if that is within your scope of responsibility).

△ The integration of new technologies in the most educationally suitable manner.

△ The physical arrangement of the library media center that allows for the maximum educational usage.

△ Efficient recruitment, training, and deployment of all library staff, including volunteers and student squad members.

As you consider acquisitions, processing, and other routines, keep in mind that you make decisions regarding streamlining of operations or complete systematic changes in order to benefit your students, teachers, administrators, and parents. Rigorous system analysis should be part of the planning process you and your library advisory committee engage in so that you can offer your patrons:

△ The recreational library services that they desire.

△ The twenty-first century research center that they require.

△ An excellent professional reference collection.

△ Exemplary parent and community collections and services.

△ Working collaborations with the public library and other community resources.

△ A production facility for student and faculty creation of materials.

△ More time for improved instructional consulting services.

△ Online access in every classroom to resources within and beyond the school building.

Materials

New Acquisitions

Acquisitions can be a time-consuming process unless you streamline the steps involved. As you collect information throughout the year on new materials that you want to acquire, enter the ordering information on a database. Using a database will prevent duplication; assist you to group your possible purchases in any one of a number of ways, including grade, subject, and theme classifications; and provide your patrons with a bibliography of new materials. Investigate some of the electronic ordering systems that are available from the major vendors to see if these meet your needs and those of your district's business office.

Determine the purchasing procedures of your district. Are you limited to purchasing from contracted vendors? Is there a procedure to obtain bids from vendors? In general, purchasing from one of the major vendors will be cost effective and economical in terms of clerical work, but from time to time you may be able to negotiate a better deal with an individual source. You may also want to obtain quotes from several of the major vendors. The major difference in discounts is generally between library and trade editions. If you decide to purchase trade editions where available, you will usually be able to purchase books at a 40 percent discount. Library editions are generally available from the vendors at a 13 to 20 percent discount. Some vendors, such as Follett and Brodart, specialize in the school library market and carry a far greater proportion of library bindings. Others such as Baker & Taylor and Book Wholesalers, Inc. (BWI) offer both bindings when available from the publisher. Many nonfiction books are only offered in library bindings and so it is important to get the best discounts available. By examining some of the books in your collection, you can see that library-bound books have their own wear-and-tear problems. Many librarians choose to purchase trade editions in order to stretch their purchasing dollars.

Although many of the major book vendors now sell computer software, CD-ROMs, videos, and other materials, consider vendors who specialize in software. (The lowest prices are sometimes available from commercial sources such as major chains.) In making your choices, consider services such as processing, cataloging, and return policies. Check prices from several sources if you have the leeway to purchase from noncontract vendors.

Check with the other librarians in your district. Have they devised any shortcuts in receiving and check-in procedures? Finding reliable aides or volunteers is often the key to doing this step efficiently. Even if you don't have a regular aide, your principal may be able to spare someone for this kind of finite task. Ask for help.

Permanent Acquisitions

Before you purchase materials consider:

Δ How you will select vendors or use direct sources.

Δ Your ordering procedures and routines.

- Budgeting
- Processing

Do not pay bills or sign that materials were received until you have verified that the order is complete and the materials are in good condition. You may need to install CD-ROMs and computer programs to determine that they operate properly.

Gifts

A written gift policy is essential. Share it with prospective donors. A gifts policy should include:

Δ A system of gift solicitation and acknowledgments.

Δ A procedure for evaluating and weeding gift materials.

Δ Check-in and processing procedures for gifts accepted.

Δ Procedures for gifts rejected.

Temporary Acquisitions

As more materials become available via online services, faxes, video copying, and other newer forms of technology, more materials will be "temporary" acquisitions. Various copyright and fair use laws may pertain to these materials. Be aware of your legal responsibilities regarding these materials. Find ways to make your students and teachers aware of all the new information possibilities.

A temporary acquisition policy should include procedures for:

△ Borrowed materials (interlibrary loans).

△ Electronic materials via the Internet and online services (downloaded for a short or long period of time).

△ Short-term video materials (taped off the air and kept for the period of time allowable under copyright restrictions).

△ Systems for downloading or borrowing.

△ A system for use and return, or erasing (specifically, for video and computer data) as needed.

△ Timely dissemination of information to all patrons regarding these resources: newsletter, memos, flyers.

Processing

Establish a standard format for processing and supply all your vendors with your specifications. Take advantage of any central processing that your district offers. Reduce or eliminate minute details of processing (stamping on a special inside page in addition to obvious places, making special notations on cards or books, etc.). What is essential?

△ Property stamping (once should do it).

△ Copy numbers on materials pocket, materials card, and shelflist card.

Once you have identified an automated system, start having new materials processed by your vendors with the correct type of bar codes. This will save you time, effort, and money down the line even if the system purchase is a year or two down the road. Define the jobs involved in in-house processing. Decide which tasks can be done by students, staff, or volunteers.

Paperbacks are generally processed in-house due to their ephemeral status. (Processing at the vendor can cost almost as much as the discounted purchase price.) For manual circulation, you will need a pocket and card marked with author, title, and classification code (if you want to use one), copy number, and an abbreviation indicating that the book is a paperback, a property stamp, and a label, if you find it useful. For fiction, perhaps just a large capital letter indicating the author's last name is needed, if you arrange your paperbacks by letter. If you use an automated system, you may opt to purchase dumb barcodes for paperbacks. They are inexpensive and quick to apply, but you will not have a record of specific paperback titles in circulation. Alternatively, you may choose to enter paperback books into your database and print smart barcodes.

Decide if you are going to reinforce paperbacks. A wide piece of tape on the outside of the spine and the back and front inside covers gives books a longer shelflife. Balance that against the time needed to do this job neatly.

Books, Audiovisual, and Electronic Materials

When materials arrive, process and put them into the hands of the students quickly. Defects in media and software may not be apparent; install and test CD-ROMs and computer programs. View videos. Process after you have determined that the item is perfect.

General procedures:

△ Check items against invoice and order.

△ Stamp.

△ Label.

Specific to manual systems:

△ Enter date, copy number, and price on shelflist cards.

△ File catalog cards.

Specific to automated systems:

△ Add bar codes for automated circulation if not done by vendor.

△ Add to database (done in-house or with diskette from outside vendor).

Systems (for paperbacks and other ephemera):

△ Minimal identification.

△ Reinforcement to extend shelf life.

△ Storage and retrieval procedures, including labeling.

△ Display.

Cataloging

Most new items are available fully processed, including catalog cards or machine-readable data from major publishers, jobbers, or specialized cataloging companies. Cards or data for the older materials in your library media center are also available. If your budget does not allow for this type of expenditure and you have enough volunteer help, you can create cards using the Library of Congress Cataloging-in-Publication (CIP) information on the verso of the title page. (This is found in most books after the early 1970s.) Software programs that enable you to produce cards in the correct format can be purchased, but this is recommended only on a very limited basis because it is time-consuming.

Your major task in cataloging is to maintain a system that will give your users up-to-date access to all the resources in your collection. This is accomplished more and more with the assistance of an online public access catalog or OPAC. Easy to update, both with new entries and withdrawals, OPACs enable children and adults to use sophisticated Boolean logic to link several terms and broaden or limit the search in a variety of ways. If you are considering an OPAC, read chapter 10, "Online Public Access Catalog and Circulation System." Although the system will certainly bring improvements to the library media center, the initial stages involve administrative and clerical work that must be included in your already busy schedule. In addition, staff (both paid and volunteer) will have to be taught new methods of entering and withdrawing data and securing the database.

If you use a traditional card catalog, you should regularly update it by both adding and withdrawing cards. Include all forms of media. Some catalogs include separate sections of videos, media kits, software, and so on. Give users subject access to these materials within the body of the regular catalog as well. You may color-code these items and assign special location codes to let users know exactly where they are located, if they are not housed on the shelves in Dewey order.

Foreign language materials should also be accessible to the user through the catalog. In a library with a small collection, 200 titles or fewer, the catalog access may be kept separate. If the collection is large, or if the school is bilingual, the librarian may choose to interfile English and non-English materials. With an automated system, the user would be able to search by language as well as subject.

Your other major decision in terms of the traditional catalog is the arrangement. If your library has a working catalog, you will probably want to leave it the way it is currently set up. If you are starting from scratch and do not feel that you will have the funds available for an online catalog, you will have to make a choice. The three major ways of organizing a card catalog are:

One Alphabet. Often called a "Dictionary Catalog," all cards are filed together with author, title, and subject cards in the same alphabet.

Two Alphabets. Sometimes called a "Divided Catalog," author and title cards may be filed in one alphabet, and subject cards are filed in a second alphabet.

Three Alphabets. Also called a "Divided or Separated Catalog," this format is used in many public library book catalogs. Authors, titles, and subjects are each filed in their own alphabet.

Instructions for using any of the cataloging systems should be clearly posted in precise language. Do not rely on printed instructions from one of the library graphics companies. Prepare your own directions, using vocabulary and examples that your students will understand.

Some librarians feel that the "three alphabet" system is easier for children to understand. It also eliminates some of the detailed filing rules needed for the "one alphabet" or dictionary catalog.

Catalog requirements:

Δ System for entry and withdrawal.

Δ Setup and maintenance of the catalog.

Δ Use of national standards (full MARC records, ALA filing rules, etc.).

Δ Dictionary or divided card catalog.

Δ Full "adult-style" OPAC vs. adapted or modified "kid's" OPAC.

Δ Services from vendors (such as alphabetizing catalog cards, smart bar codes, etc.).

Repair/Maintenance of Materials

When materials sustain minor damage—a torn or missing page, scribbled-on picture, or the like—librarians can usually make repairs with tape, glue, erasers, photocopies, and tip-in missing material as needed. Sometimes a new plastic cover or removal of an old dust jacket and plastic cover gives new life to a title. Children can make new covers using collage techniques, crayons, markers or paint, writing a blurb, and putting their own photos on the back flyleaf with a short biography of the new cover illustrator. Volunteers then cover the book, put on the proper label, and apply a new plastic cover. These books can be highlighted in a special display.

Materials with extensive damages should be discarded. (The days of sending items to an outside bindery are over, and condition is one of the main reasons for deselecting materials. Some book companies replace books with spine damage.) Some small repairs can be done for nonprint materials, but most of the time they should be discarded unless the vendor is willing to exchange them for new copies. To purchase a new copy of the discarded item, note it in your acquisitions file or database, delete the copy number from your shelflist, and leave the catalog cards or the data in your system. Otherwise, delete the item entirely from your shelflist and your catalog.

Circulation

Circulation policies and practices will need adjustment when you are adopting flexible access and promoting a new philosophy of library media center service throughout your school and the community. In setting your borrowing policies, give maximum access to the collection to your various patrons: students, teachers, and parents. Set priorities. Small collections necessitate rapid turnover and short loan periods. You will need to consider making decisions about the circulation of materials that may change your current procedures. These decisions will affect:

△ The policy on loans of materials in different formats to students, teachers, parents.

△ The adoption of manual vs. automated systems (considerations involve size of student population and volume of circulation).

△ Maximum access vs. restrictive access (open access to library, loan policies and loan periods, types of materials loaned).

△ Overdue and lost materials.

In the past when many nonprint items were expensive and students lacked access to equipment to use films and filmstrips at home, nonprint loans were usually restricted to teachers. Now new decisions must be made regarding access to materials. In some schools, nonprint materials are still only loaned to teachers. The consequence is that many of these resources sit moldering on shelves until they are fit only for the discard pile. Look at each type of resource and make some new determinations regarding loan policies. Perhaps as a start, loan out media to those students who have proven to be responsible over a stated period of time. Create special loan periods for items such as videos or cassettes, perhaps only one or two days. Find ways to get the materials circulating, not sitting on your shelves.

The other major concern about circulation relates to information about materials that are currently out of the media center. If you have an automated system, your circulation records will be available to you in a variety of formats. You can check your overdue records, see if a particular item is out, or see how many items Mary P. in class 2-223 has borrowed. If you have a manual system, this becomes a bit more complicated. Decisions about how to arrange your circulation file need to be made based on your priorities.

Children should be encouraged to return materials on time in order to give their fellow students opportunities to use the resources. To keep overdue books from turning into lost materials, you must send out overdue notices in a timely way. Every three or four weeks, clerical help should pull the overdue cards from the circulation file, separated by class, and write overdue notices. If time and staff permit, this should probably be done more often. Automated systems greatly reduce human clerical work in this area.

You should have a written policy for lost items. Parents should know in advance if your school or district requires payment for lost materials. Some schools charge full purchase price; others charge a token fee. Other systems do not charge. If there is no policy in place, you may wish to decide on a sliding scale, keeping in mind individual families' economic levels. You may also ask the student to perform some type of school service to foster a greater feeling of responsibility to the school community.

Inventory of Materials

Inventory seems like an enormous task for most busy library media specialists, but it is a vital element of collection development. It is impossible to know what to purchase if you do not know what your collection contains. The key for many is to do the job in bite-size chunks. You must enlist the help of others: aides, volunteers, or students. Some librarians take inventory of one section at a time (e.g., the 600s), going through the shelves, the circulation records, and any books returned during that specific time. Set aside time at the beginning of the year, during testing time, or at the end of the semester. If your system pays you for any days when students are not in school, that may be an opportune time. Set a regular schedule for yourself, reserving time each week or month. Start with sections that you feel need heavy weeding and new purchasing. This will make your inventory meaningful in terms of collection development.

Once you do a thorough inventory of the entire library, you can quickly add and subtract purchases and withdrawals and keep an approximate running record of the collection until another complete inventory can be done. The frequency of inventory (once a year or continuously over a period of three to five years) will depend on the size of your collection, the accuracy of your existing shelflist, or the completeness of the database of your online catalog and the number of trained staff, students, or volunteers assisting.

Factors to consider about inventory:

Δ Any special procedure for paperbacks.

Δ Full inventory vs. partial inventory spread over time.

Δ Method of accounting for each item against shelflist or computer database.

Δ Method of accounting for items when materials are still in circulation.

Δ Dealing with discrepancies between records and materials.

Δ Replacement/weeding policies as discrepancies are discovered.

Discarding Materials

Weed to maintain a collection that offers the best and most relevant materials for your school community. Consider the curricular needs of the school at the current time and your collection development plans, and the recreational interests of the students. Start with a section at a time or try to go through the whole library from beginning to end. After you are clear about your criteria, enlist the help of others, but reserve the final judgment for yourself. There are three major issues concerning weeding.

Δ Criteria for weeding: curricular and recreational needs of your school population.

Δ Disposition of discarded materials: give away vs. throw away.

Δ Replacement and renewal of the collection.

Your primary interest should be the timeliness and accuracy of the material. To keep an item simply because it is about a subject that may be requested, even though the information may be dated, is counterproductive. A school library media center should be responsive to the immediate needs of the school and cannot be comprehensive or all-inclusive. Books that pertain to topics no longer emphasized in the curriculum need to be carefully examined. Many of them, especially those tired-looking volumes that were not used even when the topic was "required," need to be discarded. Novels that were mediocre in their day are even more mediocre today. Didactic books about behavior, freedom, and brotherhood are not needed. Weeding your collection carefully but ruthlessly will allow you to show your administrators the strengths and weaknesses of the current collection and graphically show the need for additional funding.

Consider these five Cs of deselection:

△ Condition

△ Circulation

△ Currency

△ Content

△ Community

Fig. 8.1. Weeding—Difficult, Dirty, Essential. Get Help!

Condition

Books with missing or torn pages, broken spines, or shabby, unappealing covers should be removed and discarded. If the title is useful but cannot be repurchased, consider making a new jacket and plastic cover. A new design by a student artist can add life to a book with a shabby cover. If you want children to care about keeping books clean and in good repair, you must offer them the same. This is the easiest type of book to find and discard. If the book you are discarding is one you want to replace, keep a record of it for later. Don't hold on to the book.

Circulation

The next easiest reason for discarding is eliminating those materials that are shelf-sitters. Sometimes books do not circulate because the stories or ideas are not relevant, for example: fictional farm families of the 1950s, cowboy adventures, stories about retired baseball players, and former TV stars. These are not to be confused with books on former great players like Babe Ruth, or historical fiction such as *The Little House* books in which the author and illustrator make a conscious effort to re-create a time in the past. Some materials may be valuable for comparisons or to highlight a particular bias or style. (Save these titles with other professional materials, *not* on the borrowers' shelves.) No matter how carefully selection is made, there are bound to be errors in judgment. Sometimes multiple copies of a book were bought at times of peak demand. Once the popularity has worn off, it is time to reduce the number retained. Your circulation system can tell you when a book last circulated. If it was several years ago, decide if the book needs promoting, or pitch it.

Currency and Content

These are the most difficult criteria to apply to your collection. You must decide if the subject matter is accurate and timely or should be removed from the collection. Pay special attention to rapidly changing fields: technology, astronomy, transportation, communications, atomic energy, careers, ecology, and foreign governments. You will not be able to point out the outdated parts of a book to each child who is using your collection, so discard materials that present misinformation, even if it is only one part of the resource. In addition, you need to skim your collection to determine if materials provide an accurate depiction of men and women, of various age groups and ethnicities, and if the illustrations are still appealing.

Community

School populations change. Discard materials that will not or cannot be used because they are too easy or too difficult. If they are of good quality and the information is current, consider transferring them to a library where they may be used (e.g., to an early childhood program or to a middle school).

Disposal

There are three categories of weeding materials. Books that are no longer of great interest, including many novels that have been shelf-sitters for years, volumes in shabby condition, or items on topics no longer covered in the curriculum can be given away to teachers or students after they have been de-accessioned.

Materials that are outdated, biased, inaccurate, or incomplete should be processed for de-accessioning and placed in garbage bags or cartons. Discuss with your principal and custodian the best arrangements for packing and discarding these materials. Don't give them to adults or children. Don't offer them to community libraries or send them abroad.

Managing Equipment

As school library media specialist, you may be responsible for the coordination of all procedures related to equipment in the media center or the whole school. You may be the expert on acquisition, selection, distribution, or circulation, and maintenance of all media and technological equipment. You may be expected to train students and teachers. In some schools you will share the responsibility for equipment with other staff members, such as computer or technology coordinators, audiovisual technicians, or other designated teachers, paraprofessionals, or aides. Even if you are the officially designated staff member, you will need support from other staff members and adult and student volunteers. *Information Power* encourages students to produce their own information in many formats. As the production of materials (including multimedia productions) expands, you will need a trained cadre of adults and students to assist novices in the various technologies that will be available in your school. Service contracts, maintenance agreements, and access to outside consultants are also important to the success of your program.

Acquisition

Your district may have detailed procedures in place for the acquisition of equipment. Be aware of all such regulations governing companies under contract, bidding procedures, and other purchasing rules. Be familiar with what you are purchasing. If possible, try out the equipment at another school, a professional conference, or in a store. Talk to others who are already using it. Check commercial prices and educational vendors. Remember that service and reliability are important factors.

Steps in the selection process:

△ Identify types, kinds, and brands available.

△ Investigate the warranties and repair services.

△ Examine district or regional selection services.

△ Create equipment specifications and requests for proposals (RFPs).

△ Solicit bids.

When deciding between using a vendor or purchasing from direct sources, consider these factors:

△ Dealers' services and reliability.

△ Good value includes quality, service, reliability, support, and compatibility with other equipment.

△ The track record of past service (in your school and other regional schools).

When ordering, you must know your district's:

△ Procedures for bidding vs. sole source.

△ Purchasing procedures.

Processing Equipment

Unpack equipment and test all features as soon as possible. Computers may come with preloaded software. Follow manual instructions regarding backing up diskettes, or purchase backup diskettes and manuals. (Purchased programs also require backing up.) Separate storage areas should be created for backup diskettes. Settle problems with vendors before their bills are paid. All warranty registrations should be completed immediately and all forms should be photocopied and placed in several locations (e.g., the media center, general office, and so on). Another important document to be copied is the users' manual. Attach one copy to the equipment carrying case, or stand and file the other copy for your records.

Record the model and serial numbers and the purchase date on a master inventory list or database. Equipment can also be bar-coded for inventory purposes if you have an automated system. Simplified inventory numbers can also be assigned to individual pieces of equipment, for example, VCR #2.

Use a permanent magic marker or engraving device to mark each piece of equipment and all its separate components (case, speakers, etc.) with school property information and the simplified number.

You can also mark helpful information such as battery or bulb numbers and color-code such things as cables between TVs and VCRs.

Steps in processing equipment:

Δ Checking in:
  - Unpack.
  - Test all features.
  - Return defective items.

Δ Warranty registration:
  - Completion of company forms.
  - Local record of warranties.

Δ Identification labels and numbers.

Δ Entering items on master inventory lists or computer databases.

Δ Additions to insurance policies (district, school?).

Δ Tracking of spare parts and consumables (inventory and supply).

Δ System for filing instruction manuals and usage records.

Δ Paying the bills:
  - Payment of invoices.
  - Partial vs. complete payments.

Circulation

Distribution of major pieces of equipment may take place in September, but in many schools it goes on continuously as teachers borrow the equipment they need for short periods of time. Use existing forms or create new request and repair forms. Use a tracking sheet for borrowers to note problems or repairs needed. A circulation form should indicate all the parts of the unit, including cords, cables, lenses, microphones, etc. The advisory committee should help set loan policies to students or parents. Some schools loan cassette players, cameras, and even computers to students, especially those working on special projects. Weekends and vacation weeks are good times to try this out. You might want to hold a workshop with parents and have the parents sign a permission form. Think of it in the same terms as loaning band instruments to students. If your school district's policy includes deposits or rental fees for materials loaned for home or community use, you may want to explore this option for library equipment.

Policy considerations for the circulation of equipment include:

Δ Loans for school and home use.

Δ Manual vs. automated system.

Δ Maximum access vs. minimal access.

Δ Deposits, late fines, and payments for lost or damaged equipment.

Δ Amortization and replacement of equipment.

Δ Insurance coverage.

Training for Effective Use

When new equipment is received, find ways to ensure that it will be used effectively for curricular purposes. Sometimes salespeople provide on-site instruction; at other times, your district may provide special training for you and other staff members. Students, parent volunteers, and aides can all be trained to operate equipment and they can teach others, too.

△ Read the manuals and learn how to operate the equipment.

△ Ask experienced colleagues for help.

△ Hold workshops for interested staff as soon as you feel confident and urge attendees to teach other peers.

△ Attend specialized training at outside conferences, courses, and so on.

△ Train a special squad of equipment "pros."

△ Recruit older students, including those from high school or college.

△ Request services from district or vendors.

Inventory

All equipment should be inventoried on a regular basis, usually at the end of each school year, and quickly checked in September. If you have an automated system, all equipment can be bar-coded, entered on the database, and checked each year. If you don't have such a system, speak to your administrators about installing a system for library materials, textbooks, and equipment inventory. An inventory should note that equipment is in good working order. Borrowers should examine equipment when received and returned, noting problems, damage, and missing parts.

Issues involving the inventory of equipment include:

△ Frequency (by type of equipment).

△ Full inventory vs. partial inventory spread over time.

△ Manual vs. automated system (bar coding for an automated system).

△ Method of accounting for each item against master records.

△ Method of inventory when equipment is still in circulation.

△ Dealing with discrepancies between master records and actual presence of equipment.

△ Replacement policy.

Repairs and Servicing

Simple repairs and adjustments can be made on-site if you are handy or if you have other staff members, older students, or volunteers with practical skills. A basic tool kit is helpful: various screw drivers, a small hammer, machine oil, tweezers, cotton gloves, and cleaning supplies to dust and wash lenses. Extra electrical cords, adapters, batteries, and bulbs should always be available.

If machines are under warranty or service contracts, contact the vendor for repair and servicing instructions. Machines need to be examined regularly and repaired promptly. In some districts there may be a central facility for repairs. Make sure that you know what services are available to you.

Issues involving repairs and servicing include:

Δ Tracking of service contracts and warranties.

Δ Tracking of frequency of repairs to individual items.

Δ Information, tools, and supplies for simple repairs.

Δ First echelon maintenance and repair system: who is responsible?

Δ Second echelon maintenance and repair procedures: district or outside services?

Δ Replacement cycles (budget implications).

Discarding

Equipment should be checked regularly. If items no longer work and repairs are too expensive to consider, the item should be removed from the school's inventory. If parts can be salvaged for future use, save them. Follow your school or district procedures for discarding equipment. If your storage shelves are packed with equipment that is obsolete, discard these items. Ask your colleagues if they want an 8mm film-loop projector or a 45 rpm phonograph. You may find the person with a storehouse of film loops or old recordings who would find a use for them. Check the school policy to determine if you can sell obsolete equipment or give it away.

Give your administrator an accurate picture of the existing equipment available in the building and then submit a realistic wish list, perhaps drawn up by the advisory committee. That should give the school a good start on the road to the future.

Issues to consider when deselecting materials:

Δ Criteria for discarding equipment.

Δ Use of component parts.

Δ Dispose, give away, or sell.

Δ Policy regarding replacement, upgrade, or purchase of new equipment.

Providing Opportunities for Teacher and Student Productions

As emphasized in *Information Power,* students and staff should have the opportunity to use resources and create their own information in many formats. Students and staff may want to create video productions; slide and cassette presentations; multimedia programs utilizing text, graphics, and videos on the computer; and telecommunications projects. All of these programs have implications for the use of space, time, resources, equipment, and supplies. Keep up with these rapidly changing fields through professional literature, but on a practical level, think about how to integrate these activities with the rest of your busy schedule. Adult volunteers or squad members who can help individuals and small groups are useful. Perhaps you can attract students from the high school or a local college who have some expertise or strong interest. When planning for productions you need to think about:

Δ Necessary equipment.

Δ Necessary supplies.

△ Space considerations.

△ Scheduling considerations.

△ Developing a squad to assist with various types of audiovisual and technological productions.

Some basic concerns that you face in running your library media center are the physical arrangement and operation of the facility, the delineation of tasks and responsibilities for staff members including parent and student volunteers, and the introduction of new technology. In-depth discussions of each of these important topics can be found in chapter 7, "The Facility," chapter 10, "Online Public Access Catalog and Circulation System," chapter 9, "Technology," and chapter 12, "Support Staff: Filling the Need."

Bibliography

Callison, Daniel, and Jacqueline Morris. *Case Studies in Managing School Library Media Centers.* Phoenix, AZ: Oryx Press, 1989.

Craver, Kathleen W. *School Library Media Centers in the 21st Century.* Greenwood Guides in School Librarianship. Westport, CT: Greenwood Press, 1994.

Farmer, Lesley J. *When Your Library Budget Is Almost Zero.* Englewood, CO: Libraries Unlimited, 1993.

Henri, James, Edward R. Monkhouse, and Claire Louise Williams. *Managing the School Library Resource Center: A Selection of Case Studies.* Metuchen, NJ: Scarecrow Press, 1991.

Loertscher, David V. *Taxonomies of the School Library Media Program.* Englewood, CO: Libraries Unlimited, 1988.

Morris, Betty J., with John T. Gillespie and Diana L. Spirt. *Administering the School Library Media Program.* 3d ed. New Providence, NJ: Bowker, 1992.

Stein, Barbara L., and Risa W. Brown. *Running a School Library Media Center: A How-to-Do-It Manual for Librarians.* New York: Neal-Schuman, 1992.

Wallster, Dian. *Managing Time: A How-to-Do-It-Manual for Librarians.* New York: Neal-Schuman, 1993.

Weihs, Jean. *The Integrated Library: Encouraging Access to Multimedia Materials.* 2d ed. Phoenix, AZ: Oryx Press, 1991.

Woolls, Blanche. *Managing School Library Media Programs.* Englewood, CO: Libraries Unlimited, 1988.

Chapter 9 — Technology

Fig. 9.1. Joyful Exploration Through Technology.

Introduction

Welcome to the new information age! These are exhilarating and anxious times. Your library is taking on new functions and you are taking on new responsibilities. Coping with the explosion of information and new methods of accessing it, the proliferation of formats, the development of expensive and technically sophisticated equipment, and the demands for training by staff and students require a team that will create a long-range plan.

A team including administrators, classroom teachers, subject specialists, librarians, parents, students, and community partners is necessary to explore resources and determine how the school will meet the challenge of this information revolution. Some decisions will reach beyond the school to the district, state, or federal level. Some of the issues include:

Δ What skills and strategies do users need to participate effectively in the new age of information?

Δ Who will teach new skills and strategies? Where? How? When?

Δ Who will teach the librarians, teachers, and others?

Δ How will you finance new infrastructure, hardware, software, technical support, and training?

Δ What will you purchase?

Δ How can you best manage scarce resources? What are the priorities for using equipment, space, time, leased services, and training dollars?

Δ How will you keep up with new developments in technology?

In this new information age, the library may no longer serve as a central location, housing all hardware, software, and resources within its walls. Instead, equipment and access to information may be scattered throughout the building and beyond the school itself. The library media specialist has important functions as part of this information web: linking and connecting resources throughout the school, creating a communications center, serving as a doorway to long-distance resources, and teaching the school community how to provide physical and intellectual access to information.

The Changing Library Media Center

In the past, librarians taught students how information was organized in most libraries (the Dewey Decimal system, the card catalog) and in standard tools (the almanac, atlas, dictionary, encyclopedia). The library arrangement has changed little in the past 100 years. Certainly some sections have expanded and others have become less prominent, but for the most part, Melvil Dewey himself could have come into a school library 10 years ago, browsed the shelves, and located a book of interest with little assistance.

Resources in new formats, such as films, media kits, and even realia, were often catalogued and shelved "like books." Much like the grocery store shopper, the reader was advised, "What you see is what we have." The card catalog provided some additional access with "see" and "see also" references, but many readers relied on browsing. It made sense to learn the common patterns and classifications because the user could transfer and apply the skills to almost any library in the world.

The concept of similar subjects, shelved together in one room for convenient visual browsing, also influenced how users selected, refined, and explored information. A user with a general idea or topic would go to a particular area of the room and "see what there was." Student researchers frequently "worked backward," first examining sources to see what answers could be found, and then developing their questions and hypotheses. Often teacher-generated topics and questions were no better, because students were only asked things to which there were answers. This "backward research" taught children how to browse, but little about research. It resulted in research papers that were merely plagiarized, regurgitated facts and opinions. The content was frequently forgettable, and the agonizing process did not generalize into skills or strategies students could use in answering real-life information questions. Students frequently came to the conclusion that research was a school-based exercise in which you found questions to fit answers you already had. It was not a process most people needed or used in everyday life.

Mr. Dewey might have a more difficult time walking into your library today. Lots of information is not in the card catalog. Indeed, you might not even have a card catalog. It is unlikely everything is shelved "like a book." Some information is locked in CD-ROMs or computer software. It may require specialized machinery, protocols, and training to operate. Some information sources may be housed elsewhere in the school: the computer lab, production center, or office. There is information that is not even in the building, but accessed through e-mail and the Internet. The familiar library organization patterns and classifications are less useful and less transferable in the library for the twenty-first century. Instead, librarians need to teach students and teachers skills and strategies for:

△ Finding information in a variety of formats from local and long-distance locations.

△ Developing independent use of new information tools and technologies.

△ Focusing, narrowing, and defining information needs.

△ Analyzing and evaluating information gathered.

△ Interpreting information from a variety of formats.

△ Creating new products in a variety of formats.

△ Drawing conclusions and solving real problems with information gathered.

△ Communicating and sharing what they have learned.

Technology and Its Implications for Teaching the Research Process

At the start of the inquiry or research process, you need to help children understand the importance of thinking about their information needs to develop questions they would like to answer, identify keywords, and evaluate possible sources and formats of information. Activities that stimulate visual literacy; help students interpret maps, graphs, and diagrams; and give opportunities to use models and simulations are essential. It is also important that children learn about the strengths and limitations of different formats. Examining the same data in a variety of formats and representations is useful for developing competencies.

Student researchers in the past received guidance in focusing or narrowing topics, developing keywords, and selecting the most appropriate format for the content, but their choices of references were fewer. They were frequently limited to materials at hand or to those from the local public library. Where interlibrary loan was available, students were limited by the time frame of the assignment and frequently had no way of knowing what other sources existed. The problem was usually too little information.

It is not information scarcity but information overload that is now the rule. Any fourth-grader with access to a CD-ROM encyclopedia can print out 79 pages at a keystroke. A sixth-grader with access to the Internet can inadvertently download enough data to cause the system to crash or run up an exorbitant online phone bill. It is essential that you teach children how to narrow topics, focus their research, and select precise and carefully chosen keywords before they start using powerful technologies. Fuzzy thinking and poor planning frequently result in wasteful time-consuming searches that may produce no information if an improper term is selected, or reams of useless information if the topic is too broadly or poorly defined.

Using the Catalog

An automated catalog can be a useful tool for teaching students the search strategies they will need throughout their lives. The librarian can help children move along the learning progression to overcome situations in which their initial query does not have positive results. Researcher Paul Solomon in "Children,

Technology, and Instruction: A Case Study of Elementary School Children Using an Online Public Access Catalog (OPAC)" notes that both elementary school children and high school students seem to have the same problems with online and CD-ROM databases, suggesting that there may be generic approaches to the problems students face in using electronic information resources. He suggests a pattern of remediation and strategy instruction that can be used to help children succeed, noting: "Ultimately, the study OPAC—when coupled with the rich instructional strategy of integrating reading and writing with children's questions and interests—served as a vehicle for helping children find information while helping them build their information-seeking skills." (Solomon, 49)

Providing children with early exposure to OPACs and a variety of research opportunities in the elementary school can prepare them for more sophisticated data searches later in life. Practice with developing keywords, using Boolean logic, and broadening and narrowing topics can all be applied to other tools and other searches. More information on automated catalogs and circulation systems is found in chapter 10.

Using Diverse Formats

Print reference tools are generally similar in arrangement, content, and format. A reader familiar with the *World Book Encyclopedia* could, with little additional help, use *Compton's* or even a more specialized tool, such as the *Encyclopedia of Education*. Many of the new tools do not follow a standard pattern. Some are not arranged alphabetically. Others require you to browse a timeline or locate visual images, sound clips, videos, and text in separate places. Some permit you to use a variety of search strategies such as truncation, wild cards, or Boolean logic. Many programs have special icons, shortcuts, or special features.

For the student and for the librarian, nonstandard access and arrangement means that familiarity with one tool will not necessarily transfer to other tools. Students and teachers need time working with programs to practice and develop skills. Helping busy students get sufficient access and time to use machinery in limited supply will challenge your scheduling abilities. You will have to help set priorities for students and teachers.

Verifying Information

In the past, there was a fair degree of standardization in information sources. Major tools were produced by a few companies with a reputation for scholarship and authority (Wilson, Bowker, World Book, for example). Companies often had subject specialists who were experts in their field. Knowing the publisher's reputation, the reader was assured of the reliability of the information obtained from the source. There was less need to verify facts and ideas.

Today, information is coming from many sources. Almost anyone could be producing the information you are viewing on the Internet, and producers may be taking the data, opinions, audio, and images from various sources. As a selector of information, you are increasingly forced to purchase materials in new formats without preview, often before professional reviews are published and with little documentation. Even when materials are available for preview or have been formally reviewed, what do you look for? The average CD-ROM disc can hold 325,000 pages of text. The average videodisc holds 54,000 still frames. If, as an information expert, you have difficulty evaluating the resources at hand, imagine how much more confusing it is for your students and teachers!

Because it is so easy to grab and alter information using the new technologies, it is much harder to determine the original source of information. How reliable is the information, what is the bias of the producer, how current is it, who gathered it and under what conditions, what has been added or omitted in this presentation? Assessing the quality of information gathered becomes a thought-provoking and difficult task.

The library media specialist needs to help children interpret and evaluate both information packages and raw data. Programs that help students repurpose and package information are valuable for helping children analyze the process and think critically about the choices publishers make in developing information packages. Oral discussions, modeling, and evaluating sessions need to stress critical thinking about content, format, authority, and packaging of information. When the authority is not clear, students and teachers need help in locating experts who can clarify and verify the data and ideas. Students need to become critical readers, listeners, and viewers.

Using Real Data

Students are charged with the task of learning how to repurpose information, analyze, and apply it to real problems. To do so, they need access to real data and they need mentors who can help them structure their search. The mentor is not necessarily the librarian. Your task may be to locate an appropriate collaborator: an older student, a classroom teacher, a subject specialist in the school, or an expert in the community or online. If your library is online with the Internet, you may assist with locating the appropriate "gopher," help download data, or dialogue with students to help them clarify their information needs. To learn more about projects that link students, schools, the community, and experts, you may wish to explore the Internet World Wide Web pages including:

△ CoVis Project (Learning Through Collaborative Visualization), which links scientists and students in joint projects gathering and analyzing data and solving problems.

△ Geometry Forum, which puts students in direct contact with scientists and experts to get help in answering questions.

△ TERM project—students working with scientists to gather data about the environment.

Independent Learning with New Technologies

Most of the exploration and learning with new technologies is happening outside the periods of formal instruction. Students use new tools in small special interest groups and independently. Wherever computers and other specialized technologies are found, they are in heavy demand. If there are three or four computers in the library, there is usually a line of students using or waiting to use them. These students frequently watch the users and offer advice or ask questions. "If you use that icon, you can speed it up." "You've got to mark the block, or it will print out all that stuff you don't want." "I can load it for you; let me." "Man, it's showing 200 matches. You had better narrow your terms or you'll never get through all those." "You can't do that on this machine." "Oh-oh, you killed off another settler; I told you not to try to rest longer."

Students vie to be on the media squad, the video or technology team, and to help and mentor teachers and peers. Many schools have "clubs" or other special interest groups. The Chess Club, Video Writers Club, the Oregon Trail Adventurers, the Carmen Sandiego Fan Club, Radio Show Announcers, Mystery Writers, LEGO-LOGO Club, Spider Animators, Happy Hypers, Internet Surfers, Dinosaur Adventurers, KidCad Creators, Cross-Word Puzzlers, and others are found wherever there is access to resources.

Students with a strong interest in technology develop expertise quickly. Give them opportunities to demonstrate what they have discovered and to teach others. They can be an important resource for helping students and teachers learn about hardware and software. No one learns the shortcuts better than a student who is seriously interested, highly motivated, and experienced with using a particular program. Student users can also help load new programs, manage files, troubleshoot software glitches, and help maintain equipment. Often they are technically literate enough to use manuals and technical articles, and assist with technical troubleshooting calls.

Children also need time to work independently with the hardware and software. Much of the important learning requires time to explore, experiment, and tinker with the equipment and programs. Until and unless school budgets improve dramatically, or equipment and software become much cheaper and available to all children, finding ways to share inadequate resources will remain one of your biggest challenges.

Ethical Issues

Once upon a time there was a fairly clear understanding of copyright and fair use, as well as several well recognized standards for documentation of sources. Most people understood what was meant by ownership and private property. The new technologies blur many of these areas. Some computer programs, laser discs, and CD-ROMs permit you to alter or interact with the content: to hear and print sections; to repurpose by adding or altering text, visuals, video, or sound clips; or by developing Hyper-Card stacks. You can have your picture taken shaking hands with the president via computer imaging, scan a color photo of a painting by Matisse and use it as part of a greeting card you are making, add a Beatles song as a backdrop for your slide show, dub a voice track so your friend is talking with his senator, or download a copyrighted computer program from the Internet. Because it is so easy to capture, copy, and alter copyrighted information, the lines of ownership do not seem so clear. You must be clear about the new copyright laws as they apply to information in many formats, and you need to help students and teachers thoroughly understand the rights of ownership and copyright.

In the same way, you need to help students understand and respect the ethics and laws of privacy. Some young computer users view data security systems as a challenge to be overcome. Unauthorized use of passwords; viewing, altering, or manipulating other people's data without permission; introducing viruses; booby-trapping files; breaching firewalls; and causing systems to crash or freeze are all unacceptable and unethical behaviors. In some cases, they may even be illegal behaviors. Young users need to learn early in their school careers about the responsibilities that come with using sophisticated and powerful technologies.

Censorship may be of increased concern as you help students and teachers access the new technologies. Once the world of information is open to students, they have access to virtually anything anywhere in the world, including text, images, and ideas that parents or teachers may find inappropriate or unacceptable. How can you guarantee that a student will not find an objectionable image or idea among the 350,000 pages on a CD-ROM? How can you be sure that they will not access an inappropriate bulletin board on the Internet?

Some commercial services like America Online are offering schools limited access to the Internet, maintaining that they will screen out undesirable bulletin boards, chatlines, and locations. However, a recent court ruling held that providers that limit or supervise the access to the Internet assume responsibility for the content that users get online. The court ruled that services that do not monitor access have no responsibility for the content users obtain. They cannot be charged with libel, or with causing harm through providing false or dangerous information.

At present, the court's ruling means America Online and others can be held responsible for any harmful or wrong information users receive through their services. It is unlikely they will continue to monitor access if this liability is upheld on appeal.

The Telecommunications Reform Act of 1995 also has tremendous implications for access to information and censorship on the Internet. Part of the Communications Decency Act seeks to restrict indecent speech on the Internet and holds Internet service providers liable for the messages of their subscribers. Other sections provide fines or jail terms for providers who allow minors subscribing to their services to download lewd or obscene materials. Within a week of passage, the act was being challenged in the courts. The challenges and the debates will undoubtedly continue.

You can best prepare students by developing their critical-thinking skills and emphasizing personal responsibility for their actions. You can help parents understand the importance of free speech and the free flow of information in a democratic society. Look to your local, state, and national professional associations for guidance and support.

The Technologies

The Telephone

The telephone is *not* a new technology, but many school libraries still don't have one! And having one phone line is no longer enough. The telephone has become essential for reaching resources outside the physical library: experts, technical support, data, documents, and information are all available via tele-communications. Speakerphones are needed for teleconferencing with experts and authors. Multi-user phone lines and phone lines that can send and receive analog and digital data at faster baud rates are increasingly important as students and teachers require long-distance resources. Phones need to be equipped with high-speed fax/modems. The Internet beckons and the bottleneck is often the single phone line. Schools and districts must explore the options of more lines, larger lines, leased lines, and open lines.

Fig. 9.2. Searching for Information.

The Computer

Since the first Victor 20 or Commodore 64, with its awesome 64K of memory, arrived in the school set up for demonstration purposes in an office or computer lab, computers have been part of the educational scene. But because computers today are so much more powerful and versatile, there is little resemblance to the older machines. Many older computer models are junked, but others are kept although they are obsolete and unrepairable. Some are upgraded to approximate newer machines and every year, budgets permitting, a shiny new model or two is added to the collection. Such is the acceleration of progress that a six-month-old computer is being nudged aside by a still newer model. In two years, that state-of-the-art beauty will be obsolete. Rapidly changing technology means that most schools will continue to have four or five different computer models. Each may require different software, peripherals, protocols, cables, operating manuals, and parts.

You and your advisory committee need to create and maintain an inventory of equipment and software and help to develop a plan for current usage and future purchases. In most cases, districtwide planning is advisable.

The advisory committee needs to decide:

△ What old models should be junked or used for parts.

△ What aging machines should be modified or used for limited tasks.

△ What can and should be upgraded.

△ Where the newest high-powered models will be placed.

Old Apple IIe computers might be sent home with students on extended loan. They are fine for learning keyboarding skills, and there are games and applications that are old but still useful. Or some Apple IIe's might be moved to the classroom to help increase keyboarding skills, to facilitate drill and practice, or to provide access to a simple word processing program for student writing. They can be part of regular classroom learning if teachers are given guides like Dublin's *Integrating Computers in Your Classroom: Elementary Education* (1994) that provide innovative ways to use older computers in the classroom. An old TRS80, with black-and-white monitor and limited processing speed and memory, can be used in the library to send and receive e-mail. Online catalogs or other print databases like *Primary Search* can run on older Apples.

CD-ROMs

Increasingly affordable and popular, more than 10.3 million CD-ROM drives were in use in 1993. *PC Magazine* estimates sales may top 25 million drives in 1995 and may approach 60 million in 1996. CD-ROM titles are proliferating at an astounding rate. According to Paul Nicholls in an article in *Computers in Libraries* (pp. 56–60), the midyear 1995 update to TFPL Publishing's *CD-ROM Directory* lists some 10,000 CD-ROM titles produced by more than 8,000 companies. The editor expects to include 12,500 titles in the 1996 edition. They have become standard equipment on many school and home computers. CD-ROMs of many types are frequently offered as low-cost "bundles" when multimedia computers are purchased. Consequently, many young students and their families now routinely use CD-ROMs at home for school assignments and recreational activities.

Double speed CD-ROM drives, once the norm, are giving way to quad speed drives (4X), and the first 6X and 8X drives are coming on the market. In addition, companies are exploring two new technologies for digital video discs (DVD), a double-sided disc, and another that boosts CD-ROM capacity from 680MB to 10 to 15 times as much. These new technologies will require new disc drives. Major industry players finally agreed on a single format high-density disc format in August of 1995, and the first commercial high-density drives and discs are expected on the market in late 1996. With the number of CD-ROM drives in use, it is anticipated that double-speed CD-ROM discs will continue to be released well into the year 2000. A single CD-ROM disc holds up to 325,000 pages of text and offers full color, still pictures and videos, animation, music and speech, as well as text; that's a lot of information in a small, reasonably priced package.

To display information on a CD-ROM, you must have a CD-ROM player connected to a computer, a compatible sound card with speakers, a VGA or Super VGA color monitor, and a CD-ROM disc compatible with your computer operating system. Many CD-ROMs are available in Macintosh or PC (MS-DOS or Windows) format. Increasingly, they are cross-platform and can be installed on either system. Many new CD-ROMs require Pentium CPUs and lots of RAM. A careful reading of all disc specifications is essential. Unfortunately, complete specifications are hidden under shrink-wrap seals that need to be opened to be read.

Directions for installation are provided with each CD-ROM disc. Macintosh CD-ROMs are built to a single standard and they usually install without difficulty. Loading a CD-ROM on a PC computer is often more complicated because there is no single standard. An unsuspecting installer may inadvertently disable the rest of the system while trying to install a new CD-ROM. The user is advised to read the specifications carefully and install with caution. Once installed, the user need only load the CD-ROM disc in the caddy or drive and click the icon to open. Because the CD-ROMs are "Read Only" and cannot be written to or altered by the user, they are relatively impervious to damage while in operation. However, technological advances are rapidly making the name CD-ROM obsolete. The industry now produces hardware and software so that computer users can create their own CD-ROMs. According to *PC World* magazine (Quain, 107), only 18 months ago the hardware and software system cost $6,000 and individual discs cost $30 to produce. Now, half a dozen systems are available for $1,000 or less, and individual discs cost $6. It is anticipated that in the next year hardware prices will drop to less than $600 and will become more user friendly.

CD-erasables are in the works, too. In September 1995, 10 major manufacturers announced that they had reached agreement on standards and specifications for an erasable CD-ROM. The new CD-ROM drives will be capable of reading all existing CD-ROM formats; writing and reading recordable CD-Recordable media; and reading, writing, and overwriting CD-ROM erasable discs. The first commercial models are expected to become widely available in 1997.

Most drives hold a single CD-ROM, which means a user who wishes to access more than one disc must unload and load each disc he or she uses. This can be time consuming and increase the chance of damaging the disc. CD-ROM towers that have from four to 10 disc drives are an alternative. CD-ROM players networked on a LAN can provide access to more than one user at a time, or several CD-ROM drives can be daisy-chained to a single Macintosh or PC computer with a SCSI port. With either arrangement, the user can switch from one disc to another without removing the disc from the drive. Some CD-ROMs are available for networks. These are generally more expensive than the single-user version, but less expensive than buying multiple copies. (See chapter 10, "Online Public Access Catalog and Circulation System.")

Many CD-ROMs allow the user to search through an alphabetical list by topic, by keyword, by using the Boolean connectors (and, or, not), or by using truncation or wild cards. Truncation makes it possible to locate keywords with the same root but alternative endings. For example using pollut? would allow you to locate information on pollution, polluters, pollutants, and so forth. Wild cards provide alternate spellings within the word you are searching; for example, wom?n would pull up references to woman and women.

CD-ROM discs are usually not available for preview. However, review guides provide ratings and information and often a sample CD-ROM disc with selections from the programs reviewed. Most CD-ROMs are returnable if they do not install or run properly on your system. Industry experts estimated about 30 percent of all CD-ROMs purchased during the 1995 Christmas season were returned by the purchasers. Some failures are due to faulty or damaged CD-ROM discs, but others are due to incompatibilities in the disc and computer setup requirements. It is essential that you install and test CD-ROMs as soon as they are purchased so that you can return them if necessary. Save all packaging and receipts too.

Popular CD-ROMs include:

Encyclopedias. These are updated annually, though it is not always clear how many articles have been revised. All have color photos and drawings, sound and video clips, text, and multiple indexing. Children can use the notebook function to write, save, and print notes on what they are reading. They can also mark and print out sections of texts and some of the graphics found in the computer. Though the major encyclopedias are based on existing text versions and have a fifth- or sixth-grade reading level, information access is enhanced with bold type, sound selections, outlines, and hypertext. Children like using multimedia encyclopedias and enjoy browsing even when they have no research topic in mind.

Dictionaries. Some can pronounce words, provide definitions, and include illustrations. A sign language dictionary is available that provides more than 2,000 stop-action video clips of common signs, as well as drawings, audio, and written text.

Periodical Databases and Indexes. Periodical databases provide citations, annotations, and some full-text illustrated articles from magazines and newspapers. Local and regional magazine holdings can sometimes be added to the database. Bibliographic citations can be examined and marked and useful citations and full articles can be printed out.

Publishing and Presentation Tools. These combine several easy-to-use tools to let students put together their own multimedia creations. They often include word processing, painting programs for creating illustrations or enhancing clip art or photos, and the video capability to incorporate photos, clip art, soundtracks, and Quicktime clips in multimedia presentations.

Subject Resources. Many subjects are represented on CD-ROM. Some are particularly compelling. They can use virtual reality techniques to display spectacular views of the solar system; introduce students to classical music through text, sound, and pictures; and even provide a walking tour of London's National Gallery.

Simulations. These present interactive games that combine science, history, and geography.

Interactive Storybooks. These provide animated interactive stories that may be read aloud, manipulated, and listened to, often in several languages.

Benefits of CD-ROMs	Drawbacks of CD-ROMs
A large number of appealing discs are available at moderate cost. For the most part, discs are durable, easy to install, and use. Disc players are inexpensive and portable. Discs provide fast access to an enormous amount of data.	Only one user can access a disc at a time. Game applications can tie up a computer for long periods of time. Discs may lack adequate documentation. Video windows are small, and some images are fuzzy.

Fig. 9.3. Benefits and Drawbacks of CD-ROM Discs.

Interactive Videodiscs

Videodiscs (sometimes referred to as laser discs), store video information on a hard, plastic disc. The discs are read by a laser beam, enabling the user to search any segment and play it at a slow or fast speed. Videodiscs give almost instant access to any segment of the disc. Videodisc programs offer an array of video clips, still frames, sound, maps, text, and graphics that teachers and students can use to create lessons and multimedia presentations. They come in two formats:

△ CAV (constant angular velocity), which has the capacity for 30 minutes on a side or 54,000 individual frames, and permits the user to freeze on any frame or move forward or backward a frame at a time. Each frame has a unique number so that you can move directly to the point of interest.

△ CLV (constant linear velocity), which can hold up to 60 minutes on a side but cannot hold a single frame in stop action. This format is used for motion pictures and other materials, which are usually shown in a linear manner. It has embedded time codes to get the user to points of interest.

Videodiscs come in three levels of interactivity:

Level 1 The videodisc player is used without a computer. The control panel permits the user to jump from section to section, stopping as desired, much like the remote of a VCR player. The player can be programmed to play a sequence of segments. The videodisc can also be programmed by using a laser wand bar-code reader. The bar code for desired segments is scanned with the wand, much as a grocery scanner marks purchases.

Level 2   The videodisc player is not connected to a computer but has its own computer program. The disc provides images and questions for the user. The videodisc player computer jumps to the next segment depending on the user's responses.

Level 3   The videodisc player is attached to a computer that controls the player through a software program. The user can decide what segments to use in which order and can add text and graphics to create a repurposed multimedia presentation. In most cases, two separate monitors are needed because the computer monitor cannot be used to both program and display. Various peripherals can be attached to the computer, such as a keyboard, mouse, or touch pad. Software must be purchased that is specific to the computer platform being used.

Benefits of Videodiscs	Drawbacks of Videodiscs
Provide sharp images generally recorded at 350 lines of resolution. (Most videotapes are recorded at only 200-250 lines). Make it possible to freeze frames, to program which frames to go to, and permit repurposing and saving the program for future presentations. Durable and can be played again and again without loss of quality.	There is a limited amount of material available on laser discs and the number of producers seems to be shrinking. Hardware is expensive to purchase and difficult to get repaired. Discs are expensive when compared with the cost of CD-ROMs. Large-screen monitors are expensive and barely portable. When connected to a computer, a great deal of hardware is involved for a single presentation.

Fig. 9.4. Benefits and Drawbacks of Videodiscs.

Digital Images and Video

Digital and scanning equipment make it possible for you to capture text, images, and video sequences and incorporate them into a computer program. You may use a handheld or flatbed scanner, a video or still camera, or a videodisc, or a videotape recorder. Graphic scanners used with a computer will convert printed materials to a digital image on the computer. You may transfer existing documents or images into the computer. Then you may alter and manipulate the graphics and text, print them out, or send them online through a fax/modem to another computer. Less expensive scanners have fewer dots per inch (pixels), scan in black and gray, are often slow, and may scan a limited field (4" instead of an 8" x 11" page). More expensive scanners usually provide more pixels per inch, give greater clarity, are quicker, and scan in full color.

Benefits of Graphic Scanners	Drawbacks of Graphic Scanners
Scanners get text into the computer without typing and provide a way to transport text using a fax/modem rather than a fax machine. They allow text and images to be manipulated and repurposed. They allow you to capture increasingly complex graphics difficult to create with computer programs.	Quality and accuracy of scanned text and images are not always adequate. Scanners require large amounts of random access memory (RAM) to capture images and large amounts of storage space to save the images. Top of the line scanners are expensive. Scanning is slow. Users need to be aware of copyright laws when scanning materials.

Fig. 9.5. Benefits and Drawbacks of Graphic Scanners.

Video Cameras

The home or school camera usually uses a 1/2" videocassette tape. Television studios and professionals use cameras with a 3/4" videocassette tape that provide the degree of resolution in lines per screen necessary for broadcasting on television. The 3/4" videotapes must be converted to 1/2" if the cassette is to be played on the standard home VCR player. Camera features can include automatic focusing, a zoom lens, automatic adjustments for low light, motion stabilizers, and built-in microphones, as well as external ports for sound. They are versatile and may be used with portable battery packs or standard electric outlets. Videocassette tapes are inexpensive and reusable. They are played without any processing through the familiar VCR. Good quality tapes are clear and colorful with excellent sound quality, but even the best have slight imperfections in recording that appear as "snow" or "lines" in the tape. The quality of the tape deteriorates as succeeding copies of the tape are made and as the tapes are replayed.

In editing a video, you can cut and paste segments; add text; intersperse interviews, still photos, or movie or video segments; and add music or additional sound. Quality frame-by-frame editing is time consuming and requires expensive equipment.

Video editing computer software is increasingly available for a moderate to high cost. It varies in ease of use, speed, and the quality of the finished product. The computer programs provide backgrounds, screens to produce and add text and credits, dissolves and fades between cuts, and other special features.

"Quick and dirty" editing can be done by using the camera and one VCR, or two connected VCRs. The editor plays the tape marking those coordinates he wishes to keep. The second player-recorder is turned on and off at those coordinates, creating a new master tape A sound track may be added by rerecording the master while attaching the external sound port to the VCR player-recorder of the new tape being made. The cuts and fades and other transitions in this method are often abrupt and choppy, but the method is quick and inexpensive.

Benefits of Video Cameras	Drawbacks of Video Cameras
Cameras are easy to use, moderately expensive, and portable. Video gives immediate feedback about learning to students and teachers. Videos can be used to produce creative work, document research, repurpose information, and develop presentations. Videotape recorders and players are inexpensive, portable, and familiar. Videos can be produced, viewed, stored, and edited with relative ease.	Cameras are still somewhat delicate and expensive to repair and maintain. Videotapes do not retain their quality with reuse, copying, and editing.

Fig. 9.6. Benefits and Drawbacks of Video Cameras.

Digital Video

Analog video images and still images may be transported into a computer file using digital technology. Once digitized, the images can be easily manipulated. The user can change the sequence, facilitate transitions, and even "morph" the images. (Remember the ad for one product that shows a woman "morphing" or changing into a cat in succeeding frames.) While "morphing" can be used just for fun, it can also be a useful and dramatic teaching tool for showing change over time.

In digital format, video images do not lose quality when they are replayed or edited. However, digitizing the images requires enormous storage space. One frame from an analog video can take up to three-fourths of a megabyte of memory to store if uncompressed. Video grabbing requires a digitizing card and software to turn the analog signal into digital bits. The process can be tedious and time consuming. Some of the factors that influence the amount of storage space required include: the number of colors used, the size of the video window, the frame rate, and compression technique.

QuickTime Movies and Video for Windows

QuickTime (for the Macintosh) and Video for Windows (for computers using Microsoft Windows) use techniques that compress video and store digital video on the computer drive. These processes require a digitizing board as well as high speed processors with considerable RAM and storage space. The video is automatically compressed on diskette when it is captured and decompressed when it is played back. Clips from TV, commercial videos, and locally produced videos can be pasted into a variety of computer applications including word processing, spreadsheets, and hypermedia programs. The process is managed through software such as *Adobe Premier* (Macintosh) or *Adobe Premier for Windows* (PC). While hardware and software are becoming more affordable, they are still somewhat difficult and time consuming to use. Care must be taken in deciding what student and teacher products and presentations warrant the expenditure of time, technical staff, hardware, and software. New large size, expanded storage diskettes may make existing products obsolete. Inexpensive CD-ROM technology with "write-to" capabilities (now in development) will impact on this technique in the near future.

Benefits of QuickTime Movies and Video for Windows	Drawbacks of QuickTime Movies and Video for Windows
Video clips add excitement and different learning opportunities to multimedia presentations and curricula. No special additional equipment is needed to play back the presentations. The audio and video remain synchronized. Video clips can be manipulated as easily as text and graphics when repurposing.	The processes are still fairly sophisticated and time consuming. The product should justify the process. Pictures are small and somewhat blurry, and playback is somewhat choppy and limited to short segments. The process requires large amounts of RAM and large storage capacity.

Fig. 9.7. Benefits and Drawbacks of QuickTime Movies and Video for Windows.

Still Video Camera

Still video cameras are designed to take pictures that can be stored on the computer without photographic film. Most cameras like XAPShot (Canon) are analog and store images on diskettes. Images can be displayed on a television monitor or imported into a computer through a digitizing board. Many cameras include the board with the purchase of the camera. After the image has been saved on computer, it can be modified and manipulated with other computer software programs. Some schools are now using still video cameras to take photos for newsletters and multimedia projects. Cameras are slightly less expensive than other conventional video cameras.

QuickTake is a new camera produced by Apple Computer that is digital rather than analog. Images are not stored on diskette but are stored in the camera until it is downloaded directly into the modem port of the computer. Up to 32 standard resolution photos can be stored at a time. It is available in Windows and Macintosh versions.

Benefits of Still Video Cameras	Drawbacks of Still Video Cameras
Instant photos are quick and easy.	Cameras are expensive.
They add interest and immediacy to presentations and demonstrations.	Storing images takes up considerable hard drive space.
They provide documentation for learning.	
There is no film to buy, no processing costs.	
Images can be altered to meet educational needs.	
They can be printed out easily.	

Fig. 9.8. Benefits and Drawbacks of Still Video Cameras.

Creating Hypermedia

Teachers and students can create exciting interactive stacks (files) that are fun to use and serve as impressive demonstrations of learning. The process of developing a script, creating a logical sequence, researching, and deciding on the best content and format requires highly developed critical-thinking skills. Reflections on the intended audience and the purpose of the stack help the creator develop meta-cognitive skills. The well-designed stack provides opportunities for creative expression and demonstrates learning with a high degree of sophistication. However, because the process is time consuming, it is important that the content be worthy of the procedure.

Macintosh computers come with hypermedia capability installed. PC computers require add-on software like LinkWay Live! In Barron and Orwig's *New Technologies for Education: A Beginner's Guide* (2nd ed.), it states that most hypermedia development tools are based on the idea of a stack. In HyperStudio and HyperCard, a file is called a stack, and each computer screen is called a card. In Link-Way Live!, a file is called a folder and each computer screen is called a page. In either case, the screen contains fields, buttons, and graphics.

△ Fields are for text and serve as miniature word processing sites.

△ Buttons initiate actions, moving the user to another card (called branching), playing an audio file, or accessing a segment of a videodisc.

△ Graphics can be created with paint tools within the hypermedia program or imported from clip-art files or graphics programs. (Barron and Orwig, 137)

Most hypermedia programs have the "runtime" feature. This permits a user to run a stack even if the user does not own the program used to develop the stack. For example, if students create a stack on "garbage" and would like to load it on 20 computers or loan it to students in another school, they can do so without violating copyright laws if there is a runtime feature. However, they cannot legally make copies of the software they purchased to produce the stack for other users. In most cases, if you are creating stacks for educational purchases, you can distribute them with a "runtime" program without paying any additional fee. If you or your students are using a program to create stacks that you hope to sell, you need to have professional advice about copyright restrictions that apply.

Benefits of Hypermedia	Drawbacks of Hypermedia
The process of creating the media teaches and demonstrates effective information skills: gathering, evaluating, synthesizing, reformulating, and communicating. The process permits the learners to take charge of their own learning and encourages creativity. Hypermedia can help teachers and students create new information packages and learning tools for other users.	Scheduling sufficient time for interested users to create effective stacks may be difficult given existing resources. Poorly designed stacks are hyper-confusion. The old "garbage in, garbage out" maxim holds, even if the process is captivating. For group viewing, hypermedia stacks require expensive liquid crystal display (LCD) or large screen TVs. If stacks are played on a computer, only a few students at a time can use them.

Fig. 9.9. Benefits and Drawbacks of Hypermedia.

Local Area Networks

Local area networks (LANs) are a way of connecting and sharing existing computer resources to maximize speed, access, and efficiency while keeping costs down. LANs for PCs usually require a network card like Ethernet and a software program like *LANtastic* (Artisoft) or *Netware* (Novell). Macintosh computers and many Apple computers come with *AppleTalk* already installed.

In a typical system, several computers in the same room or, less commonly, in the same building are linked to a file server by cables. Running cables through walls, especially in older buildings, can be difficult and expensive. Wireless systems are in the development stage, but at present they are expensive and not very reliable. William Wright's article, "NII Watch Wireless Internet Access," in *Electronic Learning* reported that a coalition of educational leaders was asking the Federal Communication Commission to encourage the development of low-cost wireless data networks for classrooms to use to connect to the Internet. Also, Apple Computer is pushing to have the 2.4-gigahertz range exempt from licensing. This would permit small, short-distance wireless networking of computers sharing a room or a small building. Permission was granted. The race is on to see how quickly peripherals and programs can be developed. Wireless LANs would be especially useful for older school buildings where cabling through the walls is expensive and difficult.

At present, most LANs consist of cables connecting the workstations or computers and a file server that contains a large hard drive where files, programs, and data are stored. The file server can be connected to a dedicated power outlet with a surge protector, guaranteeing uninterrupted power flow. The file server also connects to a printer and other peripherals that can be accessed by any of the computers on the LAN. Each computer on the LAN calls up files as needed and more than one user can access the program at the same time, though usually not the same document. The network can share printers and CD-ROMs.

Instead of purchasing single-user programs and CD-ROMs, the LAN operator selects "network" or multiuser versions of the software or CD-ROM. Network versions are usually more expensive than single-user programs, but are generally less expensive than having to purchase multiple copies of the same program to be installed on separate computers. If the program is one that will be updated, it becomes easier to upgrade it on the file server rather than upgrading the program on each individual computer.

A library-based LAN might be used to link computers so that the library's automated catalog and circulation programs could be used from any of the computer workstations without having to load the data files on each computer's hard drive or diskettes. A LAN would be especially useful if several users need to share printers, scanners, or the same database. Similarly, computers could share a fax/modem and the phone line, although each could only be used by one person at a time. If the library has access to a T-1 line, more than one user could be online to the Internet at a time.

A LAN might connect the library network to computers available in the computer lab, offices, or classrooms, allowing students and teachers to access programs and files wherever computers are linked by cables. A student would begin taking notes on a CD-ROM encyclopedia in the library and then download his or her notes or data into the computer folder or file in the classroom. Similarly, a classroom teacher could access the library holdings by using the classroom computer to call up the library catalog.

In most libraries with fewer than six computers or a mix of computers, LANs may not be cost effective or especially efficient. The cost of wiring, Ethernet cards, and special software, as well as problems with technical support, may reduce the feasibility. However, in new schools or in those undergoing modernization, every effort should be made to put the cabling in place. Each local situation must be evaluated, but often a district or regional plan is desirable.

LANs are most useful with large numbers of computers that share software and files. In the past, individual computers were equipped with small hard drives or no hard drives, operated at slow speeds, and had only 2 or 4 MB of RAM. It made sense to try and purchase stripped-down workstations and link them to a network to take advantage of the central large hard drive and speed up the installation time for programs. With the expanding home market and the advances in technology, large, inexpensive hard drives are standard equipment on most machines, and there is little cost savings in getting a stripped-down workstation without its own hard drive. Many machines come with 16 MB of RAM, expandable to 64 MB. They have much faster operating systems, and CD-ROM players and fax/modems as standard equipment. All these factors reduce the advantages of the network. Networks also have some disadvantages that must be considered. Any system can go down; with network technology, if the file server is down, you are out of business. Every network requires some technical maintenance.

Benefits of a LAN	Drawbacks of a LAN
Computers share a large memory storage space and can share printers, files, and programs. Less time is spent loading programs or reinstalling programs if there are upgrades. Users can access data and programs from anywhere on the LAN. It reduces software piracy because software is centrally controlled. It also reduces the introduction of viruses because users do not load discs.	File servers go down, shutting down the entire system. LANs are expensive to install and require ongoing maintenance. It may not be cost effective to create a network for fewer than six computers. If a virus does get into the system, everybody gets it.

Fig. 9.10. Benefits and Drawbacks of a LAN.

Wide Area Networks

A wide area network (WAN) is a network for places and spaces too far apart for a LAN. WANs can link every room in the building, several schools, or a whole district. Telephone cables link each machine and site. When schools are connected, they use special high-speed, leased lines that allow for rapid transmission of data. It can cost several million dollars or more to link several schools with a WAN. Because the costs are so high, it usually requires state or federal grants to develop a WAN. In addition to the cost of installing lines, schools must pay leasing fees that may average $3,000-6,000 a month or more per line. The Telecommunications Reform Act of 1995 may provide new opportunities for schools.

Benefits of a WAN	Drawbacks of a WAN
Welcome to the electronic superhighway. Data, graphics, e-mail, the Internet—information and resources everywhere in the world are at your computer station. Many users can simultaneously access the data lines. No file is too big, too graphic, or too complex.	It is expensive to install. It is expensive to maintain. It requires ongoing maintenance.

Fig. 9.11. Benefits and Drawbacks of a WAN.

Telecommunications

Once you have a computer, a modem, and a telephone, you are no longer limited to the resources in your library or building. You already may have interlibrary loan, but this is incredible access to a whole new world of resources. Most telecommunications services provide:

△ Electronic mail, or e-mail: sending and receiving messages electronically.

△ File transfer: downloading and sending documents to a remote computer.

△ Remote access: searching long distance, connecting your computers to other systems, searching directories, reading files, leaving messages, and downloading data directly to your computer.

Join a local or state educational service or use a commercial provider. Some educational services have only limited access to the Internet or may provide text without graphics. This is a little like watching television without having the visual component. Some commercial services provide limited access to the Internet, monitoring and restricting what the user can access. Especially geared to the educational market, they may offer a menu of special programs of interest to children or teachers. For example, Scholastic Network, associated with America Online, provides online programs with dignitaries and authors. A recent calendar offered a chat with author R. L. Stine, and another featured an online interview with Rosa Parks. Children can type their questions to the personality and receive answers electronically. Both Prodigy and America Online (AOL) provide teacher guides and suggested lesson plans for using telecommunications.

There are national, regional, and local commercial services. Shop around for the service that meets your needs. Look for one with a local dial-up number to avoid long-distance charges.

Local service providers like PANIX in the New York metropolitan region have the advantage of a monthly flat fee with unlimited use. They provide full access to text and graphics. With so many providers available, it is essential that you investigate the services, costs, and limitations before purchasing a service.

The Internet

The Internet began in 1969 as ARPANET (Advanced Research Projects Agency Network), a communication link for government scientists working on Defense Department projects at universities around the country. In 1986, the National Science Foundation formed NSFNET, which replaced ARPANET. The rest is history! Today, more than two million people access the Internet every day. You can find almost anything on the Net, including: an online college library catalog, chat lines and bulletin boards for every topic under the sun, access to government data and legislation, full-text periodicals, curriculum units, a connection to NASA, weather data, online discussions with scientists and world newsmakers, interactive science projects, what's new in museums and art galleries around the world, and more.

World Wide Web

Once you are familiar with some of the resources of telecommunications, you may want fuller access, more time online, and the ability to use hypermedia interfaces. You will want access to the World Wide Web (WWW), which was developed to provide for hyperlinks within documents. With WWW you can click on words, pictures, or buttons in a document and jump to a related document. If you are reading a report on classroom use of LANs in science education, you can click on many of the sources in the bibliography and jump to the complete text of the article cited. Or if you are investigating a dinosaur exhibit in the Los Angeles Museum of Natural History, you might click on a button that takes you to a dinosaur exhibit in Glasgow, Scotland, or an interview with a paleontologist working in Tanzania.

Direct connections can be provided through a LAN with a web server and a special leased data line, such as a T-1 or ISDN line. The user becomes a node on the Net, connecting to other nodes. Both provide fast, multiple connections and a wide-band range. This means more than one computer user can access the service at a time, and it is possible to view and download even elaborate graphic portions of the Net. Unfortunately, both T-1 lines and ISDN lines are expensive, both to install and lease, and are not available everywhere.

You may also connect to the Net through standard telephone lines with a modem. At least a 28.8 baud modem is desirable. For graphical access, You must use a Serial Line Internet Protocol (SLIP) or a point to point protocol (PPP). You will also need a provider, for example a college or university partner, full-service commercial provider (AT&T, PIPELINE), or limited access provider (Compuserve, America Online). You will also need software. Much of it can be downloaded for free from the Internet or purchased on disc at a modest cost. You will need a TCP/IP stack (Transmission Control Protocol/Internet Protocol) if you are using an IBM/PC computer with windows. Macintosh computers typically use a proprietary software called MacTCP.

To make a successful connection to the Internet, your PC needs an application software like Netscape, a TCP/IP stack consisting of TCP/IP software, sockets software, and hardware driver software. Sockets software for PCs using Windows are usually called "Winsocks," short for Window Sockets. A typical Winsock which can be downloaded from the Internet is Trumpet. If you are using Windows 95, you will not need a Winsock; the specifications and routines have been built into the program. Connecting to the internet with Windows 95 is not yet "Plug and Play," but it is getting better. Macintosh computers use a socket called MacPPP which "plugs" your system into the host system.

Your provider will usually supply you with software and a script for making the Internet connection. Providers often supply telephone or online help as well. If possible have someone who has already connected to the Internet assist you. The process can be time consuming and frustrating. Just remember ten million Americans are using the Net. Everyone of them had to get connected. Some of them *must* live in your area (parents, teachers, teens). Surely you can find someone willing to help you!

What to Do on the Internet

E-mail. Students and teachers can connect to others around the world through e-mail. They can share letters and resources, exchange data, work together on simulations and common problems, share lesson plans and curricula, and communicate with experts.

Chat Online. Connect to long-distance experts and personalities around the world and ask and answer questions online.

Electronic Publishing. Send and receive stories online.

Basic Research. The Internet provides access not only to published resources, but also access to data from around the world.

Data and Analysis Tools. Students can access and use sophisticated tools to manipulate and display data in a visual format.

Simulations. Students participate in scientific field trips or "telepresences." Trips are accomplished through highly advanced robots that are capable of exploring the depths of oceanic vents or the inner molten reaches of volcanoes.

Original Research. Students work with scientists to gather new research data. The Global Lab Project at the Technical Education Resource Center links classrooms around the world with each other and experts to collect student data on acid rain for scientific use.

Create. Produce your own World Wide Web page.

For more information on where to go and what to do on the Internet, see the recommended titles in the bibliography. Because information changes almost hourly, you may also want to subscribe to periodicals that specialize in the Internet like *Classroom Connect* or *Internet World*.

Benefits of Telecommunications	Drawbacks of Telecommunications
Outstanding resources made available to teachers and students. Opportunities to participate in a global learning community. Opportunities to develop information skills for lifelong learning. Individualization of education giving the learner more control over learning.	Access is limited by the number of connection points. System equipment must be maintained. The enormous volume of traffic on the Internet can result in slowdown, breakdown, and frustration. So much is available, it is hard to know what to access. It is easy to become addicted; casual cruising is time consuming and not always productive.

Fig. 9.12. Benefits and Drawbacks of Telecommunications.

Teleconferencing

Three general types of teleconferencing are available:

Δ Audio teleconferencing—using standard phones and speakerphones.

Δ Audiographic teleconferencing—adding two-way image transmission to audio teleconferencing, by using a computer with a fax/modem, for example.

Δ Videoconferencing—combining two-way video with the audio. Still in the development stage, this is most expensive.

Audio teleconferencing is the least expensive and easiest. Any school library equipped with a speakerphone can arrange with outside speakers for an audio conference. Contact the speaker in advance to set up a day and time and advise the speaker about the student information needs. Have students develop questions that may be sent to the speaker in advance. Arrange to tape-record the interview and have students take notes. At the time of the interview, gather students in the library to ask their questions and hear the speaker's responses over the speakerphone. Audio calls can bring authors and outside experts into the classroom when needed, for very little cost. You may also wish to explore the conference call possibilities available from your local phone company.

Audiographic teleconferencing is moderately easy to accomplish. Using your computer, telecommunications software, phone line, and a fax/modem, you can send and receive documents, charts, and still pictures to others at a long-distance site. This technique can be useful for long-distance collaboration on writing projects, experiments, research, and the like. Documents zapped back and forth online can be jointly edited and published.

Videoconferencing is very expensive and still in the developmental stage. Video cameras at both sites send visual images between sites. At present, most systems require expensive optical cables linking sites. Some large companies are using videoconferencing to link their main and satellite offices around the world, and some universities are offering long-distance courses to other campuses using this method. Technology companies such as Creative Labs are experimenting with digital cameras and software such as ShareVision that can use standard phone lines for transmission of visual images, but as yet, the equipment is expensive and the images are marginally successful.

Other companies are exploring satellite, cable television, and microwave conferencing. At present, all are in their infancy. Pick up any newspaper or current periodical. The impossible is happening almost daily as cable networks, telephone companies, satellite access providers, and others vie for the new communications customers and stretch and expand existing technologies. An article in the *New York Times,* January 31, 1996 (Landler, D1), reported on a pilot project in Elmira, New York, in which Warner Cable has connected 200 cable customers to the Internet via TV cable. The lightning speed of coaxial cable was demonstrated in transmitting a black-and-white photo. Time required to transmit:

△ 1:33.75 minutes and seconds with a standard 28.8-baud modem and conventional copper phone wire.

△ 0:48.21 minutes and seconds with a high-capacity ISDN line.

△ 0:01.80 minutes and seconds with a T1 phone line.

△ 0:00.27 minutes and seconds with coaxial cable.

With a potential top range of speed of 25 million bits per second, the cable system can deliver data up to 800 times faster than phone companies. In many parts of the country, the needed coaxial cable is already in place. Schools may benefit in particular because many cable companies have a community access clause as part of their service contracts; in some locations, schools were wired for cable when neighborhoods were wired. Check to see if your school has been wired.

Public library systems such as in New York and Denver offer Internet access at their branches through a Wide Area Network; the state of Maryland is connecting home computer users via the Internet to all the library resources in the state. Other libraries are exploring wireless options. The State of Iowa Libraries On-line is using a portion of a $2.5 million U.S. Department of Education HEA-II-B grant to perfect a wireless LAN. Though still expensive and slower than some options, wireless LANs are a good solution for older buildings or hard-to-wire places. NASA head Daniel S. Goldin reports that the space agency is on the brink of a new, exciting era with ambitious plans for more, smaller, less expensive satellites. Meanwhile, Project Gutenberg is putting the text of 10,000 books in the Library of Congress online by the year 2001.

Within the next year, new advances in technology and competition among information providers (made possible by the Telecommunications Reform Act of 1995) will exponentially increase the innovations and choices for the delivery of information. Keep informed. Develop a network of outside experts who can advise you. We are traveling at warp speed to an unknown destination. Welcome to the Information Age!

Programs Integrating Technology

Studying the Inuit

Second-graders are learning about the Inuit as part of their social studies curriculum. Students visited the local Museum of Natural History and borrowed artifacts from the Children's Museum. Their teacher recorded a program on Alaska from C-Span, the cable television channel. In addition to books and videos, students have been paired with long-distance pen pals using America Online, e-mail, and the Internet. Getting online required help from the technical support line provided by America Online and the expertise of a retired phone company executive, who solved the problem of incompatibility with the modem baud output and the system requirements. Because the second-graders have limited keyboarding skills, e-mail messages are typed to a floppy diskette on the classroom and library computers and then downloaded in a batch to the Inuit pen pals at the end of the school day. Additional letters, drawings, photos, and videos are sent via "snail mail." Teachers report that the immediacy of e-mail is appealing to the second-graders, and that contact with Inuit children of a similar age has greatly increased student awareness of the similarities and differences between their lifestyles.

The China Dance Festival

Fourth-grade students investigated China as part of their social studies curriculum. The project included library research on the music, art, dance, games, major cities, monuments, geography, food, customs, language, and history of the country. Children used books, videos, and CD-ROM programs such as *Kodak Photo CD* (Kodak). Because the library and computer room are networked via cable and share a file server, students were able to gather data in the library, record notes, and download them into their folder in the computer room where they could access them later. Students interviewed and videotaped parents from China and performed a Chinese dance that also was videotaped. Students brought in postcards and photos of China, which were scanned into the computer lab Macintosh computer. With the help of the computer teacher, students developed hypertext stacks using the information gathered in their research. The computer teacher demonstrated how to use ClarisWorks (Claris) to import and assemble text, still photos, video clips, narration, and CD-ROM music clips to create a multimedia interactive presentation that documented the yearlong study.

Reflections on Martin Luther King Jr.

Fifth-grade students worked with the guidance counselor, librarian, music teacher, and classroom teachers to develop this special presentation for Martin Luther King Jr. Day. Students used an interactive videodisc about Martin Luther King Jr. and repurposed sections for their assembly presentation. Students participated in the America Online live teleconference with Rosa Parks, coming to the library to watch students from around the country type questions that Rosa Parks answered online. Students also interviewed and videotaped adults from the community reflecting on their memories of Martin Luther King Jr. and the civil rights movement. These oral histories were shared among the students who then used them as a basis for writing poems, prose, and rap songs. For the assembly presentation, a large LCD screen was used to project sections of the Martin Luther King Jr. videodisc that students had repurposed. Students on stage shared poems, songs, writings, and minidramas based on the reflections of parents and community people and on their own research. The entire presentation was videotaped for the school library collection.

Memoirs

Fifth-graders in a bilingual school participated in a yearlong festival studying and creating memoirs. Each student produced two books over the course of the year, either in Spanish or English, including one book using the computer program, Children's Writing and Publishing Center (Learning Company), and an interactive computer video book using HyperStudio (Roger Wagner Publishing).

Children studied and read about the genre of memoirs in the library and classroom, and wrote their own memoirs. Additional books were borrowed via interlibrary loan using the CD-ROM bibliographic database of library collections in the area. Requests were made using online telecommunications software. As part of their research, students interviewed parents and relatives. Children were also linked with Spanish-speaking pen pals in Mexico, the Dominican Republic, and Puerto Rico via telecommunications services and the Internet using computers and phone lines in the library, classrooms, and the computer lab. They received additional keyboarding instruction in the computer lab, and students and their teachers learned more about using HyperStudio through a series of workshops.

Video books were produced with the help of the computer teacher, classroom teachers, and the librarian in the computer lab. Student books included text, scanned art and photos, music, and voiceover narration. Students presented and demonstrated their video books to parents and friends during a series of special authors' celebrations.

Welcome to the Library

Sixth- and seventh-grade hard-of-hearing and deaf students produced this interactive computer orientation to the school library, which included text, graphics, video clips, still photos, and hypertext. The librarian worked with the computer teacher, language arts teacher, sign language specialist, and students to decide what students needed to know about the school library. Students helped develop a glossary of library terms, a storyboard for the orientation, and the still photos. Students were videotaped presenting the necessary text in American Sign Language. The computer teacher assisted students in using Adobe Director (Adobe Systems, Inc.) to create the interactive computer program. The user can click on glossary words or library terms to see still photos of the library and its resources. Video clips show students signing the related information in American Sign Language while the text appears on the screen. The video clip can be slowed down, enlarged, and shown a frame at a time so that the user can better understand the sign language message. Using both written text and the ASL signs helps teachers, parents, and students access the information in two modalities. Click-on buttons provide hypertext links to further explain and define the terms and orientation information.

The *Guernica* Project

Seventh- and eighth-grade hard-of-hearing and deaf students prepared this interactive computer program as part of their social studies, language arts, art history, and computer course work. The computer, art, library, language arts, social studies, and sign language teachers collaborated in this effort. Students studied Picasso, focusing on one of his most famous works, *Guernica. Guernica* was used in language arts and sign language class to explore the emotions and language of war. In social studies, students researched the life, art, and history of Picasso as well as the history of the Spanish civil war. They explored the emotions as expressed in the painting and related them to political cartoons and photos of the Vietnam War and student protests at Kent State. Students repurposed graphic and textual segments from the videodisc *A Geographic Perspective on American History* (GTV, National Geographic) and inserted them in the computer program they created. They created original art and writing on the theme of war, developed a sign language narration and glossary, added hypertext buttons and Quick-Time video clips, and produced a computer program that is both a documentation of their research and learning and a curricular tool for future students and teachers to use. The multimedia program was celebrated at an open house in which student art and writing was displayed, and the guests were invited to explore the interactive computer program on the library and computer room computers.

Bibliography

Adkins, Susan L. "CD-ROM: A Review of the Literature." *Computers in Libraries* (January 1996): 66–74.

Ayre, Rick, and Kevin Richard. "Web Browsers: The Web Untangled." *PC Magazine* 14, no. 3 (February 7, 1995): 173–96.

Barron, Ann E., and Gary W. Orwig. *New Technologies for Education: A Beginner's Guide.* 2d ed. Englewood, CO: Libraries Unlimited, 1995.

Berger, Pam, and Susan Kinnell. *CD-ROM for Schools: A Directory and Practical Handbook for Media Specialists.* Wilton, CT: Online, 1994.

"Best Web Browsers: A Guide to the World Wide Web." *PC Magazine* 13, no. 6 (March 21, 1994): 122–38.

California Media and Library Educators Association. *From Library Skills to Information Literacy: A Handbook for the 21st Century.* Castle Rock, CO: Hi Willow Research and Publishing, 1994.

Cannings, Terence R., and LeRoy Finkel, eds. *The Technology Age Classroom.* Wilsonville, OR: Franklin, Beedle, 1992.

Chae, Lee. "Off the Canvas: Wide Area Networking." *LAN: The Network Solutions Magazine* 10, no. 6 (June 1995): 69–74.

Clark, Elizabeth. "Leveling the Learning Curve: Are Cyberspace Study Halls the Wave of the Future? A Progress Report on Networks in Education." *LAN: The Network Solutions Magazine* 10, no. 6 (June 1995): 117–21.

Dean, William D. *Future Schools: Connected to the World.* Cambridge, MA: Massachusetts Institute of Technology, 1994. VHS tape. 22 min. (Distributed by Master Communications Group, Minneapolis, MN).

Desmarais, Norman. *Multimedia on the PC: A Guide for Information Professionals.* New York: McGraw-Hill, 1994.

Dickinson, Gail K. *Selection and Evaluation of Electronic Resources.* Englewood, CO: Libraries Unlimited, 1994.

Dublin, Peter, Harvey Pressman, Eileen Barnett et al. *Integrating Computers in Your Classroom: Elementary Education.* New York: International Education/HarperCollins, 1994.

Fishman, B., and Roy D. Pea. "The Interworked School: A Policy for the Future." *Technos: Quarterly of Education and Technology* 3, no. 1: 22–26.

Gordin, Douglas N., Louis M. Gomez, Roy D. Pea, and Barry Fishman. "Using the WWW to Build Learning Communities in K-12 Settings." Portions copyright ©1995 O'Reilly and Assoc., Inc. and Houghton Mifflin. Available on the WWW: http://gnn.com/gnn/meta/edu/features/covis.html. (Education Center GNN Home Page).

Grotta, Daniel, and Sally Wiener Grotta. "Kodak DC-40: The Ultimate in PC Instant Photography." *PC Magazine* 14, no. 11 (1995): 37–39.

Harris, Judi. *Ways of the Ferret: Finding Educational Resources on the Internet.* Eugene, OR: International Society for Technology in Education, 1994.

Heller, Norma. *Projects for New Technologies in Education, Grades 6-9.* Englewood, CO: Teacher Ideas Press, 1994.

Hertzberg, Lanny. "The Right to Privacy: Security Software Built to Protect Sensitive Files." *Electronic Learning: The Magazine for Technology & School Change* 14, no. 5 (February 1995): 48–56.

Hixson, Susan W. "It's Elementary! Internet in a K-5 School." *Multimedia School* 2, no. 2 (November-December 1994): 36–44.

Johnson, Doug. "Captured by the Web: K-12 Schools and the World Wide Web." *MultiMedia School* 2, no. 2 (November-December 1994): 24–30.

Landler, Mark. "It's Not Online, It's on Cable: In a Test City, Sitcoms and the Internet Travel Together." *The New York Times* Vol CXLV no. 50323 Section D (January 31, 1996): 1-4.

Mendelson, Edward. "HTML Add-Ons Bring the Power of the Internet to Word for Windows." *PC Magazine* 14, no. 11 (1995): 37.

Miastkowski, Stan. "Plextor 6X CD-ROM Takes Performance Laurels." *PC World* 13, no. 6 (March 6, 1994): 68–70.

Miller, E. B. *The Internet Resource Directory for K-12 Teachers and Librarians.* Englewood, CO: Libraries Unlimited, 1994.

Needleman, Ted. "The Newest Spin on CD-ROM Drives." *PC Magazine* 14, no. 6 (March 28, 1995): 111–65.

Nicholls, Paul. "CD-ROM and Multimedia Trends: The Year in Review." *Computers in Libraries* (November/ December 1995) 56–60.

Persky, Jim. "Hooking Macs to the Net." *LAN: The Network Solutions Magazine* 10, no. 6 (June 1993): 135–40.

Petruso, Sam. "Hybrid Fiber/Copper LAN Meets School's 25 year Networking Requirements." *T.H.E. Journal* 21, no. 10: 86–90.

Quain, John R. "Cover Story: CD-R Drives." *PC World* 15, no. 7 (April 9, 1996): 107-124.

Quain, John R. "Video over Regular Phone Lines? Creative Labs Makes the Call." *PC Magazine* 14, no. 6 (March 28, 1995): 37.

Schuster, Judy. "5 Things You Should Know About Districtwide Networking." *Electronic Learning: The Magazine for Technology & School Change* 14, no. 5 (February 1995): 32–46.

Solomon, Paul. "Children, Technology, and Instruction: A Case Study of Elementary School Children Using an Online Public Access Catalog (OPAC)." *School Library Media Quarterly* 23, no. 1 (Winter 1995): 43–51.

"The Switched-On Classroom: A Technology Planning Guide for Public Schools in Massachusetts." A Project of the Massachusetts Software Council, Inc., One Exeter Plaza, Suite 200, Boston, MA 02116. Available on paper or diskette. You may retrieve the Guide at the following ftp. address: ftp.neirl.org.

Wright, Keith. *The Challenge of Technology: Action Strategies for the School Library Media Specialist.* Chicago: American Library Association, 1993.

Wright, William W., Jr. "NII Watch Wireless Internet Access." *Electronic Learning* 14, no. 5 (February 1995): 10.

Useful Periodicals

Classroom Connect. Wentworth Worldwide Media, 1866 Colonial Village La., P.O. Box 10488, Lancaster, PA 17605-0488. (800) 638-1639; e-mail Amy Young at connect@wentworth.com for subscriptions and Chris Noonan Sturm at editor@wentworth.com for submissions. Published nine times each year. $47 for one year.

Electronic Learning: The Magazine for Technology & School Change. Published by Scholastic, Inc., 555 Broadway, New York, NY 10012. (212) 505-4900. For subscription information, call (800) 544-2917. Published eight times each year. $23.95 for one year.

Internet World: The Magazine for Internet Users. P.O. Box 713, Mt. Morris, IL 61054. (815) 734-1261. For subscriptions only, call (800) 573-3062. E-mail sub@mecklermedia.com. Editorial mail: Internet World Editorial, 20 Ketchum St., Westport, CT 06880. (203) 226-6967; fax (203) 454-5840; e-mail iwedit@mecklermedia.com. Published monthly. $29 for one year.

MacWorld. International Data Group. MacWorld Communications, Ed. Division, 5th fl., 2nd St., San Francisco, CA 94107. (415) 243-0505; access: Internet (macworld@macworld.com).

Multimedia School. Online, Inc. 462 Danbury Rd., Wilson, CT 06897-2126. Published five times each year. $38 for one year.

PC Magazine. PC Magazine. P.O. Box 54093, Boulder, CO 80322-4093. Subscriptions information: (303) 604-7445; fax (303) 604-0540. Editorial offices: PC Magazine, 1 Park Ave., New York, NY 10016-5802. E-mail Internet address: 157.9301@mcimail.com. Published 22 times each year. $49.97 for one year.

Technology & Learning. Peter Li, Inc., P.O. Box 49727, Dayton, OH 45449-0727. Monthly, except June-August, December. $24 for one year.

Technology Connection: The Magazine for School Media and Technology Specialists. Linwood Publishing, Inc., 480 East Wilson Bridge Rd., Suite L, Worthington, OH 43085-2372. Published 10 times each year. $36 for one year.

Chapter 10 — Online Public Access Catalog and Circulation System

by Carol Kroll and Kevin F. Daly

Introduction

Converting the media center to an integrated, electronic information center requires a long, thoughtful process. The intent of the information provided here is to enable library media specialists to understand the automation process so that it can be accomplished in a nonthreatening and effective manner. Library automation includes the use of technology to access CD-ROM and other electronic resources, the Internet, and connectivity throughout the building, and the district, and to the community. The information contained here will only address automation of the online catalog and circulation system. Chapter 9 discusses technology in the learning environment.

The library media specialist (LMS) and a team of educators, with a commitment to information literacy as well as an understanding of the district's instructional program, provide leadership during the yearlong automation process. The automation of the library media center is guided by a long-range plan and basic library media policies. The library media specialists must evaluate the media center selection and collection policies and revise them to include issues connected with copyright and student use of online and other electronic resources. All revisions should be adopted by the Board of Education. If such policies have not been written they must be made part of the work of a subcommittee of the long-range planning team.

Steps in the Automation Process

The planning process:

△ Define the district or school's educational objectives.

△ Locate resources describing elements of library automation.

△ Gather support and form a planning committee.

△ Prepare the library media center's collection, including weeding and inventory.

The conversion process:

△ Select an online catalog and circulation system.

△ Select a retrospective conversion process or vendor.

△ Convert the cataloging information to MARC records.

△ Bar-code library resources.

Selection of hardware and software:

△ Select and purchase hardware for the library Local Area Network (LAN).

△ Select and purchase network operating and telecommunications software.

Site preparation:

△ Determine layout.

△ Select and purchase or construct library furniture.

△ Plan for and install network cable, adequate electric supply, and telecommunication lines.

△ Install hardware, networking software, and the automation system.

△ Consider climate control and a security system.

Other considerations:

△ Purchase and distribute patron cards with bar codes.

△ Receive training to use and maintain the online catalog and circulation system.

△ Create an ongoing user group for sharing and training.

△ Design ongoing evaluation, upgrading, and extension of system.

Automation Process

The Planning Process

A library mission statement that reflects the school's and district's educational objectives should be formulated. This statement will set the tone that all technology is thought about in terms of teaching and learning. Student learning is the primary focus of library automation.

After the mission statement is written, a districtwide technology committee should be formed. The committee, made up of teachers, administrators, students, board members, community members, and business representatives, should write a three- to five-year technology usage plan. Included will be a rationale and plan for library automation. The plan has at its core a vision of how to support the school's or district's instructional program, identification of the learning needs of the students, personnel and resources needed, training of professional and support staff, facility renovation, and budgetary considerations. Central to any plan should be configurations, resources, and processes that support ease of use and equity of access. A long-range plan should include a vision of use beyond the library walls. The plan should start by connecting the resources of the media center to classrooms, labs, subject area offices, and administrative offices. It should include a plan for students and members of the community to access resources beyond the school in the district, region, and state. The plan should address a vision for Internet access.

As part of the educational process, students will develop portfolios and design reports and presentations using a variety of multimedia formats. Consideration should be given to creating a production area in or adjacent to the media center where students can produce multimedia presentations.

The Information Search

The library media specialist will want to locate current general automation information and specific information about retrospective conversion of library titles and the selection of an online catalog and circulation system. The bibliography at the end of this chapter contains reference recommendations. Beyond articles describing automation, committee members should read library and general educational literature about the use of technology for libraries and learning. When committee members have a general understanding of the automation process and its educational implications, visits to other schools should be scheduled. These visits offer committee members the opportunity to question students, library media specialists, and support staff about their experiences using the online catalog. Because each school, school district, student population, staff, and instructional program is unique, no single site will meet all needs or answer all questions. By selecting features from the sites visited and the articles read, the committee will be able to identify the best process, software, and hardware configurations to meet local needs.

Gather Support

The planning and implementation process needs lots of support. Help can be obtained from the state education department, local automation consultants, public library or university library personnel, and local professional organizations. Local businesses may offer support. Members of the committee should attend technology workshops and automation seminars.

Regional educational agencies offer critical assistance and support. In areas without cooperative educational services, consideration can be given to alignment with local districts to standardize software and hardware configurations. By standardizing, increased support can be obtained from the vendor and discounts negotiated. After automation, user groups should be formed and joint projects developed. A union catalog for sharing resources should be created. Libraries can specialize in a particular area of the curriculum or share a technology specialist.

Prepare the Collection

Once a plan is developed, the automation process will take at least a year. If there are budgetary limitations, the library titles might be converted during the first year and hardware purchased during the second. It is a good idea to begin weeding the library collection as soon as possible. The library media specialist will examine each title carefully, and decide if it should remain in the collection. Hard-to-locate titles often become visible through an electronic catalog so the collection should be carefully evaluated. The library media specialists should identify changes in the curriculum as well as faculty additions and retirements that cause changes in resource use. Sensitivity to language usage, ethnic references, global changes, and inaccuracies in statements due to a world now influenced by sophisticated technologies will result in a superior collection. (See chapter 6, "The Collection," and chapter 7, "The Facilty.")

Selecting Online Catalog and Circulation System Software

The library media specialist should learn about online catalog and circulation systems by attending workshops and meetings where they are discussed. Selecting a program is a complex decision; by listening to questions others ask and by hearing the same information many times, details will be understood. It is important to look beyond attractive screens, to evaluate program construction, and to learn about the company's management. The online catalog and circulation system salespeople, trainers, technical support staff, and programmers will affect the professional life of media center staff and the quality of the library media program. The automation vendor should be interested in education and information literacy and dedicated to supporting the information needs of children. The vendor should be responsive to the needs of media center staff and be able to provide local training for the professional and support staff. Because the online catalog is an educational tool, the media staff should become proficient in the use of the online catalog before moving on to use of the circulation system. Students can use the OPAC (online public access catalog) before the books are bar-coded.

If a consortium has been formed with other districts or schools exploring online catalog and circulation systems, vendors will be willing to provide repeated demonstrations. Selection of a system is a slow process of evaluation and self-education. As the planning committee's expertise increases, questions asked during demonstrations of software will increase in depth.

The following checklist should be considered prior to selection of an online catalog and circulation system:

△ Does the online catalog and circulation system support the following items?

- Provision for a full MARC record (if not, do not consider it).
- Networking capability.
- A fully integrated system (circulation and catalog software are not separated—changes in the database are made only once).
- High-speed access to records within the database.
- Menu-driven software.
- Keyword and Boolean searching capability.
- Possibility to add to the MARC record.
- Provision for entry of multiple databases such as periodicals and other informational databases.
- A clear and easily understood procedure and instructional manual.
- Ability to import student demographic data from the computerized attendance and grade reporting system.
- Ability to index fields such as notes, grade level, and reading level.
- Online help menu.
- Ability to merge new MARC records into the database.
- Provision for interlibrary loan management.

△ What is the reputation of the vendor?

△ Is the company stable?

△ Does the company maintain an "800" number?

△ Can the vendor make adjustments to your system online?

△ Is the cost of the automation software competitive?

△ Are there any ongoing or maintenance costs?

△ Are there semiannual upgrades to the software?

△ Are the charges for upgrades competitive?

△ Does the vendor install the resource database and automation software?

△ Does the vendor provide initial and ongoing training at a competitive cost?

△ Does the vendor have a surcharge for connection of additional workstations?

△ Have the retrospective conversion vendor and the automation vendor worked together or is the system provided by the automation vendor alone?

The Conversion Process

Overview of the Conversion Process

In order to use a library automation system, a database of the media center's resources must be created and loaded onto a file server containing online catalog and circulation system software. The database is created by converting resource titles to an electronic format. The conversion process is accomplished by matching a specific title held in the media center against a database of records. The standard database of records against which a media center's titles are matched is called MARC (machine readable cataloging). The process of converting titles already owned is called retrospective conversion. Automation software requires a database of resources to make it functional. The extent to which the online catalog can be used educationally is dependent upon the quality of both the automation software and the electronic database created during the conversion process. Those not familiar with the retrospective conversion process or with MARC records should read some of the articles noted in the bibliography at the end of this chapter.

Conversion to MARC

To begin the conversion process, each shelflist card must be examined for accuracy and fullness of information. Each card must contain either an LCCN (Library of Congress Card Number) or an ISBN (International Standard Book Number). These numbers assist in accurate conversion to MARC. All data including date of publication, place, publisher, and number of copies should be verified. Dewey numbers within the collection should be standardized as to collection code designation (e.g., reference, fiction, etc.), Cutter (number of letters used for the author's name) and Dewey extensions within a given Dewey number. Standardization is particularly significant when converting to MARC because personal interpretation of numbers is not possible when the computer arranges the shelflist. The database is formed using information found on the MARC record so that local subject headings will not appear on the converted record. The district library media specialist or a consortium may want to standardize collection codes. This will facilitate bibliographic listing from a union catalog.

In-House Conversion Versus Vendor Conversion

A decision must be made whether to convert in-house or to send the shelflist cards to a vendor. Conversion in-house is a long, slow, and tedious process. It cannot be accomplished as part of the workday when other tasks are completed. In-house conversion should only be considered if additional personnel will be hired for the task.

Whichever process is selected, the media center staff needs a working understanding of MARC in order to maintain and upgrade the catalog records on the online database. Media center staff should learn to do original cataloging and editing in the MARC format.

Other Considerations

Placement of special collections and oversized books should be reconsidered when preparing the collection for conversion to MARC. Because Library of Congress subject headings appear on converted records, the library staff may want to enhance the MARC record with additional subject headings or added analytics. This can be done during the conversion process or after the database has been loaded onto the file server. The decision should be based on time available for conversion, the professional ability of conversion personnel, funding allocated for the process, and familiarity with MARC records. Some automation software permits global changes to headings, making such changes easier once the database has been created.

When the Conversion Is Complete

After the library records have been converted to MARC, the database is sent to the automation vendor to be processed, configured, and indexed. It will be loaded into the automation software and installed on the file server. The library media specialists should be sure that the conversion vendor has worked with the software company so that all procedures are compatible.

Bar-code Library Resources

While titles are being converted, attention should be directed to the purchase of bar codes. Many automation vendors supply bar codes because this ensures compatibility with the automation system. If purchasing bar-code labels from an outside vendor, the automation vendor should be consulted first to be sure they are compatible with the selected system. Labels may include the call number of the bibliographic record, a code identifying the library, or other information.

Many schools hire outside consultants to place the bar codes on resources. In other schools, the media specialist, support staff, parents, and/or students work in teams. Ideally, the media center is closed during the process. When this is not possible, blocks of time are devoted to the project. This can best be accomplished during schoolwide testing, parent conference days, assembly periods, or summer holidays. Every effort should be made to ensure that all books are returned before bar coding begins. Work should be completed one section of the collection at a time (e.g., fiction, reference, or 500s).

Placement of bar-code labels on books and other resources can be either on the back cover at the top, or preferably on the back cover at the bottom near the spine. Each choice has an advantage and disadvantage. The first method causes less wear on the bar code; the second facilitates inventory procedures. Placement on the outside of the cover is the most popular but causes the most wear. All labels should be covered with a protective shield.

The retrospective conversion vendor or media staff (if conversion is performed in-house) should enter the bar-code numbers into the database during the retrospective conversion process. A printout of the holdings and bar-code numbers is printed in shelflist order. This listing is referred to during the barcoding process. Bar-code numbers can be added to the database either before or after the bar-codes are adhered to the resources. In all situations the collection must be in perfect shelflist order.

All bar-code label numbers should be checked against the shelflist to be certain the correct bar-code labels are being assigned. During the bar-coding process the shelflist cards, the printout, and the bar codes are used simultaneously. A check mark is made next to each barcode number on the shelflist as the bar-code label is adhered to the book. Unassigned bar-code labels are affixed to multiple copies (if they had not been listed on the printout). The bar-code number(s) on the shelflist card are noted and the shelflist card is filed in a catalog card drawer marked *multiple copies modification.* The bar-code number(s) are added to the database. If a book is on the shelflist but not on the shelf, a unique mark is placed next to the bar-code number on the list. If a book is not on the list but is on the shelf, an unassigned bar-code label is affixed to the book and the number recorded on the shelflist card. A second catalog card drawer called *not on database* is created so that the bar-code numbers can be added to the database.

When the MARC records have been converted and returned to the media center, the bar-code numbers are added to the record. The shelflist cards are removed from the *not on database* and the *multiple copies modification* drawers and are corrected and refiled in the shelflist drawers, until they are discarded at the completion of the automation process.

As new resources are added to the collection, bar coding becomes part of the processing routine. New materials are received with bar codes affixed. The vendor also supplies cataloging information on diskette or tape for uploading into the database.

Selection of Hardware

Students can have access to technology-rich environments throughout the school day. When networked computers are located fairly close to each other, the network is called a local area network, or LAN. When computers located in all parts of the school building are connected, the term "distributed local area network" is applied. A library LAN enables students and teachers to access the resources of the library media center from classrooms and labs. A file server, student and teacher workstations, printers, scanning devices, a tape backup unit, and an uninterruptible power supply are some of the devices that are needed. A wide area network, or WAN, is created when districts connect their building networks.

The library media center is the school's information center. If it is automated, it serves as an "electronic gateway" to the school's resources. Local area networks are created by connecting computers through cables, adapters, and network software. In its simplest form, a network interface card is placed inside each computer. A cable is connected to the network interface card and run from each computer to a hub or access unit. The file server, printers, scanners, and CD-ROM drives are attached in a similar manner. The network operating system acts as a "traffic cop," regulating the flow of information between all the resources on the network.

The hardware must provide the platform for the automation software. This is why the automation software is selected early in the process. Hardware selection should be discussed with the automation software vendor or with the regional center involved in the automation project. To determine specific hardware, the following should be considered:

The number of volumes in the collection. A larger hard disk in the fileserver will be needed for collections of 20,000 or more volumes.

Population of the school. The larger the school population, the greater the number of OPAC (online public access catalog) computer workstations that should be available for student use. A ratio of one OPAC workstation for every 100 students should be considered. Fewer than one OPAC per 250 students is not advised.

Circulation activity of the library media center. Schools with more than 2,000 students and significant circulation should consider purchasing a second circulation desk unit.

Commitment to a districtwide union catalog of the holdings of all component schools. If the catalogs of five or more schools are combined, the database will require additional hard disk space. The automation software vendor or regional center can help determine the size of the disk.

Telecommunication access to outside information resources such as the Internet.

Provision for remote access to the system by automation support service personnel. The operating system will sometimes be serviced by this method as will other software on the LAN. When there are problems with software, service personnel will be able to dial into the system through the modem, take over the computer, and correct problems or reconfigure software.

The rapidly changing computer technology field. Workstations need to be state-of-the-art. Workstations should be chosen with top-of-the-line processors, fast clock speeds, and lots of memory. Automation software will be continuously upgraded. Upgrades generally require more memory, larger hard disk space, and monitors with high resolution. Multimedia capability is essential because workstations will be required to run the latest graphics-based software and CD-ROM titles. Program upgrades may not only have text, but also graphics, video, and sound. The media specialist should be in close contact with the automation vendor to learn of plans for major program changes that may necessitate hardware upgrades.

The Library LAN—The Hardware Configuration

The following system design addresses the considerations previously described. The hardware configuration (pictured in fig. 10.1), includes the following components.

Library Office

The library office workstation will allow access to the online catalog and circulation system software residing on a file server. This file server, a dedicated unit, should be a top-of-the-line processor with a fast clock speed, a 2-gigabyte hard drive and 16 to 32 megabytes of memory. An uninterruptible power supply (UPS), which will allow the system to be shut down in an orderly fashion in case of an electrical outage, is placed here and the file server is attached to it. The network operating system should be menu-driven, allowing selection of various software and system options, and allowing "spool" (shared) printing at the OPAC and circulation desk.

In addition to a file server, other equipment is needed in the library office configuration. By attaching a modem to the library office workstation, access will be available to outside resources. A tape backup system (used to backup the information on the file server) is connected to this workstation. A portable bar-code scanner is needed to inventory the collection.

Student Area

The circulation workstation will handle loans, returns, overdues, and other circulation desk activities. Attached to this unit will be a scanning device that will read the bar-code labels on library resources as well as on student and teacher identification cards, and a laser printer (for administrative functions).

The student access configuration consists of several workstations. Known as OPACs, they give students access to the online catalog. The total number of OPAC stations is dependent on the size of the student population of the building. At least one OPAC workstation should be purchased per 250 students. One or more printers will be placed in this area to allow students to get printouts of their searches. A surge protector should be placed on each workstation and printer to filter electrical spikes and surges.

Network Hardware

To allow all the computers and other hardware to interact with the file server, a transmission protocol is needed to transmit information from one unit to another. The two major choices are Ethernet, which currently operates at 10 megabytes per second, or token ring, which operates at 16 megabytes per second. It is estimated that some 70 percent of local area networks are Ethernet and about 20 percent are token ring. This is a complex choice, and the library media specialist should turn to a service vendor or consultant to assess specific needs.

CD-ROM Access

Single CD-ROM drives that are attached to individual computers offer access to only one resource at a time. As more information is available in CD-ROM format, many schools want access to multiple CD-ROMs. Because there are several workstations on a local area network, teachers and students want to take advantage of this and gain access to multiple CD-ROM drives simultaneously.

To access multiple CD-ROMs, a CD-Tower is used that generally can accommodate from four to seven CD-ROM drives. The CD-Tower is a frame into which CD-ROM drives are placed. A computer is installed to act as a CD-ROM server. It has its own network interface card that allows it to communicate with the network and an interface controller card to which the CD-Tower is attached. Special software is installed that allows workstations to gain multiple, simultaneous use.

Those schools already owning individual CD-ROM devices can connect the individual drives together in a daisy-chain format instead of acquiring a tower. The CD-ROM server, interface cards, and special software are still required.

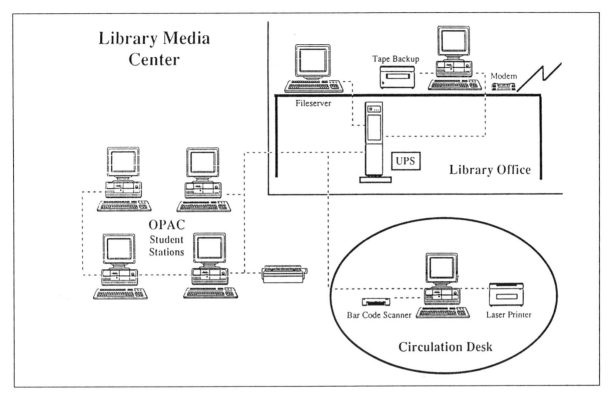

Fig. 10.1. Library Media Center.

Site Preparation

Site preparation should now be considered. Site preparation includes designing the layout of the library media center, planning and designing furniture configurations, providing adequate electric service, installing the network cable and telecommunication lines, providing proper temperature control and ventilation, and, if desired, identifying a security system.

Layout

Careful planning for the layout of the library media center is critical. It is difficult and expensive to move equipment once electric and network cable has been installed. The design of the media center must be developed from an instructional standpoint first and then from a technical perspective. Educational outcomes should not be compromised for ease of installation. For example, a decision might be made to create an island of computers so that a group of students can work collaboratively, but the installers argue that cabling and electrical installation would be more costly. Choosing the less expensive route could result in limited use of the OPAC. It would be a poor decision.

The final design should be reviewed by the buildings and grounds supervisor, and perhaps the fire marshal and building inspector, to determine compliance with safety, electrical, and fire codes.

Furniture

Plans should be made for the purchase or design of furniture early in the automation process. Some districts construct their own computer furniture. Desk and counter materials should be constructed of high-pressure plastic laminates in matte finish and be strong enough to support the equipment. Vendors can supply catalogs and diagrams and in many cases come to the media center to develop specific plans.

Space allocated to each computer should be a minimum of 3' wide and 2.5' deep. Provision should be made for enough space for the mouse and mouse pad, placement of student materials, and printers and printer paper. The "footprint" of each unit and device should be measured to determine space requirements.

Many library media specialists have found that OPAC stations should allow students to stand rather than sit while searching for information. Standing stations lead students to focus on the task at hand without getting too comfortable, which will cause shorter per-use time and allow wider student access. One or more stations with wheelchair access must be provided.

Provision for the library media specialist's workstation should allow not only for the computer but also for related equipment such as the tape backup unit and CD-ROM server and drives. The file server and related equipment require a minimum space of 5' x 3'.

Electrical Power

Following agreement on the workstation layout, proper electrical power must be provided. Computers require a reliable source of power to operate at maximum efficiency. The building maintenance supervisor and a licensed electrical contractor will develop electrical specifications. Light should be reflected light, and the light control should allow for variable lighting. Consideration should be given to the control of artificial, natural, and reflected light.

Network Cable

This is a specialized area and requires the services of a contractor, vendor, or consultant. Proper planning and installation of the network cable will promote the initial integrity of the network and its continued functioning.

The building maintenance supervisor will provide the contractor with the media center blueprints. The distances between the computer units will be measured and the vendor will design the network.

Only the cable recommended by the computer vendor should be installed. The buildings and grounds supervisor should review the specifications, check local codes, and determine if plenum-covered cable must be used.

Network cable is susceptible to interference from electrical devices and sources. Cable should not be run near fluorescent lights, electric motors, air-conditioning units, and other sources of interference.

Telecommunications

At least one direct telephone line is necessary next to the library media specialist's workstation that has the modem attached to it. This line will allow dial-out access to resources. It will also permit the software vendor or technical support company to dial into the network and perform remote diagnostics.

Students also need access to the Internet and to other electronic information services. Multiple, simultaneous access from several computers can be accomplished in a number of ways:

Δ Telecommunications software could be installed in one or more of the OPAC computers. A modem should be attached to each OPAC to be used for telecommunications. Each modem is then attached to an individual telephone line. This approach will allow students using these specially configured workstations to connect to outside resources.

∆ A "modem pool" could be attached on the LAN. A "modem pool" is a device containing several modems that allows workstations on the LAN, running appropriate telecommunications software, to bounce (jump) from one modem to another for outside information access. This approach allows modems and telephone lines to be shared by many computers.

∆ Special software is installed in each workstation on the network and a router attached to the network. The router, which directs and processes multiple, simultaneous network traffic, is then attached to a high-speed telephone line. The telephone line is connected to a point of presence (POP) on the Internet or to another information source. This approach requires a high level of technical expertise, but many schools are moving in this direction.

Climate Control

Consideration must be given to adequate ventilation. Air-conditioning with local room controls, although not mandatory, is strongly recommended. In addition to the heat generated by students and teachers, the equipment will also generate significant amounts of heat. Computer equipment responds much better and lasts longer if room temperature is kept below 78 degrees Fahrenheit.

Security

Computer equipment is expensive and thought must be given to providing adequate security. The library should be locked with keys that cannot be easily duplicated. Drapes and blinds should be drawn so that people cannot see in from the outside when classes are not in session. Consideration should be given to installing security devices on each unit.

Security should also be considered for the media center resources. This is an ideal time to consider installing a security system at the library entrances and exits. The security device or sensor can be placed on each item along with the bar code. This way books will only have to be handled once.

Other Considerations

Patron Library Cards

Many schools provide identification cards for all students and staff. Current student ID cards can be used by simply adhering a unique bar-code label. The corresponding unique bar-code label number for each student is then entered into the patron database. Many schools have student records on databases that can be electronically transferred into the circulation system along with the bar-code number. If the automation software vendor cannot provide such a process, the student records and bar-code numbers will have to be entered manually.

In elementary schools the student identification cards (each with a bar code) may be put onto a rolodex or into a loose-leaf book. Cards may be arranged by class or by student name.

Service and Support

During the network installation, all pertinent information such as model number, description, and serial number is recorded about each piece of newly acquired equipment. Plans should be made to contract for maintenance on the equipment coinciding with the expiration of the manufacturer's warranty.

The library media specialist serves as LAN manager and should be trained by the network installer or software vendor to perform minor troubleshooting activities. Contracts should be maintained with vendor or regional support providers who will answer questions about hardware and software. They should also be available to respond when software must be reconfigured, upgraded, or added, and when hardware repairs are required.

When computers are placed in the hands of teachers and students, entire programs of instruction become dependent on the technology. If the system goes down, the educational program cannot function. Therefore, it is important to enter into contracts with a group that will support the system. It is best to deal with one group who can provide telephone support, remote diagnostics, and on-site assistance. If the entire system is down, the need for assistance is immediate. A contract should be signed with a service provider that guarantees assistance within a 24-hour period.

Training to Use and Maintain the Automated System

Care should be taken that funds have been allocated for adequate training in use of both the online catalog and the circulation system. Two to three days of training are necessary for each. All members of the library staff should receive hands-on training. The more complex the system, the more training will be necessary. A deep understanding of the system by the media specialist and the staff will permit personalization of the information on the database, the generation of self-designed bibliographies, streamlined reports, and indexes to support specific instructional requirements.

The library media center must be closed during training days. Training is highly technical and complex, and interruptions should be avoided. The training process should include written materials.

Once library personnel have been trained, the media specialist will be ready to introduce the automation system to the school staff and students. Effective ways to use the online catalog, including analyzing the collection prior to assigning research, developing search strategies, and creating bibliographies, should be introduced to teachers. The automated system will facilitate the planning of instructional units between the classroom/subject area teacher and library media specialist. It will permit access to other library collections, thus encouraging interloan of resources. The media specialist will be able to emphasize evaluation and use of resources rather than location skills. Students will print out resource titles and be able to easily locate resources. Discussions with faculty during the training process should explore possible new uses of the media center.

Once the initial training of library personnel is completed, the media specialist will want to become a member of ongoing user group meetings and training sessions. If a user group does not exist in an area, a group of media specialists may want to form one. Bimonthly meetings to discuss educational implications, procedures, and strategies are very beneficial. If many users of an automation system are located in a particular area, the vendor may send a trainer to the user meetings. In this way users can learn about upgrades and how to use them, review procedures, and receive answers to technical and instructional concerns.

The Library Media Center: Part of the Schoolwide Design

The library automation LAN is just one part of the schoolwide technology picture designed to facilitate learning (see fig. 10.2). The schoolwide use of technology should include:

Δ A school backbone network that acts as a conduit for once separate instructional networks and classroom computers as well as administrative computing.

Δ The automated library media center with an online catalog and circulation system connected to banks of computers used by students for writing and research. The school community would have access not only to in-house databases but to regional, state, national, and international resources.

Δ Networked "labs" of computers designed for individual or large group instruction and skills acquisition. For example, language arts departments would use the computer system to enhance writing using word processing; social studies departments to record, analyze, and graph data using spreadsheets; and science departments using probes attached to workstations could record experiment results in spreadsheets and databases.

△ Computers in each classroom with a display device so that the teacher can instruct groups. An individual student can also access library resources or use the computer for other purposes.

△ Computers in teacher work areas, departmental offices, and in resource centers for teacher and administrative use.

△ Provision for connecting students' notebook computers.

△ Provision for teachers and students to dial-in from home whether or not school is in session. This would be an excellent way for an absent teacher to forward lesson plans to substitute teachers, for students to work together on a school project, or for community members to use the media center's resources.

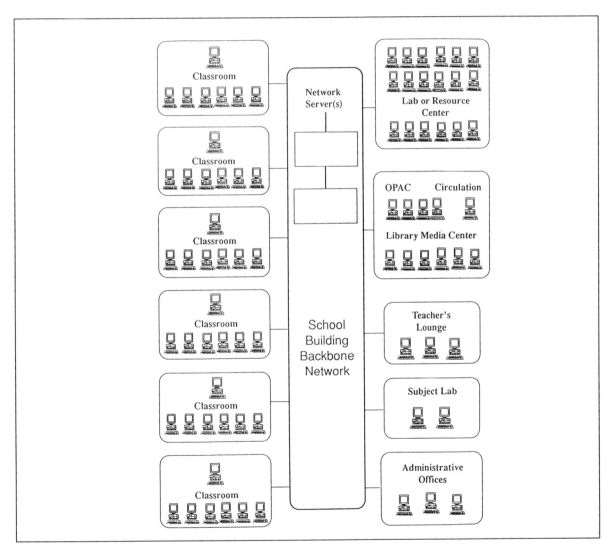

Fig. 10.2. School Building Backbone Network.

Conclusion

In a school with the resources described above, students and teachers with appropriate passwords will be able to access software and information on any file server in the building. For example, a student who began research on a project in the library media center in the morning could check references from a workstation in a writing lab or classroom in the afternoon. A teacher or administrator could access a file on an instructional or administrative server from the faculty lounge, or from home in the evening, for that matter.

When walking into their school with an automated library, planning committee members would know that all their hard work, endless hours of preparation, and long process was worthwhile. Students can locate resources not found previously; they will understand the general nature of online searching and will be familiar with keywords and narrowing and broadening topics. They will understand Boolean operators. Parents and other visitors will see students using the online catalog to design effective search strategies that enable them to find resources once beyond their reach. Students and teachers will be able to identify researchable topics that are supported by the school's resources.

Teachers, administrators, and community members would want to continue their exploration of the school's information access. They would find teachers and students busily accessing the resources housed in the library media center from remote locations. Students who come to the library media center find resources to support classroom curricula because their teacher has prechecked the collection and the media specialist has interloaned requested resources. In fact, visitors find themselves in the center of a vibrant, integrated, electronic learning atmosphere.

Glossary

Backbone network. A framework or skeleton that traverses the center or periphery of a building to which various networks can be attached.

CD-ROM. An acronym for "Compact Disc-Read Only Memory." Generally refers to an optical disc that is capable of holding 650 MB or more of information including video, audio, text, and graphics.

File server. A hardware and software device that acts as an interface between a local area network and peripheral devices. The server receives requests for peripheral services and manages the requests so that they are handled in an orderly manner.

Gigabyte. A unit of measure equal to 1,000 megabytes.

LAN. Local area network.

Local area network. A geographically confined, computer-based communications system.

Megabyte. A unit of measure equal to one million bytes.

Menu-driven. Software in which information necessary for its operation is displayed in a menu. This typically restricts available options while at the same time makes the program easier for a novice to use.

Modem. MOdulator/DEModulator. A device that converts digital signals from a computer to modulated signals for transmission over a telephone line. At the receiving end, another modem converts the modulated signals back to digital signals and passes them to a receiving computer.

OPAC. Online public access catalog.

Peripheral. A device, such as a printer or tape drive, that is connected to a computer and controlled by it.

Plenum. A cable coating or cover that, if ignited, would not emit harmful toxic fumes.

Protocol. A set of defined parameters for establishing and controlling communications. In a local area network, major protocols cover the hardware level (Ethernet, token ring, etc.) and transport levels (TCP/IP).

RAM. Random access memory.

Software. The instruction programs that tell a computer what to do.

Topology. The physical layout of a local area network. Bus, ring, and star are some common topologies.

Bibliography

Adams, Helen. "Media Magic: Automating a K-12 Library Program in a Rural District." *Emergency Librarian* 21, no. 5 (May-June 1994): 24–29.

Barron, Ann E., and Gary W. Orwig. *Multimedia Technologies for Training: An Introduction.* Englewood, CO: Libraries Unlimited, 1995.

Berger, Pam, and Susan Kinnell. *CD-ROM for Schools.* Wilton, CT: Eight Bit Books, 1994.

Byrne, Deborah J. *MARC Manual: Understanding and Using MARC Records.* Englewood, CO: Libraries Unlimited, 1991.

Connolly, Bruce. "Review Roundup—Ask the Experts! Choosing the Right CD-ROM Drive." *Multimedia Schools* 1, no. 2 (September/October 1994): 29–38.

Daly, Kevin F. "A Planning Guide for Instructional Networks, Part I." *The Computing Teacher* 22, no. 1 (September 1994): 11–15.

Daly, Kevin F. "A Planning Guide for Instructional Networks, Part II" *The Computing Teacher* 22, no. 2 (October 1994): 10-15.

Duggan, Brian. "A Measured Approach to Microcomputer Lab Design." *Tech Trends* 39, no. 4 (September 1994): 24–28.

Espinosa, Leonard J. *Microcomputer Facilities in Schools.* Englewood, CO: Libraries Unlimited, 1990.

Hooten, Patricia A., ed. *Perspectives on School Library Automation.* Chicago: American Library Association, 1990.

Intner, Sheila, and Richard Smiraglia, eds. *Policy and Practice in Bibliographic Control of Nonbook Media.* Chicago: American Library Association, 1987.

Kroll, Carol. "Preparing the Collection for Retrospective Conversion." *School Library Media Quarterly* 18, no. 2 (Winter 1990): 82–83.

Kurshan, Barbara L. and Marcia A. Harrington. *An Educator's Guide to Electronic Networking: Creating Virtual Communities.* Revised and updated by Peter G. Milbury. Syracuse, NY: ERIC Clearinghouse on Information and Technology, 1994.

McCroskey, Marilyn. *Cataloging Nonbook Materials with AACR2R and MARC: A Guide for the School Library Media Specialist.* Chicago: American Library Association, 1994.

McKain, Ted, and Mark Ekelund. *Computer Networking for Educators.* Eugene, OR: International Society for Technology in Education, 1993.

Martinsen, K., and Helen Adams. "Creating a District Plan for Technology." *The Book Report* 12, no. 2 (September/October 1993): 25–27.

Mendrinos, Roxanne. *Building Information Literacy Using High Techonology.* Englewood CO: Libraries Unlimited, 1994.

Mendrinos, Roxanne Baxter. "CD-ROM and the School Library Media Center." *School Library Media Annual 12,* ed. by Carol Collier Kuhlthau (Englewood, CO: Libraries Unlimited, 1994), 21–32.

Solomon, Paul. "Children, Technology, and Instruction: A Case Study of Elementary School Children Using an On-line Public Access Catalog (OPAC)." *School Library Media Quarterly* 23, no. 1 (Fall 1994): 43–51.

Chapter 11 — The Library Budget

Introduction

The library media center budget, to a large extent, determines the staffing, program, services, and resources. Because there is fierce competition for scarce school funding, the library media specialist must be an articulate, vocal, and persuasive advocate for the library media center if there is to be adequate funding to meet the needs of the school community.

It is essential that you learn who plans and determines the budget, when it is planned, when modifications are accepted, how to submit written documentation, and when you may appear at meetings to support your budget requests.

You may be given very little information on the budget other than the total amount to be spent and the deadline for spending it. It will be up to you to get more information. Ask questions! The financial officer may not fully understand the media center's mission and its place as the educational hub of the school. By working closely with your principal, advisory committee, and district library supervisor you can help get that message across.

The more you know and the more you network, the better your chances will be to enhance the library budget. Remember, you are fighting to meet the learning needs of the whole school community. You cannot do it properly without adequate resources.

Where the Money Comes From

Most public school libraries derive their budgets from local tax levy funds. Libraries also may receive supplemental funding from state and federal sources including funding for bilingual education, special education, early childhood programs, and so on. If state or federal funding is coming into the school but not to the library, find out who is getting the money. With persuasive advocacy you may be able to redirect some of these funds to the library. Grants, gifts, and fund-raising are other ways to generate additional funds.

The Master Budget

The master budget gives you an overview of anticipated income from all sources. The budget may be presented as a *lump sum,* giving the librarian the flexibility to determine what amounts are to be spent for materials, furniture, and equipment. More often, the budget allocation uses a *line item budget format* that indicates how much is available for salaries, equipment, materials, and supplies. In some cases, the budget allocation uses *program-based budgeting,* which emphasizes the program to be undertaken rather than specific items requested.

It is helpful to record the current year's anticipated income, compare it to the past year's income, and project income for the year following.

Library Media Budget for Excel School, 1995–96

Anticipated Income Source	Amount	Purpose
Tax Levy: (All Codes)	$8,645.00	All codes excluding salaries
State Textbook Fund	$2,000.00	Books
State Computer Software Funds	$1,000.00	Computer software
PTA gift	$600.00	Unrestricted funds
PTA	$720.00	To purchase scanner
Birthday Books Donations	*$600.00	Books and materials
+Corporate Match	$200.00	Books and materials
Lost and Damaged Materials	*$400.00	Materials
Book Fair	*$600.00	Unrestricted funds
Flea Market Fun Day	*$400.00	Unrestricted funds
After-School Reading Buddy District Grant (See program analysis page 215.)	$3,750.00	
Apple Technology Grant	$1,000.00	Computer software and supplies
PTA Funds for Authors' Visit Celebrations	$1,200.00	Honorariums, publicity, postage, refreshments, books
Totals (All Sources)	$21,115.00	

*Note: Anticipated income is based on last year's revenues for similar projects.
+ Some major corporations match employee contributions to school libraries.

Fig. 11.1. Library Media Budget for Excel School, 1995–96.

Line Item Accounting

A portion of the Excel School library budget has been expanded in figure 11.2 on page 213 to show line item accounting. The line item budget may be very specific, providing a different code for each material format, or it may be general, using one code for all materials. The line item may be unique to the library media center or refer to all similar purchases within the school or district. The latter practice may cause difficulties if there are no ways to indicate the library's special needs. For example, if all books in the school are purchased under one code number, there may be no way to indicate that library books must be supplied with book pockets, plastic covers, and bar codes. Also, if more than one person or department is authorized to spend from a single budget code, there may be instances where monies intended for library materials are actually expended for materials used elsewhere in the school.

Example of Line Item Accounting

Line item accounting expands a portion of a budget. Figure 11.2 shows not only the current year's anticipated income but also compares it to the past year's income and to the projected income for the following year.

Tax Levy Budget for Excel School Library Media Center
1994–95, 1995–96, 1996–97
Note: All 301 codes refer to the library media center

Account Number	Line Item	Last Year	Current Year	Next Year	Justification
301.101	Books	$3,000.00	$3,500.00	$4,000.00	Cost of books increasing
301.102	Periodicals	$900.00	$995.00	$520.00	Reduce titles
303.103	Nonprint	$2,000.00	$2,200.00	$2,800.00	Expand CD-ROM periodical holdings
303.104	Supplies	$150.00	$200.00	$600.00	Need for more computer paper, supplies
301.105	Furniture	$200.00	$200.00	$600.00	New computer table
303.106	Equipment	$600.00	$600.00	$1,100.00	Add scanner
303.107	Repairs, Service Contracts	$500.00	$600.00	$900.00	New computer
303.108	Memberships	$50.00	$50.00	$50.00	State Library Association dues
303.110	Conferences	$300.00	$300.00	$300.00	

Fig. 11.2. Tax Levy Budget for Excel School Library Media Center.

Most line item budgets distinguish between materials and supplies that are consumable, and equipment and furnishings that are considered durable. In some cases, the financial officer or purchasing committee has developed specifications and selected a particular model and brand of equipment, for example, Gaylord book truck XX or Califone cassette player YY. They may also have determined the supplier and negotiated a set price. You will need to examine the specifications of each item you are considering to determine if the item meets your requirements. If you have additional or different specifications, you will need to inform the financial officer and follow the guidelines for such purchases. For large equipment purchases or items unique to the library or system, the financial officer may request that you submit specifications so that bids can be solicited for the item. You will find more about this in the section of this chapter describing bidding.

Some line items do not appear in this budget, for example, salaries and fringe benefits of staff, or electricity and heat for the library. These items usually do not show up in the budget given to the library, but they do appear in the line item budget for the school and the district.

Keep in mind that items and services you want and need for the library may be available in the school budget even if they do not appear in your budget lines. For example, the principal may have a budget line for equipment repairs that could get the library VCR fixed, or a line for building repairs that would cover replacement of damaged floor tiles. Often there are discretionary funds that will cover needed supplies and emergency purchases. An active library advisory committee and ongoing communications with your principal or district library supervisor can make a tremendous difference in your budget allocations.

Program Budget Accounting

Other portions of the master budget may use *program budget accounting,* which emphasizes the program or product to be undertaken rather than the items requested. This type of budget is most frequently used in grants and is designed to help the financial officers understand what programs or products they are buying and what the cost is of each. Program budgeting is closely allied to the planning process. The librarian and members of the advisory committee determine what they hope to accomplish, how they will accomplish it, and what it will cost. This process includes discussion of specific programs and services, why the programs are needed, and how they fit into the larger context of the school's learning objectives. Often the librarian provides a specific justification for the individual program, documenting need and anticipated outcome.

The program budget request is designed to persuade funders and financial officers that a project or activity you would like to implement is fiscally sound, well thought-out, and will result in the stated outcomes. Financial officers expect balanced budgets, cost documentation, and, whenever possible, measurable outcomes. Program budgets often require that you show in-kind and other financial support for the program. Thus, the sample program budget below and on page 215 gives a dollar value to the hourly help of parents who volunteer. If the program is funded, it may be at any one of the three levels noted below or at some figure in between. Be prepared to reevaluate the essential components of the program and have a fallback position in the event that funding is not received at the level requested.

Level of Service in Program Budget Accounting

Program budget accounting usually offers a choice of levels of service specifying:

Maintenance level. Costs and benefits involved in continuing the service at the current level.

Enhanced level. Costs and benefits involved in increasing the service by 50 percent.

Reduced level. Costs and decreased benefits if the service is continued at the lowest level.

In a fully developed program budget, every cost should be calculated and assigned to a program, including behind the scenes technical tasks. If you are using a program budget either as your general budgeting tool or as part of a grant application, it is important that you prepare a budget that lists both direct and indirect costs.

Direct costs are those easily attributed to the specific program or activity (such as materials, personnel, and supplies).

Indirect costs are those not easily assignable to one program (including both operating expenses and support services).

Sample Program Budget

The sample budget, figure 11.3 on page 215, expands one program of the Excel School conducted in the library, the "After-School Reading Buddies Program," funded through a small grant.

Note that the sample budget lists direct costs of keeping the library open after school (staffing the library, additional custodial help, money for books, postage, printing, electricity, and heat) and indirect costs (additional clerical time needed to generate increased overdue slips, repair of equipment getting additional heavy use, materials lost in circulation, and additional demand for help or service during the school day by parents made familiar with the library resources).

After-School Reading Buddies Program
October-June 1996,
Tuesdays and Thursdays, 3:00-4:30 P.M.

Direct Costs	Amount	Method of Computation	In Kind Contribution
Salaries			
LMS	$2,000.00	Hourly rate @ $20.00	$1,000.00
Aide	$600.00	Hourly rate @ $6.00	
Custodian	$100.00	Flat rate	
Parent Volunteers		Hourly rate @ $6.00	$1,000.00
Postage	$100.00		
Printing	$100.00		$300.00
Materials	$800.00		$200.00
Indirect Costs			
Electricity	$300.00	% of average bill	
Equipment wear	$200.00	10%	
Clerical services	$100.00	Hourly rate	
Material replacement	$200.00	10% of damaged materials	
Costs	$4,500.00		$2,500.00
Total costs	$7,000.00		

Fig. 11.3. After-School Reading Buddies Program.

The Reduced-Cost Budget

If funding is received at the reduced-cost level, the program will be offered one day a week. Some costs can be reduced, for example, salaries, but others will remain relatively constant even with reduced hours or days, for example, postage and printing. Some services can be reduced or eliminated, for example, rewinding videotapes. This does not mean the work is unnecessary. The elimination of this budget amount will mean aides will rewind when time permits during their regular work hours. The users will have to wait longer before tapes are again available for loan. Materials will be repaired and additional overdues will be sent, staff time permitting. It is anticipated there will be substantial delay that may inconvenience users.

Enhanced Budget

With the enhanced budget, the hours of the program could be extended to serve students from 3 to 5:30 P.M., or alternatively, a third day could be added during the winter months. Additional money in the indirect cost service section of the budget would mean faster processing of overdues, faster repairs, and more timely shelving of materials.

Keeping Track of Expenditures

Whatever budget method or methods you use, you will need to keep track of income and expenditures. Either an account ledger or a computer database or spreadsheet program may be used. Record the beginning balance, budget code (if used), and the source of the funding. Keep records of expenditures noting the date of the order, vendor or source, purchase order number (if used), amount encumbered, invoice date, actual cost, and the remaining balance. The same information is kept if you are using program budget accounting or line item accounting. Figure 11.4 is a sample of an Expense Record Summary.

Line Item Budget: Expense Record Summary

Excel School Library Media Center 1995–96

Budget Code: 301.101

Books

Budgeted Amount $3,500.00

P.O. #	Date Ordered	Vendor/ Source	Encumbered Balance	Invoice Date	Actual Cost	Actual Balance
201	9/17	Baker and Taylor	$800.00	10/20	$653.00	$2,847.00
202	9/18	Bowker	$300.00	10/25	$290.00	$2,557.00
203	10/3	Scholastic	$199.00	11/8	$199.00	$2,358.00
204	11/9	Book Wholesellers, Inc.	$1,000.00			
205	12/5	World Book	$699.00	12/20	$699.00	$1659.00

Budget Code: 303.106

Equipment

Budgeted Amount $600.00

P.O. #	Date Ordered	Vendor/ Source	Encumbered Balance	Invoice Date	Actual Cost	Actual Balance
206	12/8	Califone Cassette Player	$54.20	1/12	$54.20	$545.80
211	1/13	Dukane FS Projector	$329.20	2/18	$342.00	$203.80

Budget Code: 303.108

Memberships

Budgeted Amount $50.00

P.O. #	Date Ordered	Vendor/ Source	Encumbered Balance	Invoice Date	Actual Cost	Actual Balance
101	9/5	State Library Association Dues	$50.00	10/1	$50.00	$0.00

Fig. 11.4. Line Item Budget: Expense Record Summary.

Other Budget Procedures

You need to be familiar with local regulations governing the purchase of equipment, materials, and services. Frequently, financial officers have developed a list of approved vendors and jobbers that you are required to use for purchases. The business office may have already established accounts and procedures for back orders, cancellations, substitutions, returns, shipping, processing, and billing. They may have negotiated a standard discount. For larger items or one-of-a-kind purchases, most systems have established a bidding method.

Bidding

In the bidding process, the librarian and financial officer delineate the specifications and descriptions for the items needed. The proposals are then sent to two or more vendors or jobbers. Vendors who are interested in supplying the item submit a bid specifying the item to be supplied, conditions of sale, and the costs. The financial officer and the librarian then evaluate the bids and select the one that best meets the conditions and specifications. The bid selected is often, but not always, the one offering the lowest price. Extreme care should be taken in developing the specifications for any item put out to bid. If possible, request the assistance of a specialist and examine previous bids for similar products or services. Consider:

△ Size, weight, desired configuration, portability, durability, color, and composition.

△ Energy consumption, electrical requirements, mechanical operations, capacity, volume, and speed of operations.

△ Policies on returns, service, repairs, and replacement.

△ Guarantees and warranties.

△ Training, tutorials, manuals, documentation, and technical assistance.

△ Delivery dates required.

△ Shipping, delivery, and setup charges.

△ Previous record of the vendor or jobber.

Requests for Proposals

When equipment such as an automated circulation system or networked computer system is being considered, you should examine the equipment in a library similar to your own before you write the proposal. Specifications should include:

△ Specific language regarding performance.

△ Successful passing of benchmark tests, including the actual running of the equipment under various conditions, with attention to speed of response.

Bidding information and specifications are compiled in a Request for Proposal, or RFP. Extra care taken in writing the RFP can enhance your chances of receiving quality equipment and quality service. A network of professional colleagues can also be extremely helpful. You will be able to exchange bid information; sample RFPs; and discuss projects, successes, and concerns.

Budget Adjustments

During the course of the year, usually midway, most budgets are adjusted to reflect actual expenditures. For example, you anticipated spending $995 on periodical subscriptions, but because of increased costs, you actually spent $1,025. You may be able to take money from one of the other budget accounts and transfer it to the periodical subscriptions line at midyear.

School districts vary in the flexibility permitted in their budget transfers. Be guided by your financial office and experienced colleagues. Sometimes funds cannot be transferred and the rule is "use it or lose it."

At the end of the fiscal year, you may be required to clear a budget or program line. Any money left in the account after the deadline will be lost. You may overorder intentionally, but ask that vendors "do not exceed" a certain dollar amount. Vendors must also be informed of closing dates for billing and your requirements regarding items that are out of stock. Funding from some budget accounts and budget lines may be held over to the next fiscal year. Again, it is important to get clear guidelines from your financial office.

Planning Budget Needs

Most of this chapter has dealt with how the library media specialist handles budget income and expenses that have already been allocated. The next step is to determine the current budget requirements for the library media center and then plan for the future. You should:

Δ Examine previous budgets.

Δ Be familiar with the rules, budgeting procedures, forms, deadlines, and contact people.

Δ Review the library and school mission statements and objectives.

Δ Review your selection policy and collection map.

Look at your resources, staffing, programs, and services with a fresh eye. Do not be deterred by cries of "There isn't any money!" or "We've never done that!" Use the collection map and collection plan you developed to review your needs and plan priorities. Consider not only the rising costs of existing materials and services but also anticipate future services, resources, and staffing needs. Many librarians keep a journal or folder in which they record specific requests they were unable to fill and information on new equipment, products, and services. Speak with members of the school community to get an understanding of their interests and needs.

Gather Information on Programs and Services

Ask your colleagues in other libraries about the programs and resources they offer. Visit other libraries in your region and district and attend regional and national conferences. Compare your expenditures with those from other schools in the area, region, state, and nation. Examine *Information Power* and the professional literature for a discussion of services, goals, and objectives.

Justifying Budget Needs

Once you have gathered information on interests and needs, prioritize the needs, develop a plan of action, and anticipate the costs. Justify any budget increase request and specify how the increase will result in improved service and enhanced educational outcomes. Careful record keeping, including circulation figures, programs, and services offered; materials added and weeded; and requests will help you justify budget increases. Document changing conditions that will have an impact on services, costs, or resources. For example, if more classes are using a whole-language approach to reading, additional resources will need to be purchased. Changing conditions that may have an impact on the library media center can be noted in the annual report you file with your principal and with the district library supervisor. Use evidence from the professional literature to document costs. It is helpful to prepare three sample budgets. The budgets should illustrate:

△ The current year's allotment, demonstrating how continuation at the same level of funding will actually result in a reduction of services.

△ The level of funding needed to maintain existing services.

△ How services would be enhanced with additional funding. (See fig. 11.5.)

Tax Levy Budget for the Excel School Library Media Center
Funding at the Same Level as Last Year
Inflation Adjusted
Enhanced Funding
Note: All 301 codes refer to the library media center

Account Number	Line Item	Same as Last Year	Inflation Adjusted	Enhanced	Description
301.100	Salary				
301.101	Books	$3,000.00	$3,500.00	$4,000.00	Projected inflation 20% for books
301.102	Periodicals	$900.00	$995.00	$520.00	Projected inflation 15% for periodicals. Purchase some on CD-ROM if funds permit.
303.103	Nonprint	$2,000.00	$2,200.00	$2,800.00	Expand CD-ROM periodical holdings; add new computer programs.
303.104	Supplies	$150.00	$200.00	$600.00	Computer paper, supplies
301.105	Furniture	$200.00	$200.00	$600.00	New computer table
303.106	Equipment	$600.00	$600.00	$1,100.00	Add scanner
303.107	Repairs, Service Contracts	$500.00	$600.00	$900.00	New computer
303.108	Memberships	$50.00	$50.00	$50.00	State Library Assoc. dues
303.110	Conferences	$300.00	$300.00	$300.00	

Fig. 11.5. Tax Levy Budget for the Excel School Library Media Center.

Narrative

If this year's funding is maintained at last year's level, the library will need to:

△ Reduce book purchases by 18 percent, purchasing approximately 164 books instead of 200 purchased this year.

△ Reduce periodical subscriptions by 15 percent, purchasing 25 instead of 30.

△ Reduce hours of service by five percent, closing Wednesday at 3 P.M. instead of 4:30 P.M.

△ Reduce aide time. A five percent increase in the hourly rate of aides will result in a reduction of service hours, which will necessitate the reduction of special services, for example, limit teacher reserves and preparing bibliographies for teachers. Last year, 312 teacher reserves were filled and 23 specialized bibliographies were prepared at teacher requests.

If funding is inflation adjusted as indicated above, there will be no reduction in purchases or services. If funding is provided at the enhanced level:

∆ Book purchases will increase from 200 to 238 and we will be better able to serve the new bilingual class.

∆ Periodicals will be purchased on CD-ROM to extend holdings, reduce storage problems, and enhance access for students and teachers.

∆ A computer table for mobility-impaired students will be purchased, making the computers more accessible to special populations.

∆ An additional computer will be purchased for student use.

∆ The new computer HyperStudio program will be used for enhancing research skills.

∆ A color flatbed scanner will be added to the computer for students and teachers creating materials using graphics.

Persuading Others

Now that you have developed a budget, the next step is to persuade others to support it. You know how! You are an expert in communications and public relations. You are not requesting more money for books because *you* need more books, but because more books are essential so that all children can reach their learning potential. Discuss budget requests with your library advisory committee, administrator, and district library supervisor, and include other faculty, parents, students, and community people. Encourage wide support and argue that:

∆ Every school library in the district has this except us!

∆ This supports the goals outlined by the district superintendent, city commissioner, and state education chairman.

∆ The regional, state, or national guidelines require or suggest this.

∆ No other school in the district has anything like this!

∆ We would be on the cutting edge.

∆ It would help students with special needs.

∆ Parents would love it! Teachers would love it! Kids would love it! The newspapers would love it!

∆ It would help teachers with:
- the new outcome-based learning
- inclusion
- whole language
- authentic assessment
- multicultural awareness
- conflict resolution

△ It would promote:
- lifelong learning
- higher-level thinking skills
- building self-esteem
- collaborative learning
- visual literacy
- vocational skills

△ It would cut costs.

△ It would increase efficiency.

△ It would be a wonderful experiment.

You increase the chances of new or expanded budget items being adopted if other members of the school community view the items as enhancing their own programs and learning objectives. Do not get discouraged if your budget proposals do not meet with instant success. Persistence counts, and change takes time.

Other Funding Sources

Other funding options may also be available. Many librarians, with the help of their advisory committees, engage in fund-raising to supplement library budgets. Book fairs, birthday book programs, raffles, bake sales, flea markets, and magazine sales are common ways of raising cash. Discuss any ideas for fund-raising with your administrator who will be able to advise you on local regulations and procedures including:

△ Getting permission for fund-raisers.

△ Restrictions on kinds (and numbers) of fund-raisers, publicity, space, and time.

△ Who may sell.

△ What may be sold.

△ Insurance.

△ Charging admission.

△ How to handle cash and receipts.

△ How and where to deposit funds.

The library advisory committee should help plan a fund-raising event. It is an excellent source of ideas, practical help, and support. Consider the real costs of staging a fund-raising event, including the time and energy you will spend planning, publicizing, supervising, and cleaning up after any event, and the actual dollar return. Consider your hourly salary. Can you afford to spend 50 hours planning and supervising a book fair for a total profit of $200? When parent volunteers or students supervise the event, consider whether this is the most productive use of their time.

If the event is scheduled in the library space, you will also need to consider the time the library will be unavailable for regular circulation, reference needs, and programs. And most of all, decide whether the activity enhances and supports the educational objectives of the library and the school.

Book Fairs

Book fairs are among the more common fund-raising events sponsored by libraries. Properly planned and run, book fairs offer children, parents, and teachers access to many beautiful new books at reasonable costs. They provide the librarian with an opportunity to do booktalks, introduce titles, give reader guidance, and celebrate books and reading. Book fairs can raise money, but their purpose should be to enhance access to quality books and promote reading.

Beware of companies that promote stickers, stamps, erasers, puzzles, and posters with little educational value. Junk items are often alluring to children. Parents who have given their children money to select a book are justifiably annoyed when their children come home with an array of junk instead. But what about children who come with little or no money? Keep a box of discards, acceptable gifts, or donated magazines and books that children can purchase at a very reduced price or have free. Some libraries arrange for a "book swap" to be held at the same time as the book fair but in another place. Children are invited to come with a book they no longer want and swap it for one someone else has brought in. As a general caveat for all sales: Don't buy junk or sell junk!

Not all book fair companies provide the same quality products, services, and profits. Before you select, discuss different companies with other librarians who have used their services. Consider:

The Quality and Choice of Merchandise:

∆ Are the books of excellent quality and of current interest to your students and teachers?

∆ Are you able to select titles or series?

∆ Are books available to meet the interests of a wide range of students?

∆ Are books available that are multicultural? In different languages?

∆ Are the books affordable?

∆ Will the company supply additional copies of titles quickly if you run out during the sale?

Space and Time:

∆ How long will the books be available for sale?

∆ Where will you hold the fair?

∆ How far in advance must you book?

∆ Will the company deliver inside, upstairs?

∆ Will you be able to schedule around holidays or during parent-teacher conferences?

Publicity:

∆ Will the company provide publicity posters and signs?

∆ Will the company send a printed list to parents in advance of the sale?

Display and Sale:

∆ How easy is it to set up displays, inventory, pack up, and ship?

∆ Are books supplied in attractive display racks that can be easily stored and secured?

∆ Will sales help be available from the company?

Profits and Service:

∆ Does the company accept checks?

∆ What profits are offered? What discounts are offered purchasers?

∆ How does the percentage of profit compare with other companies?

∆ Are profits offered in cash, books, or a combination of your choice?

∆ Is the company reliable, helpful, and prompt in pickup and delivery?

∆ Must you total books sold and count books returned, or can you just send the percentage of profit agreed on with the company?

Be sure to evaluate the book fair after it is over, as with any other library program or service. You may want to offer two book fairs a year, one charging the full cover price and the second at which purchasers receive a discount. Profits are reduced for the second sale, but purchasers benefit. Ask parents, teachers, and students if they were satisfied with the selection, price, and quality of the books. Do they have suggestions for future sales? Keep notes in your journal and log comments, detailing suggestions, criticisms, and problems. This information will be useful in planning next year's events. Relay the criticisms and compliments to the company. They should be appreciative and promise to redress the problems to retain your business.

Book Donation Programs

Some school libraries supplement the library collection with donations, for example, a birthday books program. Parents are invited to donate money to the library for the purchase of a book in honor of their child's birthday or other special event. The librarian sets aside books newly added to the collection, including books at a variety of reading levels that reflect different interests. From these, the child selects one to be his or her birthday book. This method has several advantages for the busy librarian: The titles are those that you want for your collection, they are purchased at full discount from the vendor, and they arrive fully processed. The librarian need only add the book plate and write the thank you note. The child has the immediate gratification of examining and selecting.

In some cases, children want a particular title or a book by a favorite author, and efforts are made to accommodate the request. However, placing an order for a single title takes time and effort; the child needs to be aware that it may be a month or more before the material is received.

Still another option is to allow children and parents to purchase a book at a local bookstore and donate it to the library. The books will need processing, and usually the purchasers pay the full list price for the titles, making this method a more expensive option. Some librarians feel the excitement generated makes the added cost and effort worthwhile. It is helpful to have a list of desired titles from which parents and children can select. Do not purchase or accept any title that does not meet the standards set forth in your selection policy.

A special book plate is put in the book indicating:

> *A Birthday Book*
> *In Honor of Alita Galvez's Birthday*
> *September 1, 1996*

The birthday child receives a personal thank you letter and has the opportunity to read the book first. Then it becomes part of the regular circulating collection. Children often select a title that reflects their personal reading interests. The program builds pride and a sense of ownership in the library and celebrates books as an appropriate and valued gift. Before instituting any program like birthday books, discuss it with your administrator and advisory committee.

Corporate Donations

Some major corporations encourage contributions to libraries and match employee gifts. Query parents about whether their employers give matching funds or contributions. Local corporations, banks, and utilities also may make donations. Not all contributions are cash. Be on the lookout for useful gifts in-kind. Are there companies discarding computers, audio or video equipment, furniture, paper, or art, or display materials? Would companies loan a photographer or video camera, sound equipment, stage, or folding chairs for a special event? Can they supply refreshments or pay for printing costs?

Parent, Teacher, and Community Contributions

Parents and others in the community may be wonderful sources for donated materials. Are they weeding their home libraries? Have they back issues of magazines for reference or art projects? Do they want to donate puzzles, maps, audiotapes, educational toys, rocking chairs, rocks, shells, or other realia? Have they slides, photos, or postcards from trips? As with all additions to the collection, donated materials should meet the criteria set forth in the library selection policy.

Community members may also share their expertise and talents. They can share their expertise in law, medicine, electronics, current history, countries, and cultures. They can install a CD-ROM or computer program, upgrade computer memory, help with a snag on the Internet, reformat computer discs, or provide computer or technology training for teachers or students. If you have not yet developed a card file or computer database "People Resource File," you may wish to start one with the help of your advisory committee. As with all activities involving volunteers, be generous in your praise and make sure you recognize their valuable contributions.

Grants

Many librarians write grants to supplement their budgets. Books about fund-raising and grant writing of special interest to librarians are listed in the bibliography. Many of the books are published by the Foundation Center. The center is a service organization established and supported by foundations to provide an authoritative source of information about corporate and foundation giving. It publishes many reference books including:

△ Directories that describe specific funders.

△ Grant indexes that list and classify by subject the recent foundation and corporate awards.

△ Guides and monographs that introduce the reader to proposal writing, funding research, and nonprofit management issues.

You may wish to visit the closest Foundation Center regional library for information and help in locating grants of interest. To locate the center nearest you, call the Foundation Center at 800-424-9836.

The center maintains two extensive information databases that are available online. These can be reached through DIALOG Information Services and through many online utilities. For further information on accessing the center's databases directly through DIALOG, contact DIALOG at 415-858-2700.

Other sources of grants include the PTA, local civic and social groups, banks, businesses, elected officials, professional organizations, and state and Federal agencies. Often your professional association, or state and national magazines have listings of grant possibilities. Your district office or regional library may also keep a file. Encourage colleagues and parents to be on the lookout for grants that fit the school's educational mission and objectives. The *best grants* are those that enable you to do what you need to do more easily, successfully, or with greater intensity. The *worst grants* are those that drain resources, time, and energy from other worthwhile projects and do not enhance the ongoing educational mission.

Tips for Grant Writing

Check with your principal and library supervisor before you apply for any grant and get the necessary approval. If you plan to use school staff, space, resources, or time, they will want to be involved early on in the process.

Develop a team of grant writers to share the work. District office staff, administrators, teaching colleagues, and parents can all be helpful members of a grant writing team. Some parents and teachers have grant writing experience. Collaborate and use the skills they have already developed. Some of the more successful library grants are those done with other teachers or groups. If you assist others with their grant writing, there may be an opportunity to add a library component. You will have a better idea of the teachers' interests and build a network of expertise. Teachers will appreciate your involvement and may be willing to pull you into other projects or help you. Use your talents as an information expert and master teacher to help determine the grant focus, research a topic, and gather the information you need to write a grant. Once you have gathered the information, don't throw it away! It often is possible, with minor adjustments, to use the same data to apply for other related grants. Some administrators put a library component into every grant proposal.

Maximizing Success

Filling out grant applications requires time and effort. You enhance the potential for success with careful planning when you:

Δ Collect grant proposal forms and samples of successful grant applications.

Δ Analyze the kinds of information required and the elements of the successful proposals.

Δ Investigate the number of grants to be offered.

Δ Apply for those for which you have a special edge.

Δ Take note of filing deadlines, matching requirements in money, staff, resources, and record-keeping requirements.

Δ Evaluate if the grant is worth the time and effort necessary for implementation and record keeping.

Reducing Time and Effort

Recycle and reuse grant proposals as often as possible. Gather the information that is frequently requested and save the following on the computer:

△ Demographic information on the students, school, and community.

△ Information about the school's educational mission and objectives.

△ A summary of other special programs and grants in place.

△ Information that documents the unique and special features of your school, community, and program.

Some funders provide assistance in grant writing through grant writing workshops. Talk directly with the sponsors to get a clear understanding of what is expected. If the grant has been awarded in the past, ask if you can have copies of winning proposals. Follow the directions exactly as requested. Answer all questions. Many applications are eliminated from consideration because the form is incompletely filled out or the grant writer doesn't follow directions. Members of the staff, your administrator, and friends should read the application before you file it. While professional educators may notice inconsistencies in the education philosophy and objectives, friends may be better able to spot educational jargon that is unclear or weakens the whole. Keep a copy of all applications. **Be sure to file on time!!**

Success or Rejection

If you are awarded the grant, work closely with your administrator, financial officer, and advisory committee to plan out implementation. Be clear on deadlines, documentation, and kinds of evaluation that are required by the grantor. Be sure to tell colleagues, students, parents, and community people about the success of the proposal. Positive publicity often helps promote other funding opportunities.

If you are not awarded a grant, ask if the sponsor will critique your proposal. What didn't you do or say? How did it differ from winning grants? Would they advise you to try again or even try elsewhere?

Conclusion

The proactive librarian needs to take on many roles during the course of the workday. It may seem strange to you that it has become part of your job to drum up the money to do the work for which you were trained. Some veteran librarians complain: "Why should I have to lobby for the budget? I should be given the resources necessary to do the job for which I was hired!" Perhaps in a better world with surpluses rather than shortages, it would be possible to sit back and let others hand you your budget. In this world, however, the choice is often to take a strong position of advocacy and improve your budget, or to accept the budget as given and deny your patrons vital services and resources. It is your decision.

Bibliography

Foundation Center Staff. *National Guide to Funding in Elementary and Secondary Education.* 2d ed. New York: Foundation Center, 1993. The Foundation Center is a national service that maintains free funding information centers in New York City, Washington, San Francisco, and Cleveland. For information on hours and services, phone (800) 424-9836. The Foundation Center maintains up-to-date and authoritative data online through DIALOG Information Services. For further information on accessing the center's databases directly through DIALOG, contact DIALOG at (415) 858-2700.

Morris, Betty J., John T. Gillespie, and Diana L. Spirt. *Administering the School Library Media Center.* 3d ed. New Providence, NJ: Bowker, 1992.

Olson, Stan, and Ruth Kovacs, eds. *National Guide to Funding for Libraries and Information Services.* 2d ed. New York: Foundation Center, 1993.

Smith, G. Stevenson. *Managerial Accounting for Libraries and Other Not-for-Profit Organizations.* Chicago: American Library Association, 1991.

Steele, Victoria, and Stephen D. Elder. *Becoming a Fundraiser: The Principles and Practice of Library Development.* Chicago: American Library Association, 1992.

Stein, Barbara L., and Risa W. Brown. *Running a School Library Media Center.* New York: Neal-Schuman, 1992.

Weingand, Darlene E. *Managing Today's Public Library: Blueprint for Change.* Englewood, CO: Libraries Unlimited, 1994.

Woolls, Blanche. *Supervision of District Level Library Media Programs.* Englewood, CO: Libraries Unlimited, 1990.

Chapter 12

Support Staff: Filling the Need

Introduction

Your primary responsibility as librarian is to administer the library program. How can you adequately direct the program and also tend to the clerical and other library-related tasks that should be performed regularly to enable the library to operate smoothly? You cannot! Clerical staff and volunteers relieve you of the nonprofessional tasks so that your time and energy can be devoted to working with children and teachers. This support enables the program to continue and develop. Clerks, paraprofessionals, teachers, interns, parents, relatives, caregivers, students, and community volunteers can provide the necessary support you require.

School Support Staff

Clerical support should be built into your program. If it has not been, you should appeal to school and community leaders to help you obtain sufficient assistance. In your requests, be clear and specific about why you need clerical and program support. Describe the duties and responsibilities of the personnel you require as well as the skills and time allocations needed to perform the duties.

Clerks who are paid to work in the school (also called school aides) are excellent choices to provide library support. They work in the school and may already be proficient at some of the required clerical tasks. One or more full-time clerks should be assigned to the library. If that is just not possible, request that several part-time aides be assigned on a permanent schedule. Clerical support should be available throughout the day to ensure that the library stays open, even when you are not available.

Paraprofessionals or educational assistants also may be excellent support staff. They may be assigned to work in the library full time, when particular classes or small groups are there, or when classroom teachers do not require their assistance.

Tasks, Duties, and Opportunities

What routines and tasks in your library can be performed by others? Become familiar with local policies concerning clerks and teaching assistants. May they supervise students in a nonteaching environment or must a teacher supervise whenever students are in the library? The tasks, duties, and opportunities for nonprofessional staff are enumerated below.

Circulation

△ Monitor and/or help checking materials in and out.

△ Arrange book cards in the circulation file, if used.

△ Print and distribute overdue notices at designated intervals.

△ Shelve books (usually done by library squad).

△ Read (organize) shelves on a regular basis to keep books in proper order.

△ Compile circulation statistics.

Book Ordering and Processing

△ Assist as needed in verifying prices, ISBNs (International Standard Book Numbers), authors, titles, publishers.

△ Type orders or place electronic orders. (Orders should be on a computer database to facilitate good record keeping.)

△ Check in new books and materials.

△ Do any necessary processing tasks.

△ Apply bar codes as necessary.

Cataloging

△ Import data into automated systems.

△ Add new titles or additional copies to automated systems.

△ Print bar-code and spine labels.

△ Assist with retrospective conversion.

△ Sort, alphabetize, and file catalog cards, if still used.

Weeding

△ Assist in weeding as directed.

△ Delete titles no longer in the collection from the catalog.

△ Remove cards from books to be discarded.

△ Stamp or write "DISCARD" on the pocket.

Inventory

△ Scan bar codes of materials to verify holdings.

△ Work with the librarian or other partner to check shelves against shelf list.

△ Make duplicate shelflist cards, when necessary.

△ Remove from holdings materials not located.

Miscellaneous Tasks

△ Assist with the organization and maintenance of audiovisual and other equipment.

△ Prepare materials for the vertical file (pictures, pamphlets, clippings), label folders, stamp items to be included, file items.

△ Construct decorations, bulletin boards, and displays.

△ Help prepare the library for renovations or room rearrangement.

△ File publishers' catalogs.

△ Check in magazines; keep older copies in order.

△ Assist with book fair arrangements, orders, and record keeping.

△ Process interlibrary loan requests.

△ Copy materials or arrange to have it done by office staff.

△ Maintain, organize, and distribute software, CD-ROMs, videos, and other nonprint media.

△ Install software and CD-ROMs.

Working with Children

△ Assist children with requests.

△ Work with small groups—read a story, videotape a puppet show, use CD-ROMs, assist with research or other projects.

△ Train and oversee library squad members.

△ Assist students on computers.

△ Teach computer-related skills.

Work-Study Programs and Internships

Students in college work-study programs may be eligible to receive financial aid for working at off-campus sites such as schools. Contact your local college financial aid office for information. In many work-study programs, prospective employers submit applications and the interns select their work sites. Write an exciting job description that describes a stimulating program and list diversified duties that will whet the interest of the potential intern, because there could be more employers than interns. There may be a charge to the school or district for this program, so research how college work-study operates in your area.

Some colleges offer credit for community service. Call college career and cooperative education offices for more complete information. Some secondary schools also have community service requirements or work-study programs. Contact local schools for information.

In some areas, governmental agencies provide job training programs for people on welfare or with disabilities. They are placed at sites to learn skills that will facilitate employment. Learning to do the clerical tasks in a library can help people gain the skills that are necessary in the workplace. Learning to use the computer is an additional skill. As an intern's supervisor, you may be responsible for time sheets and other records. Discuss all possibilities with your administration before applying.

Consider contacting your alma mater or other universities that offer degrees in library science about becoming a mentor. As the mentor you would provide learning experiences in all areas of school library media service for the students and teach them how to use the library to integrate instruction. Some colleges offer free or reduced cost college courses for mentors. Perhaps you could also convince schools to place student teachers in the library.

Fig. 12.1. Student Monitors Improve Their Skills and Have the Satisfaction of Helping Others.

Students

Student squads should assist in the daily operation of the library. Students who work in the library improve their information literacy skills and reading ability, learn new skills, and have the satisfaction of helping others. When choosing student monitors, select students from more than one grade so that:

△ There are always experienced monitors in the squad.

△ The experienced monitors can teach the new squad members.

△ Even if students in one grade graduate or are unavailable, you still have other assistants.

Even young students can be monitors. If students know what their tasks are, know how to accomplish them, and *want* to do them, you will have the ingredients of a successful squad. Children often feel it is an honor to be a library monitor.

Students are learners, not indentured servants. They require tasks that will challenge them as well as teach work-related skills.

Circulate your procedure for selecting students to work in the library to students, teachers, and parents. This may make students more interested in becoming monitors and enhance respect for the position.

Interview student monitors or volunteers before choosing them. Request applications and resumes, or have students write about why they want to be monitors. Ask teachers to submit letters of recommendation for the students, and have both parents and teachers give permission for students to be on the squad. Maintain a waiting list of prospective monitors in case students do not work out. Some librarians accept all volunteers and schedule them on alternate days or use them at different periods of the day.

The following are examples of resumes from fifth-grade children in Public School 254 in Brooklyn, New York.

Sample 1. *"My name is M. H. I love to baby-sit for little kids. I'm a monitor in Ms. S's class (pre-k). That is why I think I could bring little kids up to the library. In class my teacher taught us how to use card catalogs. Also at home my sister and I made a library and had to check in and out our books. We did that so our books wouldn't get lost. So I also have experience in helping kids do that. I also know the difference between fiction, nonfiction, biographies, etc. so I could help organize books. I also do a good clean-up job (I help my mom clean the house). Just in case we need to clean the library I could help."*

Sample 2. *"I want to be a library monitor because I have had many experiences in shelving and alphabetizing. When at school or at home I alphabetize my spelling words. I have experience in shelving. When I get some magazines and books I always shelve them and organize them. I have experience in stamping books. I helped my teacher stamp papers and books and my dad stamp letters."*

It is important to acknowledge the contributions of student monitors and there are many ways to do so. You might announce the names of selected students over the loudspeaker, as if they had won a contest, or list their names in the school, library, and/or parents' association newsletter. Certificates of merit and graduation honors reinforce the concept that library monitors make significant contributions to the school. Monitors can be first to borrow new books and get discards. Occasional lunchtime gatherings or other social events also say thank you.

Diversify the monitors' tasks to prevent boredom and to extend skills. Children who have not grasped a particular task might be paired with a more proficient student. Monitors can help students select books or work on projects as well as complete clerical tasks and shelve books. They might teach other students how to use electronic tools or produce videos. They can help with computer graphics programs, troubleshoot equipment failure, or assist with classroom collection exchanges. Working with other children helps monitors extend their own knowledge and skills and learn to work cooperatively. Give students responsibilities that challenge their talents and strengths. Many students who are square pegs in classroom round holes fit very nicely in the library squad. It is important to acknowledge *attempts* as well as successes and model the social skills you want children to emulate.

It takes time to develop a strong library squad. Once it is in place, however, it can be very rewarding for you and your students.

Fig. 12.2. Student Monitors Learn to Work Cooperatively.

How Strong Is Your Library Squad?

This self-assessment will help you successfully deploy student monitors. If you have not used monitors previously, the tool suggests ways to organize and utilize a squad.

1. Describe your current squad:

    a. How many students? _____

    b. From what grades/classes? _____

2. Check when squad members work:

    _____ During your preparation time

    _____ Before school

    _____ After school

    _____ At lunchtime

    _____ At scheduled times throughout the day

    _____ Other _____

3. Check how you recruit and select squad members:

    _____ Teacher recommendation

    _____ Personal knowledge

    _____ Application form or resume

    _____ Student request

    _____ Student recommendations

    _____ Other _____

4. When do you recruit squad members? _____

    _____

5. Do you maintain a waiting list of possible squad members? _____

    _____

6. How do you announce your squad selections to the school? _____

    _____

7. How do you inform parents?

    _____ Letter

    _____ Notice

    _____ Newsletter

    _____ Other _____

8. Must parents give consent for their children to be a monitor? _____

    Has this been a problem? _____

9. Must teachers or administrators give their consent? _____

    Has this been a problem? _____

10. Check all activities your squad members have some responsibility for:

    _____ Book processing   _____ Book shelving   _____ Decorating

    _____ Circulation   _____ Cataloging   _____ Bulletin boards

    _____ Read-alouds   _____ Lib. newsletter staff   _____ Tour guide

    _____ Hall escort   _____ Book selection   _____ Computer aide

    _____ Reading shelves   _____ Overdues   _____ Special projects

    _____ AV production   _____ Computer graphics   _____ Troubleshooter

    _____ Other (explain) _____

    _____

11. Check the methods you use to train students

    _____ Peer training   _____ Training manual

    _____ Computer program (tutorial)   _____ Minicourse for small groups

    _____ Individual training   _____ Other

12. How is the squad member's performance evaluated?

    _____ Self-evaluation   _____ Personal interview

    _____ Evaluation form   _____ Other _____

13. Check all that you do to maintain enthusiasm and high morale:

    _____ Present awards to squad members at graduation and/or special assemblies

    _____ Provide squad identification (e.g., buttons, T-shirts)

    _____ Present awards at other times throughout the year

    _____ Give squad members parties, gifts for service, and so on

    _____ Additional privileges

    _____ First choice of new books

    _____ Discard priorities

    _____ Other

14. How do you keep interest in tedious jobs like shelving? _____

    _____

15. What perks do you give teachers of squad members? _____

    _____

16. What steps will you take to enhance the role of your squad in your program? _____

    _____

Fig. 12.3. How Strong Is Your Library Squad?

Volunteers

Volunteers are a major source of support in the elementary school. They are often the parents of students currently enrolled in your school but might be caregivers, relatives, senior citizens, or members of volunteer organizations or community residents. Their reasons for volunteering will be diverse. They might want to:

△ Be involved in their children's school.

△ Participate in a worthy activity.

△ Feel useful or needed.

△ Acquire or hone skills.

△ Become familiar with a school in which they would like to teach.

Whatever their personal reasons, adult volunteers provide valuable assistance and can be strong advocates for your school and your library media program. Volunteers are essential, even though you may have paid clerical staff. They lend expertise, assistance, a fresh perspective, and an air of informality.

Schools have varying degrees of success attracting parents. The *desire* to include community volunteers and parents as partners in the school is an important factor in securing involvement.

Circumstances such as working parents, lack of fluency in English, personal problems, unfamiliarity with school routines, and small children at home often deter parents. Two schools in the same neighborhood with similar populations may have very different volunteer experiences. Schools that attract volunteers have strategies that make people feel welcome. They:

△ Establish a climate of welcome that is apparent to all visitors.

△ Encourage teachers and administrators to send home positive comments about children and not contact parents only when there are problems.

△ Communicate in the language that is spoken at home.

△ Encourage participation and attendance in festivals such as "International Night" dinners, talent shows, parent and child courses, read-alouds, tutoring students, etc.

△ Ask volunteers to share their knowledge, skills, and experiences in a variety of ways.

△ Invite parents to view science fairs, room and library displays, shows, and so on.

△ Have parent and community representation on school governance committees.

△ Encourage parents to strengthen the parent association.

If your school community has initiated outreach activities with limited success, suggest the above activities. Other successful strategies:

△ Hold events at night and on weekends.

△ Pair non-English-speaking parents with those fluent in both languages.

△ Present workshops, G.E.D. and English as Second Language classes, computer training, and other workshops of interest to adults.

△ Welcome pre-school siblings.

△ Develop parent projects that can be accomplished at home.

Tips for Recruiting

△ Involve your advisory committee.

△ Speak at parent association meetings.

△ Contact senior citizen groups, political offices, or community agencies.

△ Develop grandparent, baby-sitter, aunt, or uncle programs.

△ Write a letter to all parents.

△ Solicit volunteers through your parent association, school, district, and local newspapers or newsletters.

△ Visit pre-K and other parent rooms to enlist parental help.

△ Haunt the schoolyard at dismissal time to speak with parents and caregivers.

Interviewing

When interviewing possible volunteers, describe the library program and your requirements. Your needs and expectations should be clear in your mind. Request that they list or detail their goals, interests, areas of expertise, strengths, and task preferences. When potential volunteers fill out an interest and abilities inventory, you can compare their individual skills, experiences, and interests to the jobs that must be done. Volunteers with a hobby, interest, or particular subject knowledge may be willing to share their expertise with students. With the volunteers' permission, you might circulate a list of your potential specialists to the faculty so that they can call on the volunteers when their skills are needed. Consider the hours that people are available and whether they want to work with children do clerical work, teacher training, or multiple activities. Delegate the tasks to the people who can do them best.

The sample Volunteer Letter on page 238 is a form that you may adapt to your own needs. It will give you information about prospective volunteers and will focus the applicant's attention on the skills and interests they can share with others.

Dear Volunteer:

Thank you for your interest in a voluntary position in the Excel School Library. There will be many opportunities for you to play a vital role in the lives of many students, both directly and indirectly. Please answer the following questions so that we can best use your knowledge and interests. You certainly will be able to modify the specific items you include at any time in the future.

PERSONAL INFORMATION

NAME _____

ASSOCIATION TO SCHOOL _____ (father, mother, relative, etc.)

CHILDREN IN CLASSES _____

ADDRESS _____

_____

TELEPHONE: HOME _____ WORK _____

I am available: Day(s) _____ AM _____ PM _____ BOTH _____

I cannot come to school but I could work at home doing _____

INTERESTS

1. What hobbies, talents, interests, and/or specialties do you have that you would like to share with students, teachers, or parents? For example: computers, desktop publishing, dance, opera, folk music, cooking, languages, poetry, crafts, needlework, science, reading aloud, storytelling, history, geography.

   _____

2. Are you interested in performing clerical tasks in the library media center? _____

   _____

3. Have you worked with groups of children before? _____

   In what capacity? _____

4. In what other localities, states, countries have you lived? _____

5. Would you speak with children/classes about your experiences? _____

6. What languages do you speak? _____

   _____

7. Would you like to talk (write) with children in this (these) language(s)? _____

   _____

Please add any comments or additional ways that you would like to be involved. I look forward to working with you in the library.

Sincerely,

Fig. 12.4. Volunteer Letter.

Fig. 12.5. Volunteers Work with Groups of Children.

Volunteers can learn to do many of the library clerical routines. It is important that you use a variety of teaching methods to accommodate diverse learning styles so that volunteers feel at ease as they learn. It is equally important to make sure that clerks also have a clear understanding of what is expected of them.

Prepare a manual that details how your library operates. Include library routines and tasks for those who learn best visually. Model or demonstrate how to perform routines and tasks. A library video similar to the manual will help people who learn visually and aurally and may be especially helpful for those who do not speak English fluently. It can be played as often as necessary without requiring your involvement.

Encourage volunteers to work in pairs or small groups to make it easier for them to learn from each other. They may find it more comfortable to ask questions of other volunteers than you. Invite questions. As you teach your staff how to perform their duties, have them practice the tasks. It is easier to catch mistakes in the beginning than to redo an entire project. Do not assume that support staff understand your directions until you see that they are able to do the work, then continue to monitor! One librarian found out too late that a volunteer had pasted in innumerable pockets—upside down.

Volunteers must be told precisely what is expected of them, in deportment as well as performance. State orally and in your manual that volunteers must go directly to the library and not wander through the building, unless on a specific assignment, nor visit classrooms without passes. They should not discipline students, nor should they accept jobs from others that are not within their scope as library helpers.

Occasionally support staff will not carry out the required tasks or work out as well as expected. Every effort should be made to evaluate on an ongoing basis and to develop a strong staff development program, but if a volunteer (or clerk) is not completing the assigned work, either provide different tasks or try to place the person in a different assignment. Ask your administration for help in working out problems you cannot solve alone.

Sometimes a volunteer creates difficulties. A parent might be trying to advance a political or personal ambition and try to use the volunteer position for this end. A personality clash may create interpersonal problems. Be prepared to act if there are complaints from staff, administration, students, or parents. Mediate between the volunteer and your complainant, or if the situation warrants, involve someone else. If the situation is not resolved satisfactorily, the volunteer should be asked to leave.

Retaining Volunteers

Include many opportunities for feedback and reflection. Ask the volunteers how successful they feel and if they are satisfied. Would they like to take on more advanced or challenging tasks? Can they complete their assignments within the time allotted? Is the work stimulating? Do they need additional assistance? Students need the same opportunities for reflection and discussion as other support staff. A volunteer who seems interested in the library or teaching profession might be invited to attend a library or education workshop or visit the public library with students and teachers. Compliments and praise are always welcome and create good working relationships. Make the working atmosphere enjoyable. A pot of coffee, tea, or juice is welcoming. Patience, a genuine interest in people, and a sense of humor will help build positive relationships. Remember: Praise in public, criticize in private.

When a volunteer leaves to go to work, in part because of skills learned or renewed in your library, the difficulties of finding a replacement should be mitigated by the knowledge that you have helped someone improve his or her life. You might offer to write a letter of recommendation for the volunteer. You also might ask the departing volunteer to find a replacement.

It takes time to learn, so be patient. Even if it appears to be easier to do the job yourself, it isn't. Remember that volunteers and support staff become advocates for your program, especially if they have positive experiences.

Coordinating Support Staff and Volunteers

When your staff includes paid clerical help and an active group of adult and student volunteers, setting up lines of communication, supervising, and coordinating their efforts takes thought and organization. Sometimes a volunteer will coordinate the volunteers. The person should have leadership qualities and good interpersonal skills. The coordinator can devise schedules, be called if a volunteer will be absent and a substitute is needed, and organize and teach new volunteers. Two people might share the coordinator's job.

Look at the library routines that must be done on a daily, weekly, or monthly basis. Consider the skills, experiences, interests, and schedules of all available support people. Set up a schedule. Decide who can best do the required tasks. Generate a schedule with names, times, and tasks clearly stated. Post it where it is accessible to all support staff. This will help everyone know what is expected.

Staff also need to be aware of supervisory lines that you have set up to ensure that everything goes smoothly. You may not want everyone to report to you directly. The library aide might supervise the student squad. The volunteer coordinator might assign tasks to the volunteers. If volunteers or aides have supervisory responsibilities, additional training in this area may be necessary. Always be aware of individual needs and personalities when supervision is an issue.

Mentoring

Mentoring support staff is an ongoing process. With the proper encouragement and instruction, people will grow as they take on more challenging jobs. Make your "staff" feel professional. The children and adults who work in the library should feel a sense of ownership, be able to carry out their duties independently, and be knowledgeable about the resources and the facility. They should have a good understanding of the importance of the library media center and its relationship to the school's educational program. They need to feel that they are part of a cooperative group whose mission is to run the library in the most effective way possible.

Good organizational skills will help you develop, maintain, and expand a library program that satisfies the demands of the school community. These skills combined with good "people skills" will help you to motivate your staff to do their best. When library aides, parent and community volunteers, and student monitors work closely together, your library will work well for the entire school community.

Bibliography

Chadbourne, Robert. "Volunteers in the Library: Both Sides Must Give in Order to Get." *Wilson Library Bulletin* 57 (June 1993): 25–26.

McCune, Bonnie F. "The New Volunteerism: Making It Pay Off for Your Library." *American Libraries* 24, no. 9 (October 1993): 822–24.

McHenry, Cheryl P. "Library Volunteers: Recruiting, Motivating, Keeping Them." *School Library Journal* 35 (May 1988): 137–38.

White, Herbert S. "The Double-Edged Sword of Library Volunteerism." *School Library Journal* 119 (April 1993): 55–56.

Wilson, Patricia J., and Ann C. Kimzey. *Happenings: Developing Successful Programs for School Libraries.* Englewood, CO: Libraries Unlimited, 1987.

Chapter 13 — Public Relations

Introduction

Public relations communicates the library's programs, services, and goals to the school and the larger community. Every successful school librarian needs to be an expert at providing information and attracting an audience. You are the most important factor in the public relations program. Your knowledge, enthusiasm, good humor, persuasiveness, extraordinary stamina, and caring attitude are essential. Fortunately, you are that special individual *Information Power* describes as the *typical* school librarian: "Bright, capable, somewhat reserved, yet projecting an aura of warmth and enthusiasm, confident, stable, not dependent on the group, attentive, able to communicate effectively."

The library space is special, too. It is a little like the oval office in the White House. It is a command post for information, a working space, and frequently a public reception area. The multiple functions offer many challenges as you simultaneously strive to meet the demands of the public, maintain resources, assist with ongoing projects, anticipate future needs, and on a moments notice, welcome a parent tour, teachers' conference, or third-grade puppet presentation. With so many demands on your time, talents, and space, it is essential that you plan ahead.

There are many strategies to communicate the value of your library to your school board, administrators, teachers, parents, students, and community groups in order to ensure continuing support throughout the school year.

The flyer on page 244 can help you design the public relations campaign that is appropriate for your school and purposes.

Getting Started

A successful public relations program requires analysis, research, planning, action, and evaluation. It also requires help! Do not try to do it alone. Use your advisory committee. Reach out to teachers, students, administrators, parents, and community people. If there is a schoolwide publicity committee, become a member. Time management is a serious concern for every school librarian. The more successful you are at publicizing and sharing your program and resources, the more you will be in demand, and frequently, the more you will be invited to join in other publicity efforts within the school and in the community. There is a great risk of overload. You can avoid serious problems with burnout and provide more effective programs and services if you enlist the help of others and share the responsibilities for public relations and publicity. Some guidelines, practical tips, and sources of additional information are provided here.

W I S E !

RITE

- grants and proposals
- a library newsletter
- press releases
- a column in your school or district newsletter
- an article for your local paper
- a library pamphlet
- letters to your district library coordinator
- letters to local elected officials to secure additional funds to support new or continuing activities

NVITE

- everyone!
- parents to browse through adult/ professional collections
- an author to read an original story
- an illustrator to conduct an art workshop
- the superintendant, politicians, local celebrities, press, and local merchants to library opennings, library tours, read-alouds, and storytelling contests
- student to form a library committee

HARE

- display library products in local markets, banks and public libraries
- offer the library as a meeting place for teachers and PTA meetings
- display before and after renovation photographs of the library room projects made in the library throughout the school: books from a bookmaking unit, research projects or murals
- students' computer art
- link to interlibrary loan
- give presentations about the library at union, grade level, and faculty meetings, and at local, state, and national conferences

VENTS

- organize a book fair, a nutrition or career day, a multicultural festival
- throw a breakfast for parents
- have a poetry festival
- have an open house or read-aloud day
- sponsor a yearlong project to be based in the library (*i.e. Books Across America, Count on Reading*)
- have a naming ceremony or an official opening
- write and produce a radio show
- begin a joint reading or oral history project with community senior citizen centers or another school

Fig. 13.1. A WISE Guide to Public Relations.

Developing a Focus

As a local public relations expert, you wear many hats and serve many audiences. Public relations within the school includes:

△ Alerting library users to library resources, services, and programs.

△ Connecting teachers and students in different classes to enrich learning and sharing. You are in a unique position to know what is happening in the school. If first- and fourth-grade classes are studying the environment, link their teachers in a collaboration on an Ecology Expo.

△ Facilitating change in teaching and learning by serving as an information specialist for new educational ideas including school restructuring and curricular change. Circulate professional periodicals, serve on committees, and post information on workshops and other professional development opportunities.

△ Creating a community of learners by sharing the processes and products of learning and teaching throughout the school community.

△ Documenting and saving the processes and products of learning.

The librarian is frequently an important member of the team publicizing the library and the school to the larger community. The team may be:

△ Informing the larger community about the school's philosophy, mission, and objectives.

△ Celebrating the teaching and learning process and products.

△ Advocating support for enhanced resources to further educational objectives.

△ Linking learning in the school to real-life learning opportunities, needs, and situations.

The focus of a public relations campaign might center on one facet of the school's educational philosophy and program. The focus might include:

△ Reading—how reading widely and often makes a difference.

△ Resource-Based Teaching—making a difference in how teachers teach.

△ Resource-Based Learning—making a difference in how students learn.

△ Information Literacy—how students are attacking information-rich problems.

△ Problem-Solving Abilities—learning strategies and skills to deal with new situations.

△ Real-Life Learning—teaching students how to generalize and transfer learning to new situations and authentic concerns.

△ Enhanced Self-Esteem, Tolerance, and Understanding—helping children value themselves and others.

Analyzing Your Needs

Think of school activities, events, displays, products, and happenings that have demonstrated and exemplified student learning. Think about your audience and your objectives. Analyze the past and plan for the future. What are the benefits of publicizing various events or activities? How much time, staff, and resources will publicizing the event require? Who will do it?

Who needs to hear about a program or event? What is the best way to let them know? What do you want them to know? Do you want them to: Participate? Attend? Send money? Donate a video camera? Write a feature story for the community paper?

It is impossible to highlight every event, exemplary teaching and learning practice, and product. Be selective. Time and resources are limited. Advance planning is essential.

Gathering the Resources

Word of mouth, bulletin boards, exhibits, flyers, news releases, conference presentations, publications, TV and radio spots, workshops, special events, and contests can all be used to get your message to the intended audience. You and your team will need to decide what your message, media, audience, and objectives are. As the resource and information specialist in your school, you are the logical person to gather information on publicity sources, submission requirements, people to contact, deadlines, and the like. Keep a public relations file and share it! What TV channel covers education news? Which radio station will give free publicity spots? Which community paper will send a reporter or photographer? Which bank will display student art or writing? It is not hard to incorporate publicity into the planning of a unit, program, or learning activity. Once you have done it a few times, it becomes so routine that with only a little extra effort, it can result in great benefits, not only for your program but also for learners.

Evaluating the Effort

Ongoing evaluation is essential. Are you reaching your intended audience? Is your audience growing? Does the program, service, or resource meet their needs? Are there new avenues to be explored? Should your goals or objectives be modified? How can your program, services, or resources be improved? How does this program or service fit into the larger goals and mission of the library and the school?

Visual Displays

Professional-looking bulletin boards and displays can inform members of the school community about library programs, resources, services, and goals. Visual displays can celebrate books and learning, the world of ideas, and the work of children. Whenever possible, displays should show the process and products of student learning and work: writing samples, artwork, reports, explanations, puzzles, dioramas, mobiles, photos of trips, assembly programs, demonstrations, and more.

Displays should be changed frequently and reflect current work and projects. Throughout the year, be sure exhibits highlight the work and activities of many children and many teachers. Some of the more effective displays are collaboratively planned with classroom teachers and students. Because classroom teachers sometimes have difficulty locating attractive visuals for displays, many libraries provide a useful service by keeping a file of quality visuals that teachers may borrow for bulletin boards or classroom use.

Fig. 13.2. Eye-Catching Displays Promote Interest.

Acquiring Visuals for Display

△ Many magazines include free posters.

△ *Instructor* contains a pullout art poster and calendar each month.

△ *National Geographic* has pullout maps.

△ *Odyssey* contains pullout space photos.

△ *School Library Journal* publishes a monthly column called, "Checklist," which features free and inexpensive posters, pamphlets, bookmarks, and the like.

△ Publishers' catalogs contain free and inexpensive material on books and authors.

△ Professional conferences, workshops, and book fairs often provide free visuals.

△ Display materials can be purchased from the Children's Book Council, ALA Graphics (a division of ALA), and many private companies.

△ Museum gift shops often sell posters and prints.

△ Children's artwork can be effectively used for display. Cultivate a relationship with art and classroom teachers. Encourage joint projects that produce appealing visuals.

△ Use photos of children. Commercial photo shops will enlarge photos to poster size at a reasonable cost. Have parents sign a release form whenever photographs are published.

△ Collect old art and theme calendars; many have stunning color illustrations.

∆ Use computer graphics, especially computer art designed by children. Banner-making programs make it possible to enlarge drawings and designs to gigantic size.

∆ Book jackets, and the books themselves, make visually appealing displays.

∆ Download from the Internet.

Lettering

In the old days, librarians struggled to trace and cut letters using stencils, hoarded pin-back plastic letters, or bribed students and teachers with exceptional skill to draw freehand signs. Those days are past! Teachers' stores provide inexpensive punch-out letters in vivid colors and many styles. School supply catalogs market letter punches that produce plastic letters to order. There are electronic signs that can be programmed via a computer to scroll a message in lights. Best of all, most schools have computer programs for making banners with letters of almost any size. Encourage students and parents to help design and produce computer graphics. Use a color printer if available. If not, invite students to color and decorate the letters.

Flyers, Bookmarks, and Letters

Flyers are an inexpensive and effective way to publicize programs and services. Because flyers relay the library's message, it is important that the information presented be correct, complete, and clear. Ask a colleague to examine the flyer before it is printed. Have you:

∆ Corrected all grammar and spelling errors?

∆ Indicated: Who, What, Where, When, How, and Why?

∆ Made clear if a response is required: to whom, by when?

∆ Listed any deadlines or limitations?

∆ Included the school logo, complete address, and other information required?

∆ Used a pleasing blend of text and graphics?

∆ Respected copyright laws if graphics are used?

∆ Credited student artists if their work is used?

Be sure to keep a copy of all flyers you have used in the past. Keep templates on diskette if the work was produced on the computer. It is easy to edit existing copy. Just use a glue stick or rubber cement and paste over information not needed. Insert new copy or graphics and you are ready to run. The computer template is easy to edit on screen.

Student Graphics

Students are often the best source of graphics for flyers. Keep a supply of unlined white paper and fine-line black felt-tipped markers in the library. Invite students to make designs and illustrations and keep them on file. Students should sign their names on every drawing so proper credit can be given. If the illustrations are too large or too small, you can use a photocopy machine to reduce or enlarge the illustration. Many students use computer drawing programs. Their drawings can be saved for later use. Student drawings can be scanned into the computer and manipulated on screen to fit into flyers. With enough advance warning, students can design graphics as a classroom, art, or computer project.

Dependent on local school policies, school photocopy, spirit duplicating, or mimeograph machines may be used to print flyers. Often the PTA has printing equipment and parents may have access to equipment at their homes or offices. Sometimes there is money for professional copying or printing; ask parents to investigate local stores and businesses for the best prices. Sometimes, if local school policies permit, costs are covered by advertising.

Communications

An important way to let people know about the library programs, services, resources, and goals is just to talk with them. Formal presentations at faculty meetings, student assemblies, and parent meetings can provide useful opportunities. However, informal contacts are often even more important. You may not have thought of it, but YOU are enhancing the library program whenever you:

Δ Make an enthusiastic comment in the teacher's room about a new book or multimedia product.

Δ Sponsor a high school student doing community service.

Δ Assist a student teacher with a class project.

Δ Ask local businesspeople or parents to speak about their careers.

Δ Give positive feedback to students about their research.

Δ Invite parents to see their children's work on display.

Δ Ask your administrator to visit the library while a class shares its research.

Δ Offer to help with a program, project, or activity.

Δ Thank a parent for volunteering in the library.

Δ Encourage faculty members or parents to meet in the library.

Just as you are an ambassador for the library, every paid employee, student and adult volunteer, and member of your advisory committee is an ambassador, too. Make sure they all recognize their importance. Take the time to compliment them on work well done and to express your appreciation of their efforts. A warm welcome and a sympathetic ear can reduce many problems to a manageable level.

Forms of Communication

Using the Airwaves

Most schools have public address systems or video news shows with daily announcements. Ask to make a brief announcement about library special events or pose a puzzle of the day to stimulate library research. Some schools allow students to give minibook reviews or share a short story, riddle, or poem over the loudspeaker. It is an excellent way to arouse interest in books and to develop oral language skills. A one-minute biography of a famous African American or woman in history, broadcast by a student, helps everyone in the school share in the learning and spreads the library's message. Some schools have developed programs for public interest radio, commercial shows, or even established their own school radio or TV station.

Online

If you have access to telecommunications anywhere in the school, use it to publicize your message. Use local bulletin boards, chat lines, and e-mail to connect with colleagues, obtain long-distance resources, and share information about your program and services. Teach a squad of students to be your online experts. They can send and receive messages, request interlibrary loan materials, download news items and curriculum units, and help other students, teachers, and parents communicate via computer.

Video

Many schools have video cameras. They are important tools for recording the process and product of learning in the school. Use them to document library programs and activities. Students can use them to create information in new formats and to share their learning with their classmates, parents, and the larger community. Videos can be used at parent and teacher workshops to show authentic examples of students' learning and demonstrate teaching techniques. Some schools maintain video pen pals, sending locally produced videos to schools and individuals in other locations to enhance long-distance learning. Computer techniques make it possible to insert video clips in computer programs to create new interactive learning materials. It is important to keep informed about this area of technology that is revolutionizing traditional ideas of communication.

Public Appearances and Workshops

Public appearances and workshops can be opportunities to provide others with information about the library. Encourage your advisory committee to share information about the library services, programs, and needs as they meet people at events in their neighborhood, at social and fraternal organizations, at political rallies and block parties, and as they go about their jobs and professional commitments. Say "yes" to assignments that help make the library a visible and prominent part of the school community. When you assist on a committee, act as a judge for the social studies fair, host a schoolwide event, do staff development, judge the storytelling contest, referee a debate, present student awards for essay writing at an assembly, or help select the PTA Good Citizen Award recipient, YOU are an ambassador for the library and its program.

Publications

Some librarians find that newsletters or magazines are an effective way to publicize the library program and activities. Because they can be extremely time consuming and expensive to produce, you may wish to investigate:

△ Writing a column for the PTA newsletter.

△ Writing for the school faculty newsletter or district news letter.

△ Writing a book review column or events column for the student or local newspaper.

△ Using e-mail or a computer bulletin board service.

Fig. 13.3. Participation in Staff Development Extends the Librarian's Role in the District.

If you decide to produce a library newsletter or magazine, work closely with your advisory committee and your administrator to determine how it can be funded, and identify staff and volunteers available to help. Involve classroom teachers, the art and computer teacher, and students and parents so that the writing, editing, layout, and graphic design become part of the learning experience across curriculum areas. Ask for parental involvement with editing, funding, printing, folding and stapling, and distribution. A student editorial board is also desirable. Decide how frequently the newsletter will be published, who will receive it, how it will be funded and distributed, and, most importantly, what types of articles and information it will contain.

Publications Beyond the School

Some local newspapers, shopper guides, and community newsletters publish articles about what is happening in local school libraries. Discuss the school policy on publicity with your administrator and then find out the resources of your local community. Have members of your library advisory committee:

△ Collect samples of neighborhood publications.

△ Ask others in the community about special interest publications: religious institutions' bulletins, hobby and club publications, neighborhood association newsletters, and fraternal organizations' publications.

△ Establish a publicity contact with each publication.

The Best Public Relations Is Sharing What You Do Each Day

It is important to show those who are not teachers the excitement and joy of children discovering books—sharing, learning, and finding new things to wonder about. Forge relationships with the community to foster understanding and broaden children's contact with the "real" world. To further these ends, you can:

△ Set up a collection of parenting books and invite parents to borrow them.

△ Invite an author, illustrator, or educator to speak.

△ Invite the principal, guidance staff, district office staff, and others to see children at work.

△ Ask a community person to speak about his or her career, travel, culture, or hobbies or view student presentations in his or her field.

△ Host a children's art display, puppet performance, musical presentation, or skit in the library.

△ Celebrate storytelling for all ages.

△ Visit a celebrity somewhere in the world via the Internet.

△ Create parent and child workshops or book browsing times.

Fig. 13.4. Parent Workshops Increase Parent Participation in the Library and School.

Saying Thank You

Every public relations program needs to consider how committee members, volunteers, students, staff, and community people who provide assistance will be recognized and acknowledged throughout the year. It is important to say "Thank you," but just a verbal thank you may not be enough:

△ Take the time to let individuals know how much their contribution matters and how they fit into the larger picture.

△ Give praise and thanks in front of others. Thank a student in front of his or her teacher, a teacher in the presence of his or her supervisor or administrator, and a parent in a group of peers.

△ Acknowledge help and express thanks in writing in programs, flyers, and news articles.

△ Send letters of thanks to community sponsors, elected officials, parents, staff, and volunteers. Send a letter to the local newspaper.

△ Send a letter to the boss, the district office, mayor's office, or the president.

△ Write an article for the school or district newspaper.

△ Celebrate contributions in articles written for state and national publications.

△ Give certificates, pins, badges, mugs, T-shirts, boutonnieres, stickers, and plaques.

△ Organize an appreciation assembly, pizza party, luncheon, coffee, or reception.

△ Help with resumes, job applications, and references.

△ Invite volunteers to attend workshops, conferences, and seminars.

△ Provide perks: first opportunity to check out new books, extra time using the library computer, overnight borrowing of videos, renewals, preference for topics for book discussions or storytelling programs.

△ Involve volunteers in planning future events and training. Acknowledge their ideas and provide opportunities for professional growth. Give them a meaningful role in setting the direction of the library. Make them partners in achieving the library mission.

Designing a Formal Celebration

The formal opening, dedication, Founder's Day, or birthday observance is a celebration that dramatizes and publicizes your vision for the library as central to the educational process. It emphasizes your leadership role within the educational community as an agent for school reform and educational change. An annual celebration is a milestone that encourages you and every member of your school community to look backward at where you have been and forward to where you would like to be. The celebration gives you a chance to reach a larger audience, to recognize and honor those who have been helpful in making your vision possible and successful, and to encourage and solicit additional help and support. Rather like arranging a wedding, an annual celebration requires extensive planning and help from a great many people. Do not be deterred; it is really worth it! If you have not organized such an event, you may find the following recipe and timetable useful in getting started.

Planning

A successful event requires six to eight weeks of advance preparation and involves the help and cooperation of many people. Include your administrator, district library staff, advisory committee, a member of the custodial staff, parents' association officers, parents, and children on your planning committee. A planning committee will result in increased interest and public awareness. It will generate additional ideas and distribute the workload. With the help of your planning committee:

∆ Decide on a date, time, and guest for the event.

∆ Arrange for publicity.

∆ Organize a program.

∆ Plan decorations and displays.

∆ Arrange for refreshments and documentation.

∆ Send thank you letters.

Invitations and Publicity

Clear the date and time with important guests before the invitations are sent to ensure that your most important guests are able to attend. You may want to include local dignitaries and elected officials, school board members, school administrators and faculty, district office personnel, parents, and the press as guests. Ask special guests to RSVP and contact the school for more information. Give speakers advance notice and a time limit.

Invitations may be handmade, professionally printed, mimeographed, or photocopied. A child's drawing or computer graphic adds visual appeal. Always double-check spelling, grammar, and accuracy of the information before invitations are sent. For those who might not be familiar with your program, be sure to include a summary or information flyer. Then, even if a prominent guest does not attend, he or she will be aware of the special happenings at your library. If prominent individuals are unable to attend, ask them to send a representative and write a letter of support or congratulations. Indicate that it will be read at the program.

The News Release

Write a news release for school and local newspapers, magazines, and community groups. As soon as you know of prominent people who have agreed to speak and/or attend, alert the press. Request a reporter or photographer. Make flyers or posters for distribution to teachers, parents, and children and for local store windows and community organizations. When possible have a child design the flyer or poster. To help you publicize an event, keep a file on the local press that includes:

∆ A contact person, phone number, and mailing address.

∆ Information on the kinds of articles they publish.

∆ Whether they will send a photographer or reporter.

∆ How much advance warning is needed for a story.

∆ Information on deadlines: daily, weekly.

△ Whether they publish special sections: a calendar of community events, school news, book columns.

△ The preferred format for new releases.

△ Whether they accept articles or features submitted for publication.

△ Whether they will print photos submitted; information on the size and kind of photos or negative.

Reporters and Photographers

If you are able to secure a reporter or photographer for a special event or activity, here are some things you can do to make the experience more successful:

△ Learn the name of the reporter and photographer in advance and send or fax background information on the program and the event or activity they will be covering.

△ Include the names and titles of prominent people who will be attending.

△ Include travel directions, the name and phone number of a contact person, and the exact times and place the program will be occurring.

△ If the program cannot be interrupted once begun, explain in advance and offer to set up a photography session or interview before or after the program.

△ Offer to take pictures and provide captions.

△ Provide the reporter with a copy of the program, the names of guest speakers, and brief quotes from speeches.

△ Make sure someone is assigned to greet the reporter and the photographer and escort them to the site of the program.

△ Introduce the reporter to prominent guests and explain the guests' relevance to the program.

△ Give a brief summary of the project and explain why it is newsworthy.

△ Be available to assist the reporter with the correct spelling of names and titles.

△ Offer refreshments. Though often too busy to accept, many reporters appreciate the gesture.

△ Be sure to say thank you.

△ After the story appears, write a note of thanks to the reporter and the editor.

△ Encourage others to write a letter to the editor, complimenting the reporter and the paper on the coverage.

Post the story and reprint copies for teachers, parents, district office staff, and others who might have missed it. If you feel the event might merit wider coverage, ask your administrator or district public relations staff to assist with preparing a news release for a national publication.

Radio and Television Coverage

Some programs are so novel, timely, or interesting that they might command coverage on the radio or television. Ask the help of your advisory committee in investigating local resources to determine if there is:

△ A public service radio station or local television that provides public service announcements or a community calendar.

△ A specialty reporter or commentator who might be interested in the event at your school.

△ A high school or college radio or television station.

△ A local cable television station with a public access facility.

△ A parent or other community person who has personal or professional contacts with reporters, disc jockeys, sports personalities, or others willing to make contacts to help publicize school programs.

The Ceremony

The ceremony may have a lasting effect on both the presenters and the audience. The following tips can maximize the positive memories and make the day worth the effort.

△ Have students act as hosts to greet guests at the door and escort them to the library.

△ Prepare name tags for invited guests and encourage them to sign a guest book (name, address, title, phone number). This becomes a useful reference for future volunteers.

△ Present a proclamation or plaque to add to the festivities. A ribbon-cutting ceremony is one of the many events you can plan effectively.

△ Include children in programs; remember it is their library.

△ Solicit teachers' help in organizing students to present: music, art, skits, poems, choral readings, essays, and stories.

△ Hand out a program that lists all participants and planners.

△ Keep formal speeches to a minimum, but allow a few minutes for administrators, elected officials, community leaders, and parents.

△ Give recognition to your planning committee and to others who have helped. A certificate of appreciation is a welcome and inexpensive token of thanks.

Fig. 13.5. Children Participate in Dedication Ceremonies as Presenters and Hosts.

Decorations and Special Effects

Δ The library is on display! Take extra time to see that it looks spectacular. Invite members of the library squad and colleagues to tour the library in advance. Remove shabby books and magazines, straighten and tidy shelves, dust and polish shelves and tables, and freshen signs and bulletin boards. Plan an exciting new display featuring new books and children's work.

Δ Have available literature about your program as well as bookmarks, flyers, and information on upcoming library events. Display completed and in-progress student art, research, and writing projects throughout the room.

Δ Refreshments add a festive note, but keep them simple. Ask committee members or parents to provide simple foods: punch and cookies, crackers and juice, sheet cake, or other easy-to-serve refreshments. Remember to have: paper goods, cutting and serving utensils, and cleanup supplies for accidents. Ask older children or parents to help set up, serve, and clean up.

Essential Details

Be sure to consult with your administrator and custodial staff well before the event. With their help, make a list of needed equipment and supplies: extra chairs, tables, microphone or loudspeaker, the video camera, and so on. Request help with furniture moving and extra cleaning before and after the event. Try to anticipate other assistance needed. Ask members of your committee to help with planning refreshments, name tags, a guest book, and room decorations.

Documentation

△ Ask the district office, parents, or teachers to videotape the entire event and to take photographs.

△ Encourage students to interview guests for the school paper or for a writing assignment. Use tape recorders to record the program and tape the comments of guests.

△ Urge local newspapers to send a reporter and a photographer.

△ Duplicate copies of children's writing that are part of the program and distribute.

△ Write follow-up articles for local newspapers.

△ Encourage others to write letters to the editor.

△ Help children create a scrapbook and bulletin board display documenting the entire event.

Showing Your Appreciation

△ Send thank you notes to all who helped or participated.

△ Use your guest book to recruit future volunteers.

Countdown for a Successful Event

Eight Weeks Before

Involve your administrator. Select your committee. Choose a tentative date and time and confirm it with special guests.

Six Weeks Before

With your committee, plan a program, finalize the guest list, and prepare a news release. Request a reporter and photographer. Design invitations and arrange for printing. Request special equipment and cleaning help. Plan information handouts.

Four Weeks Before

Send out invitations. Include parents and request their help with arrangements, refreshments, and assistance the day of the event. Arrange for photos or videotaping. Work with classroom teachers and students on the program. Notify parents of children who will be performing.

Two Weeks Before

Phone special guests who have not responded. Confirm press coverage. Finalize the program, refreshments, and special equipment. Prepare bulletin boards and special displays.

One Week Before

Rehearse the program and send reminders to parents of children who will be participating. Make name tags, award certificates, guest book, and sign-up sheets. Assemble special equipment (extension cords, extra film, tapes, batteries). Explain duties to student hosts.

One Day Before

Meet with your committee to review last minute changes. Review everyone's assignment. Straighten, decorate, and arrange the room. Meet with student hosts for a final review and have a dress rehearsal.

The Big Day Arrives

Station greeters and hosts. See that additional name tags are available. Test sound and audiovisual equipment in advance. Enjoy the program.

And After

Write thank you cards and notes. Help students arrange photos for a bulletin board display or scrapbook. Write a follow-up for local papers and the school newspaper. Contact those who offered to volunteer for special programs. You did a super job! **Take a bow! It's not too early to start thinking about your next extravaganza!**

Bibliography

ALA Graphics. American Library Association. 50 E. Huron Street, Chicago, IL 60611. Provides a catalog of display and promotional items to celebrate and publicize reading and libraries.

Bradbury, Phil. *Border Clip Art for Libraries.* Englewood, CO: Libraries Unlimited, 1989.

————. *Button Art: Reading and Libraries.* Englewood, CO: Libraries Unlimited, 1993.

Edsall, Marian S. *Practical PR for School Library Media Centers.* New York: Neal-Schuman, 1994.

Frohardt, Darcie Clark. *Books, Books, Books: A Treasury of Clip Art.* Englewood, CO: Libraries Unlimited, 1995.

Kohn, Rita, and Krysta A. Tepper. *Have You Got What THEY Want? Public Relations Strategies for the School Librarian/Media Specialist: A Reference Tool.* 2d ed. Metuchen, NJ: Scarecrow Press, 1990.

Laughlin, Mildred Knight, and Kathy Howard Latrobe. *Public Relations for School Library Media Centers.* Englewood, CO: Libraries Unlimited, 1990.

Appendices

261

American Association of School Librarians

Position Statement on:

THE VALUE OF LIBRARY MEDIA PROGRAMS IN EDUCATION

School library media specialists are an integral part of the total educational team which prepares students to become responsible citizens in a changing global society. In today's information age, an individual's success, even existence, depends largely on the ability to access, evaluate and utilize information. Library media specialists are leaders in carrying out the school's instructional program through their separate but overlapping roles of information specialist, teacher and instructional consultant.

The *Goals 2000* challenge our nation to make education a top priority in preparing students to compete in the worldwide marketplace and make informed decisions about problems facing society. To guarantee every young person an equal and effective educational opportunity, officials must provide each school with library media facilities and resources to meet curriculum needs. Officials must also ensure that each school's staff includes library media professionals and support personnel to carry out the mission of the instructional program.

The American Association of School Librarians is committed to the development and improvement of strong library media programs in all schools. The ability to locate and use information in solving problems, expanding ideas and becoming informed citizens depends on access to adequate library media facilities, appropriate resources and qualified personnel. Recent studies, such as *The Impact of School Library Media Centers on Academic Achievement* show a strong positive correlation between library media programs and student achievement.

The American Association of School Librarians urges all administrators, teachers, school board members, parents and community members to recognize the power of information and the critical need for strong professionally staffed library media programs so all students become effective users of information.

Suggested Readings:

American Association of School Librarians and Association for Educational Communications and Technology. *Information Power: Guidelines for School Library Media Programs.* Chicago: ALA, 1988.

Lance, Keith Curry et al. *The Impact of School Library Media Centers on Academic Achievement.* Castle Rock, CO: Hi Willow Research & Publishing, 1993.

"Restructuring and School Libraries." (Special Section) *NASSP BULLETIN 75* (May 1991): 1-58. (A Special Section on the School Library for the Nineties). PHI DELTA KAPPAN 73 (March 1992): 521-537.

Stripling, Barbara K. *Libraries for the National Education Goals.* Syracuse, NY: ERIC Clearinghouse on Information Resources, Syracuse University, 1992.

American Association of School Librarians, American Library Association • 50 East Huron Street • Chicago, IL 60611 • 1-800-545-2433 x4386

AASL

American Association of School Librarians

Position Statement on:

APPROPRIATE STAFFING FOR SCHOOL LIBRARY MEDIA CENTERS

The success of any school library media program, no matter how well designed, depends ultimately on the quality and number of the personnel responsible for the program. A well-educated and highly motivated professional staff, adequately supported by technical and clerical staff, is critical to the endeavor.

Although staffing patterns are developed to meet local needs, certain basic staffing requirements can be identified. Staffing patterns must reflect the following principles:

1. **All students, teachers, and administrators in each school building at all grade levels must have access to a library media program provided by one or more certificated library media specialist working full-time in the school's library media center.**

2. **Both professional personnel and support staff are necessary for all library media programs at all grade levels.** Each school must employ at least one full-time technical assistant or clerk for each library media specialist. Some programs, facilities, and levels of service will require more than one support staff member for each professional.

3. **More than one library media professional is required in many schools.** The specific number of additional professional staff is determined by the school's size, number of students and of teachers, facilities, specific library program. A reasonable ratio of professional staff to teacher and student populations is required in order to provide for the levels of service and library media program development described in *INFORMATION POWER: GUIDELINES FOR SCHOOL LIBRARY MEDIA* programs.

Other Position Statements Available from AASL -

- Role of the School Library Media Specialist in Site-Based Management

- Role of the School Library Media Specialist in the Whole Language Approach-Resource Based Instruction

- Role of the School Library Media Program

- Preparation of School Library Media Specialist

- Flexible Scheduling

- Value of Library Media Programs in Education

- Confidentiality of Library Records

- Information Literacy: Information Problem Solving

- Access to Resources and Services in the School Library Media Program

- School Library Media Supervisor

- Value of Independent Reading in the School Library Media Program

- Role of the Library Media Specialist in Outcomes-Based Education

All school systems must employ a district library media director to provide leadership and direction to the overall library media program. The district director is a member of the administrative staff and serves on committees that determine the criteria and policies for the district's curriculum and instructional programs. The director communicates the goals and needs of both the school and district library media programs to the superintendent, board of education, other district-level personnel, and the community. In this advocacy role, the district library media director advances the concept of the school library media specialist as a partner with teachers and promotes a staffing level that allows the partnership to flourish.

Adopted April, 1991

American Association of School Librarians, American Library Association • 50 East Huron Street • Chicago, IL 60611 • 1-800-545-2433 x4386

Position Statement on:

AASL
American Association of School Librarians

FLEXIBLE SCHEDULING

Schools must adopt the educational philosophy that the library media program is fully integrated into the educational program. This integration strengthens the teaching/learning process so that students can develop the vital skills necessary to locate, analyze, evaluate, interpret, and communicate information and ideas. When the library media program is fully integrated into the instructional program of the school, students, teachers, and library media specialists become partners in learning. The library program is an extension of the classroom. Information skills are taught and learned within the context of the classroom curriculum. The wide range of resources, technologies, and services needed to meet students' learning and information needs are readily available in a cost-effective manner.

The integrated library media program philosophy requires that an open schedule must be maintained. Classes cannot be scheduled in the library media center to provide teacher release or preparation time. Students and teachers must be able to come to the center throughout the day to use information sources, to read for pleasure, and to meet and work with other students and teachers.

Planning between the library media specialist and the classroom teacher, which encourages both scheduled and informal visits, is the catalyst that makes this integrated library program work. The teacher brings to the planning process a knowledge of subject content and student needs. The library media specialist contributes a broad knowledge of resources and technology, an understanding of teaching methods, and a wide range of strategies that may be employed to help students learn information skills.

Cooperative planning by the teacher and library media specialist integrates information skills and materials into the classroom curriculum and results in the development of assignments that encourage open inquiry.

The responsibility for flexibly scheduled library media programs must be shared by the entire school community. THE BOARD OF EDUCATION endorses the philosophy that the library program is an integral part of the district's educational program and ensures that flexible scheduling for library media centers is maintained in all buildings and at all levels.

THE DISTRICT ADMINISTRATION supports this philosophy and monitors staff assignments to ensure appropriate staffing levels so that all teachers, including the library media specialists, can fulfill their professional responsibilities.

THE PRINCIPAL creates the appropriate climate within the school by advocating the benefits of flexible scheduling to the faculty, by monitoring scheduling, by ensuring appropriate staffing levels, and by providing oint planning time for classroom teachers and library media specialists.

THE TEACHER uses resource-based instruction and views the library media program as a integral part of that instruction.

THE LIBRARY MEDIA SPECIALIST is knowledgeable about curriculum and classroom activities, and works cooperatively with the classroom teacher to integrate information skills into the curriculum.

Adopted June, 1991

American Association of School Librarians, American Library Association • 50 East Huron Street • Chicago, IL 60611 • 1-800-545-2433 x4386

Position Statement:

AASL

American Association of School Librarians

ACCESS TO RESOURCES AND SERVICES IN THE SCHOOL LIBRARY MEDIA PROGRAM
AN INTERPRETATION OF THE LIBRARY BILL OF RIGHTS

The school library media program plays a unique role in promoting intellectual freedom. It serves as a point of voluntary access to information and ideas and as a learning laboratory for students as they acquire critical thinking and problem solving skills needed in a pluralistic society. Although the educational level and program of the school necessarily shape the resources and services of a school library media program, the principles of the LIBRARY BILL OF RIGHTS apply equally to all libraries, including school library media programs.

School library media professionals assume a leadership role in promoting the principles of intellectual freedom within the school by providing resources and services that create and sustain an atmosphere of free inquiry. School library media professionals work closely with teachers to integrate instructional activities in classroom units designed to equip students to locate, evaluate, and use a broad range of ideas effectively. Through resources, programming, and educational processes, students and teachers experience the free and robust debate characteristic of a democratic society.

School library media professionals cooperate with other individuals in building collections of resources appropriate to the development and maturity levels of students. These collections provide resources which support curriculum and are consistent with the philosophy, goals, and objectives of the school district. Resources in school library media collections represent diverse points of view and current as well as historical issues.

While English is by history and tradition the customary language of the United States, the languages in use in any given community may vary. Schools serving communities in which other languages are used make efforts to accommodate the needs of students for whom English is a second language. To support these efforts, and to ensure equal access to resources and services, the school library media program provides resources which reflect the linguistic pluralism of the community.

Members of the school community involved in the collection development process employ educational criteria to select resources unfettered by their personal, political, social, or religious views.

Students and educators served by the school library media program have access to resources and services free of constraints resulting from personal, partisan, or doctrinal disapproval. School library media professionals resist efforts by individuals to define what is appropriate for all students or teachers to read, view, or hear.

Major barriers between students and resources include: imposing age or grade level restrictions on the use of resources, limiting the use of interlibrary loan and access to electronic information, charging fees for information in specific formats, requiring permission from parents or teachers, establishing restricted shelves or closed collections, and labeling. Policies, procedures, and rules related to the use of resources and services support free and open access to information.

The school board adopts policies that guarantee access to a broad range of ideas. These include policies on collection development and procedures for the review of resources about which concerns have been raised. Such policies, developed by the persons in the school community, provide for a timely and fair hearing and assure that procedures are applied equitably to all expressions of concern. School library media professionals implement district policies and procedures in the school.

Adopted July, 1986
Amended January, 1990, by the ALA Council
ISBN 8389-7053-2

American Association of School Librarians, American Library Association • 50 East Huron Street • Chicago, IL 60611 • 1-800-545-2433, x4386

CONFIDENTIALITY OF LIBRARY RECORDS

The members of the American Library Association,* recognizing the right to privacy of library users, believe that records held in libraries which connect specific individuals with specific resources, programs or services, are confidential and not to be used for purposes other than routine record keeping: i.e., to maintain access to resources, to assure that resources are available to users who need them, to arrange facilities, to provide resources for the comfort and safety of patrons, or to accomplish the purposes of the program or service. The library community recognizes that children and youth have the same rights to privacy as adults.

Libraries whose record keeping systems reveal the names of users would be in violation of the confidentiality of library record laws adopted in many states. School library media specialists are advised to seek the advice of counsel if in doubt about whether their record keeping systems violate the specific laws in their states. Efforts must be made within the reasonable constraints of budgets and school management procedures to eliminate such records as soon as reasonably possible.

With or without specific legislation, school library media specialists are urged to respect the rights of children and youth by adhering to the tenets expressed in the Confidentiality of Library Records Interpretation of the Library Bill of Rights and the ALA Code of Ethics.

*ALA Policy 52.4, 54.16

American Association of School Librarians, American Library Association • 50 East Huron Street • Chicago, IL 60611 • 1-800-545-2433 x4386

American Library Association Code of Ethics

As members of the American Library Association, we recognize the importance of codifying and making known to the profession and to the general public the ethical principles that guide the work of librarians, other professionals providing information services, library trustees and library staffs.

Ethical dilemmas occur when values are in conflict. The American Library Association Code of Ethics states the values to which we are committed, and embodies the ethical responsibilities of the profession in this changing information environment.

We significantly influence or control the selection, organization, preservation, and dissemination of information. In a political system grounded in an informed citizenry, we are members of a profession explicitly committed to intellectual freedom and the freedom of access to information. We have a special obligation to ensure the free flow of information and ideas to present and future generations.

The principles of this Code are expressed in broad statements to guide ethical decision making. These statements provide a framework; they cannot and do not dictate conduct to cover particular situations.

I. We provide the highest level of service to all library users through appropriate and usefully organized resources; equitable service policies; equitable access; and accurate, unbiased, and courteous responses to all requests.

II - We uphold the principles of intellectual freedom and resist all efforts to censor library resources.

III. We protect each library user's right to privacy and confidentiality with respect to information sought or received and resources consulted, borrowed, acquired or transmitted.

IV. We recognize and respect intellectual property rights.

V. We treat co-workers and other colleagues with respect, fairness and good faith, and advocate conditions of employment that safeguard the rights and welfare of all employees of our institutions.

VI. We do not advance private interests at the expense of library users, colleagues, or our employing institutions.

VII. We distinguish between our personal convictions and professional duties and do not allow our personal beliefs to interfere with fair representation of the aims of our institutions or the provision of access to their information resources.

VIII. We strive for excellence in the profession by maintaining and enhancing our own knowledge and skills, by encouraging the professional development of co-workers, and by fostering the aspirations of potential members of the profession.

Adopted by the ALA Council
June 28, 1995

Reprinted by the permission of the American Library Association.

Library Bill of Rights

The American Library Association affirms that all libraries are forums for information and ideas, and that the following basic policies should guide their services.

1. Books and other library resources should be provided for the interest, information, and enlightenment of all people of the community the library serves. Materials should not be excluded because of the origin, background, or views of those contributing to their creation.

2. Libraries should provide materials and information presenting all points of view on current and historical issues. Materials should not be proscribed or removed because of partisan or doctrinal disapproval.

3. Libraries should challenge censorship in the fulfillment of their responsibility to provide information and enlightenment.

4. Libraries should cooperate with all persons and groups concerned with resisting abridgment of free expression and free access to ideas.

5. A person's right to use a library should not be denied or abridged because of origin, age, background, or views.

6. Libraries which make exhibit spaces and meeting rooms available to the public they serve should make such facilities available on an equitable basis, regardless of the beliefs or affiliations of individuals or groups requesting their use.

Adopted June 18, 1948.
Amended February 2, 1961, June 27, 1967, and January 23, 1980,
by the ALA Council.

THE FREEDOM TO READ

The freedom to read is essential to our democracy. It is continuously under attack. Private groups and public authorities in various parts of the country are working to remove books from sale, to censor textbooks, to label "controversial" books, to distribute lists of "objectionable" books or authors, and to purge libraries. These actions apparently rise from a view that our national tradition of free expression is no longer valid; that censorship and suppression are needed to avoid the subversion of politics and the corruption of morals. We, as citizens devoted to the use of books and as librarians and publishers responsible for disseminating them, wish to assert the public interest in the preservation of the freedom to read.

We are deeply concerned about these attempts at suppression. Most such attempts rest on a denial of the fundamental premise of democracy: that the ordinary citizen, by exercising critical judgment, will accept the good and reject the bad. The censors, public and private, assume that they should determine what is good and what is bad for their fellow-citizens.

We trust Americans to recognize propaganda, and to reject it. We do not believe they need the help of censors to assist them in this task. We do not believe they are prepared to sacrifice their heritage of a free press in order to be "protected" against what others think may be bad for them. We believe they still favor free enterprise in ideas and expression.

We are aware, of course, that books are not alone in being subjected to efforts at suppression. We are aware that these efforts are related to a larger pattern of pressures being brought against education, the press, films, radio and television. The problem is not only one of actual censorship. The shadow of fear cast by these pressures leads, we suspect, to an even larger voluntary curtailment of expression by those who seek to avoid controversy.

Such pressure toward conformity is perhaps natural to a time of uneasy change and pervading fear. Especially when so many of our apprehensions are directed against an ideology, the expression of a dissident idea becomes a thing feared in itself, and we tend to move against it as against a hostile deed, with suppression.

And yet suppression is never more dangerous than in such a time of social tension. Freedom has given the United States the elasticity to endure strain. Freedom keeps open the path of novel and creative solutions, and enables change to come by choice. Every silencing of a heresy, every enforcement of an orthodoxy, diminishes the toughness and resilience of our society and leaves it the less able to deal with stress.

Now as always in our history, books are among our greatest instruments of freedom. They are almost the only means for making generally available ideas or manners of expression that can initially command only a small audience. They are the natural medium for the new idea and the untried voice from which come the original contributions to social growth. They are essential to the extended discussion which serious thought requires, and to the accumulation of knowledge and ideas into organized collections.

We believe that free communication is essential to the preservation of a free society and a creative culture. We believe that these pressures towards conformity present the danger of limiting the range and variety of inquiry and expression on which our democracy and our culture depend. We believe that every American community must jealously guard the freedom to publish and to circulate, in order to preserve its own freedom to read. We believe that publishers and librarians have a profound responsibility to give validity to that freedom to read by making it possible for the readers to choose freely from a variety of offerings.

The freedom to read is guaranteed by the Constitution. Those with faith in free people will stand firm on these constitutional guarantees of essential rights and will exercise the responsibilities that accompany these rights.

We therefore affirm these propositions:

1.   **It is in the public interest for publishers and librarians to make available the widest diversity of views and expressions, including those which are unorthodox or unpopular with the majority.**

Creative thought is by definition new, and what is new is different. The bearer of every new thought is a rebel until that idea is refined and tested. Totalitarian systems attempt to maintain themselves in power by the ruthless suppression of any concept which challenges the established orthodoxy. The power of a democratic system to adapt to change is vastly strengthened by the freedom of its citizens to choose widely from among conflicting opinions offered freely to them. To stifle every nonconformist idea at birth would mark the end of the democratic process. Furthermore, only through the constant activity of weighing and selecting can the democratic mind attain the strength demanded by times like these. We need to know not only what we believe but why we believe it.

2.   **Publishers, librarians and booksellers do not need to endorse every idea or presentation contained in the books they make available. It would conflict with the public interest for them to establish their own political, moral or aesthetic views as a standard for determining what books should be published or circulated.**

Publishers and librarians serve the educational process by helping to make available knowledge and ideas required for the growth of the mind and the increase of learning. They do not foster education by imposing as mentors the patterns of their own thought. The people should have the freedom to read and consider a broader range of ideas than those that may be held by any single librarian or publisher or government or church. It is wrong that what one can read should be confined to what another thinks proper.

3.   **It is contrary to the public interest for publishers or librarians to determine the acceptability of a book on the basis of the personal history or political affiliations of the author.**

A book should be judged as a book. No art or literature can flourish if it is to be measured by the political views or private lives of its creators. No society of free people can flourish which draws up lists of writers to whom it will not listen, whatever they may have to say.

4.   **There is no place in our society for efforts to coerce the taste of others, to confine adults to the reading matter deemed suitable for adolescents, or to inhibit the efforts of writers to achieve artistic expression.**

To some, much of modern literature is shocking. But is not much of life itself shocking? We cut off literature at the source if we prevent writers from dealing with the stuff of life. Parents and teachers have a responsibility to prepare the young to meet the diversity of experiences in life to which they will be exposed, as they have a responsibility to help them learn to think critically for themselves. These are affirmative responsibilities, not to be discharged simply by preventing them from reading works for which they are not yet prepared. In these matters taste differs, and taste cannot be legislated; nor can machinery be devised which will suit the demands of one group without limiting the freedom of others.

5.   **It is not in the public interest to force a reader to accept with any book the prejudgment of a label characterizing the book or author as subversive or dangerous.**

The ideal of labeling presupposes the existence of individuals or groups with wisdom to determine by authority what is good or bad for the citizen. It presupposes that individuals must be directed in making up their minds about the ideas they examine. But Americans do not need others to do their thinking for them.

6.   **It is the responsibility of publishers and librarians, as guardians of the people's freedom to read, to contest encroachments upon that freedom by individuals or groups seeking to impose their own standards or tastes upon the community at large.**

It is inevitable in the give and take of the democratic process that the political, the moral, or the aesthetic concepts of an individual or group will occasionally collide with those of another individual or group. In a free society individuals are free to determine for themselves what they wish to read, and each group is free to determine what it will recommend to its freely associated members. But no group has the right to take the law into its own hands, and to impose its own concept of politics or morality upon other members of a democratic society. Freedom is no freedom if it is accorded only to the accepted and the inoffensive.

7.   **It is the responsibility of publishers and librarians to give full meaning to the freedom to read by providing books that enrich the quality and diversity of thought and expression. By the exercise of this affirmative responsibility, they can demonstrate that the answer to a bad book is a good one, the answer to a bad idea is a good one.**

Reprinted by the permission of the American Library Association.

The freedom to read is of little consequence when expended on the trivial; it is frustrated when the reader cannot obtain matter fit for that reader's purpose. What is needed is not only the absence of restraint, but the positive provision of opportunity for the people to read the best that has been thought and said. Books are the major channel by which the intellectual inheritance is handed down, and the principal means of its testing and growth. The defense of their freedom and integrity, and the enlargement of their service to society, requires of all publishers and librarians the utmost of their faculties, and deserves of all citizens the fullest of their support.

We state these propositions neither lightly nor as easy generalizations. We here stake out a lofty claim for the value of books. We do so because we believe that they are good, possessed of enormous variety and usefulness, worthy of cherishing and keeping free. We realize that the application of these propositions may mean the dissemination of ideas and manners of expression that are repugnant to many persons. We do not state these propositions in the comfortable belief that what people read is unimportant. We believe rather that what people read is deeply important; that ideas can be dangerous; but that the suppression of ideas is fatal to a democratic society. Freedom itself is a dangerous way of life, but it is ours.

This statement was originally issued in May of 1953 by the Westchester Conference of the American Library Association and the American Book Publishers Council, which in 1970 consolidated with the American Educational Publishers Institute to become the Association of American Publishers.

Adopted June 25, 1953; revised January 28, 1972, January 16, 1991, by the ALA Council and the AAP Freedom to Read Committee.

A Joint Statement by: American Library Association & Association of American Publishers

Subsequently Endorsed by:

American Booksellers Association
American Booksellers Foundation for
  Free Expression
American Civil Liberties Union
American Federation of Teachers AFL-CIO
Anti-Defamation League of B'nai B'rith
Association of American University Presses
Children's Book Council
Freedom to Read Foundation
International Reading Association
Thomas Jefferson Center for the Protection
of Free Expression

National Association of College Stores
National Council of Teachers of English
P.E.N. - American Center
People for the American Way
Periodical and Book Association of America
Sex Information and Education Council of the
U.S.
Society of Professional Journalists
Women's National Book Association
YWCA of the U.S.A.

Index

NATIONAL GEOGRAPHIC KIDS

EVERYTHING BIG CATS

NATIONAL GEOGRAPHIC

NATIONAL GEOGRAPHIC
KIDS™

EVERYTHING BIG CATS

BY ELIZABETH CARNEY

NATIONAL GEOGRAPHIC

WASHINGTON, D.C.

CONTENTS

A lioness and her cubs take a cool drink from a watering hole in Serengeti National Park.

A female tiger, or tigress, sneaks up on a potential meal.

INTRODUCTION

KINGS OF THE JUNGLE.
GHOSTS OF THE SAVANNA. RULERS OF THE RAIN FOREST.
No matter where they're found, the world's big cats command titles of respect and awe. A fearsome foursome—lions, tigers, jaguars, and leopards—makes up the feline family's roster of heavyweights. With powerful, streamlined bodies built for killing, these cats sit at the top of their ecosystems' food chains.

Nothing comes easily to some of nature's most feared predators, however. Experts worry that some big cats are running down the last of their "nine lives." How did these mighty cats find themselves scratching at extinction's door? And what makes them so special? Let's find out EVERYTHING about big cats!

EXPLORERS' CORNER

Hi! We're Beverly and Dereck Joubert.
We've spent more than 25 years studying, filming, and photographing big cats. We can read a big cat's twitch of the tail or curl of the lip and know whether it's just playing or ready to charge. When you see us, we'll share our experiences with big cats in the wild. Look for this Explorers' Corner, and you'll be one step closer to being a big cat expert.

A leopard bounds through the grass in the Masai Mara National Reserve in Kenya.

1

BRING ON THE BIG CATS

A young male jaguar drools in anticipation of a meal.

CATNIP   AN ADULT LION'S ROAR CAN BE HEARD UP TO 5 MILES (8 KILOMETERS) AWAY.

WHAT'S A BIG CAT?

JAGUARS

PEOPLE MIGHT CONSIDER YOUR NEIGHBOR'S 25-POUND TABBY A "BIG CAT," BUT TO WILDLIFE EXPERTS, THE TERM HAS A SPECIFIC MEANING. Big cats are often defined as the four living members of the genus Panthera: tigers, lions, leopards, and jaguars. These cats have the ability to roar. They cannot purr the way house cats do. Big cats can only make a purring noise while breathing out.

All big cats are carnivores, which means they survive solely on the flesh of other animals. To do this, they have adaptations that make them excellent hunters, like powerful jaws, long, sharp claws, and dagger-like teeth. All big cats need a lot of land to roam and abundant prey to hunt.

LEOPARDS

TIGERS

LIONS

WHO'S WHO?

BIG CATS MAY HAVE A LOT OF FEATURES IN COMMON, BUT IF YOU KNOW WHAT TO LOOK FOR, YOU'LL BE ABLE TO TELL WHO'S WHO IN NO TIME.

FUR

TIGERS

Most tigers are orange-colored with vertical black stripes on their bodies. This coloring helps the cats blend in with tall grasses as they sneak up on prey. Tigers are the only big cats that have stripes. These markings are like fingerprints; no two stripe patterns are alike.

JAGUARS

A jaguar's coat pattern looks similar to that of a leopard. Both have dark spots called rosettes, but there's a way to spot the difference. Jaguars' rosettes have irregularly shaped borders and at least one black dot in the center.

LEOPARDS

A leopard's yellowy coat has dark spots called rosettes on its back and sides. In leopards, the rosettes' edges are smooth and circular. This color combo helps leopards blend into their surroundings.

LIONS

Lions have a light brown, or tawny, coat and a tuft of black hair at the end of their tails. When they reach their prime, most male lions have shaggy manes that help males look larger and more intimidating. Scientists have found that female lions prefer males with long, dark manes.

CATNIP JAGUARS AND TIGERS LOVE TO GO FOR A SWIM. THEY ARE TWO OF THE FEW CAT SPECIES THAT ENJOY WATER.

LEOPARD
66 to 176 pounds,
(30 TO 80 KG)
3 to 6 feet long
(0.9 TO 1.8 M)

JAGUAR
70 to 300 pounds
(32 TO 136 KG)
3.8 to 6 feet long
(1.2 TO 1.8 M)

Siberian, or Amur, tigers hold the title for biggest of the big cats. They can weigh up to 660 pounds and be as long as a station wagon. Leopards are the smallest, but they're no house cats. They weigh up to 176 pounds and measure up to six feet in length.

TIGER
200 to 660 pounds
(90 TO 300 KG)
7 to 13 feet long
(2.1 TO 4 M)

LION
265 to 420 pounds
(122 TO 191 KG)
4.6 to 8.3 feet long
(1.4 TO 2.5 M)

WHAT ABOUT BLACK PANTHERS?

These black beauties are actually either jaguars or leopards, just darkly dressed. "Black panther" is a term for a black-colored big cat. It isn't a separate animal. Both black jaguars and black leopards still have spots; they're just harder to see within their dark fur. A black coat comes from a specific combination of genes inherited from a cat's parents. In the wild, black jaguars are more common than black leopards.

WHERE TO FIND BIG CATS

NORTH AMERICA

ATLANTIC

NORTH

PACIFIC OCEAN

SOUTH AMERICA

BIG CATS CAN BE FOUND AROUND THE WORLD IN MANY TYPES OF HABITATS

and climates. Tigers can be found the farthest north, with one type inhabiting the snow-covered forests of Siberia. Jaguars favor the steamy rain forests and sunny grasslands of Central and South America. Lions primarily prowl the plains of central and southern Africa. Leopards—the most widespread of all the big cats—can be found in large parts of Africa and Asia.

EXPLORERS' CORNER

Some big cats are experts at camouflaging themselves, so they can sneak up on prey. (We should know; sometimes we've had to spend days in the bush waiting for a glimpse.) Consequently, counting them is not an easy task. Experts don't know exactly how many of each species remain in the wild. But scientists can make well-informed guesses, and they're not pretty. Over the past century, humans have relentlessly hunted big cats, causing their numbers to drop. Humans have also converted big cat habitats into homes, businesses, and farmland, which has left many of these animals without a place to rest their paws.

JAGUARS

This big cat lives in dense forest habitat where it is hard to find. For this reason, it has been difficult for scientists to estimate the size of the jaguar population.

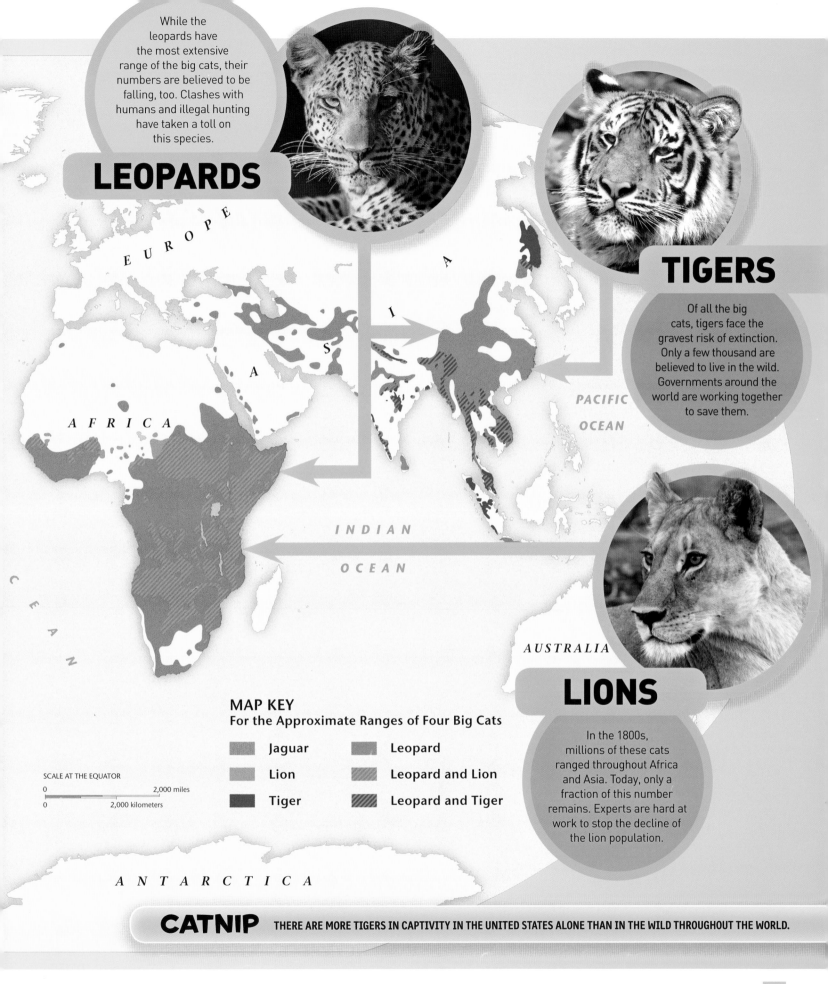

LEOPARDS

While the leopards have the most extensive range of the big cats, their numbers are believed to be falling, too. Clashes with humans and illegal hunting have taken a toll on this species.

TIGERS

Of all the big cats, tigers face the gravest risk of extinction. Only a few thousand are believed to live in the wild. Governments around the world are working together to save them.

LIONS

In the 1800s, millions of these cats ranged throughout Africa and Asia. Today, only a fraction of this number remains. Experts are hard at work to stop the decline of the lion population.

MAP KEY
For the Approximate Ranges of Four Big Cats

▨	Jaguar	▨	Leopard
▨	Lion	▨	Leopard and Lion
▨	Tiger	▨	Leopard and Tiger

SCALE AT THE EQUATOR
0 ——————— 2,000 miles
0 ——————— 2,000 kilometers

EUROPE
ASIA
AFRICA
PACIFIC OCEAN
INDIAN OCEAN
OCEAN
AUSTRALIA
ANTARCTICA

CATNIP THERE ARE MORE TIGERS IN CAPTIVITY IN THE UNITED STATES ALONE THAN IN THE WILD THROUGHOUT THE WORLD.

LIGER
MALE LION + FEMALE TIGER

This super-size offspring inherits Mom's stripes, Dad's shaggy mane, and a tendency to grow to gigantic proportions. Ligers can weigh almost as much as a lion and tiger combined. The world record holder for the biggest cat is a liger named Hercules. He was 12 feet long and tipped the scales at 900 pounds! The colossal cats look amazing, but their bulky frames and risk of health problems usually give them a short life expectancy.

MIXED SIGNALS

One reason tigers and lions don't mate in the wild is they have very different mating signals. Tigers are solitary, spending most of their time avoiding one another and sticking to their own territories. They signal a readiness to mate by spraying urine or other fluids around an area. Lions, on the other hand, are the social butterflies of the cat kingdom. They live in large groups and communicate with a range of social cues. A lioness might paw at the jaw of a prospective mate or brush her head against his.

CATNIP A LION'S TOP RUNNING SPEED IS 36 MILES PER HOUR.

BIG CAT COMBO

WHILE THE NUMBER OF WILD BIG CATS IS DECLINING, THEIR NUMBERS IN CAPTIVITY ARE ON THE RISE.

Many zoos and parks try very hard to give big cats homes that feel as natural as possible. Occasionally, however, big cat keepers experiment with unnatural cat combinations. The result: Cat hybrids that wouldn't exist in the wild.

The most popular cat combos happen when tigers and lions are bred together. In nature, a tiger and a lion would be an odd couple and they wouldn't mate. Their offspring's mismatched genes would make the cubs vulnerable to health problems such as blindness, deafness, and heart problems. That's why most scientists think these peculiar pairings aren't a good idea.

TIGON
MALE TIGER + FEMALE LION

This cat crossing results in average-size offspring outfitted with stripes, and, on males, a mini-mane. Tigons normally grow no larger than their parents. These hybrids are not as common as ligers (perhaps because they don't grow up to be giants). Unfortunately, tigons are vulnerable to the same health problems that plague ligers.

It's no yawning matter. These ligers have no way of knowing that their very existence is controversial.

A PHOTOGRAPHIC DIAGRAM

BIG CATS UP CLOSE

BIG CATS ARE DESIGNED
TO BE FAST, INTELLIGENT, AND POWERFUL.
They need these qualities to be successful hunters. Here are some of the features that give big cats their feline superpowers.

Long tails help big cats balance while leaping, climbing, and running. They're also used to communicate.

Sheaths at the top of each toe protect claws as sharp as knife points. In big cats, the claws retract, or move back into, the sheaths when the animals aren't using them.

Long muscular legs allow big cats to jump long distances and take big strides while running.

Fur coats protect big cats' sensitive body parts, shelter them from nasty weather, and provide camouflage in their home environments.

A Bengal tiger shows off an impressive physique as it sprints for its supper.

A rounded head encloses a brain that is large in relation to big cats' body size. Cats need a lot of brainpower to outsmart prey.

Eyes have an extra layer of light-absorbing cells. This feature allows cats to see six times better at night than humans do.

Long canine teeth are used to stab prey.

A big cat nose has more than 100 million scent-sensing cells. That's 20 times more smelling power than humans have.

A flexible spine allows cats to make quick twists and turns during high-speed chases. It also helps cats land on their feet if they tumble from a high perch.

Ears can detect many sounds that humans would never notice. Cats can even tell by listening when disasters like earthquakes and volcanic eruptions are about to occur.

Sensitive whiskers help cats find their way in the dark and squeeze in and out of tight spaces.

2

LIFE
OF A
BIG CAT

Female lions and cubs wade
through floodwaters of the
Okavango Delta in Botswana.

A leopard mother gently gives her cub a lift.

BRINGING UP BABY

BIG CATS MIGHT RULE

THEIR TERRITORY, BUT THEY DON'T START OUT THAT WAY.

At birth, cubs are blind and helpless. Big cats usually have between two and four cubs per litter. Just as with human babies, caring for cubs is a full-time job. Big cats are mammals, so mothers must nurse cubs for several months. Then, the cubs move on to meat meals. When a big cat has multiple mouths to feed, she has to hunt more frequently.

Moms must protect cubs from predators such as hyenas, baboons, and other big cats. They move their babies frequently to keep enemies off guard. To do this, mothers gently lift cubs by loose skin on their necks. Cubs relax their muscles and hang quietly. Wigglers would feel a pinch.

Cubs stay under their mothers' care for up to two years. During this time, cubs have a lot to learn. Their mother teaches them the best hunting locations and strategies. They learn which animals are dangerous and which make a good meal. They find out where the safest resting places and watering holes are. It's like Big Cat University and Mom's the professor!

Legadema

Two lion cubs roughhouse with their mother.

EXPLORERS' CORNER

What do you do when a fearless leopard cub crawls into the front seat of your jeep? We had this experience while we were filming and photographing in Botswana. A courageous cub, called Legadema (pronounced LOCK-ah-DEE-ma), became used to our presence. She would lie in the cool shadow of our jeep, while her mom was off hunting. One day, she jumped onto the passenger seat, like a dog going for a ride. We wanted to discourage this behavior, which could get her into trouble with tourists or, worse, poachers. Dereck tried to teach her some manners the way her mother would; he hissed at her. She ignored him. So we turned on the jeep's heater, which made a louder noise. She got the message.

We returned to the area after Legadema had grown up and had cubs of her own. It didn't take long before she was lounging in the shade of our jeep, just like she used to. We had made a friend for life.

CATNIP LARGE CATS' OFFSPRING ARE CALLED CUBS, WHILE SMALL CATS' YOUNGSTERS ARE KNOWN AS KITTENS.

ALONE ON THE PROWL

Tigers tend to hunt and patrol their territory solo.

CATNIP A LION PRIDE CAN BE AS FEW AS 3 LIONS OR AS MANY AS 30!

A solitary jaguar pads through the grass.

MOST CATS PREFER THE SINGLE LIFE.

USUALLY, BIG CATS ONLY TOLERATE COMPANY IN ORDER TO

mate or to raise their cubs. Big cats communicate with scent marks or roars to let their neighbors know, "This is my space. Keep out!"

But there's one big exception: lions. Lions are the only cats that live in social groups, called prides. Within a pride, nearly every female is related. Moms, sisters, aunts, and cousins all work together to raise cubs and hunt for enough food to support the pride. A dominant male or two will guard the pride's territory. He also babysits the cubs while their mothers are off hunting.

Young males are forced to leave the pride once they are old enough to hunt for themselves. These lions sometimes form small, all-boy gangs, called bachelor groups. The youngsters stay together until they're big enough to challenge a dominant male for control of a pride.

..OR THE MORE THE MERRIER?

LION AROUND

A LION'S TO-DO LIST

Snoozing	16 hours a day
Hunting for food	2 hours
Grooming and socializing	1 hour and 10 minutes
Eating	50 minutes

A pride's lionesses turn raising cubs into a group effort.

WHAT'S FOR LUNCH?

There's no fast food in the places where big cats live, but there is food that moves fast. Big cats have to work to snag their supper. Here are some of the favorite hard-earned meals in their diet.

JAGUAR

  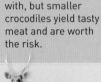

Fish A favorite dish; jaguars will dive right into water to catch a seafood meal.

Small crocodiles Large crocs are too dangerous to tangle with, but smaller crocodiles yield tasty meat and are worth the risk.

Peccarries These pig-like animals of North and South America are another jaguar favorite.

TIGER

Chital Deer This spotted deer is native to Asia and is popular tiger prey.

Sambar Deer This is another deer that is a common meal for tigers.

Water Buffalo Tigers' most challenging quarry, water buffalo will charge and have been known to injure and even kill tigers.

LION

Zebras If a lion can separate a young or sick zebra from the herd, it will gladly take this striped snack.

Wildebeests This variety of antelope is another popular choice for lions.

Cape Buffalo This animal is dangerous prey for lions, but some strictly prefer this meaty prize.

LEOPARD

Impalas These speedy antelopes are common prey for leopards.

Monkeys Leopards already lounge in trees, so they might as well hunt there, too. A quick leopard can snag a vervet monkey off its guard.

Porcupines This prickly snack can only be hunted very carefully, unless the leopard wants a muzzle full of spines.

JAW DROPPER

CATS CAN'T LIVE OFF

PLANTS, SO THEY MUST HUNT FOR EVERYTHING THEY EAT. Cats usually stalk their prey by crouching low to the ground and silently sneaking up on it. When the moment is right, the cat will strike. It leaps on to the prey, baring sharp fangs and claws. Sometimes cats will chase their prey for short distances. Oftentimes, a cat's efforts will fail and its potential prey escapes. The cat will go hungry until a hunt is successful.

Even though big cats use hunting strategies that aren't for the faint of heart, these top predators actually make their habitat healthier. In fact, big cats serve a very important role in the ecosystem. Cats such as lions and tigers keep the numbers of plant-eating animals in check, so plants have a chance to grow and thrive. They also keep grazing herds healthier by picking off sick and wounded members. Without big cats, delicate ecosystems would be out of balance.

STEAK DINNER

Tigers can eat more than 80 pounds (36 kg) of meat in one sitting. That's the equivalent of about 70 T-bone steaks!

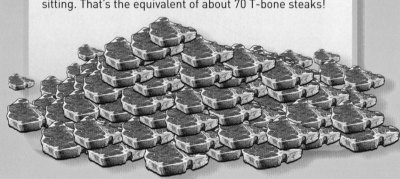

CATNIP A LEOPARD CAN DRAG PREY AS HIGH AS 50 FEET (15 METERS) UP A TREE—EVEN IF ITS MEAL IS LARGER AND HEAVIER THAN ITSELF!

Female lions team up to bring down a Cape buffalo.

BIG CATS' HUNTING METHODS **MAY SEEM HARSH TO US,** BUT THEY'RE JUST DOING WHAT THEY NEED TO DO IN ORDER TO EAT.

A tiger crouches low to the ground in an attempt to make a stealthy strike.

A leopard heaves a heavy impala up a tree.

CLASHING
WITH BIG CATS

Amazon rain forest trees are chopped down and burned in Brazil.

EVERY BIG CAT SHARES
ONE BIG PROBLEM: HABITAT LOSS.
AS HUMAN POPULATIONS GROW, PEOPLE

take over land for homes, businesses, and farms. This leaves fewer wild places for animals. To cope with their shrinking world, big cats sometimes prey on valuable livestock. This upsets farmers because livestock are often the only way of supporting their families. As a consequence, some feline offenders are shot or poisoned.

CATNIP SOMETIMES BIG CATS ARE POACHED FOR THEIR BODY PARTS, SUCH AS SKIN, WHISKERS, TEETH, AND BONES.

Disappearing Habitats

3 tiger subspecies have become extinct in the past century.

300 Asiatic lions remain in the Gir Forest in India. This subspecies of lion is almost extinct.

1/2 of jaguars' natural habitat has been lost over the last hundred years.

45 Amur leopards, an Asian subspecies, are probably all that remain in the wild. This leopard is one of the world's rarest cats.

A Bengal tiger rests in a tangle of mangrove trees in Bangladesh.

Can humans and big cats live together peacefully? Many people think they can; it just might take extra effort on our part. In some areas, wildlife conservationists pay farmers for lost livestock, so long as they don't kill big cats. Conservationists also teach farmers ways to keep livestock safe, such as building pens with metal fences and keeping wild pigs (which attract cats) out of crops.

In many countries, governments have set aside large areas of land as reserves. There, animals are protected from habitat loss and hunting. Animal-related tourism such as safaris may help big cats, too. Travelers pay money to see big cats up close. Local people who work at lodges and tour companies make money. For them, this makes big cats more valuable alive than dead—and worth protecting.

A PHOTO GALLERY

ALL THE CATS

BIG CATS MAKE UP
ONLY 4 OF THE 36 SPECIES OF CATS.
These other cats may not be as large, but they're still feared hunters in their habitats. Keen senses, sharp claws, and pointed teeth give all cats an edge in the search for prey.

A caracal has distinctive tufts of long, black hair on its ears. Fittingly, the name comes from a Turkish word meaning "black eared."

The territorial ocelot can be found in North and South America. It is also known as a painted leopard.

The elusive Asiatic golden cat mainly lives in forests and is rarely seen.

The shy, nocturnal marbled cat lives in thick forests of Southeast Asia.

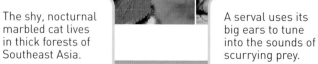

A serval uses its big ears to tune into the sounds of scurrying prey.

A fast cheetah keeps a sharp lookout.

Half the size of a house cat, the rusty spotted cat is a pint-size feline. Most members of the species can be found only on the island of Sri Lanka.

One-month-old Pallas Cat kittens hiss for the camera.

A sand cat lives in the deserts of North Africa and the Middle East. It gets most of its water from its food.

The Canada lynx has a short, bobbed tail tipped with black fur.

BEYOND THE BIG CAT

A bobcat descends a rocky slope in Colorado. These feisty cats can only be found in North America. Bobcats are one of four species of lynx.

33

CAT FAMILY TREE

Paramachairodus

Metailurus

Proailurnus

Pseudaelurus

ALL CATS, FROM THE MIGHTY TIGER TO THE COMMON HOUSE CAT, EVOLVED FROM A SMALL,

catlike creature that lived 12 million years ago. Eventually, the feline family split into two types. One branch grew into the smaller cats such as pumas, lynx, and domestic cats. The big cats sprang out of the other branch. Today's domestic cats are actually big cats' cousins. Cats really are one big family!

SMALL CAT, TALL CAT

One of the smallest living cats is the teacup-sized domestic breed Singapura. Its towering cousin, the Siberian tiger, is the largest living cat. One of the biggest cats to ever exist was the American cave lion. It may have tipped the scales at 1,100 pounds (500 kg).

36.5–23.5 MILLION YEARS AGO	23.5–5.3 MILLION YEARS AGO

Machairodus

Homotherium

Smilodon

Megantereon

Dinofelis

Leopardus

Miracinonyx

Puma

Felis

Acinonyx

Panthera

5.3–1.6 MILLION YEARS AGO   1.6 MILLION YEARS AGO–PRESENT

A MOUTHY RELATIVE

With two dagger-like teeth that didn't even fit inside their mouths, saber-toothed cats might be felines' most infamous ancestor. Several of these long-fanged species lived between 2.5 million and 10,000 years ago. The cats' canine teeth grew up to 7 inches (18 centimeters) long. The fangs had one drawback: such long teeth were prone to breaking. To protect them, saber-toothed cats didn't grab prey with their mouths. They pinned their prey down with sharp claws and strong paws. Then, the cats used their teeth to slash their victims.

MARSUPIAL

NIMRAVID

SABER-TOOTHED CAT

A wide-set jaw with dagger-like fangs evolved independently in some unrelated animals. Marsupials (pouched animals), an extinct meat eater called nimravid, and cats all sported the tapered teeth at some point in history.

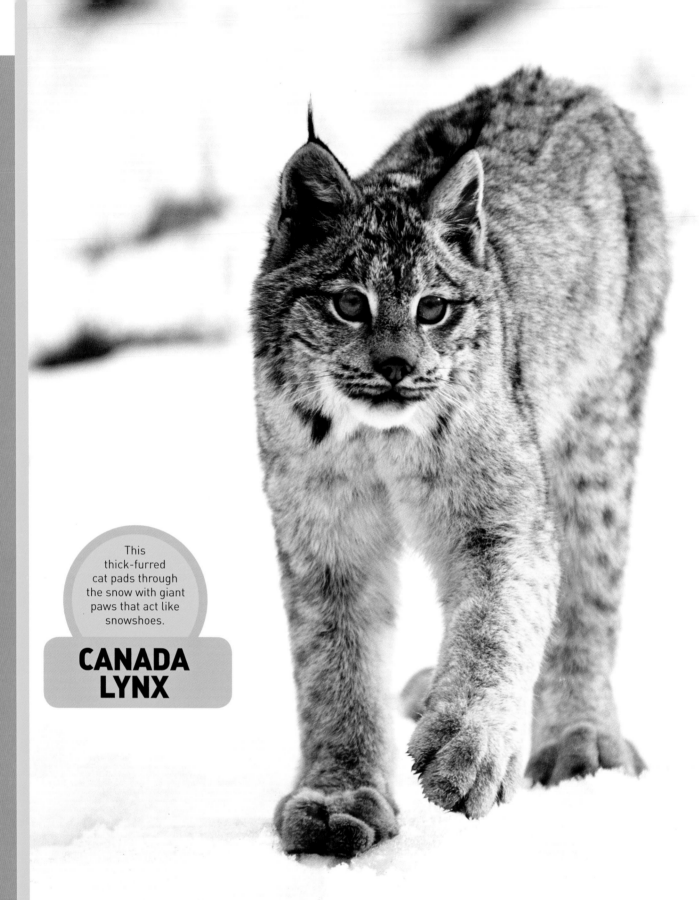

This thick-furred cat pads through the snow with giant paws that act like snowshoes.

CANADA LYNX

CATNIP CHEETAHS CAN REACH SPEEDS UP TO 70 MPH (112 KPH) IN LESS THAN THREE SECONDS, FASTER THAN A RACE CAR CAN ACCELERATE.

NOT-SO-BIG CATS

BIG CATS MIGHT HAVE SIZE
ON THEIR SIDE, BUT WHEN IT COMES DOWN TO
THE NUMBERS, SMALL CATS HAVE THEM BEAT.

Most cats in the feline family tree belong to the small-cat branch. These cats have a different throat structure from big cats. They can't roar, but they have a different ability. Smaller cats can purr continually. Small cats can be found in almost any environment on Earth—from the desert-dwelling sand cat to the rain forest–residing margay. Cats such as the Canada lynx can even brave bone-chilling winters in the northern tundra.

Classifying cats isn't always clear-cut. Snow leopards have the same throat structure as big cats but have never been known to roar. Pumas are usually classified with small cats—they don't roar either. But these super-sized kitties can weigh up to 230 pounds (104 kg), more than an average leopard.

Cheetahs aren't closely related to either big or small cats. They descend from a line of running cats and are the last of their kind. Body features such as extra-long legs, a long spine, and claws that work like runner's spikes allow these cats to hold the title of world's fastest land animal.

Crouching low, the caracal stalks birds and rodents in short savanna grass.

CARACAL

This cat hunts during the day when its prey is most active.

PALLAS CAT

The largest of the "small cats," the puma has a giant range that stretches from the tip of South America to the top of the Canadian Rockies.

PUMA

LISTEN TO THE CATS!
A ROAR OR PURR INDICATES BIG CAT OR SMALLER COUSIN.

WILD CAT

HUNTING HEAVYWEIGHTS

Many wild cats can take down prey that are often more than twice their size.

TRY, TRY AGAIN

For many types of wild cats, only a small portion of hunting attempts are successful. About 10 to 20 percent of tiger hunts end in a kill.

SMELLY MESSAGES

Many wild cat species prominently mark their territory with urine and droppings.

MANY SPECIES

Scientists have tallied 35 species of wild cats in the world.

NOT FIT FOR LIVING ROOMS

Keeping wild cats as pets is a dangerous idea. Wild cats have complex needs that are best met in their natural environment. They can seriously injure or kill people when handled incorrectly.

TAME TABBY

STICKING WITH SMALL SNACKS
Domestic cats often hunt pint-sized critters such as mice, birds, and lizards.

HOTSHOT HUNTERS
Domestic cats can be very efficient hunters. At the top of their game, one in three attempts results in a kill.

DISCREETLY DOING THEIR BUSINESS
Domestic cats neatly bury their droppings.

ONE SPECIES, MANY BREEDS
Domestic cats all belong to a single species (*Felis catus*), but they come in more than 80 breeds.

PERFECT PETS
Domestic cats have been living with humans for 9,000 years and are practiced companions for many people.

CATNIP THERE ARE APPROXIMATELY 93.6 MILLION PET CATS IN THE UNITED STATES.

CAT CARE

Zoo cats often receive a lot of hands-on care to keep them fit and healthy, including a teeth cleaning!

WITH THEIR STRENGTH AND BEAUTY, WILD CATS HAVE STAR POWER AMONG HUMAN ADMIRERS. VISITORS TO ZOOS AND wildlife parks often scramble to see cat exhibits. Zoos allow millions of people to get close to animals they would likely never see in the wild. With expert care, zoos and animal parks can provide environments that help captive cats feel at home.

Most zoos use techniques called animal enrichment that help animals tap into their natural instincts. Zoo animals spend their days in the same enclosure. This could get very boring for intelligent animals like big cats. So how do you help a lion in a city zoo feel like it's prowling the African savanna? Keepers can stuff a cardboard "zebra" with meat or scatter antelope dung in the lions' enclosure. Interaction with scents and sights of prey animals allow the cats to act like their wild counterparts.

Zookeepers also train cats to follow commands such as come, sit, stand, and lie down. Training gives cats a mental workout. It also allows veterinarians to visually check out the animals without resorting to drugs to make them sleepy.

FOR THE FIRST SIX WEEKS OF THEIR LIVES, YOUNG CUBS CAN **FEED UP TO EIGHT TIMES A DAY.**

YOU BE THE ZOOKEEPER

Many pet owners often practice animal enrichment without even knowing it. Like zoo animals, pets thrive in environments where they get to use their instincts and smarts. How can you help a pet cat connect with its wild side? Provide safe, pet-friendly toys and change them frequently. Challenge your cat with interesting scents like catnip. Use treats as food rewards for good behavior or create food puzzles, like treats in an empty open water bottle.

A white tiger cub drinks milk from a bottle.

CATNIP ZOO SCIENTISTS HAVE DEVELOPED A DRUG THAT ALLOWS FIELD RESEARCHERS TO SEDATE AND SAFELY FIT WILD TIGERS WITH RADIO COLLARS.

YOU DON'T

HAVE TO ROAR WHEN YOU'RE ANGRY OR

purr when you're content to have some things in common with cats. Both humans and cats are mammals. That means both nurse their young with milk, have body hair, and are warm blooded. Let's see some other ways big cats compare with your world.

CAT COMPARISONS

CHANNELING YOUR INNER CAT

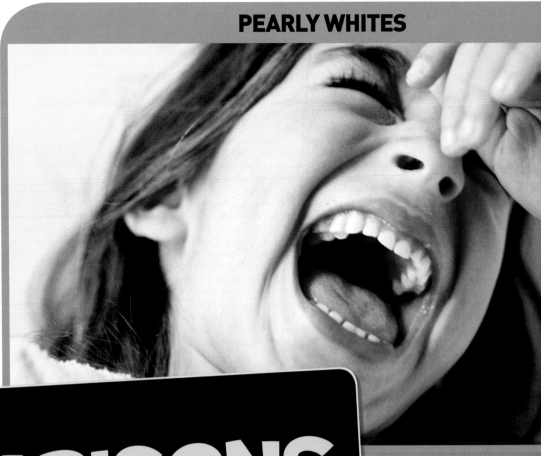

Young children have 20 teeth. Human teeth are shaped for a mixed diet of plants and meat. Lions and tigers have 30 teeth. Their large stabbing teeth, called canines, are used to catch and kill prey.

SLEEPING

It's no coincidence that "catnap" is a term for sleep. Cats are experts at getting their zzz's. By sleeping in short stretches at a time, cats sleep as many as 20 hours a day. Most kids sleep for about 9 or 10 hours a night. But while a leopard snoozes in a tree, you likely prefer a comfy bed.

STRETCHING

Your gym teacher may have you stretch before a workout to keep your muscles flexible. Cats stretch for similar reasons. But for them, no yoga mat is required.

GROOMING

You likely need a brush or comb to tame your strands. Big cats have a brush built in to their tongues! A cat's tongue is covered with backward-facing spines that act like bristles. Cats lick their fur to remove loose hair and dead skin.

NAIL CARE

You probably trim your nails with nail clippers. Big cats need something more heavy-duty for their sharp, curved claws. To keep their nails sharp and clean, big cats dig their claws into a tree, flex them, and pull down.

During playtime, a leopard cub toys with its mother as the pair rests in the shade.

4

FUN
WITH
BIG CATS

CATCH A CAT— IF YOU CAN!

EACH SPECIES
OF BIG CAT HAS A UNIQUE

cat pattern. This camouflage helps the cat blend into its environment. Cats would go hungry if their prey were able to spot them easily and escape. Do you have what it takes to spot big cats? Put your skills to the test. How many big cats can you find on this page?

WHAT'S YOUR CAT PURR-SONALITY?

HAVE YOU EVER

WONDERED WHAT TYPE of feline you would be? Take this quiz to find out!

1 What type of meal sounds the most delicious to you?

A. An extra-large steak, the rarer the better
B. Sharing a family-style supper
C. Chowing down while perched on a high countertop
D. Nibbling on several small snacks throughout the day

2 Which statement best describes your approach to social interactions?

A. I'm a loner and most comfortable by myself.
B. The more the merrier; I like to hang out with big groups.
C. I'm solitary, but I don't mind when others come into my space.
D. I prefer to be around only a couple of my favorite folks.

3 Where is your perfect living spot?

A. No preference. I'll live where it's hot or cold.
B. I like sunny grasslands.
C. I like warm, wooded places such as jungles and forests.
D. I just want to be indoors!

4 What do you like to wear?

A. Stripes
B. Solid colors
C. Spots
D. A variety of patterns

5 What describes your approach to physical fitness?

A. I focus on strength and power.
B. I need both power and speed.
C. I concentrate on flexibility and power.
D. I aim to be fast and graceful.

CATNIP LION CUBS ARE BORN SPOTTED FOR EXTRA CAMOUFLAGE AS THEY HIDE IN THE BUSH. THESE SPOTS MOSTLY FADE BY ADULTHOOD.

WHAT'S YOUR PLACE IN THE FELINE FAMILY?

IF YOU SCORED MOSTLY A's: You're like the mighty tiger. A solitary yet powerful force, you're comfortable in a variety of environments.

IF YOU SCORED MOSTLY B's: You're like the majestic lion. At ease in a crowd, you like to use your power and speed to race through sunny savannas.

IF YOU SCORED MOSTLY C's: You're like the stealthy leopard. You're not strictly territorial, but you're no social butterfly either. You often sport your spots in steamy climates.

IF YOU SCORED MOSTLY D's: You're like the cunning house cat. Ever resourceful, you like to cuddle up with your favorite humans and take advantage of easy meals.

PHYSICAL FEATS

A large tiger can leap more than **30 FEET** (9.1 meters) to pounce on its prey. That's about the length of three mini-vans parked in a row.

BIG CATS USE
MUSCULAR LEGS AND

a superb sense of balance to leap extraordinary distances. If animals were allowed in the Olympics, big cats could definitely compete in the jumping events. Which cat would likely take first prize in the long jump?

JUMPING CONTEST

How far can you jump compared to big cats? Use a tape measure to see how you measure up against these four-legged jumping champs. Just remember, what goes up must come down. Be sure to practice your jumping safely and on level ground.

Jumping contestants not to scale.

5 FEET   **10 FEET**   **15 FEET**

Lions can jump up to **36 FEET** (11 meters). They can clear the length of a school bus in a single bound.

GOLD MEDAL WINNER!

Snow leopards are able to soar through the air as far as **45 FEET** (14 meters)—the length of a humpback whale. They have to be champion leapers to hunt among the cliffs and ravines of their mountainous home.

Jaguars and leopards are able to leap **20 FEET** (6 meters). That's the height of many two-story buildings!

MORE COOL CAT TRICKS

In one stride, a cheetah can cover up to **26 FEET** (7–8 meters).

Tigers are capable swimmers and divers. They can swim across lakes while dragging heavy prey in their mouths.

Leopards are the strongest climbers of the cats. They can carry prey twice their weight up a tree.

CATNIP BIG CATS HAVE THE BEST 3-D VISION OF ALL CARNIVORES, WHICH HELPS THEM CORRECTLY GAUGE DISTANCES WHILE JUMPING.

20 FEET   **25 FEET**   **30 FEET**   **35 FEET**   **40 FEET**   **45 FEET**

CATS IN CULTURE

HUMANS HAVE RESPECTED CATS' IMPRESSIVE LOOKS AND PHYSICAL ABILITIES FOR THOUSANDS OF YEARS.

Some cultures even believed cats had supernatural powers. The Maya, a Central American people, believed a powerful jaguar god guided the dead to the afterlife. For ancient Romans, some gods rode atop great cats or used felines to pull their chariots. The Egyptians believed cats were so sacred that they carefully mummified their bodies while the whole family mourned their death.

Cats' reputation among humans, however, wasn't always positive. During the late Middle Ages, large numbers of cats were killed because people believed cats were associated with witchcraft and evil. Cats had a tough time again in the early Renaissance period, when the Christian church wanted to stamp out reminders of a cat-related pagan symbol.

Today, most people don't believe in feline superstitions, such as black cats causing bad luck. Now, many humans accept cats for what they are—animals that are just trying to survive in a changing world.

Giant carved jaguar heads adorn a Maya temple in Mexico.

Many ancient Egyptians believed cats represented the goddess Bastet. Dead cats were often mummified in preparation for the afterlife.

CATNIP THE BENGAL TIGER IS INDIA'S NATIONAL ANIMAL.

MAKE YOUR OWN CATNIP

Catnip is an herb that's been used for centuries as a treat for cats. The plant, which is related to mint, contains a chemical that attracts some cats like crazy. To have a fresh supply for your cat, you can grow your own catnip. Plant catnip seeds in a sunny area and water them daily. After the plant grows several inches, pinch off budding leaves and lay them out to dry. Crumple the leaves and sew them into a felt pouch to make a mouse toy for your cat.

In this 180 A.D. mosaic, the Greek god Dionysus is pictured riding a leopard.

PHOTO FINISH

FILMMAKERS
AND PHOTOGRAPHERS

who follow big cats all share one goal: to let people to see these animals from the safety of their television sets or the pages of books and magazines. They wish to share the cats' fierce beauty and fascinating behaviors with the world. It's a noble undertaking, but it's not easy.

Most photographers and filmmakers crave adventure. In places where big cats live, there's plenty of that to go around. Beverly and Dereck Joubert film and photograph leopards and lions in Botswana. Most days, they sleep in tents and bathe in crocodile-infested rivers. Every morning, they have to shake out their shoes (in case a scorpion snuck in) and double lock their tent zippers (in case baboons try to get in). The midday heat climbs to a scorching 128°F (53°C), while overnight temperatures plunge to below freezing. Sometimes, things can get too exciting if a cranky elephant or startled lion mounts a charge. Misjudging either the weather or the wildlife can be a fatal mistake.

But when the filmmakers get the perfect shot of a lion hunt or capture the gaze of a leopard's wild, golden eyes, they don't want to be anywhere else.

CANDID CAPTURE!
A lion cub hangs from a tree in Botswana.

AFTERWORD

LIVING WITH BIG CATS

AS THE HUMAN

POPULATION SOARS, BIG CATS' numbers have tumbled worldwide. There is a chance these felines are going the way of the saber-tooth, yet this time, humankind would be responsible. But don't count out big cats yet! Some of the world's most respected biologists are on the case. Advances in the methods of studying big cats have led to a more accurate understanding of cat biology and population estimates. While the numbers currently look grim, many experts see signs of hope. And armed with accurate information, conservationists know the best places to focus their efforts.

In Central and South America, conservationists are working with governments to connect fragmented pieces of jaguar habitat. Safe routes between these wild places mean jaguars can breed and hunt throughout their range, even though humans live in large parts of it. Clear paths for jaguar migration can help ensure the big cat remains genetically strong and diverse.

In Southeast Asia, scientists have identified vast areas of healthy tiger habitat. There is enough wild land and prey to support an estimated 15,000 to 20,000 tigers. Community reforestation projects in Nepal are creating tiger habitat out of previously cleared land. If the world's remaining tigers can be protected, there are areas where they can thrive and rebound.

In Africa, ecotourism is helping local people make a living from showing off big cats in action. Simple changes in farming and ranching practices can keep livestock safe from big cats. Plus, new projects like the

Conflict between lions and the Maasai people of eastern Africa have contributed to cats' decreasing numbers in Kenya and Tanzania. With herding as their means of survival, Maasai warriors feel forced to retaliate against cats when a tribe's livestock has been attacked.

Mbirikani Predator Compensation Fund offer herding tribes immediate compensation for cattle lost to hunting lions. This reduces the chance of people killing the cats for threatening their livelihood.

Big cats have been around for hundreds of thousands of years. They are adaptable, intelligent, and tough. Plus, they reproduce quickly. Tigers, for example, can produce a litter of cubs every year. This means cats' numbers can rebound quickly under the right conditions. With a little bit of help, big cats just might have a few of their "nine lives" left.

If you would like to help, visit http://animals.nationalgeographic.com/animals/big-cats **for more information.**

BIG CAT INITIATIVE

THE NATIONAL GEOGRAPHIC SOCIETY HAS HEARD the desperate roar of the big cat community. To help lions, tigers, leopards, jaguars, and the world's other large felines, National Geographic launched the Big Cat Initiative. This program aims to stop the free fall of lion population numbers by 2015. Eventually, it hopes to bring lion numbers back to healthy levels. But that's not all. Through conservation projects, education, and spreading the word about the big cats' plight, the Big Cat Initiative hopes to ensure the long-term survival of all big cats. The program is working to involve local people in the regions where cats live. That way, the communities in direct contact with cats have an important role to play.

A veterinarian listens to a sedated African lion's heartbeat at a Namibian wildlife park.

A lion mother and cub watch the sun rise at the dawn of a new day.

AN **INTERACTIVE GLOSSARY**

Female lions lounge in the mud. The bond between these pride members is strong.

THESE WORDS ARE
COMMONLY USED AMONG BIG CAT experts.

Use the glossary to see what each word means and go to page numbers listed to see the word used in context. Then test your big cat smarts!

1. Adaptation
(PAGES 10-11)
An evolutionary change in an animal or plant that helps it live in a particular environment.

Which adaptation helps big cats hunt well in the dark?
a. long fangs
b. long legs and sharp claws
c. spotted or striped coats
d. extra light-sensing cells in their eyes

2. Camouflage
(PAGES 18-19, 46-47)
A body shape or coloring that conceals animals from predators or prey

What is the main reason big cats use camouflage?
a. to signal other animals
b. to be more successful hunters
c. to attract mates
d. all of the above

3. Carnivore
(PAGES 10-11, 26-27)
An animal that eats the flesh of other animals

What kind of teeth would you expect a carnivore to have?
a. sharp and pointy
b. square and flat
c. a mix of sharp and flat teeth
d. no teeth, only gums

4. Conservationist
(PAGES 28-29, 56-57)
A person who works to protect and manage Earth's natural resources and the wildlife that depends on those resources

What quality would be important for a person who wants to be a conservationist?
a. likes to work outside
b. good at communicating with people
c. likes to work with animals
d. all of the above

5. Diet
(PAGES 26-27)
The foods eaten by a particular group of animals

Which is part of a leopard's diet?
a. cat food
b. tater tots
c. small forest animals
d. scrub grass

6. Dominant
(PAGES 24-25)
The status of being an animal that exerts authority and control over other animals in a group

A dominant lion might exhibit which behavior?
a. backing off when another cat challenges it
b. fighting other cats for the juiciest pieces of a kill
c. letting other cats mate with members of the pride
d. all of the above

7. Ecosystem
(PAGES 6-7)
All the living things in a community and the environment in which they live

A lion can share an ecosystem with which animal?
a. leopards
b. Cape buffalo
c. zebras
d. all of the above

8. Gene
(PAGES 12-13, 16-17)
A unit of hereditary information that encodes the traits passed from parents to offspring

Which jaguar feature is certain to be determined by genes?
a. taste for crocodiles
b. black fur
c. success in raising cubs to adulthood
d. all of the above

9. Mammal
(PAGES 22-23, 42-43)
A warm-blooded animal whose young feed on milk that is produced by the mother

Which of the following is a feature of mammals?
a. cold-bloodedness
b. bodies covered in scales
c. high level of maternal care
d. very successful carnivores

10. Nocturnal
(PAGE 30)
The state of being active at night

Nocturnal animals spend a lot of time sleeping ___.
a. in caves
b. in short bursts
c. in groups
d. during the day

11. Poacher
(PAGES 22-23)
A person who illegally hunts animals, usually to sell their meat, skins, or other body parts

Hunting is only considered poaching when it ___.
a. occurs at night
b. violates laws
c. results in the killing of multiple animals
d. is practiced with guns

12. Prey
(PAGES 10-11, 26-27, 46-47)
An animal that is hunted and eaten by another

Which of the following can be a jaguar's prey?
a. peccary
b. wildebeest
c. impala
d. chital deer

13. Predator
(pages 6-7)
An animal that hunts and eats other animals

Which of the following would a predator not eat?
a. wheat
b. deer
c. porcupines
d. monkeys

14. Pride
(PAGES 24-25)
A group of lions

A lion pride is generally made up of ___.
a. young males
b. an equal number of males and females
c. related females
d. cubs

15. Reserve
(PAGES 28-29)
A tract of public land set apart for conservation purposes

Which of the following activities would probably not be allowed in a reserve?
a. camping
b. sightseeing
c. logging
d. hiking

ANSWERS: 1. d, 2. b, 3. a, 4. d, 5. c, 6. b, 7. d, 8. b, 9. c, 10. d, 11. b, 12. a, 13. a, 14. c, 15. c.

Amur leopards, like this one, are the world's rarest big cats.

FIND OUT MORE

BOOKS AND ARTICLES

Face to Face With Leopards.
Dereck Joubert and Beverly Joubert
National Geographic Children's Books, AUGUST 2009.
Face to Face With Lions.
Dereck Joubert and Beverly Joubert
National Geographic Children's Books, MARCH 2010.
"Leopards: Nature's Supercats"
Crispin Boyer, *National Geographic Kids.*
Washington, D.C.: MAY 2009.
"Path of the Jaguar"
Mel White, *National Geographic*. Washington, D.C.:
MARCH 2009.
Mountain Lions.
Erika L. Shores, Capstone Press. Bloomington,
MN: AUGUST 2010.
Cheetahs.
Deborah Nuzzolo, Pebble Plus. Bloomington,
MN: FEBRUARY 2010.
Big Cats (Xtreme Predators).
S. L. Hamilton, Abdo Publishing Company.
Edina, MN: JANUARY 2010.
Big Cats: Wild Reads.
Kenneth Ireland, Oxford University Press, USA.
New York: OCTOBER 2009.

MOVIES TO WATCH

"Eye of the Leopard"
National Geographic. Washington, D.C.: FEBRUARY 2007
"Tigers of the Snow"
National Geographic. Washington, D.C.: FEBRUARY 2000
"In Search of the Jaguar"
National Geographic. Washington, D.C.: OCTOBER 2006

WEB SITES

National Geographic Big Cats Initiative
This program works to help ensure that there is enough land
and resources for both humans AND big cats.
http://animals.nationalgeographic.com/animals/big-cats/

WWF's Tiger Initiative
To mark 2010 as the Year of the Tiger, the WWF launched a
new campaign to save the most endangered of big cats.
**http://wwf.panda.org/what_we_do/endangered_species/
tigers/tiger_initiative/**

Panthera
This conservation organization is dedicated to protecting the
world's 36 species of wild cats. **http://www.panthera.org/**

PLACES TO VISIT

The most exciting way to learn about big cats is to see them
yourself! Find out if your local zoo or wildlife park has a big cat
exhibit. Here are a few where visitors can "roar" with delight.

San Diego Zoo's Africa Rocks (Big Cat), San Diego, California
Smithsonian National Zoo's Great Cats Exhibit, Washington, D.C.
The Bronx Zoo's Tiger Mountain, Bronx, New York
Pittsburgh Zoo's Asian Forest, Pittsburgh, Pennsylvania
Oklahoma City Zoo's Cat Forest, Oklahoma City, Oklahoma

For those who work tirelessly to ensure the survival of the world's wild cats—EC

Published by the National Geographic Society
John M. Fahey, Jr., *President and Chief Executive Officer*
Gilbert M. Grosvenor, *Chairman of the Board*
Tim T. Kelly, President, *Global Media Group*
John Q. Griffin, *Executive Vice President;*
    President, Publishing
Nina D. Hoffman, *Executive Vice President;*
    President, Book Publishing Group
Melina Gerosa Bellows, *Chief Creative Officer,*
    Kids and Family, Global Media

Prepared by the Book Division
Nancy Laties Feresten, *Vice President,*
    Editor in Chief, Children's Books
Jonathan Halling, *Design Director, Children's Publishing*
Jennifer Emmett, *Executive Editor, Children's Books*
Carl Mehler, *Director of Maps*
R. Gary Colbert, *Production Director*
Jennifer A. Thornton, *Managing Editor*

Staff for This Book
Priyanka Lamichhane, *Project Editor*
James Hiscott Jr., *Art Director*
Lori Epstein, Annette Kiesow, *Illustrations Editors*
Erin Mayes, Chad Tomlinson, *Designers*
Kate Olesin, *Editorial Assistant*
Grace Hill, *Associate Managing Editor*
Lewis R. Bassford, *Production Manager*
Susan Borke, *Legal and Business Affairs*
Madeleine Franklin, *Editorial Intern*
Janice Gilman, *Illustrations Intern*

Manufacturing and Quality Management
Christopher A. Liedel, *Chief Financial Officer*
Phillip L. Schlosser, *Senior Vice President*
Chris Brown, *Technical Director*
Nicole Elliott, *Manager*
Rachel Faulise, *Manager*
Robert L. Barr, *Manager*

Captions
Page 1: Do you think this snarling male lion looks funny or fierce?
Pages 2-3: A leopard lounges in a tree. From this perch, leopards can eat and sleep undisturbed.
Cover: A tiger splashes through the water.
Back cover: A lion yawning.

The National Geographic Society is one of the world's largest nonprofit scientific and educational organizations. Founded in 1888 to "increase and diffuse geographic knowledge," the Society works to inspire people to care about the planet. National Geographic reflects the world through its magazines, television programs, films, music and radio, books, DVDs, maps, exhibitions, live events, school publishing programs, interactive media and merchandise. *National Geographic* magazine, the Society's official journal, published in English and 32 local-language editions, is read by more than 35 million people each month. The National Geographic Channel reaches 310 million households in 34 languages in 165 countries. National Geographic Digital Media receives more than 13 million visitors a month. National Geographic has funded more than 9,200 scientific research, conservation and exploration projects and supports an education program promoting geography literacy. For more information, visit nationalgeographic.com.

For more information, please call 1-800-NGS LINE (647-5463) or write to the following address:
National Geographic Society
1145 17th Street N.W.
Washington, D.C. 20036-4688 U.S.A.

Visit us online at www.nationalgeographic.com/books

For librarians and teachers: www.ngchildrensbooks.org

More for kids from National Geographic: kids.nationalgeographic.com

For information about special discounts for bulk purchases, please contact National Geographic Books Special Sales: ngspecsales@ngs.org

For rights or permissions inquiries, please contact National Geographic Books Subsidiary Rights: ngbookrights@ngs.org

Library of Congress Cataloging-in-Publication Data
Carney, Elizabeth, 1981-
 NGK everything big cats / by Elizabeth Carney.
   p. cm.
 Includes bibliographical references and index.
 ISBN 978-1-4263-0805-5 (hardcover : alk. paper) —
 ISBN 978-1-4263-0806-2 (library binding : alk. paper)
 1. Felidae—Juvenile literature. I. Title. II. Title: Big cats.
 QL737.C23C348 2011
 599.75'5—dc22
                                  2010026963

Scholastic edition ISBN: 978-1-4263-0875-8

Printed in United States of America
11/WOR/2